Shojo Beat

2

Story & Art by
Taeko Watanabe

Contents

Story Thus Far

It is the end of the Bakumatsu era, in the third year of Bunkyu (1863), in Kyoto. The Mibu-Roshi (later to become the Shinsengumi) is created to protect the shogun in this chaotic time.

Both Tominaga Sei's father and brother are killed by anti-Shogunate rebels. Sei then joins the Mibu-Roshi Party disguised as a boy with the name Kamiya Seizaburo to avenge her family. She comes to regard Okita Soji as her mentor after he saves her from being attacked. Sei aspires to become a true bushi, but she finds herself surrounded by "animals." Further, Soji soon discovers Sei is a girl. Soji agrees to keep her secret after she tells him her tragic story. He looks after Sei in the Mibu-Roshi, and she finds herself starting to have feelings for him…

Characters

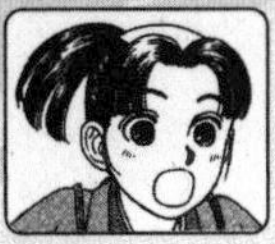

Tominaga Sei
She disguises herself as a boy to enter the Mibu-Roshi. Sei wants to become a warrior so she can avenge her father and brother. She trains under Soji and aspires to become a true bushi.

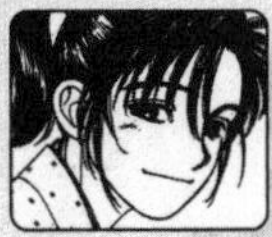

Okita Soji
Assistant vice captain of the Mibu-Roshi and the selected successor of the Ten'nen Rishin-ryu school of sword fighting. He is the only member of the Mibu-Roshi who knows Sei's secret.

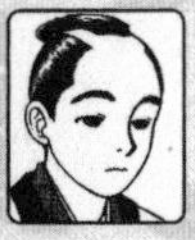

Saito Hajime
Assistant vice captain. He was a friend of Sei's older brother, Yuma, to whom he bears a striking resemblance.

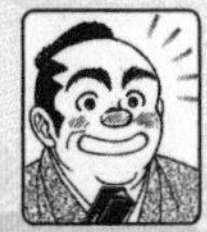

Serizawa Kamo
Captain of the Mibu-Roshi. Captain Serizawa of the Mito clan has a lackadaisical—and often inebriated—facade that belies his cunning and calculating mind.

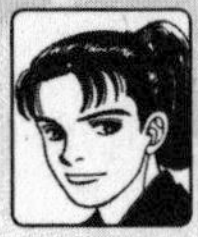

Hijikata Toshizo
Vice captain of the Mibu-Roshi. He commands the Mibu-Roshi with strict authority.

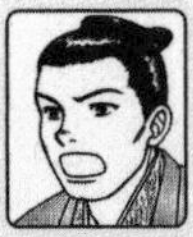

Kondo Isami
Captain of the Mibu-Roshi and fourth master of the Ten'nen Rishin-ryu. Has a very calm temperament and is highly respected.

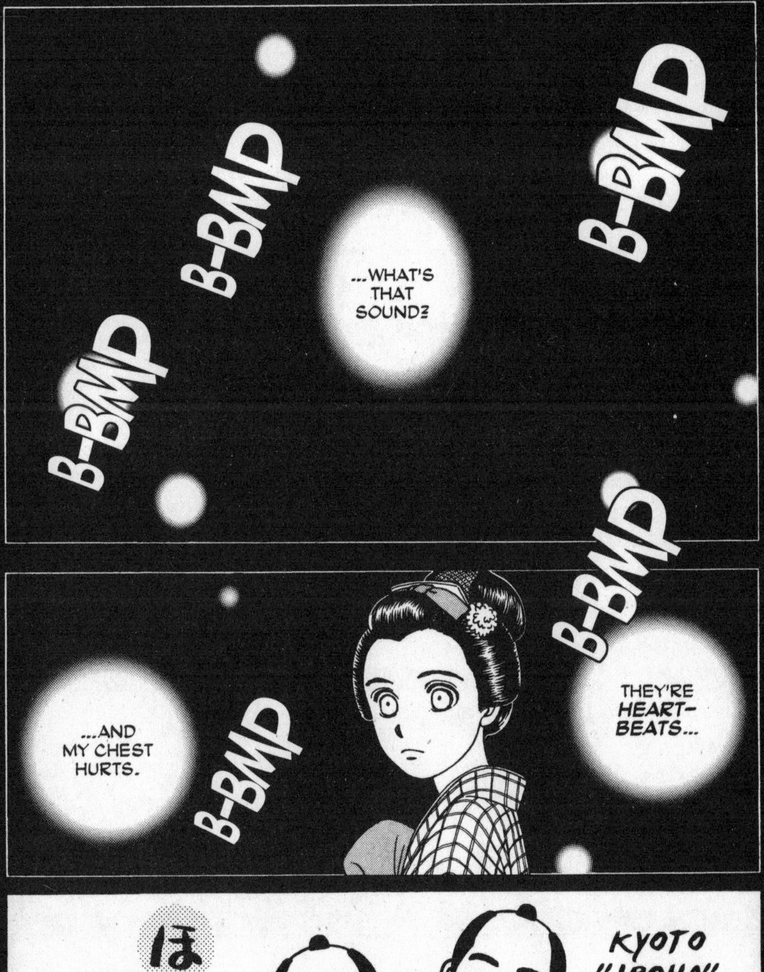
B-BMP
...WHAT'S THAT SOUND?
B-BMP
B-BMP
B-BMP
THEY'RE HEART-BEATS...
B-BMP
...AND MY CHEST HURTS.
KYOTO "IROHA" KARUTA GAME!
は
"HO" HOTOKE NO KAO MO SAN DO "TO TRY THE PATIENCE OF A SAINT"

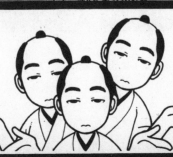

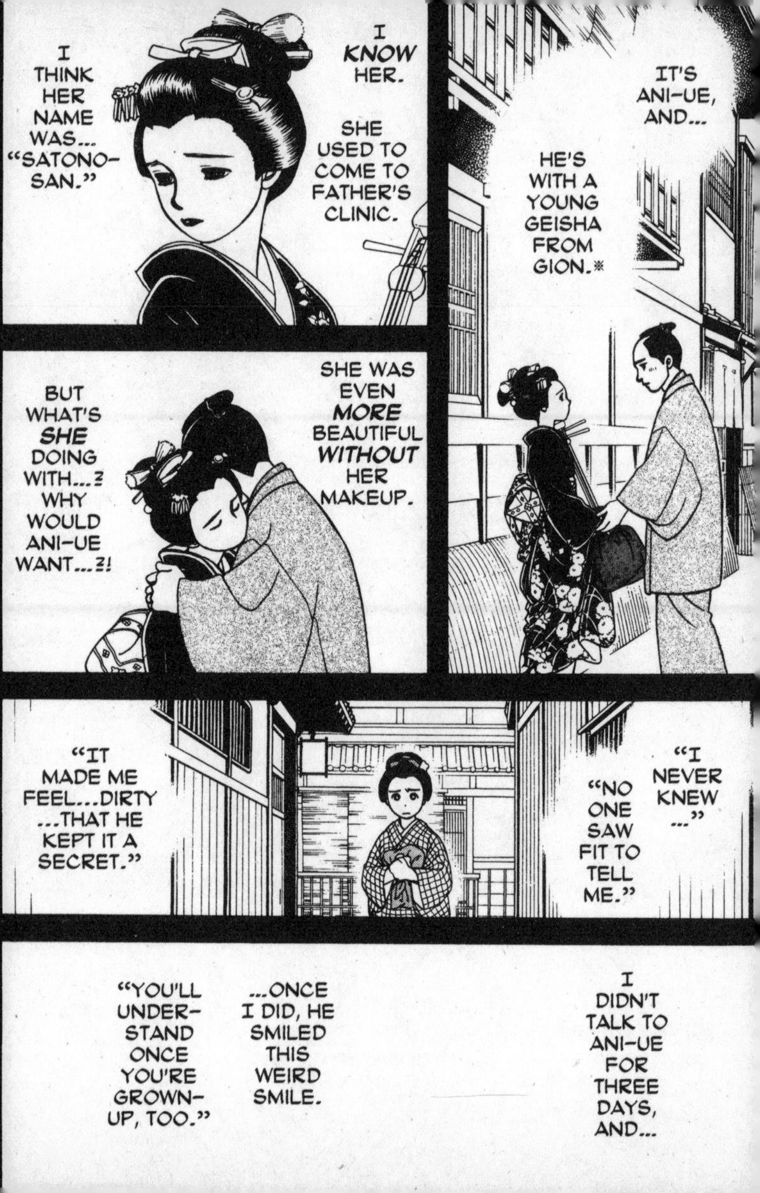
IT'S ANI-UE, AND...
HE'S WITH A YOUNG GEISHA FROM GION.※
I KNOW HER.
SHE USED TO COME TO FATHER'S CLINIC.
I THINK HER NAME WAS... "SATONO-SAN."
SHE WAS EVEN MORE BEAUTIFUL WITHOUT HER MAKEUP.
BUT WHAT'S SHE DOING WITH...? WHY WOULD ANI-UE WANT...?!
"I NEVER KNEW..."
"NO ONE SAW FIT TO TELL ME."
"IT MADE ME FEEL...DIRTY ...THAT HE KEPT IT A SECRET."
I DIDN'T TALK TO ANI-UE FOR THREE DAYS, AND...
...ONCE I DID, HE SMILED THIS WEIRD SMILE.
"YOU'LL UNDER-STAND ONCE YOU'RE GROWN-UP, TOO."

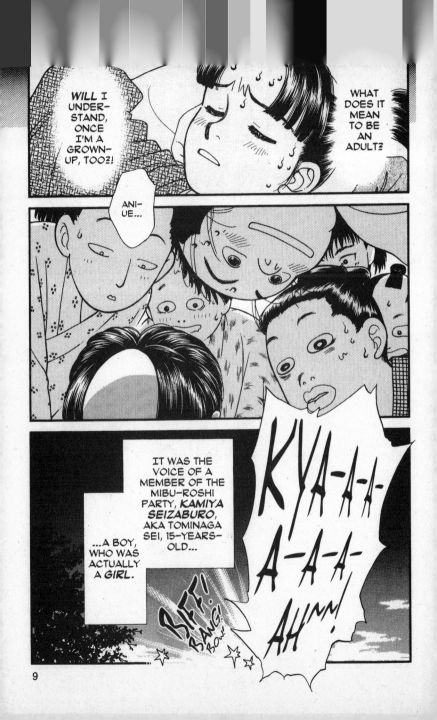

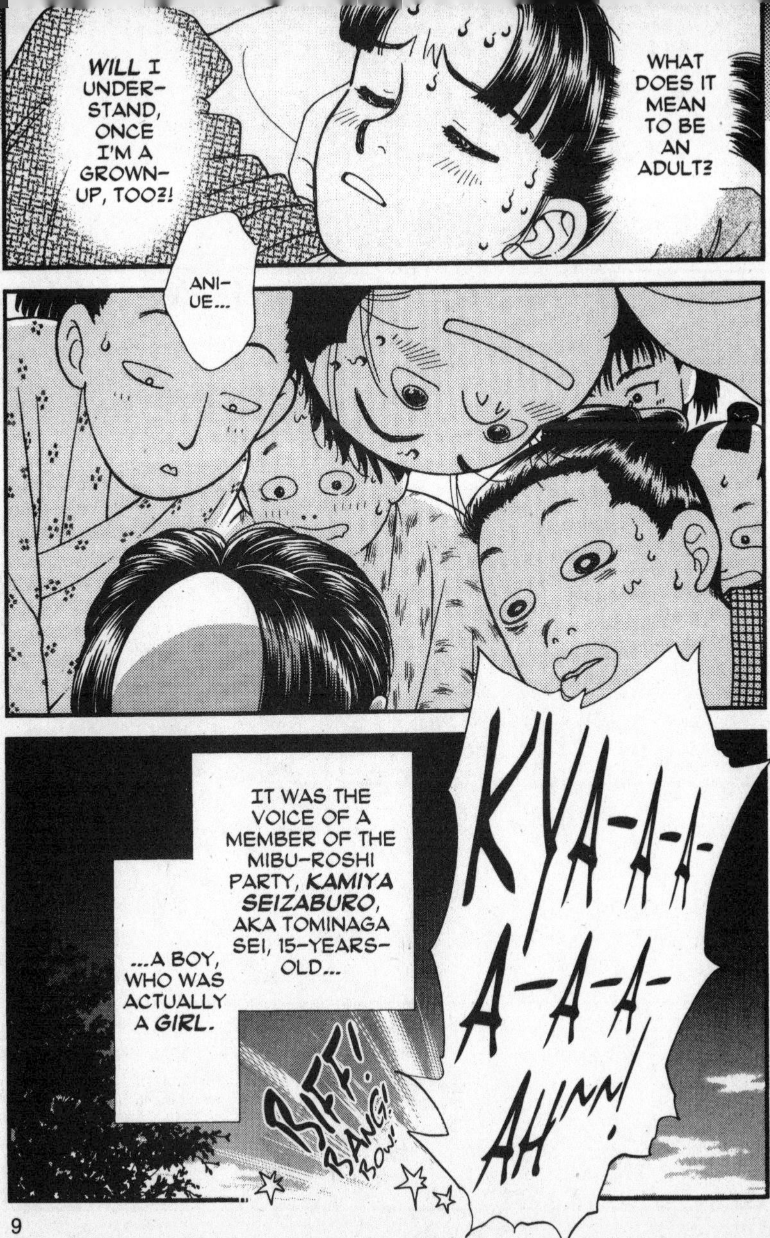
WHAT DOES IT MEAN TO BE AN ADULT?
WILL I UNDERSTAND, ONCE I'M A GROWN-UP, TOO?!
ANI-UE...
KYA-A-A-A-A-A-AHN!
IT WAS THE VOICE OF A MEMBER OF THE MIBU-ROSHI PARTY, KAMIYA SEIZABURO, AKA TOMINAGA SEI, 15-YEARS-OLD...
...A BOY, WHO WAS ACTUALLY A GIRL.
BIFF! BANG! BOW!

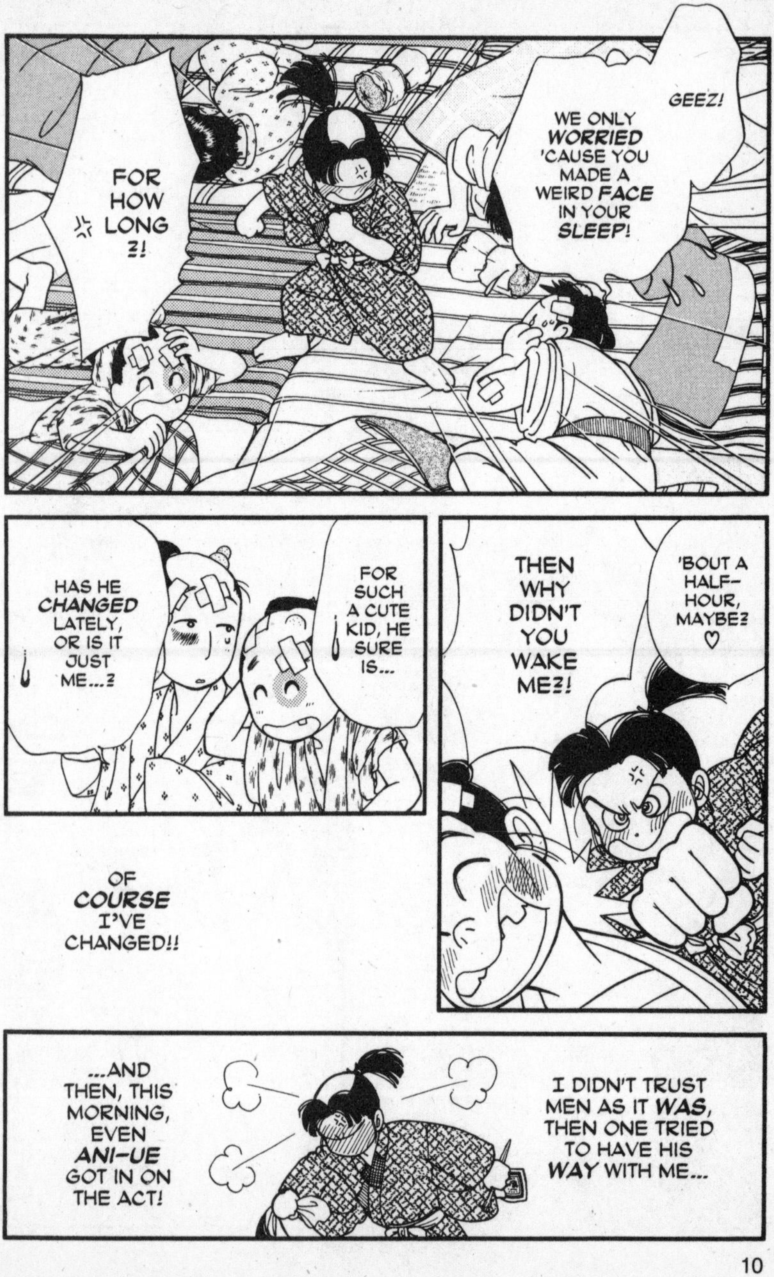
GEEZ!
WE ONLY WORRIED 'CAUSE YOU MADE A WEIRD FACE IN YOUR SLEEP!
FOR HOW LONG?!
'BOUT A HALF-HOUR, MAYBE? ♡
THEN WHY DIDN'T YOU WAKE ME?!
FOR SUCH A CUTE KID, HE SURE IS...
HAS HE CHANGED LATELY, OR IS IT JUST ME...?
OF COURSE I'VE CHANGED!!
I DIDN'T TRUST MEN AS IT WAS, THEN ONE TRIED TO HAVE HIS WAY WITH ME...
...AND THEN, THIS MORNING, EVEN ANI-UE GOT IN ON THE ACT!

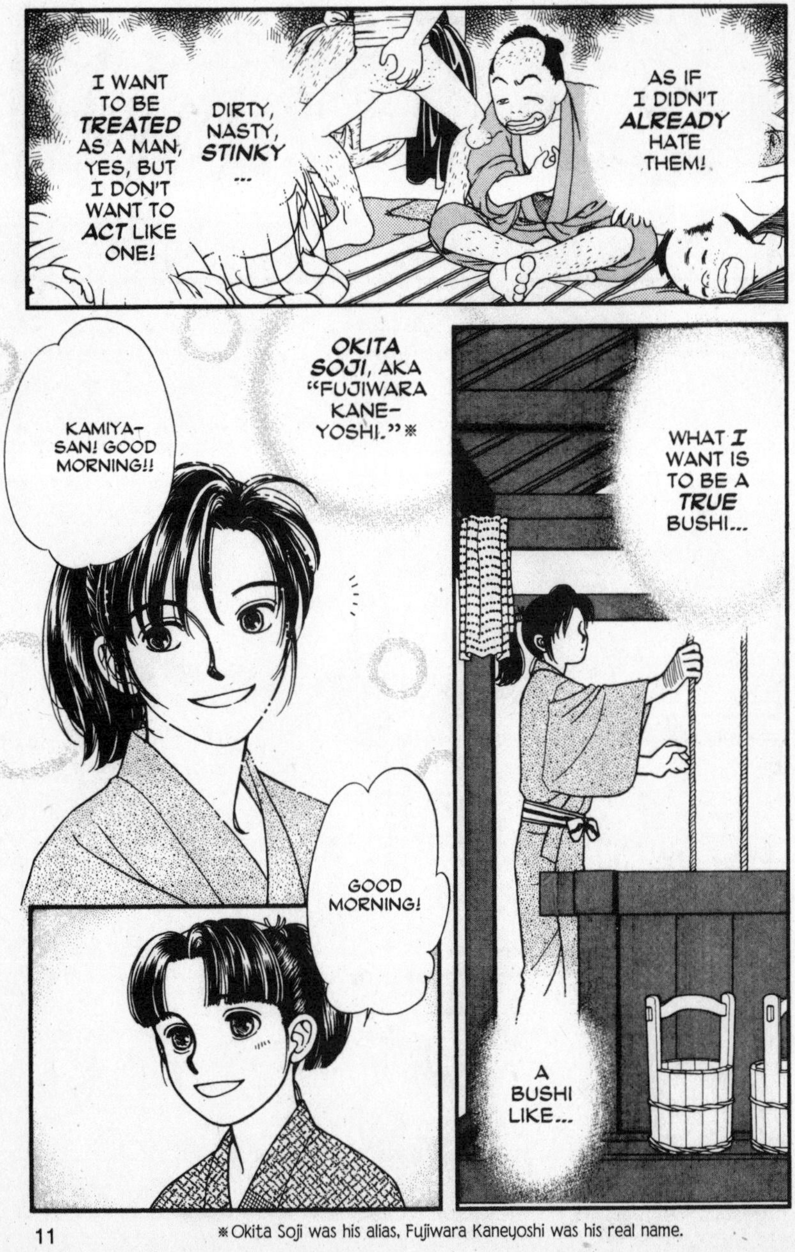
AS IF I DIDN'T ALREADY HATE THEM!
DIRTY, NASTY, STINKY ...
I WANT TO BE TREATED AS A MAN, YES, BUT I DON'T WANT TO ACT LIKE ONE!
WHAT I WANT IS TO BE A TRUE BUSHI...
A BUSHI LIKE...
OKITA SOJI, AKA "FUJIWARA KANE-YOSHI."※
KAMIYA-SAN! GOOD MORNING!!
GOOD MORNING!

※Okita Soji was his alias, Fujiwara Kaneyoshi was his real name.

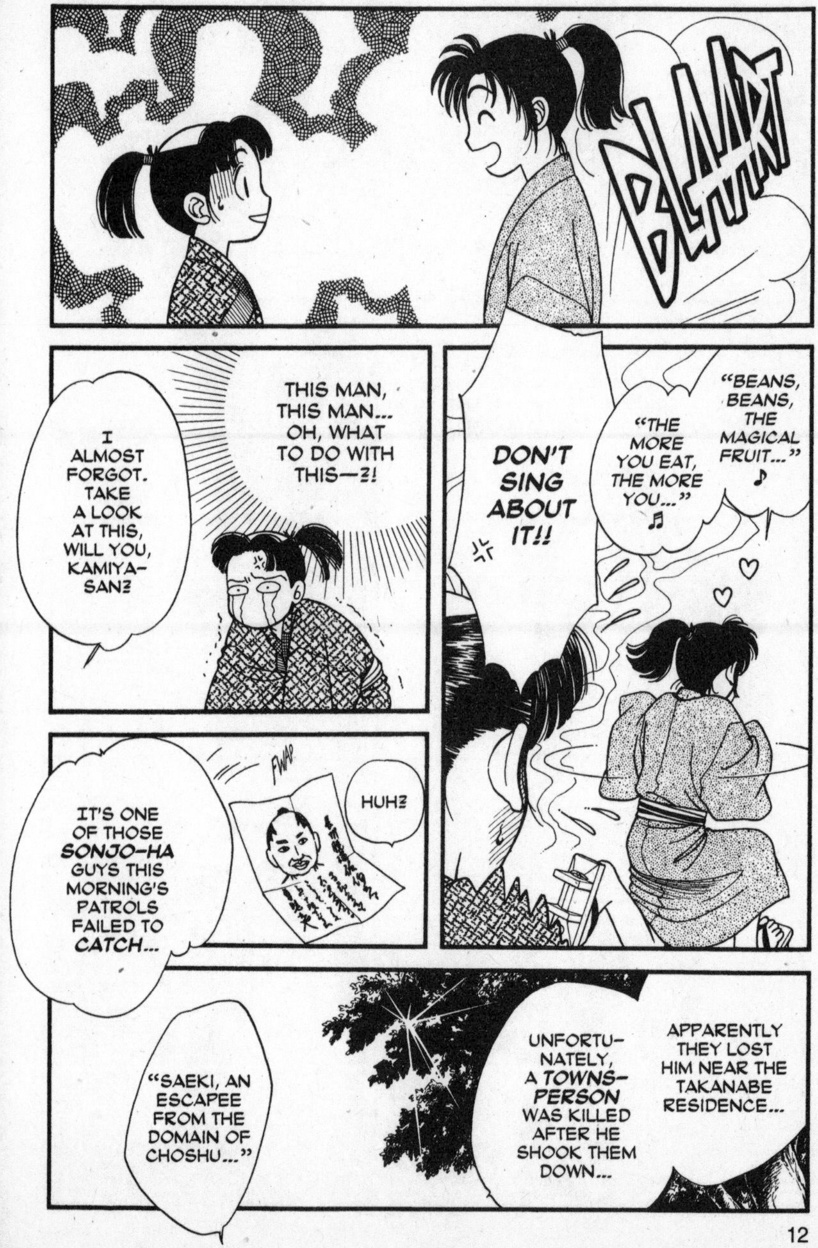
"BEANS, BEANS, THE MAGICAL FRUIT..." ♪
"THE MORE YOU EAT, THE MORE YOU..." ♬
DON'T SING ABOUT IT!!
THIS MAN, THIS MAN... OH, WHAT TO DO WITH THIS—?!
I ALMOST FORGOT. TAKE A LOOK AT THIS, WILL YOU, KAMIYA-SAN?
FWAP
HUH?
IT'S ONE OF THOSE SONJO-HA GUYS THIS MORNING'S PATROLS FAILED TO CATCH...
APPARENTLY THEY LOST HIM NEAR THE TAKANABE RESIDENCE...
UNFORTUNATELY, A TOWNSPERSON WAS KILLED AFTER HE SHOOK THEM DOWN...
"SAEKI, AN ESCAPEE FROM THE DOMAIN OF CHOSHU..."

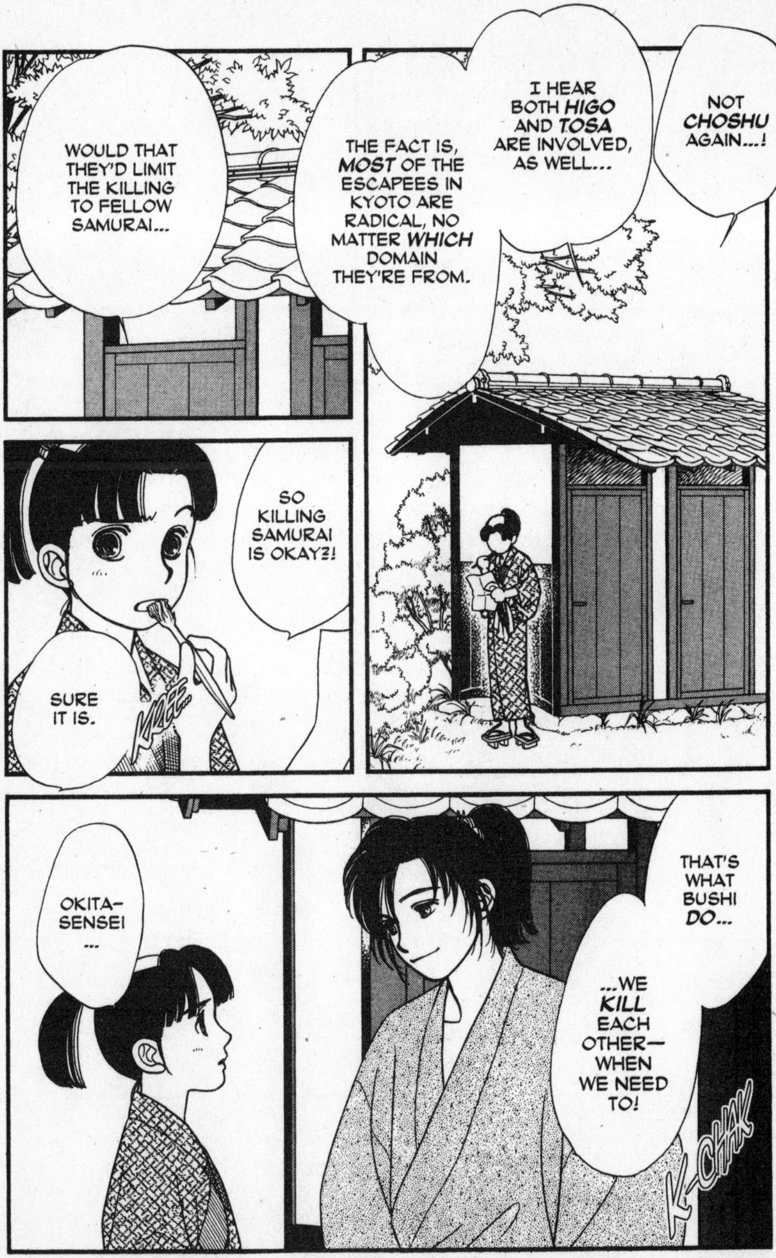
NOT CHOSHU AGAIN...!
I HEAR BOTH HIGO AND TOSA ARE INVOLVED, AS WELL...
THE FACT IS, MOST OF THE ESCAPEES IN KYOTO ARE RADICAL, NO MATTER WHICH DOMAIN THEY'RE FROM.
WOULD THAT THEY'D LIMIT THE KILLING TO FELLOW SAMURAI...
SO KILLING SAMURAI IS OKAY?!
SURE IT IS.
THAT'S WHAT BUSHI DO...
...WE KILL EACH OTHER— WHEN WE NEED TO!
K-CHAK
OKITA-SENSEI ...

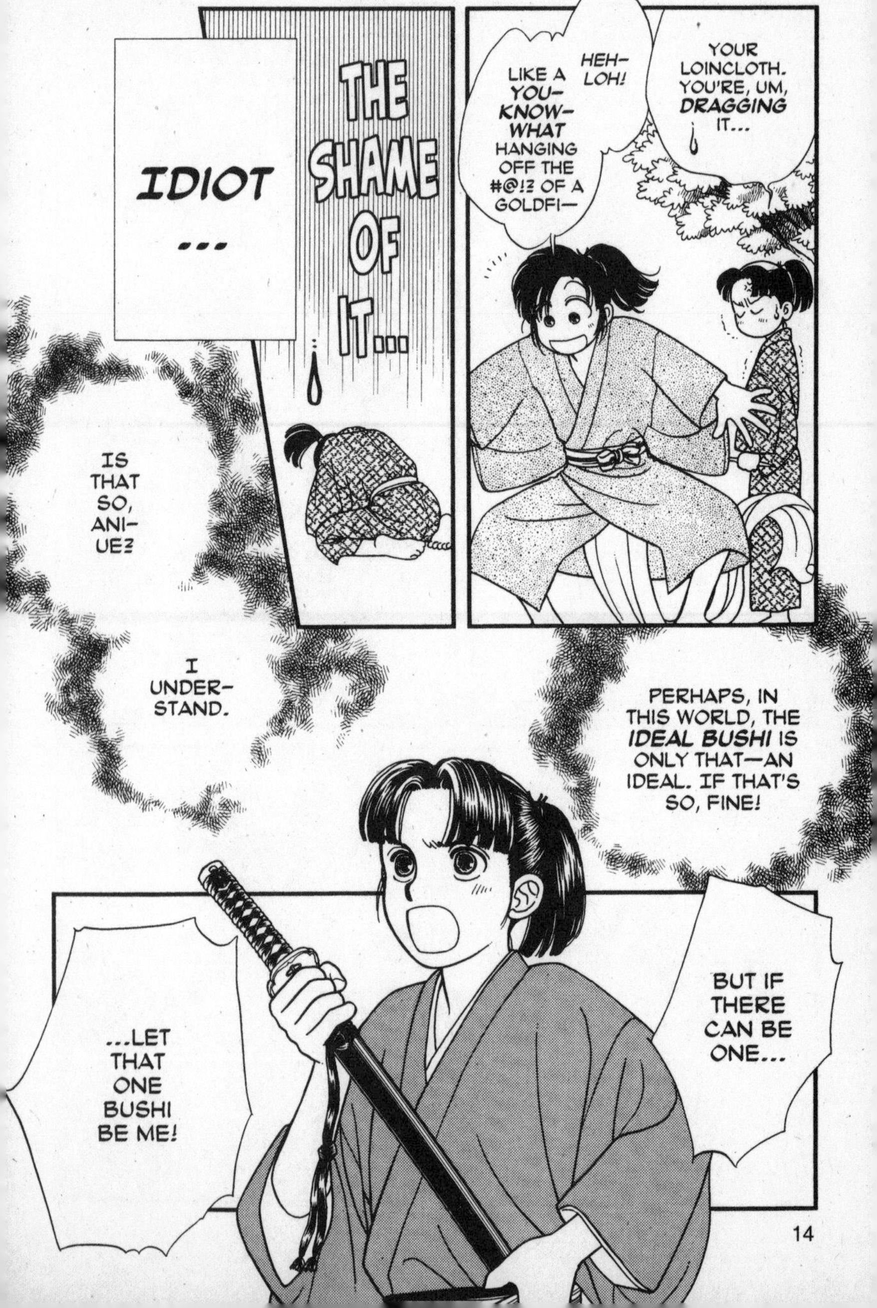
YOUR LOINCLOTH. YOU'RE, UM, DRAGGING IT...
HEH-LOH! LIKE A YOU-KNOW-WHAT HANGING OFF THE #@!? OF A GOLDFI—
THE SHAME OF IT...
IDIOT ...
IS THAT SO, ANI-UE?
I UNDER-STAND.
PERHAPS, IN THIS WORLD, THE IDEAL BUSHI IS ONLY THAT—AN IDEAL. IF THAT'S SO, FINE!
BUT IF THERE CAN BE ONE...
...LET THAT ONE BUSHI BE ME!

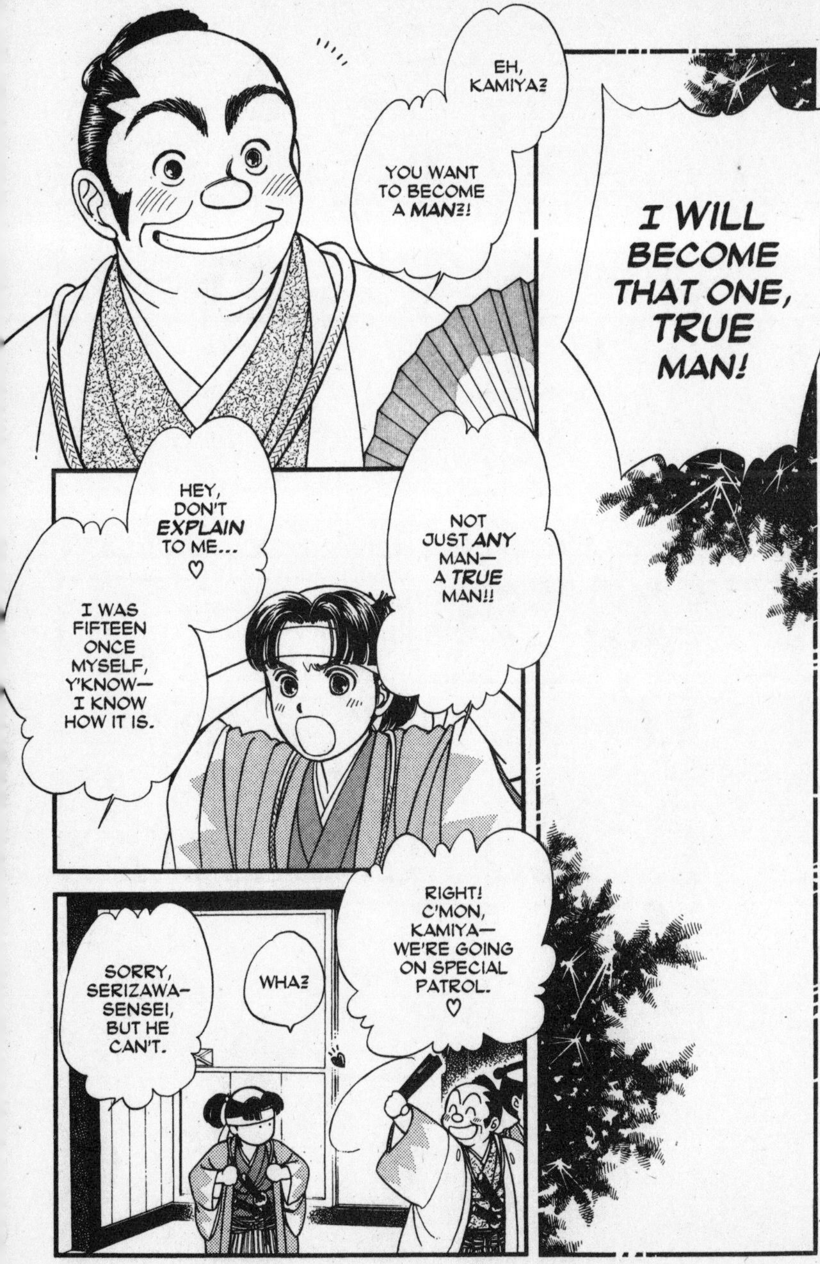
I WILL BECOME THAT ONE, TRUE MAN!
EH, KAMIYA?
YOU WANT TO BECOME A MAN?!
NOT JUST ANY MAN— A TRUE MAN!!
HEY, DON'T EXPLAIN TO ME... ♡
I WAS FIFTEEN ONCE MYSELF, Y'KNOW— I KNOW HOW IT IS.
RIGHT! C'MON, KAMIYA— WE'RE GOING ON SPECIAL PATROL. ♡
WHA?
SORRY, SERIZAWA-SENSEI, BUT HE CAN'T.

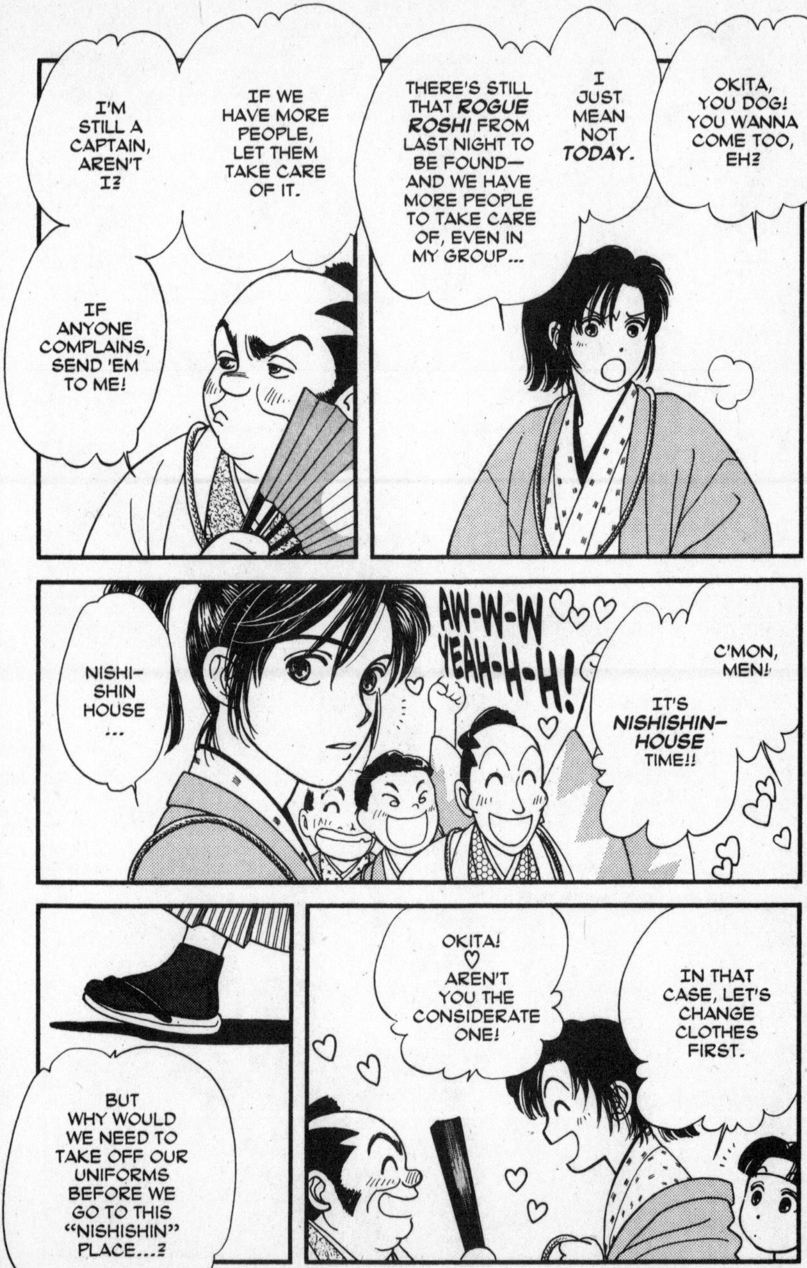
OKITA, YOU DOG! YOU WANNA COME TOO, EH?
I JUST MEAN NOT *TODAY*.
THERE'S STILL THAT *ROGUE ROSHI* FROM LAST NIGHT TO BE FOUND—AND WE HAVE MORE PEOPLE TO TAKE CARE OF, EVEN IN MY GROUP...
IF WE HAVE MORE PEOPLE, LET THEM TAKE CARE OF IT.
I'M STILL A CAPTAIN, AREN'T I?
IF ANYONE COMPLAINS, SEND 'EM TO ME!
C'MON, MEN!
IT'S *NISHISHIN-HOUSE* TIME!!
AW-W-W YEAH-H-H!
NISHI-SHIN HOUSE ...
IN THAT CASE, LET'S CHANGE CLOTHES FIRST.
OKITA! ♡ AREN'T YOU THE CONSIDERATE ONE!
BUT WHY WOULD WE NEED TO TAKE OFF OUR UNIFORMS BEFORE WE GO TO THIS "NISHISHIN" PLACE...?

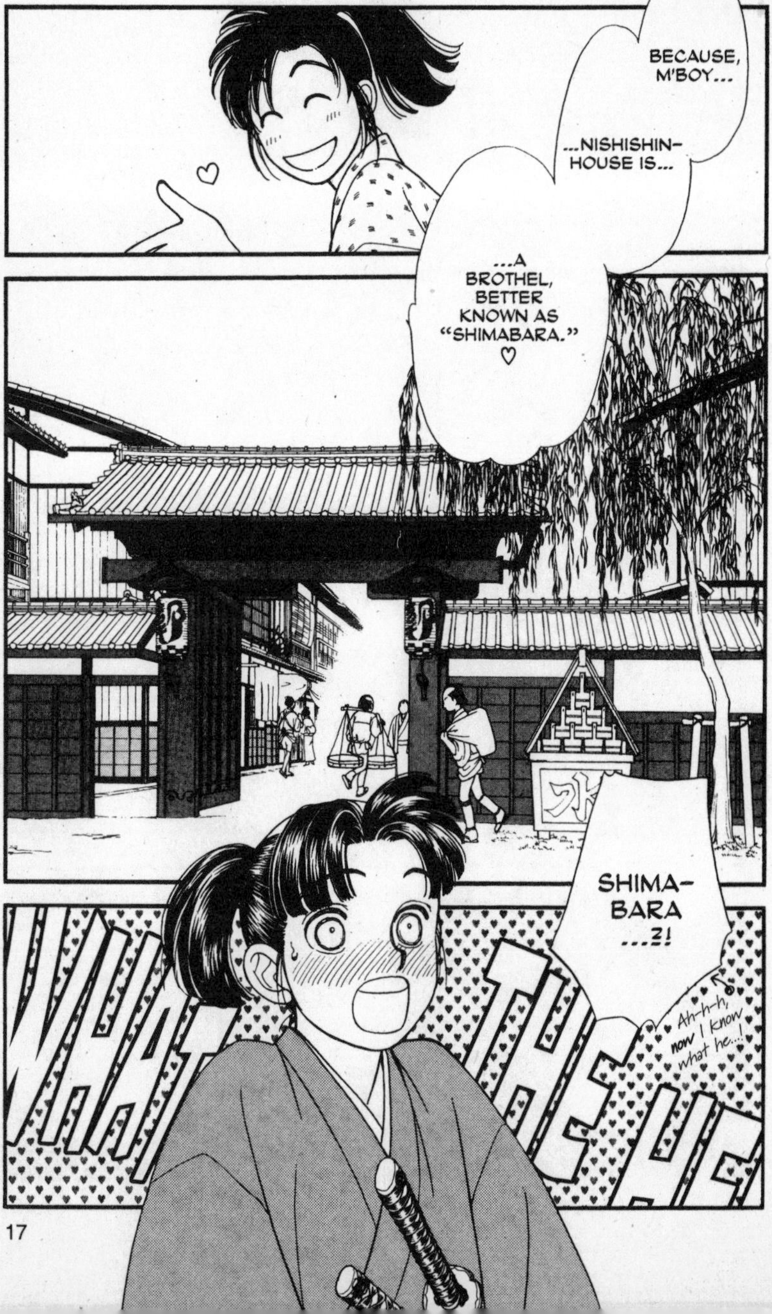
BECAUSE, M'BOY...
...NISHISHIN-HOUSE IS...
...A BROTHEL, BETTER KNOWN AS "SHIMABARA." ♡
SHIMA-BARA ...?!
Ah-h-h, **now** I know what he...!
WHAT THE HE

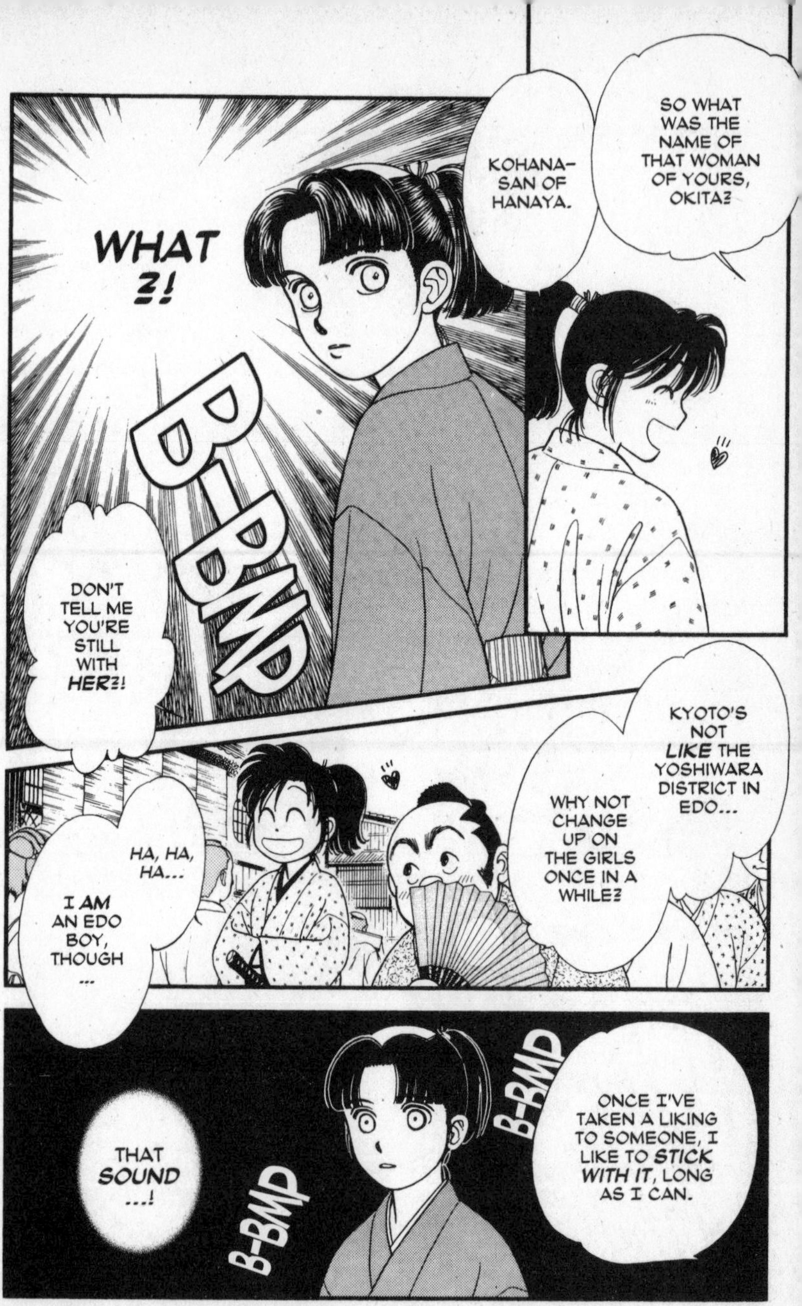
SO WHAT WAS THE NAME OF THAT WOMAN OF YOURS, OKITA?
KOHANA-SAN OF HANAYA.
WHAT?!
B-BMP
DON'T TELL ME YOU'RE STILL WITH HER?!
KYOTO'S NOT LIKE THE YOSHIWARA DISTRICT IN EDO...
WHY NOT CHANGE UP ON THE GIRLS ONCE IN A WHILE?
HA, HA, HA...
I AM AN EDO BOY, THOUGH ...
ONCE I'VE TAKEN A LIKING TO SOMEONE, I LIKE TO STICK WITH IT, LONG AS I CAN.
B-BMP
B-BMP
THAT SOUND ...!

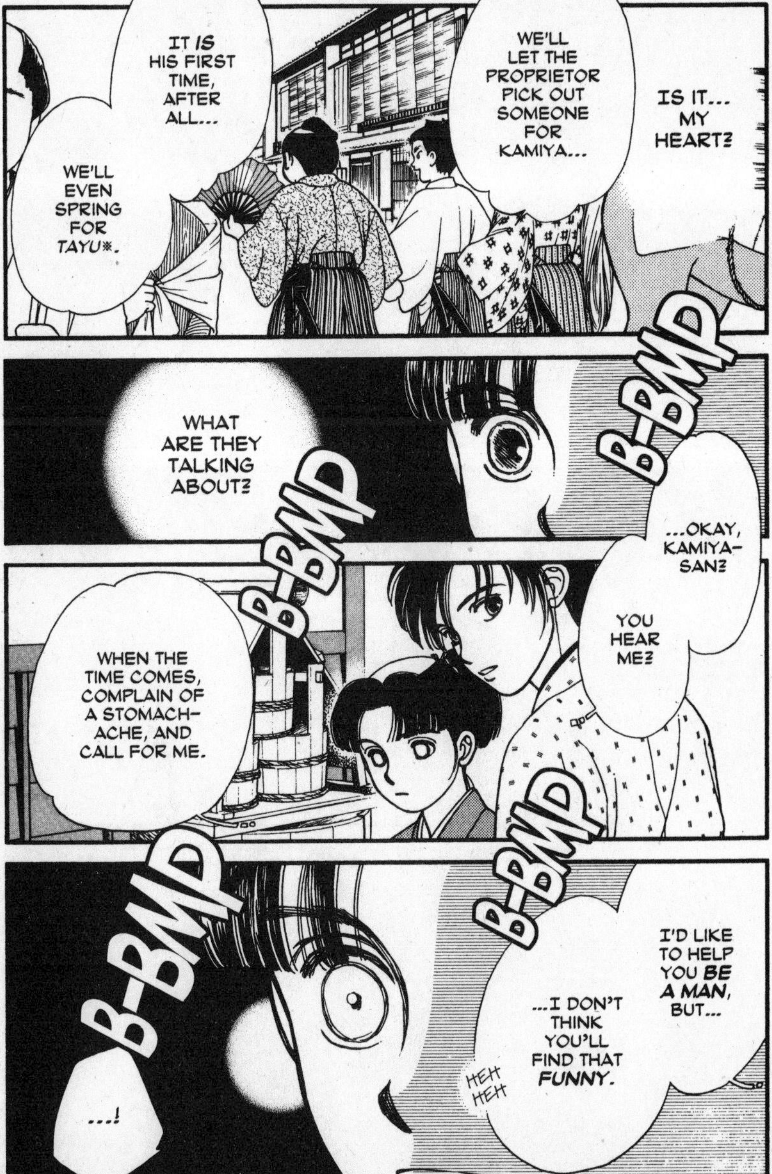
IS IT... MY HEART?
WE'LL LET THE PROPRIETOR PICK OUT SOMEONE FOR KAMIYA...
IT *IS* HIS FIRST TIME, AFTER ALL...
WE'LL EVEN SPRING FOR *TAYU*※.
B-BMP
B-BMP
WHAT ARE THEY TALKING ABOUT?
...OKAY, KAMIYA-SAN?
YOU HEAR ME?
B-BMP
WHEN THE TIME COMES, COMPLAIN OF A STOMACH-ACHE, AND CALL FOR ME.
B-BMP
B-BMP
I'D LIKE TO HELP YOU **BE A MAN**, BUT...
...I DON'T THINK YOU'LL FIND THAT **FUNNY**.
HEH HEH
...!

※*Tayu*: The highest rank of a Shimabara courtesan, followed by "*tenjin*" and "*kakoi*."

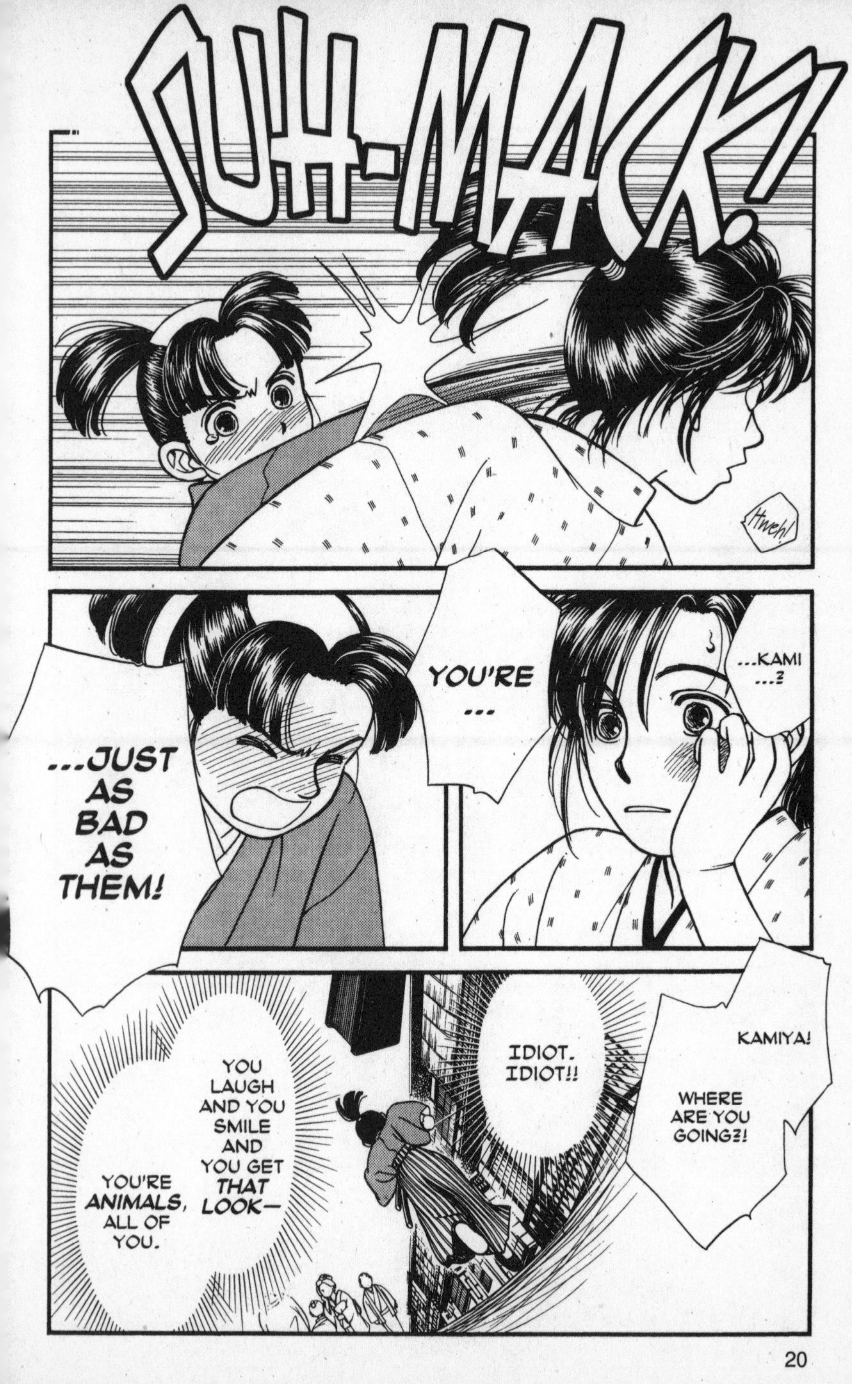
SUH-MACK!
Hweh!
...KAMI...?
YOU'RE...
...JUST AS BAD AS THEM!
KAMIYA!
WHERE ARE YOU GOING?!
IDIOT. IDIOT!!
YOU LAUGH AND YOU SMILE AND YOU GET THAT LOOK—
YOU'RE ANIMALS, ALL OF YOU.

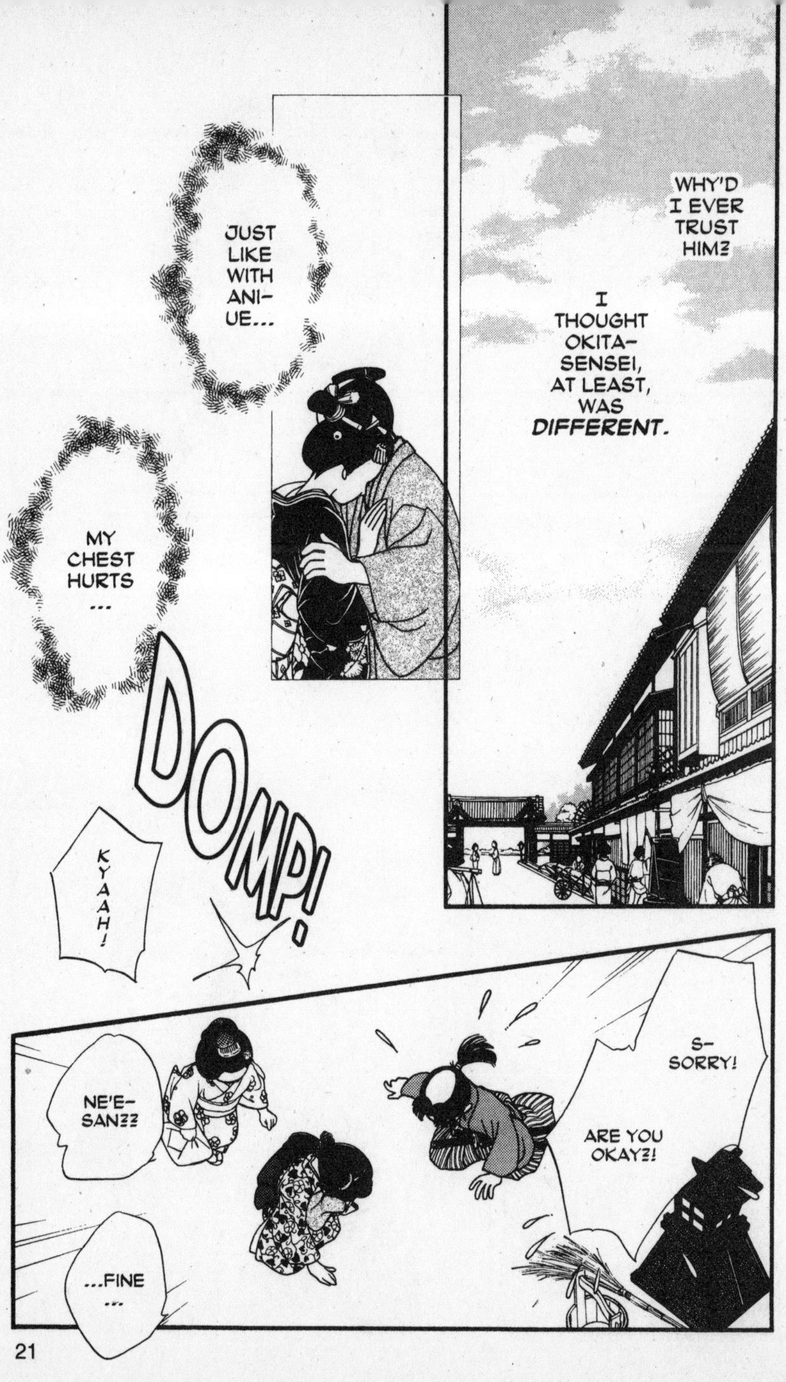

WHY'D I EVER TRUST HIM?
I THOUGHT OKITA-SENSEI, AT LEAST, WAS DIFFERENT.
JUST LIKE WITH ANI-UE...
MY CHEST HURTS...
DOMP!
KYAAH!
S-SORRY!
ARE YOU OKAY?!
NE'E-SAN??
...FINE...

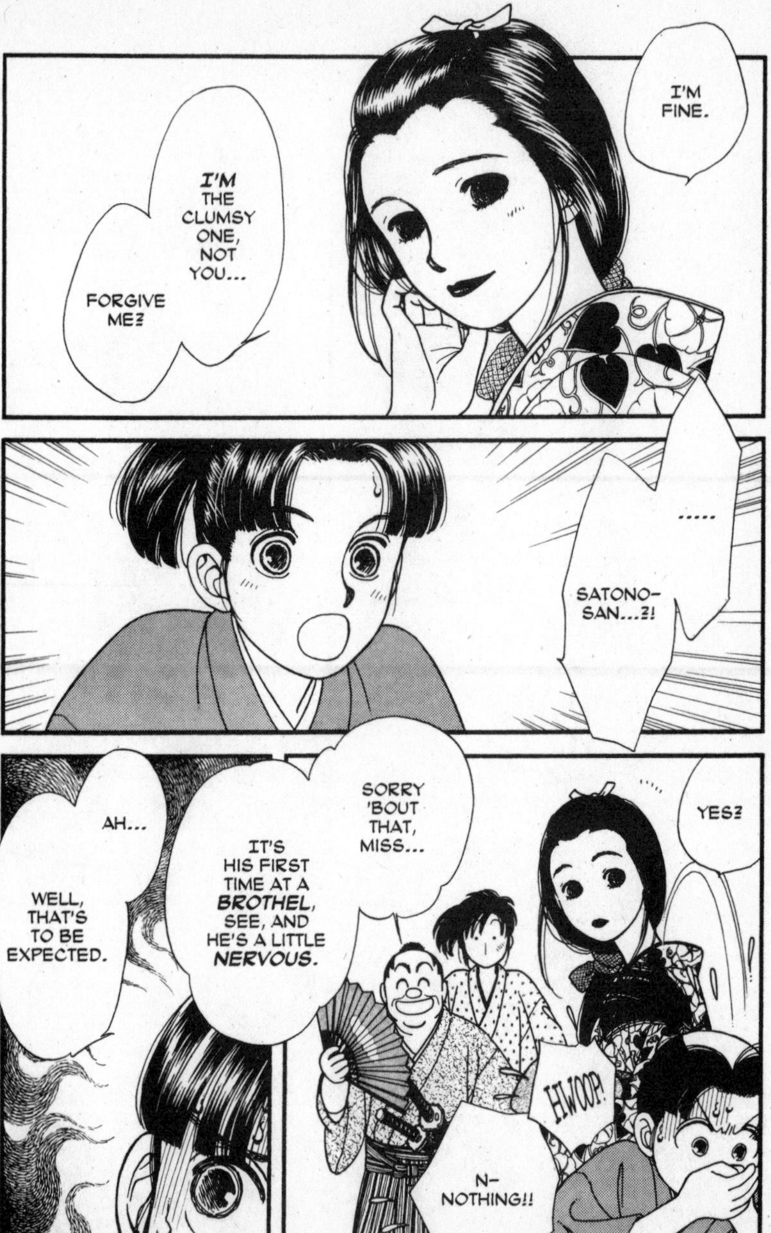
I'M FINE.
I'M THE CLUMSY ONE, NOT YOU... FORGIVE ME?
.....
SATONO-SAN...?!
YES?
SORRY 'BOUT THAT, MISS...
IT'S HIS FIRST TIME AT A BROTHEL, SEE, AND HE'S A LITTLE NERVOUS.
HWOOP!
N-NOTHING!!
AH...
WELL, THAT'S TO BE EXPECTED.

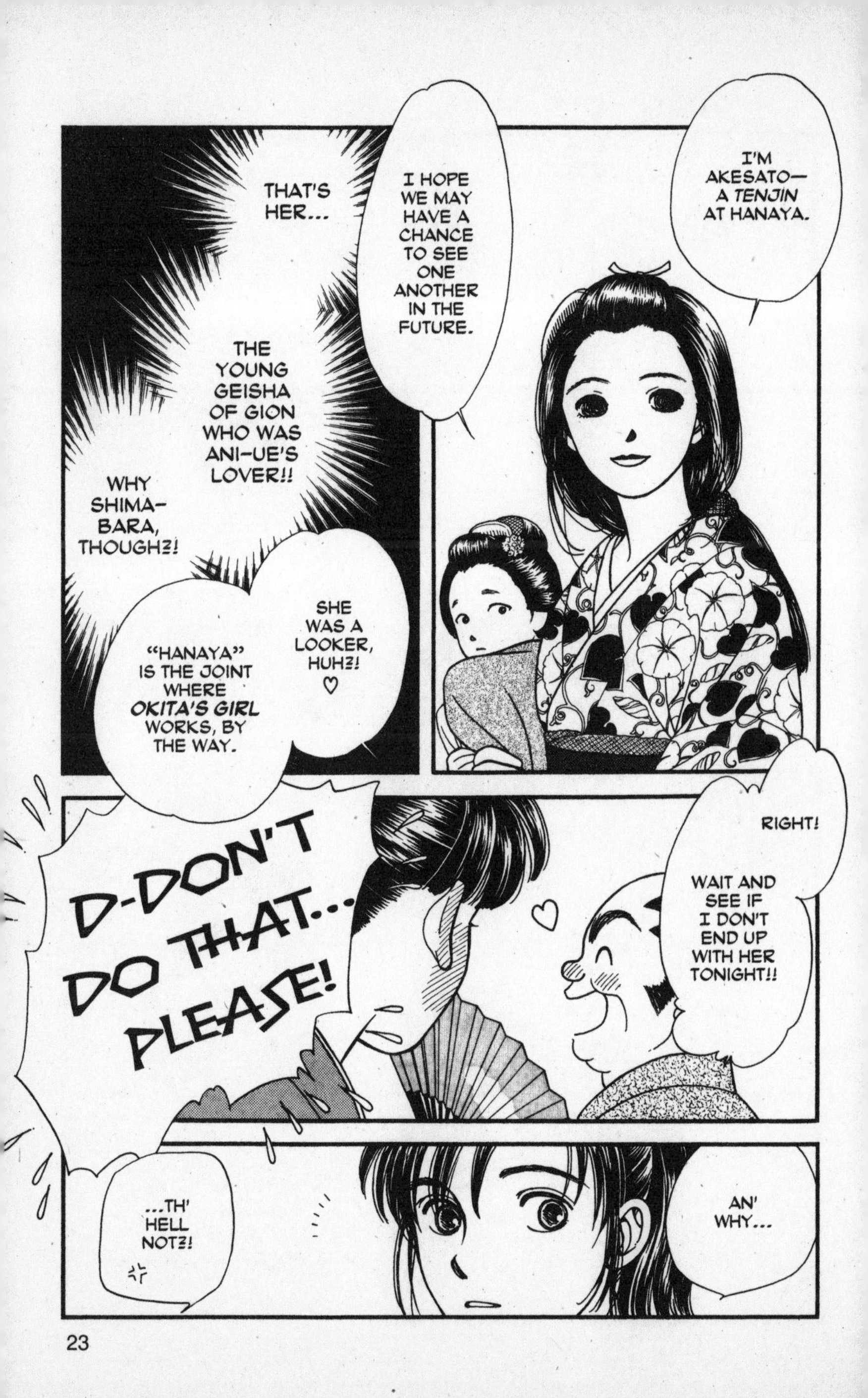
I'M AKESATO— A *TENJIN* AT HANAYA.
I HOPE WE MAY HAVE A CHANCE TO SEE ONE ANOTHER IN THE FUTURE.
THAT'S HER...
THE YOUNG GEISHA OF GION WHO WAS ANI-UE'S LOVER!!
WHY SHIMA-BARA, THOUGH?!
SHE WAS A LOOKER, HUH?! ♡
"HANAYA" IS THE JOINT WHERE ***OKITA'S GIRL*** WORKS, BY THE WAY.
RIGHT!
WAIT AND SEE IF I DON'T END UP WITH HER TONIGHT!!
D-DON'T DO THAT... PLEASE!
AN' WHY...
...TH' HELL NOT?!

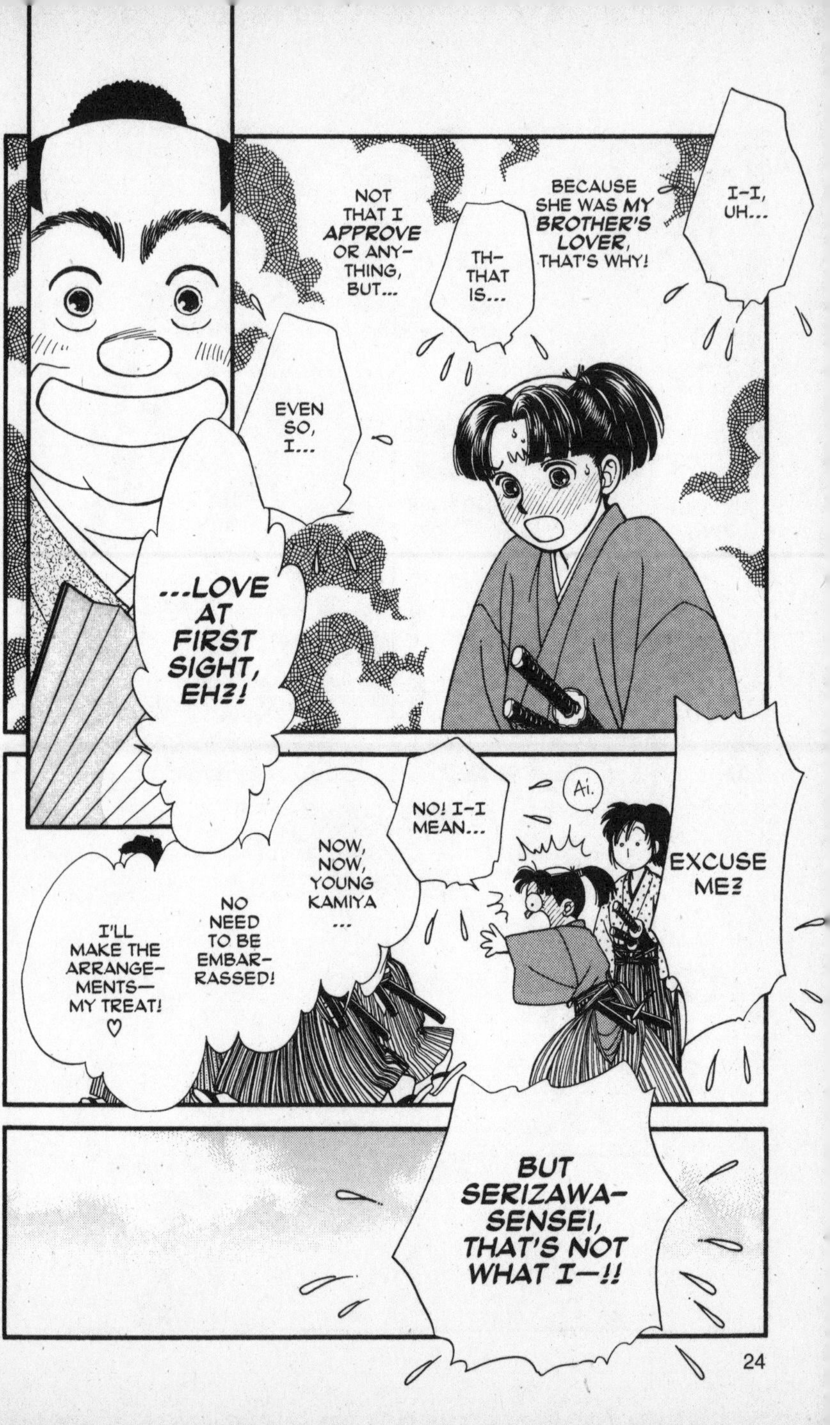
I-I, UH...
BECAUSE SHE WAS MY BROTHER'S LOVER, THAT'S WHY!
TH- THAT IS...
NOT THAT I APPROVE OR ANYTHING, BUT...
EVEN SO, I...
...LOVE AT FIRST SIGHT, EH?!
EXCUSE ME?
Ai.
NO! I-I MEAN...
NOW, NOW, YOUNG KAMIYA...
NO NEED TO BE EMBARRASSED!
I'LL MAKE THE ARRANGEMENTS— MY TREAT! ♡
BUT SERIZAWA-SENSEI, THAT'S NOT WHAT I—!!

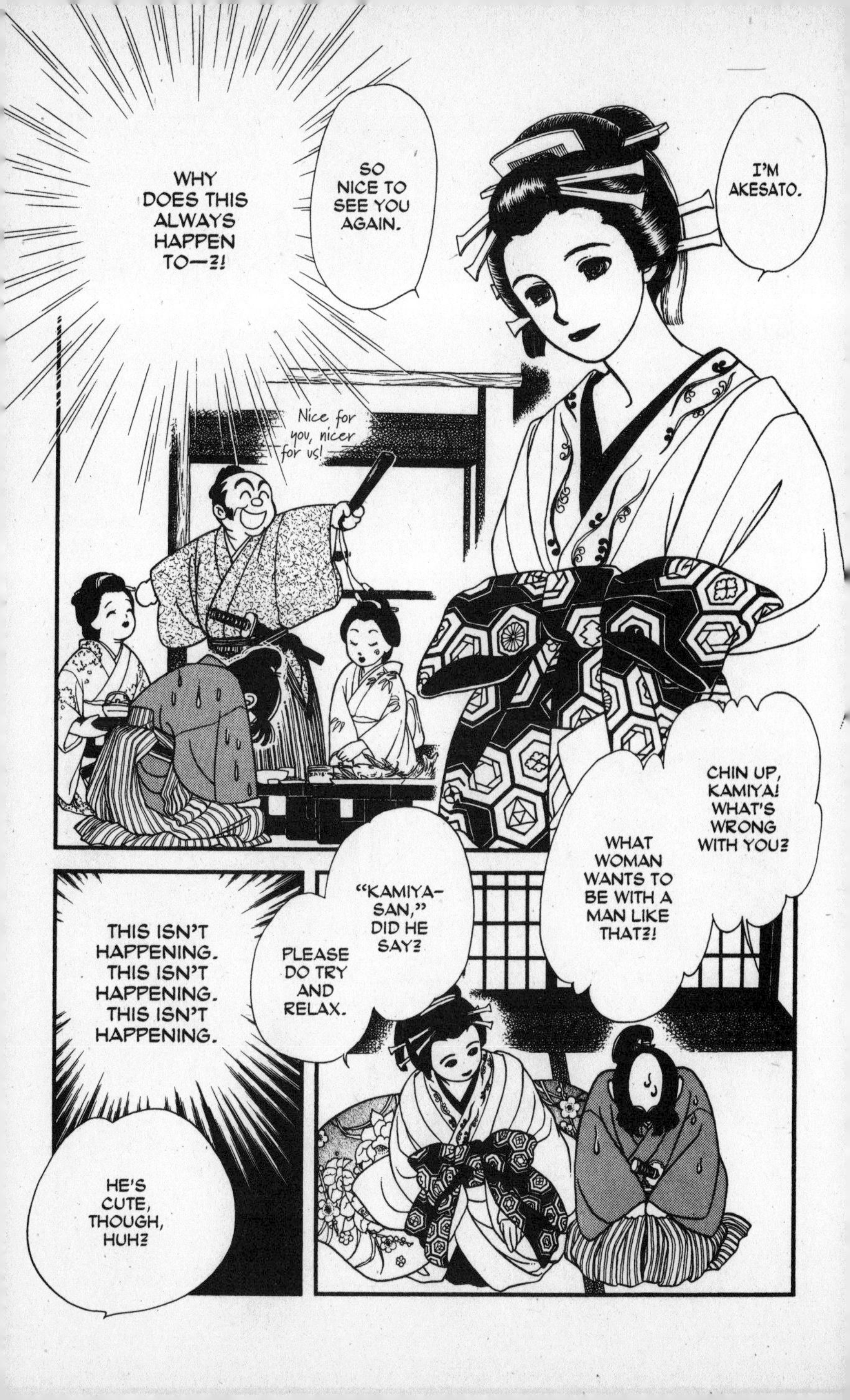
I'M AKESATO.
SO NICE TO SEE YOU AGAIN.
WHY DOES THIS ALWAYS HAPPEN TO—?!
Nice for you, nicer for us!
CHIN UP, KAMIYA! WHAT'S WRONG WITH YOU?
WHAT WOMAN WANTS TO BE WITH A MAN LIKE THAT?!
"KAMIYA-SAN," DID HE SAY?
PLEASE DO TRY AND RELAX.
THIS ISN'T HAPPENING. THIS ISN'T HAPPENING. THIS ISN'T HAPPENING.
HE'S CUTE, THOUGH, HUH?

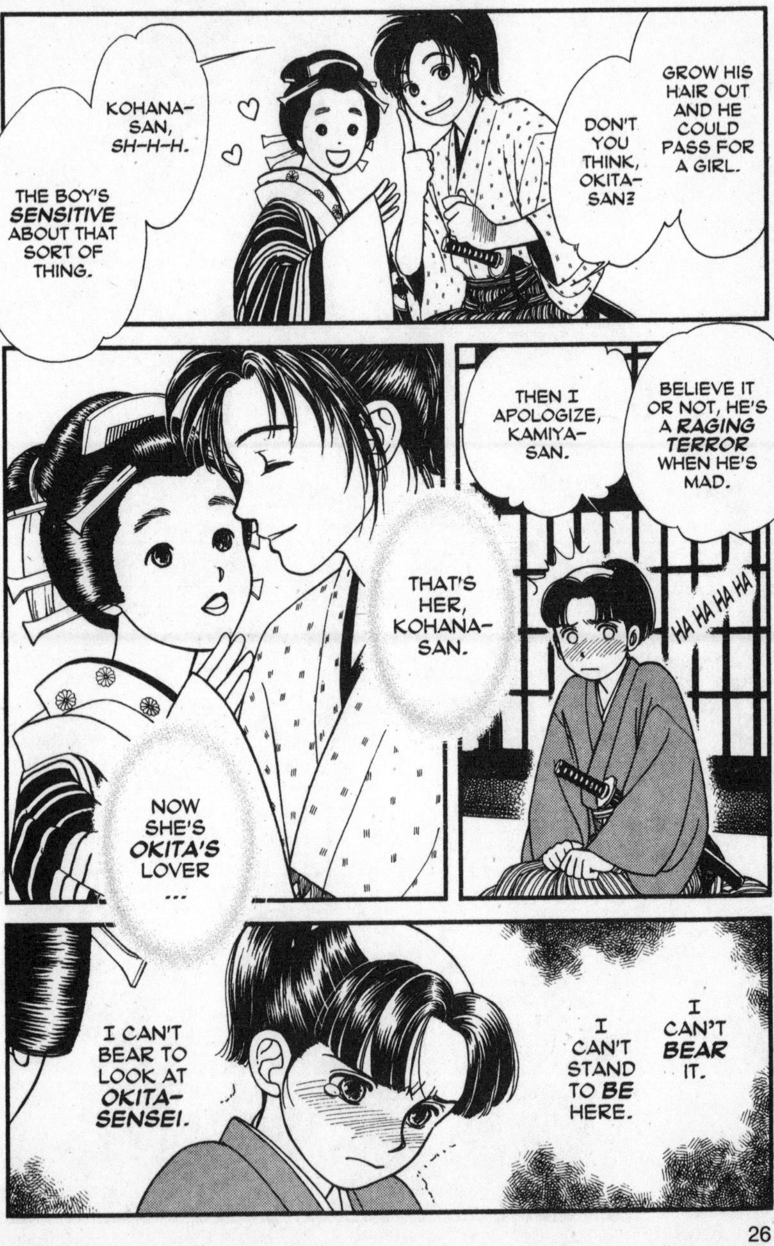
GROW HIS HAIR OUT AND HE COULD PASS FOR A GIRL.
DON'T YOU THINK, OKITA-SAN?
KOHANA-SAN, SH-H-H.
THE BOY'S SENSITIVE ABOUT THAT SORT OF THING.
BELIEVE IT OR NOT, HE'S A RAGING TERROR WHEN HE'S MAD.
THEN I APOLOGIZE, KAMIYA-SAN.
HA HA HA HA
THAT'S HER, KOHANA-SAN.
NOW SHE'S OKITA'S LOVER ...
I CAN'T BEAR IT.
I CAN'T STAND TO BE HERE.
I CAN'T BEAR TO LOOK AT OKITA-SENSEI.

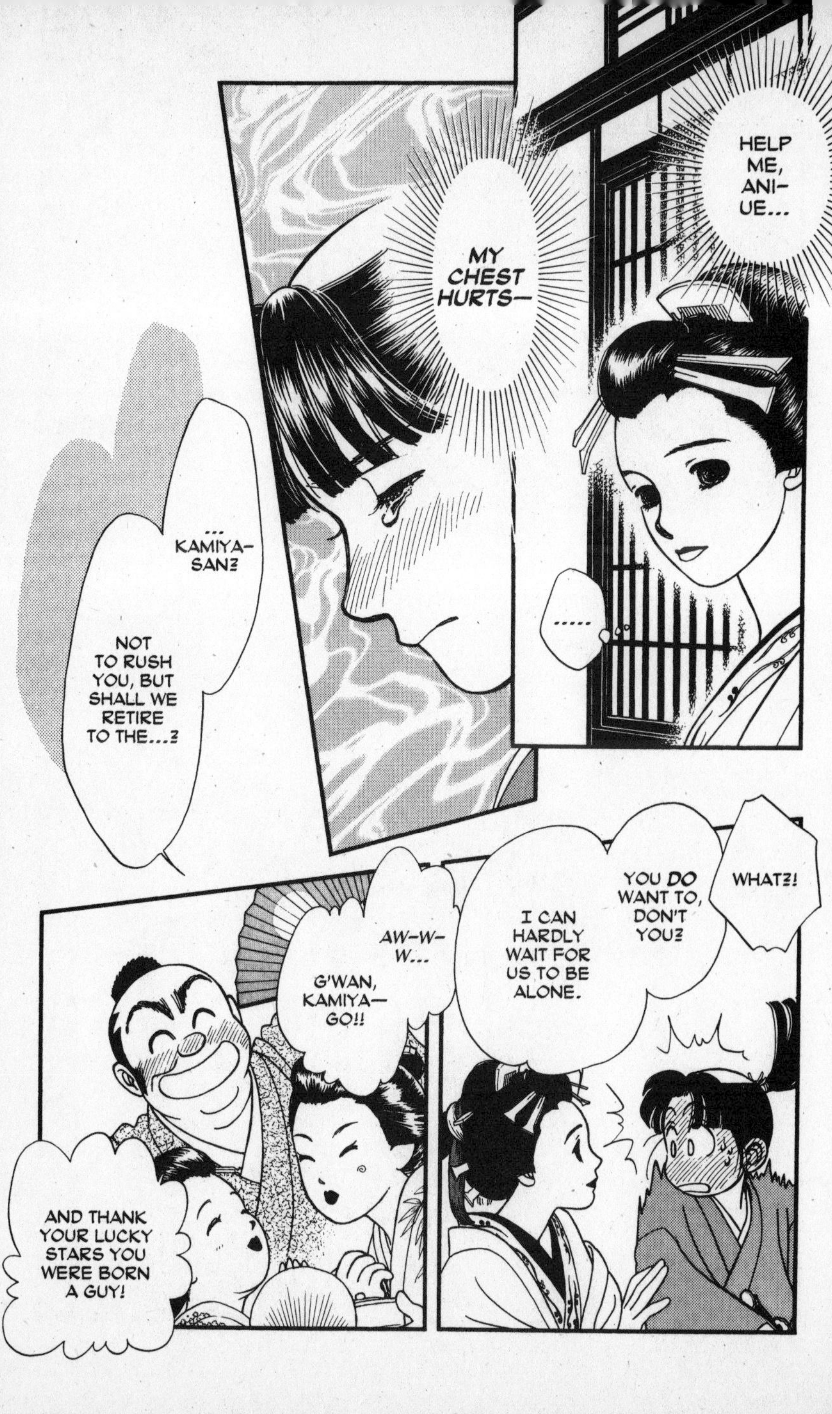
HELP ME, ANI-UE...
MY CHEST HURTS—
.....
...KAMIYA-SAN?
NOT TO RUSH YOU, BUT SHALL WE RETIRE TO THE...?
WHAT?!
YOU DO WANT TO, DON'T YOU?
I CAN HARDLY WAIT FOR US TO BE ALONE.
AW-W-W...
G'WAN, KAMIYA—GO!!
AND THANK YOUR LUCKY STARS YOU WERE BORN A GUY!

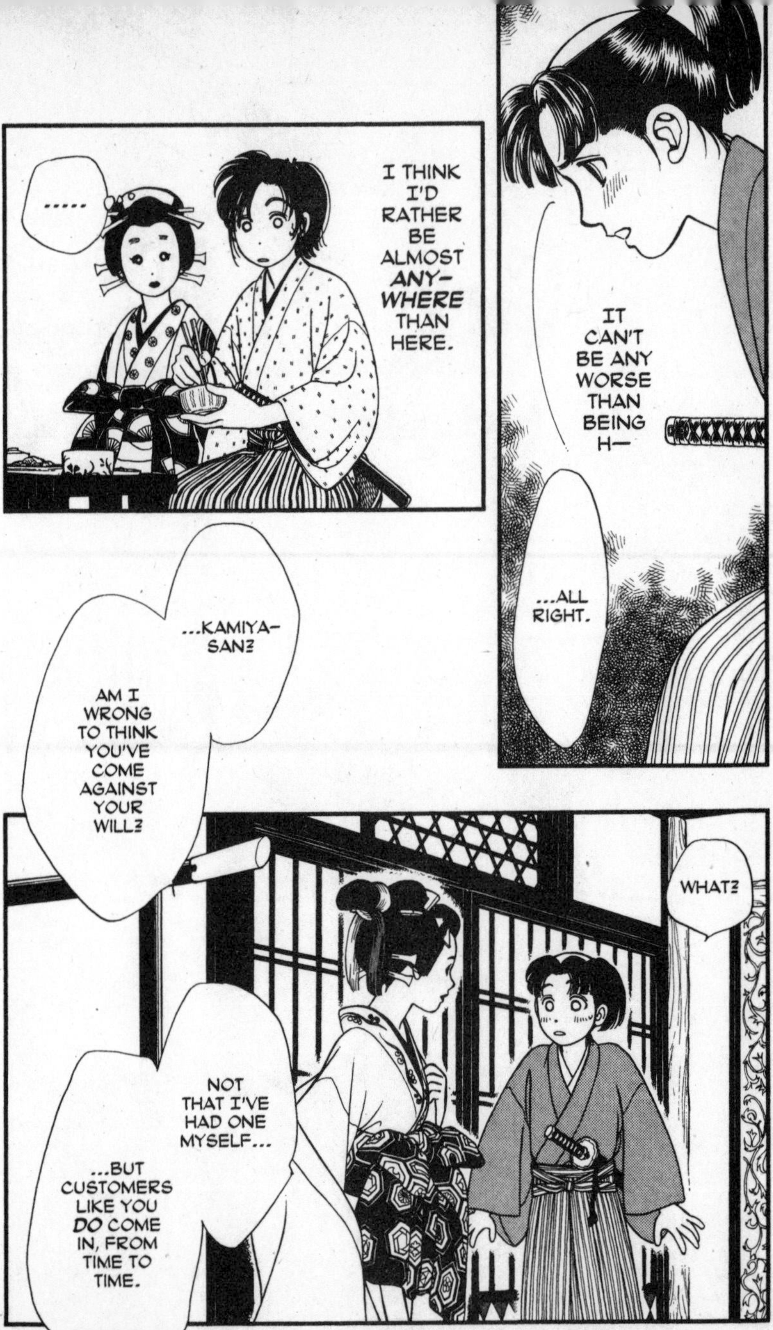
IT CAN'T BE ANY WORSE THAN BEING H—
...ALL RIGHT.
......
I THINK I'D RATHER BE ALMOST *ANY-WHERE* THAN HERE.
...KAMIYA-SAN?
AM I WRONG TO THINK YOU'VE COME AGAINST YOUR WILL?
WHAT?
NOT THAT I'VE HAD ONE MYSELF...
...BUT CUSTOMERS LIKE YOU *DO* COME IN, FROM TIME TO TIME.

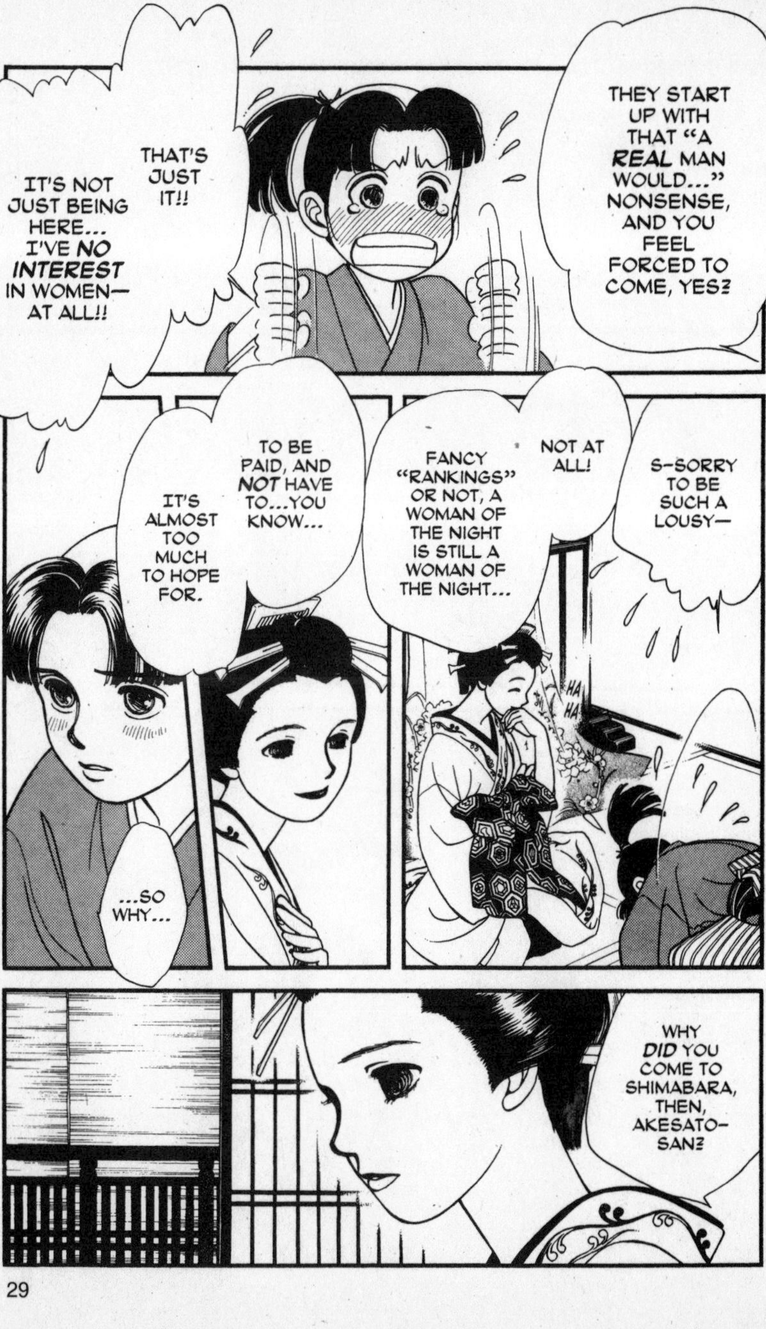
THEY START UP WITH THAT "A **REAL** MAN WOULD..." NONSENSE, AND YOU FEEL FORCED TO COME, YES?
THAT'S JUST IT!!
IT'S NOT JUST BEING HERE... I'VE **NO INTEREST** IN WOMEN— AT ALL!!
S-SORRY TO BE SUCH A LOUSY—
NOT AT ALL!
FANCY "RANKINGS" OR NOT, A WOMAN OF THE NIGHT IS STILL A WOMAN OF THE NIGHT...
HA HA
TO BE PAID, AND **NOT** HAVE TO...YOU KNOW...
IT'S ALMOST TOO MUCH TO HOPE FOR.
...SO WHY...
WHY **DID** YOU COME TO SHIMABARA, THEN, AKESATO-SAN?

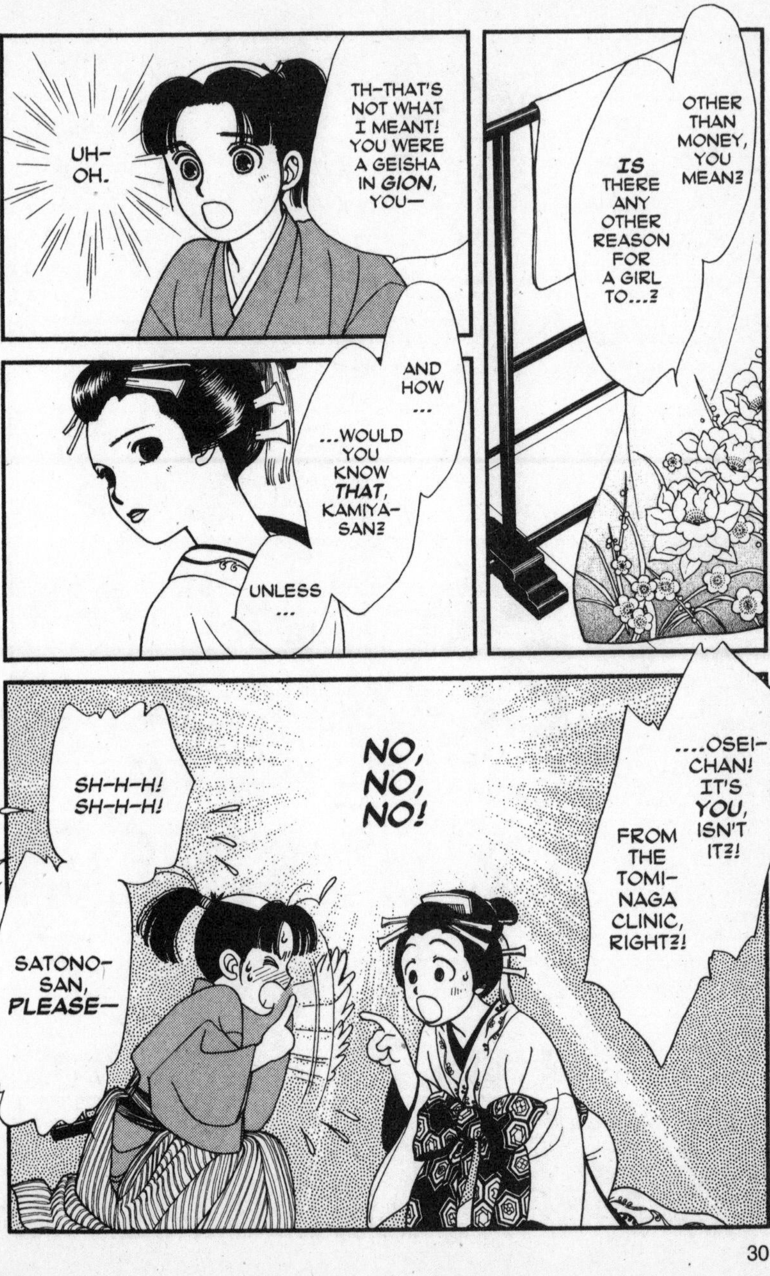
OTHER THAN MONEY, YOU MEAN?
IS THERE ANY OTHER REASON FOR A GIRL TO...?
TH-THAT'S NOT WHAT I MEANT! YOU WERE A GEISHA IN GION, YOU—
UH-OH.
AND HOW ...
...WOULD YOU KNOW THAT, KAMIYA-SAN?
UNLESS ...
....OSEI-CHAN! IT'S YOU, ISN'T IT?!
FROM THE TOMI-NAGA CLINIC, RIGHT?!
NO, NO, NO!
SH-H-H! SH-H-H!
SATONO-SAN, PLEASE—

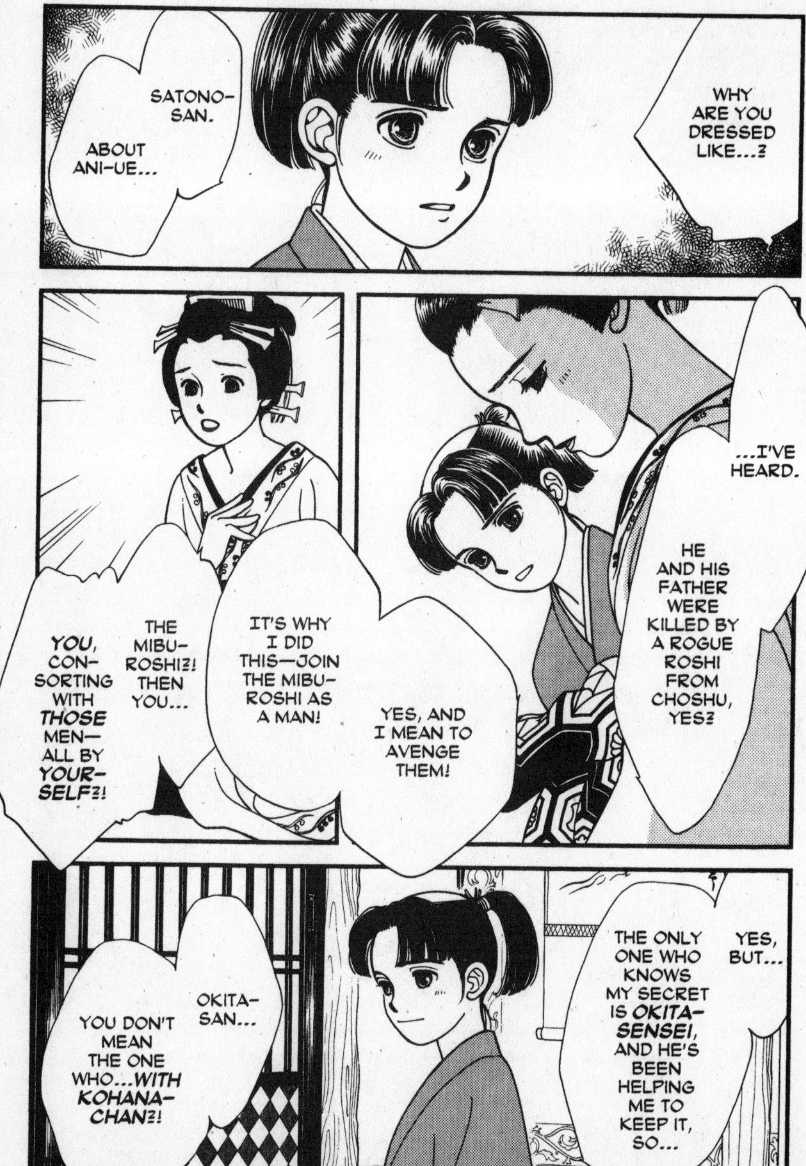
WHY ARE YOU DRESSED LIKE...?
SATONO-SAN.
ABOUT ANI-UE...
...I'VE HEARD.
HE AND HIS FATHER WERE KILLED BY A ROGUE ROSHI FROM CHOSHU, YES?
YES, AND I MEAN TO AVENGE THEM!
IT'S WHY I DID THIS—JOIN THE MIBU-ROSHI AS A MAN!
THE MIBU-ROSHI?! THEN YOU...
YOU, CONSORTING WITH *THOSE* MEN—ALL BY *YOURSELF*?!
YES, BUT...
THE ONLY ONE WHO KNOWS MY SECRET IS *OKITA-SENSEI*, AND HE'S BEEN HELPING ME TO KEEP IT, SO...
OKITA-SAN...
YOU DON'T MEAN THE ONE WHO...*WITH KOHANA-CHAN*?!

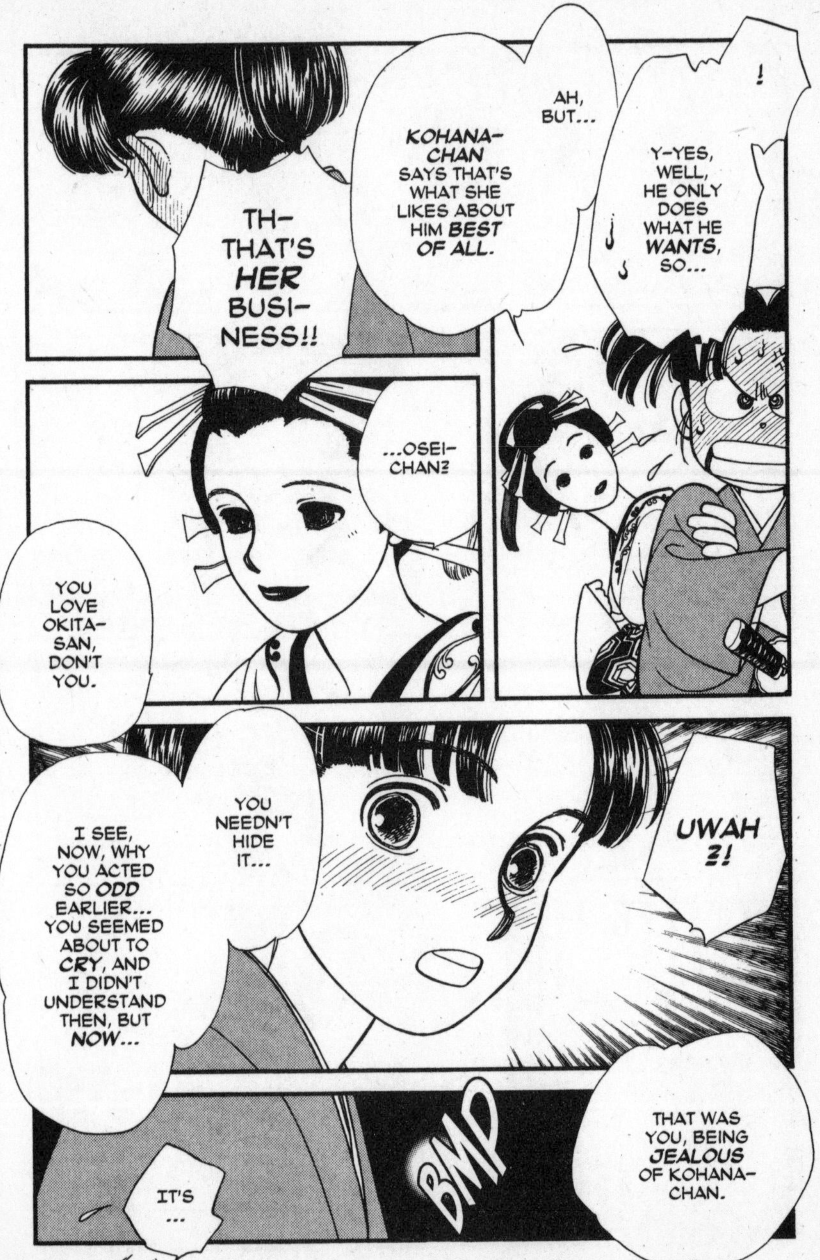
!
Y-YES, WELL, HE ONLY DOES WHAT HE WANTS, SO...
AH, BUT...
KOHANA-CHAN SAYS THAT'S WHAT SHE LIKES ABOUT HIM BEST OF ALL.
TH-THAT'S HER BUSINESS!!
...OSEI-CHAN?
YOU LOVE OKITA-SAN, DON'T YOU.
UWAH?!
YOU NEEDN'T HIDE IT...
I SEE, NOW, WHY YOU ACTED SO ODD EARLIER... YOU SEEMED ABOUT TO CRY, AND I DIDN'T UNDERSTAND THEN, BUT NOW...
THAT WAS YOU, BEING JEALOUS OF KOHANA-CHAN.
BMP
IT'S...

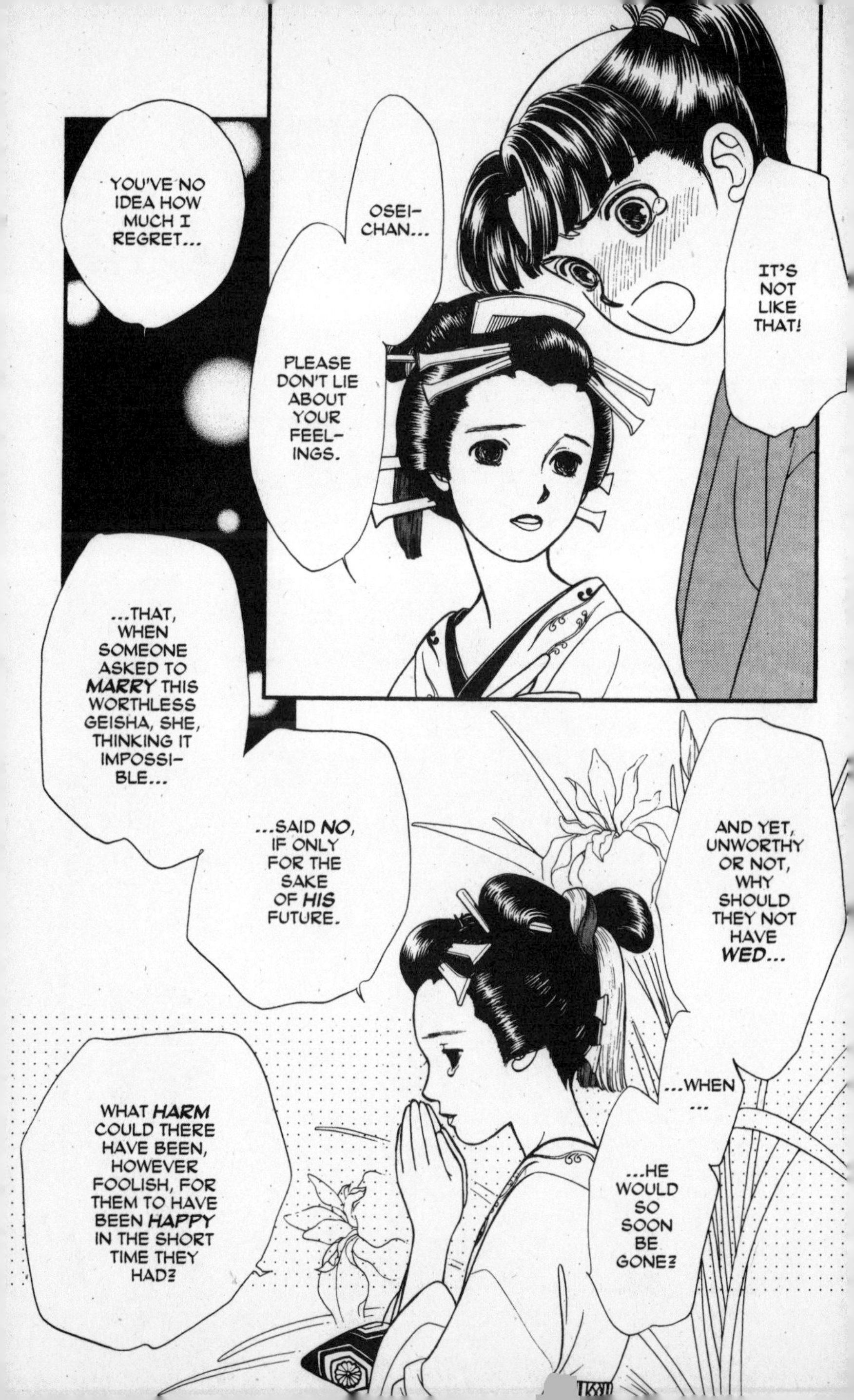
IT'S NOT LIKE THAT!
OSEI-CHAN...
PLEASE DON'T LIE ABOUT YOUR FEELINGS.
YOU'VE NO IDEA HOW MUCH I REGRET...
...THAT, WHEN SOMEONE ASKED TO ***MARRY*** THIS WORTHLESS GEISHA, SHE, THINKING IT IMPOSSIBLE...
...SAID ***NO***, IF ONLY FOR THE SAKE OF ***HIS*** FUTURE.
AND YET, UNWORTHY OR NOT, WHY SHOULD THEY NOT HAVE ***WED***...
...WHEN...
...HE WOULD SO SOON BE GONE?
WHAT ***HARM*** COULD THERE HAVE BEEN, HOWEVER FOOLISH, FOR THEM TO HAVE BEEN ***HAPPY*** IN THE SHORT TIME THEY HAD?

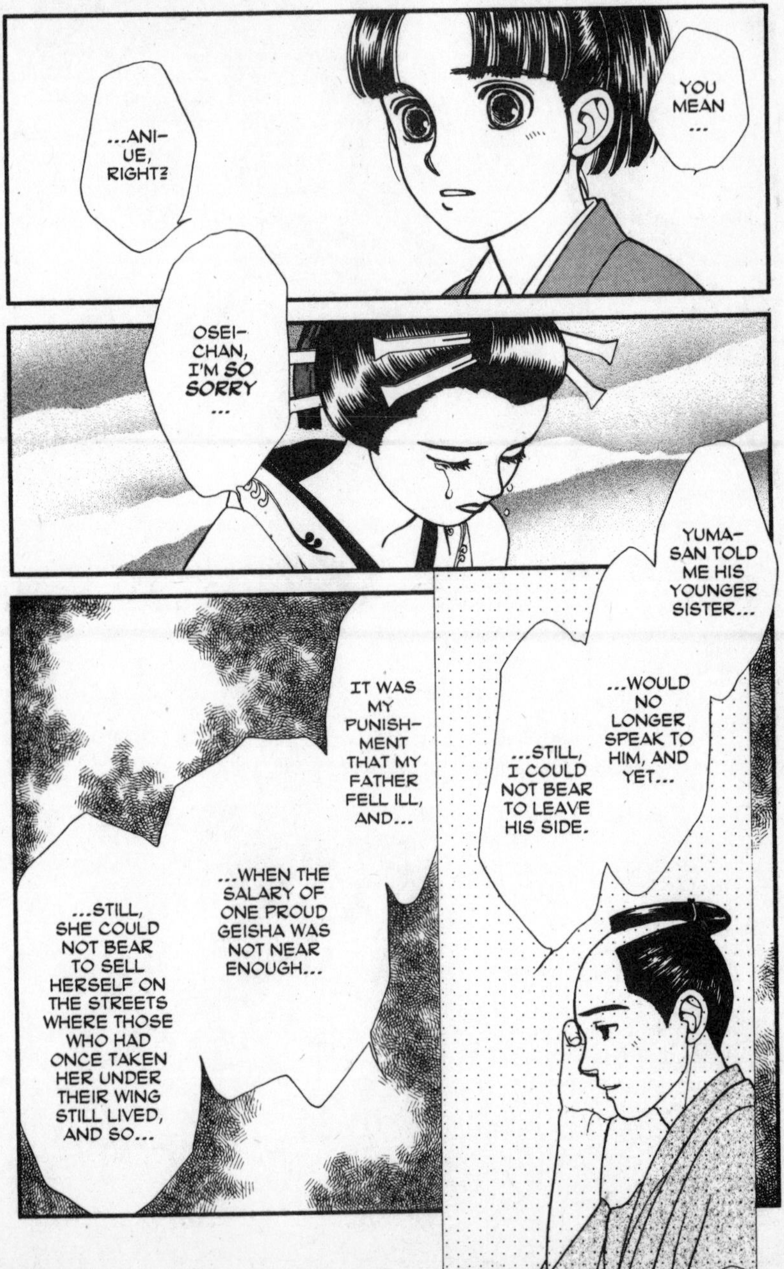
YOU MEAN ...
...ANI-UE, RIGHT?
OSEI-CHAN, I'M SO SORRY ...
YUMA-SAN TOLD ME HIS YOUNGER SISTER...
...WOULD NO LONGER SPEAK TO HIM, AND YET...
...STILL, I COULD NOT BEAR TO LEAVE HIS SIDE.
IT WAS MY PUNISHMENT THAT MY FATHER FELL ILL, AND...
...WHEN THE SALARY OF ONE PROUD GEISHA WAS NOT NEAR ENOUGH...
...STILL, SHE COULD NOT BEAR TO SELL HERSELF ON THE STREETS WHERE THOSE WHO HAD ONCE TAKEN HER UNDER THEIR WING STILL LIVED, AND SO...

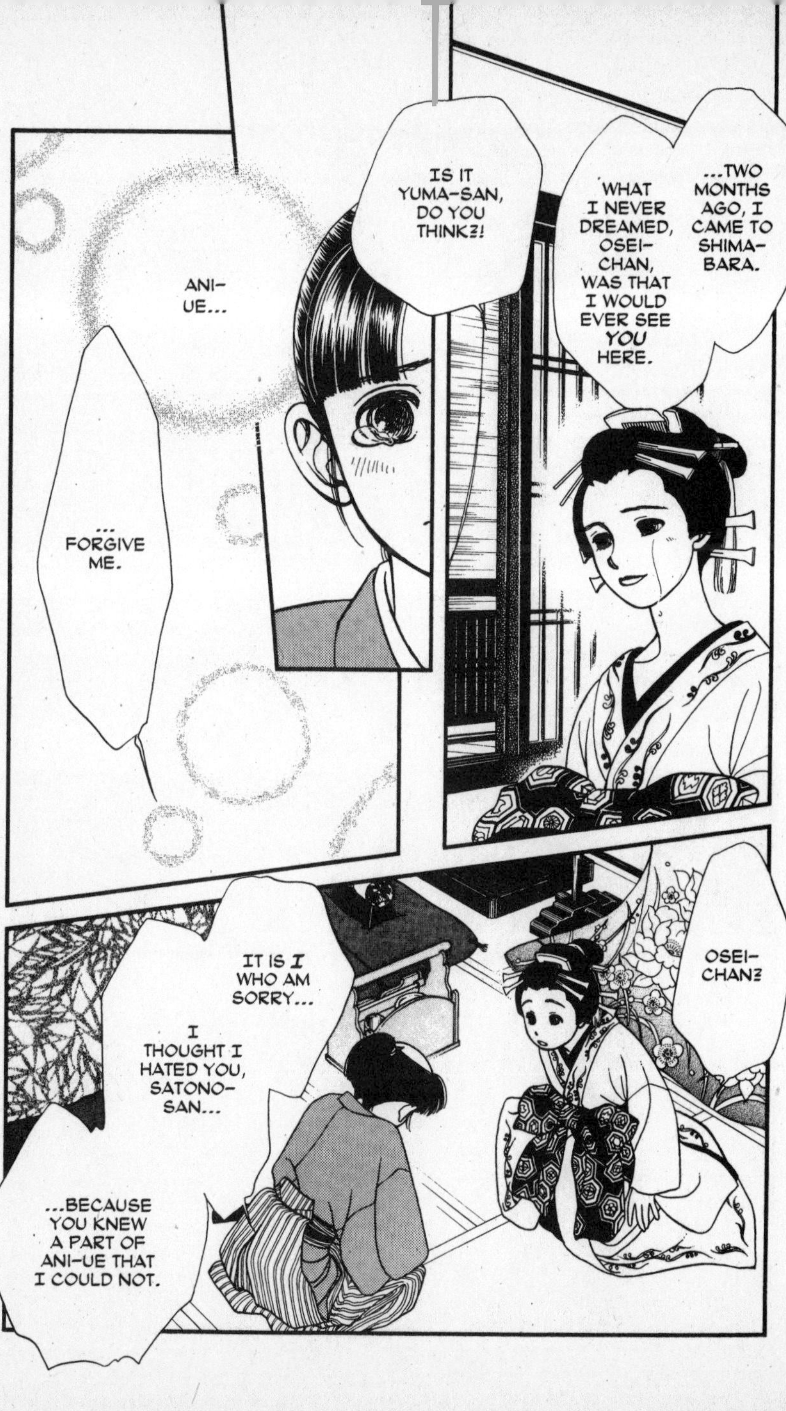
...TWO MONTHS AGO, I CAME TO SHIMABARA.
WHAT I NEVER DREAMED, OSEI-CHAN, WAS THAT I WOULD EVER SEE *YOU* HERE.
IS IT YUMA-SAN, DO YOU THINK?!
ANI-UE...
...FORGIVE ME.
OSEI-CHAN?
IT IS *I* WHO AM SORRY...
I THOUGHT I HATED YOU, SATONO-SAN...
...BECAUSE YOU KNEW A PART OF ANI-UE THAT I COULD NOT.

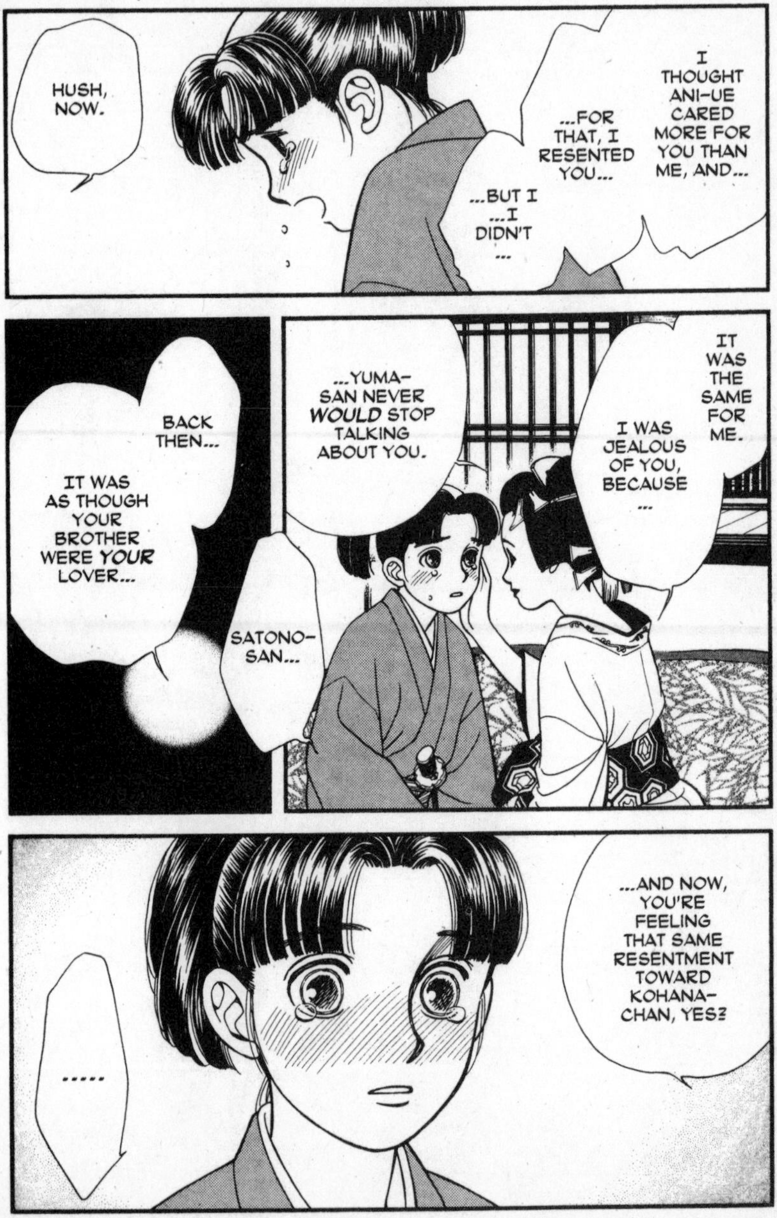
I THOUGHT ANI-UE CARED MORE FOR YOU THAN ME, AND...
...FOR THAT, I RESENTED YOU...
...BUT I ...I DIDN'T ...
HUSH, NOW.
IT WAS THE SAME FOR ME.
I WAS JEALOUS OF YOU, BECAUSE ...
...YUMA-SAN NEVER *WOULD* STOP TALKING ABOUT YOU.
SATONO-SAN...
BACK THEN...
IT WAS AS THOUGH YOUR BROTHER WERE *YOUR* LOVER...
...AND NOW, YOU'RE FEELING THAT SAME RESENTMENT TOWARD KOHANA-CHAN, YES?
.....

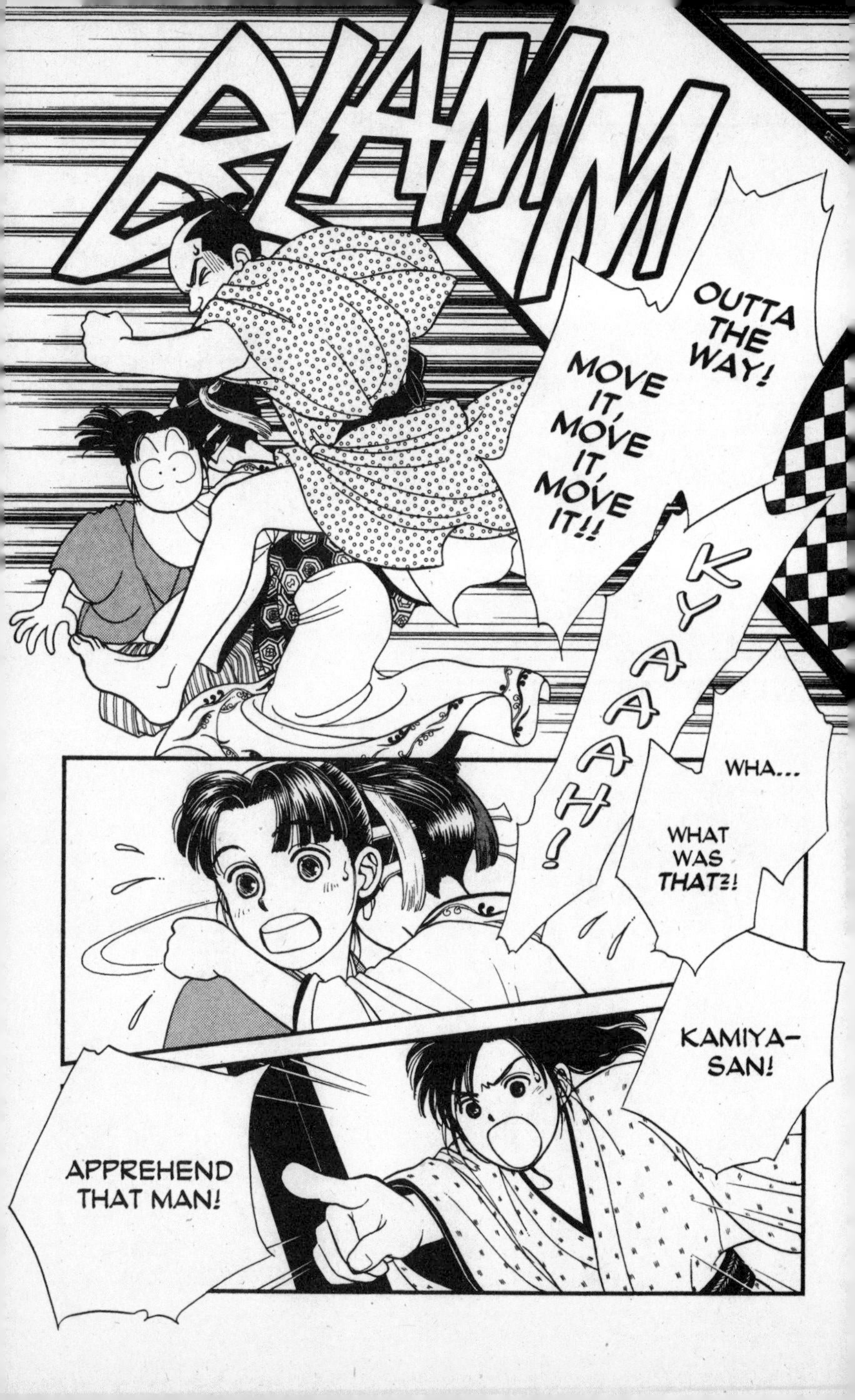
BLAMM
OUTTA THE WAY!
MOVE IT, MOVE IT, MOVE IT!!
KYAAAAH!
WHA...
WHAT WAS THAT?!
KAMIYA-SAN!
APPREHEND THAT MAN!

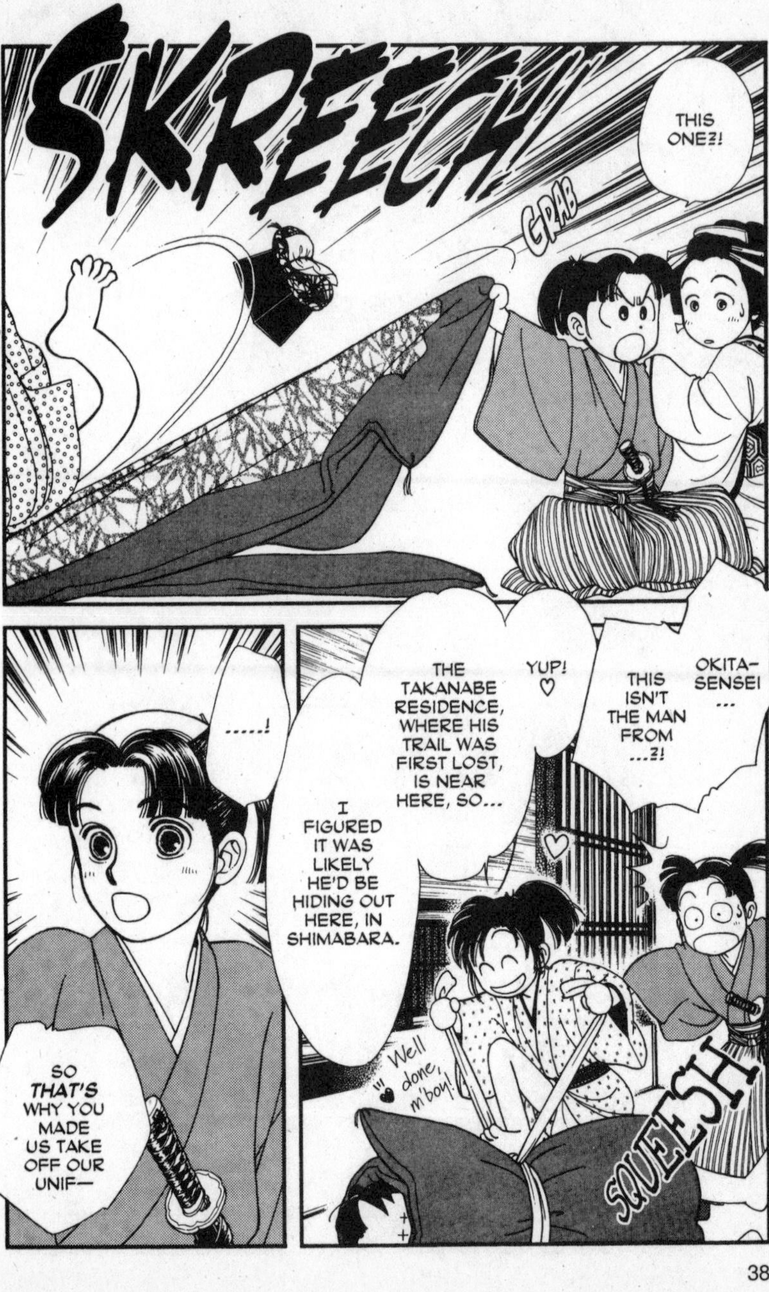
THIS ONE?!
SKREECH
GRAB
OKITA-SENSEI...
THIS ISN'T THE MAN FROM...?!
YUP! ♡
THE TAKANABE RESIDENCE, WHERE HIS TRAIL WAS FIRST LOST, IS NEAR HERE, SO...
I FIGURED IT WAS LIKELY HE'D BE HIDING OUT HERE, IN SHIMABARA.
Well done, m'boy!
SQUEESH
......!
SO *THAT'S* WHY YOU MADE US TAKE OFF OUR UNIF—

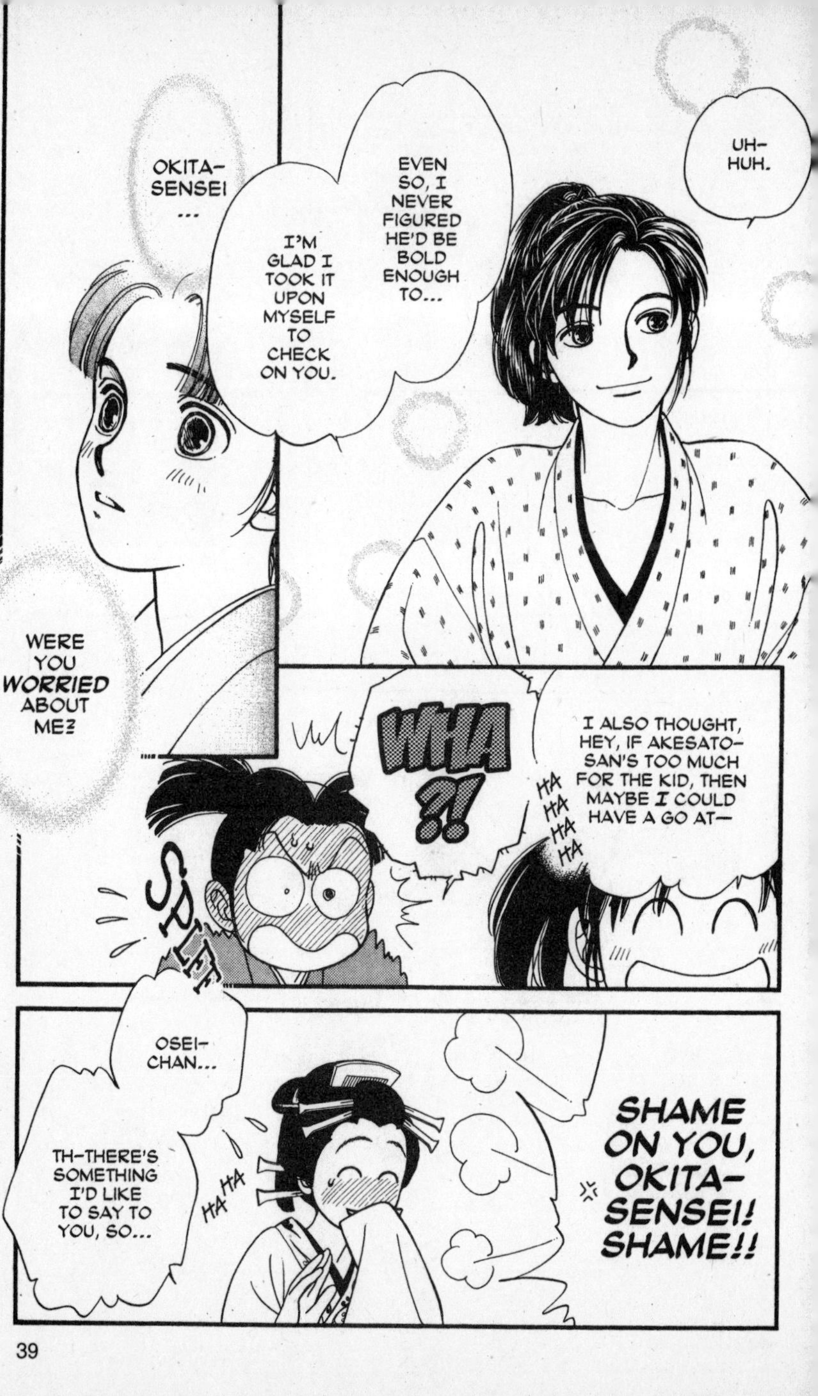
UH-HUH.
EVEN SO, I NEVER FIGURED HE'D BE BOLD ENOUGH TO...
I'M GLAD I TOOK IT UPON MYSELF TO CHECK ON YOU.
OKITA-SENSEI ...
WERE YOU *WORRIED* ABOUT ME?
I ALSO THOUGHT, HEY, IF AKESATO-SAN'S TOO MUCH FOR THE KID, THEN MAYBE *I* COULD HAVE A GO AT—
HA HA HA HA
WHA ?!
SPLIFF
SHAME ON YOU, OKITA-SENSEI! SHAME!!
HA HA
OSEI-CHAN...
TH-THERE'S SOMETHING I'D LIKE TO SAY TO YOU, SO...

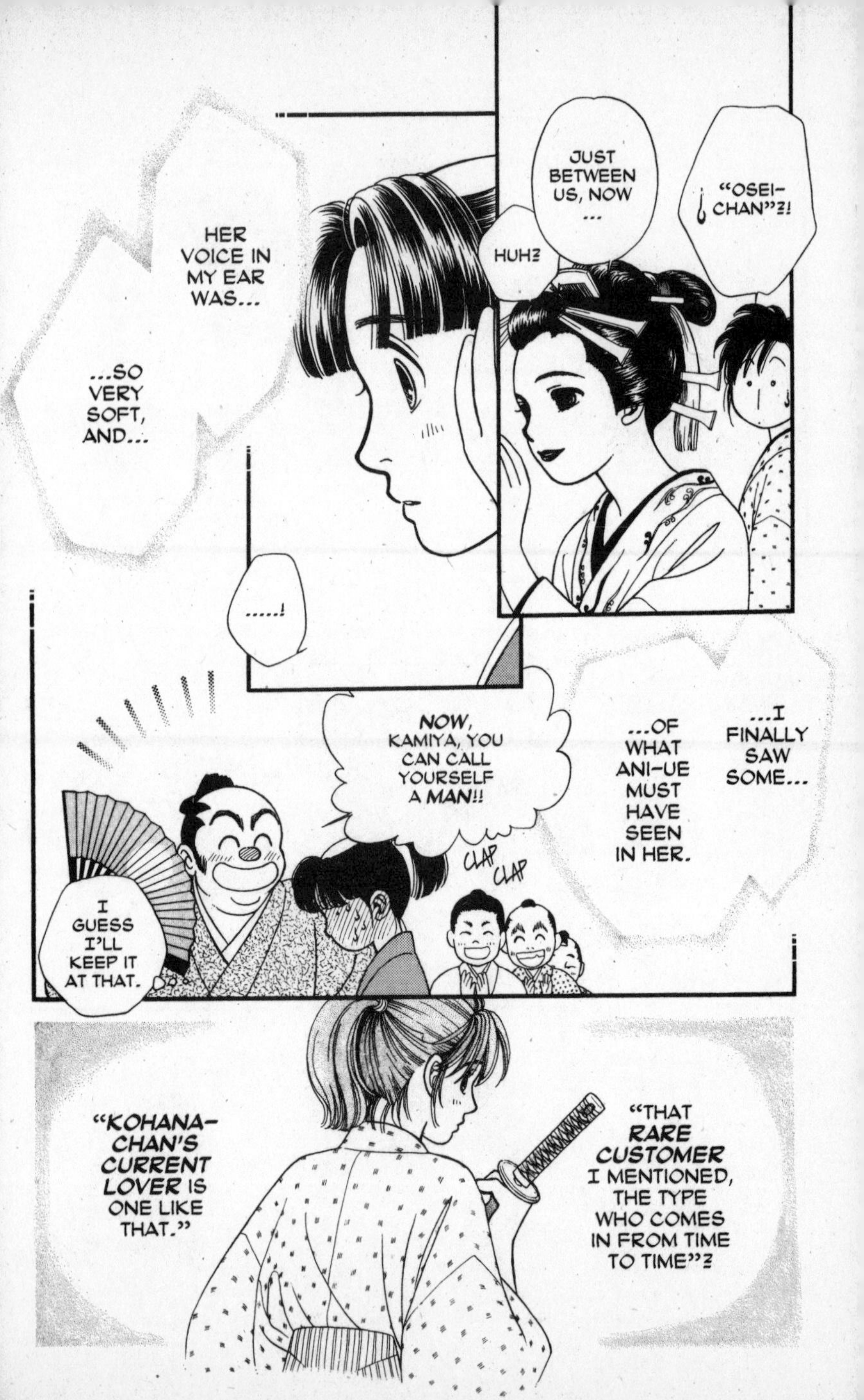

“OSEI-CHAN”?!
JUST BETWEEN US, NOW...
HUH?
HER VOICE IN MY EAR WAS...
...SO VERY SOFT, AND...
......!
...I FINALLY SAW SOME...
...OF WHAT ANI-UE MUST HAVE SEEN IN HER.
CLAP CLAP
NOW, KAMIYA, YOU CAN CALL YOURSELF A MAN!!
I GUESS I'LL KEEP IT AT THAT.
“THAT RARE CUSTOMER I MENTIONED, THE TYPE WHO COMES IN FROM TIME TO TIME”?
“KOHANA-CHAN'S CURRENT LOVER IS ONE LIKE THAT.”

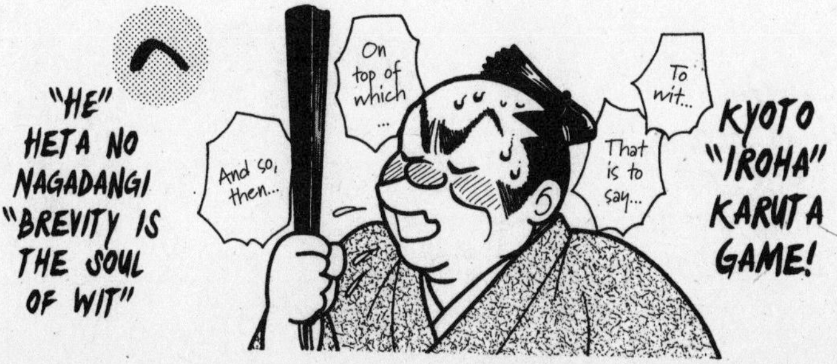
KYOTO "IROHA" KARUTA GAME!
To wit...
That is to say...
On top of which...
And so, then...
へ
"HE"
HETA NO NAGADANGI
"BREVITY IS THE SOUL OF WIT"

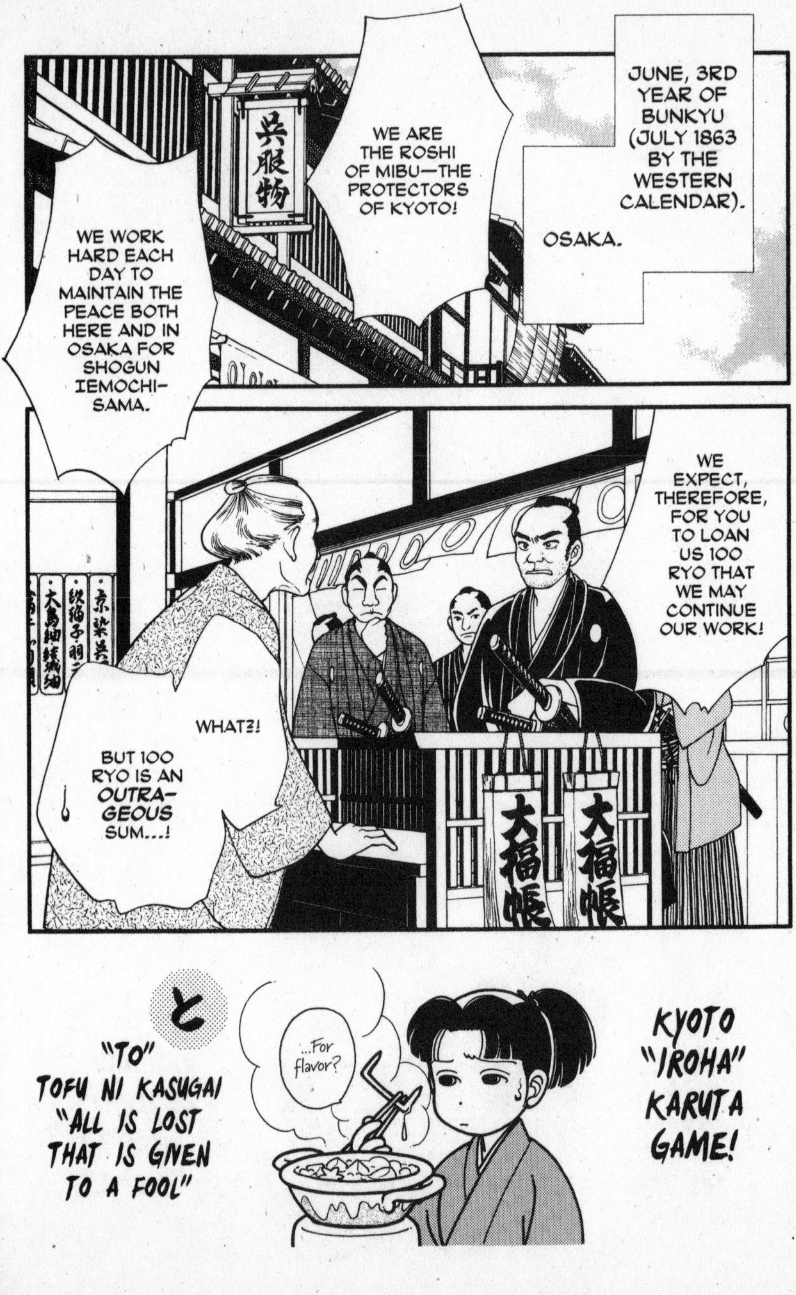
JUNE, 3RD YEAR OF BUNKYU (JULY 1863 BY THE WESTERN CALENDAR).
OSAKA.
呉服物
WE ARE THE ROSHI OF MIBU—THE PROTECTORS OF KYOTO!
WE WORK HARD EACH DAY TO MAINTAIN THE PEACE BOTH HERE AND IN OSAKA FOR SHOGUN IEMOCHI-SAMA.
WE EXPECT, THEREFORE, FOR YOU TO LOAN US 100 RYO THAT WE MAY CONTINUE OUR WORK!
大福帳
大福帳
WHAT?!
BUT 100 RYO IS AN OUTRAGEOUS SUM...!
KYOTO "IROHA" KARUTA GAME!
...For flavor?
と
"TO"
TOFU NI KASUGAI
"ALL IS LOST THAT IS GIVEN TO A FOOL"

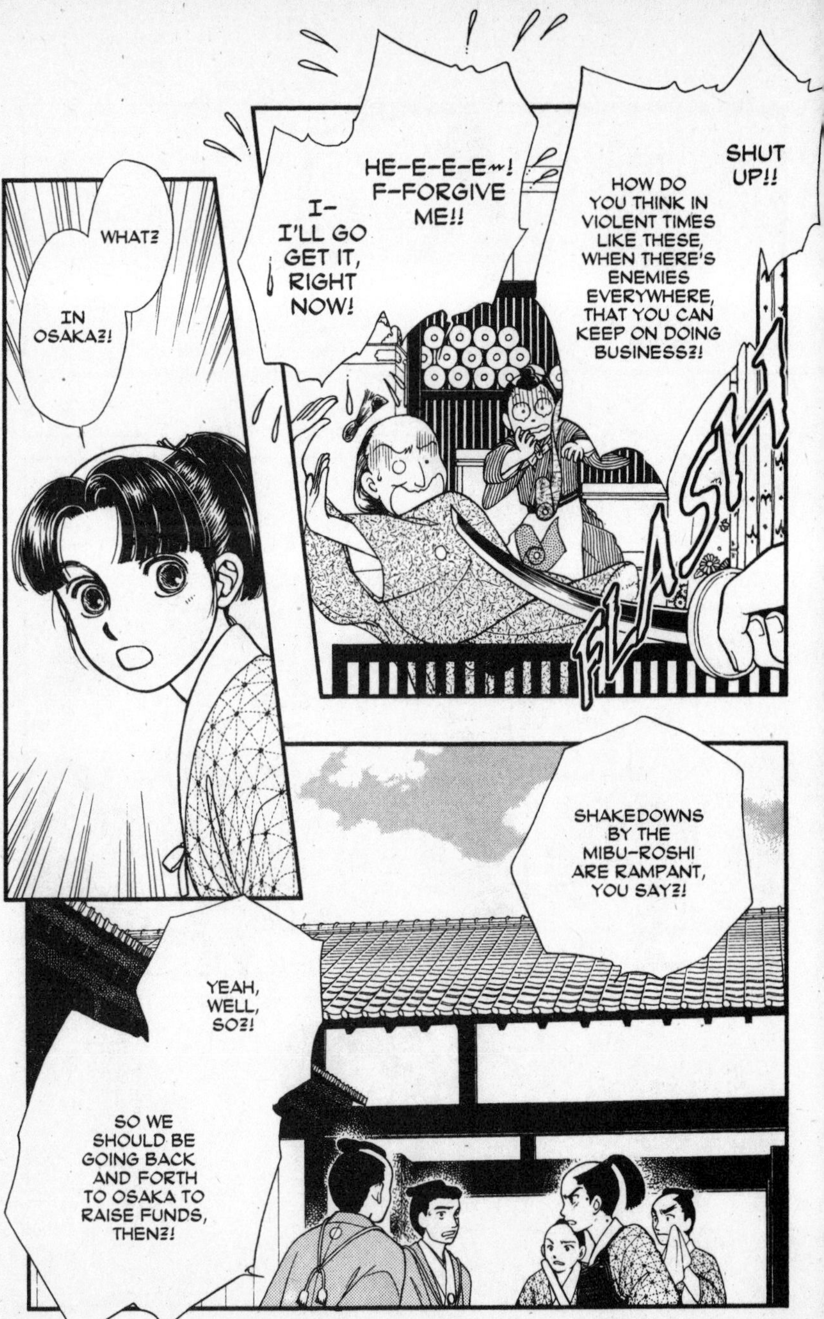
SHUT UP!!
HOW DO YOU THINK IN VIOLENT TIMES LIKE THESE, WHEN THERE'S ENEMIES EVERYWHERE, THAT YOU CAN KEEP ON DOING BUSINESS?!
FLASH
HE-E-E-E~! F-FORGIVE ME!!
I- I'LL GO GET IT, RIGHT NOW!
WHAT?
IN OSAKA?!
SHAKEDOWNS BY THE MIBU-ROSHI ARE RAMPANT, YOU SAY?!
YEAH, WELL, SO?!
SO WE SHOULD BE GOING BACK AND FORTH TO OSAKA TO RAISE FUNDS, THEN?!

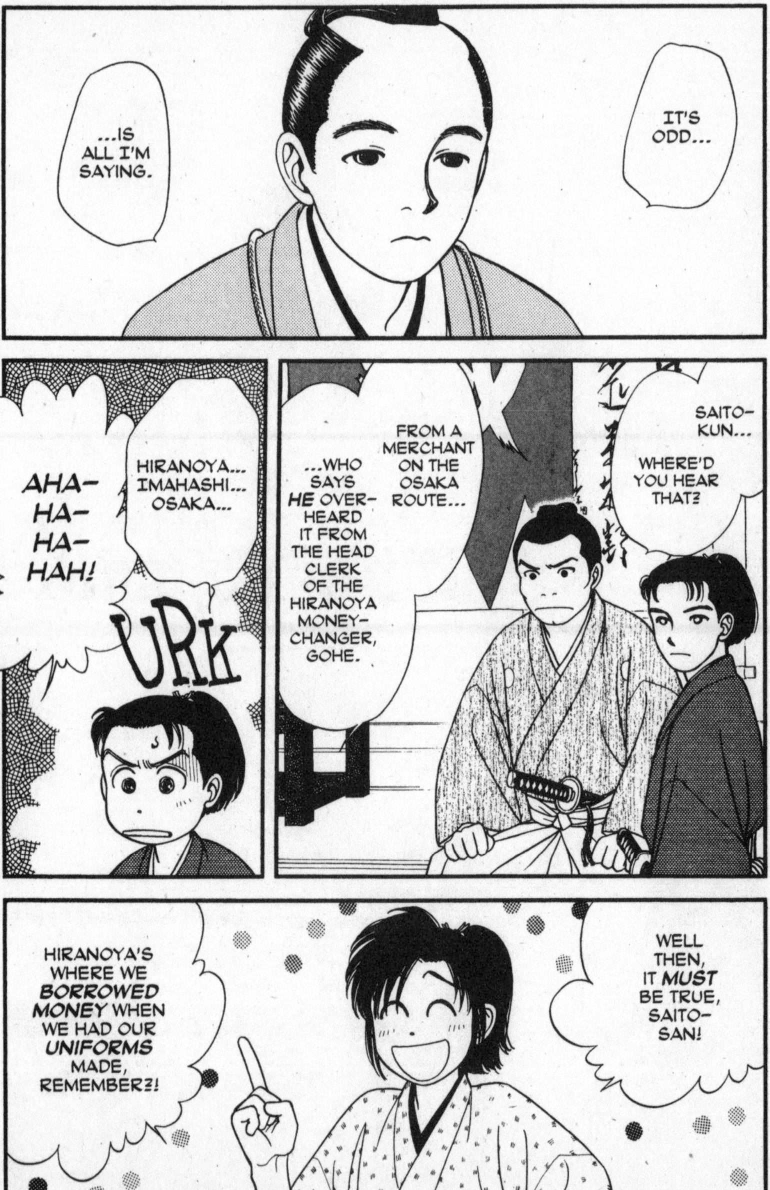
IT'S ODD...
...IS ALL I'M SAYING.
SAITO-KUN... WHERE'D YOU HEAR THAT?
FROM A MERCHANT ON THE OSAKA ROUTE...
...WHO SAYS *HE* OVERHEARD IT FROM THE HEAD CLERK OF THE HIRANOYA MONEY-CHANGER, GOHE.
HIRANOYA... IMAHASHI... OSAKA...
AHA-HA-HA-HAH!
URK
WELL THEN, IT *MUST* BE TRUE, SAITO-SAN!
HIRANOYA'S WHERE WE ***BORROWED MONEY*** WHEN WE HAD OUR ***UNIFORMS*** MADE, REMEMBER?!

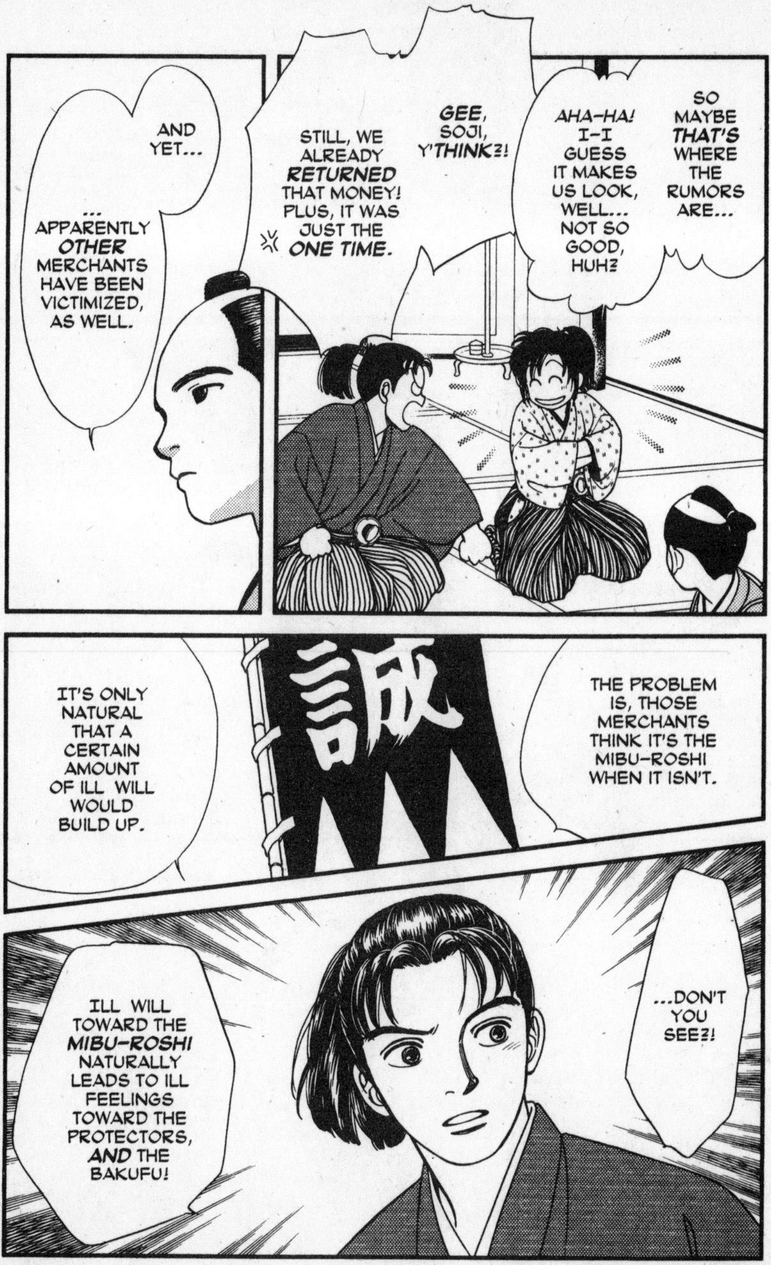
SO MAYBE THAT'S WHERE THE RUMORS ARE...
AHA-HA! I-I GUESS IT MAKES US LOOK, WELL... NOT SO GOOD, HUH?
GEE, SOJI, Y'THINK?!
STILL, WE ALREADY RETURNED THAT MONEY! PLUS, IT WAS JUST THE ONE TIME.
AND YET...
...APPARENTLY OTHER MERCHANTS HAVE BEEN VICTIMIZED, AS WELL.
THE PROBLEM IS, THOSE MERCHANTS THINK IT'S THE MIBU-ROSHI WHEN IT ISN'T.
IT'S ONLY NATURAL THAT A CERTAIN AMOUNT OF ILL WILL WOULD BUILD UP.
...DON'T YOU SEE?!
ILL WILL TOWARD THE MIBU-ROSHI NATURALLY LEADS TO ILL FEELINGS TOWARD THE PROTECTORS, AND THE BAKUFU!

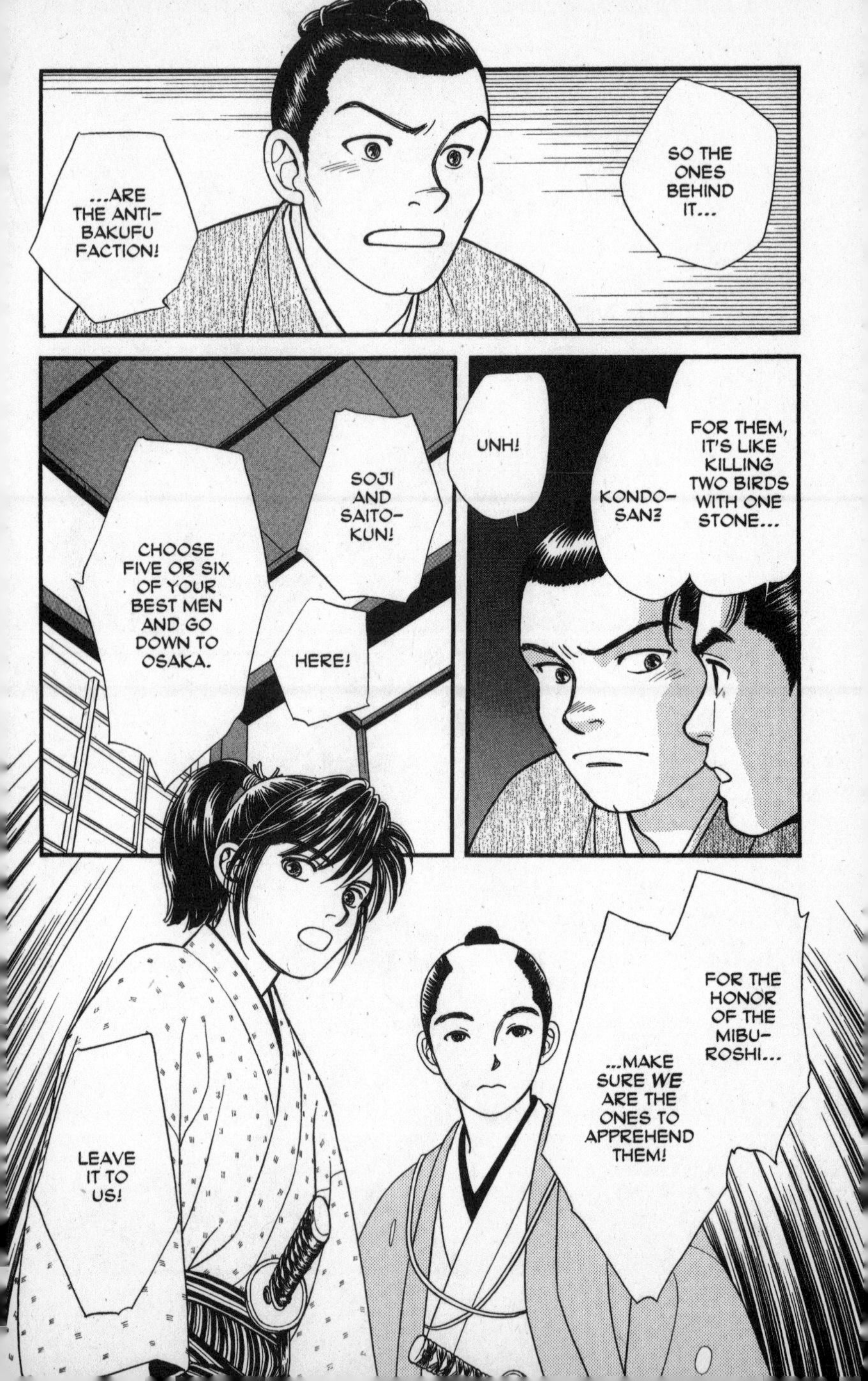

SO THE ONES BEHIND IT...
...ARE THE ANTI-BAKUFU FACTION!
FOR THEM, IT'S LIKE KILLING TWO BIRDS WITH ONE STONE...
KONDO-SAN?
UNH!
SOJI AND SAITO-KUN!
CHOOSE FIVE OR SIX OF YOUR BEST MEN AND GO DOWN TO OSAKA.
HERE!
FOR THE HONOR OF THE MIBU-ROSHI...
...MAKE SURE *WE* ARE THE ONES TO APPREHEND THEM!
LEAVE IT TO US!

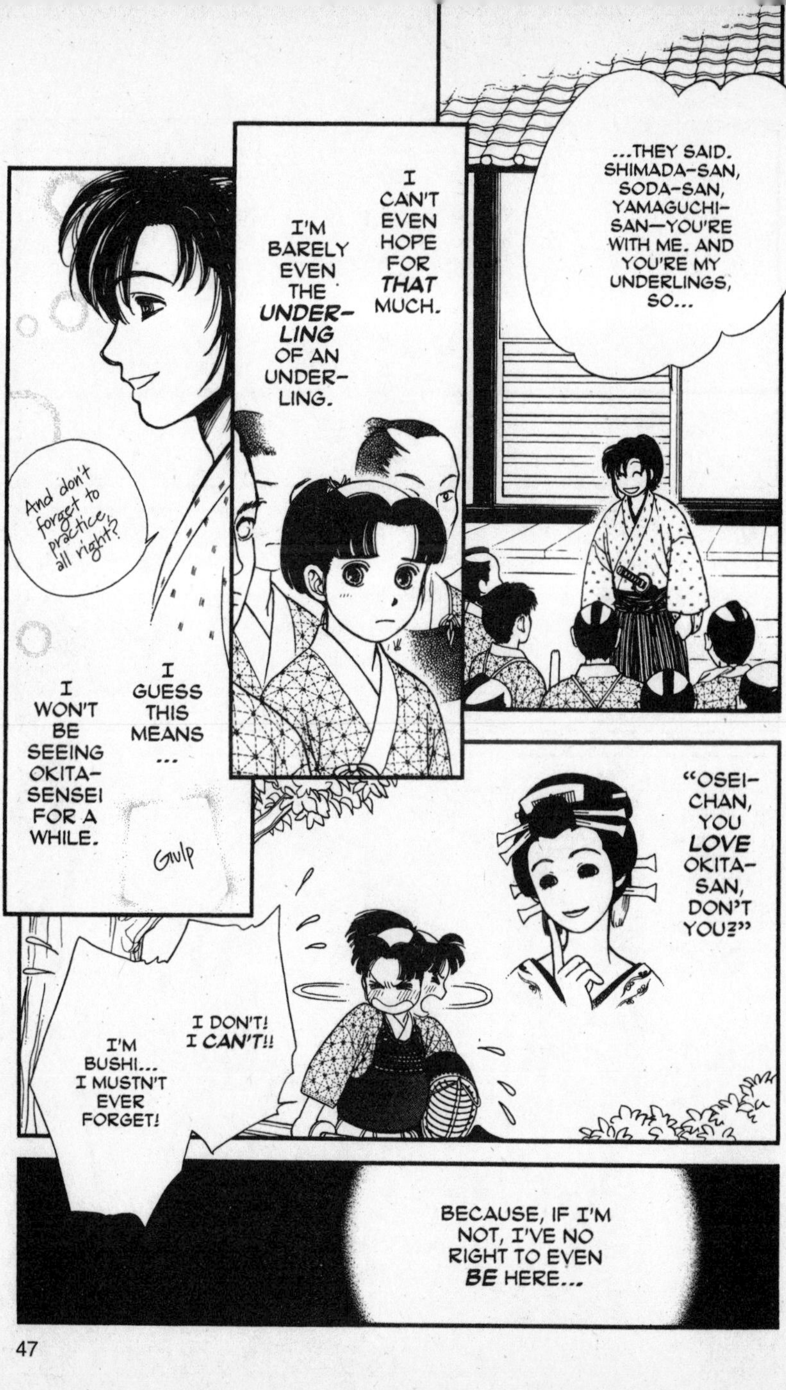
...THEY SAID. SHIMADA-SAN, SODA-SAN, YAMAGUCHI-SAN—YOU'RE WITH ME. AND YOU'RE MY UNDERLINGS, SO...
I CAN'T EVEN HOPE FOR THAT MUCH.
I'M BARELY EVEN THE UNDER-LING OF AN UNDER-LING.
And don't forget to practice, all right?
I GUESS THIS MEANS...
I WON'T BE SEEING OKITA-SENSEI FOR A WHILE.
GULP
"OSEI-CHAN, YOU LOVE OKITA-SAN, DON'T YOU?"
I DON'T! I CAN'T!!
I'M BUSHI... I MUSTN'T EVER FORGET!
BECAUSE, IF I'M NOT, I'VE NO RIGHT TO EVEN BE HERE...

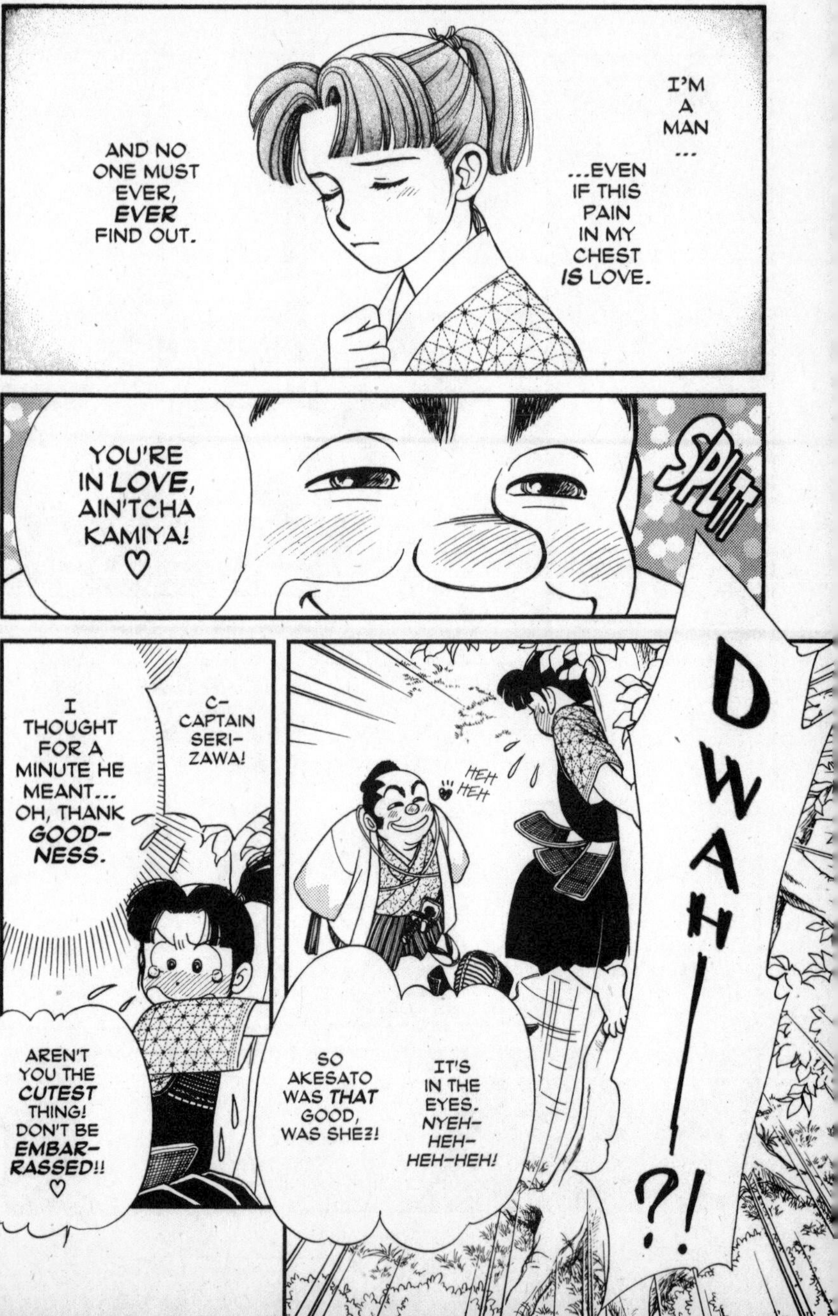
I'M A MAN...
...EVEN IF THIS PAIN IN MY CHEST IS LOVE.
AND NO ONE MUST EVER, EVER FIND OUT.
SPLIT
YOU'RE IN LOVE, AIN'TCHA KAMIYA! ♡
DWAH—!?!
HEH HEH
IT'S IN THE EYES. NYEH-HEH-HEH-HEH!
SO AKESATO WAS THAT GOOD, WAS SHE?!
C-CAPTAIN SERI-ZAWA!
I THOUGHT FOR A MINUTE HE MEANT... OH, THANK GOOD-NESS.
AREN'T YOU THE CUTEST THING! DON'T BE EMBAR-RASSED!! ♡

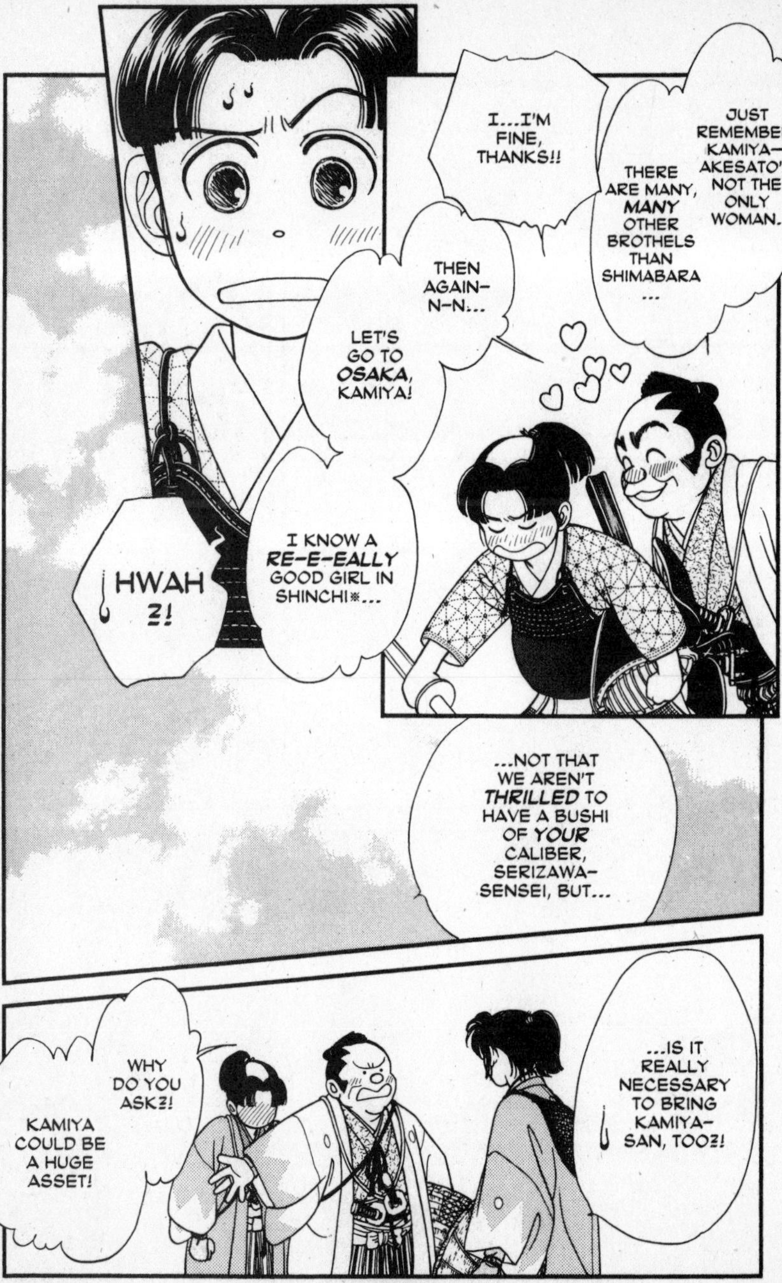
JUST REMEMBER, KAMIYA— AKESATO'S NOT THE ONLY WOMAN.
THERE ARE MANY, MANY OTHER BROTHELS THAN SHIMABARA ...
I...I'M FINE, THANKS!!
THEN AGAIN-N-N...
LET'S GO TO OSAKA, KAMIYA!
I KNOW A RE-E-EALLY GOOD GIRL IN SHINCHI※...
HWAH?!
...NOT THAT WE AREN'T THRILLED TO HAVE A BUSHI OF YOUR CALIBER, SERIZAWA-SENSEI, BUT...
...IS IT REALLY NECESSARY TO BRING KAMIYA-SAN, TOO?!
WHY DO YOU ASK?!
KAMIYA COULD BE A HUGE ASSET!

※A brothel in Osaka.

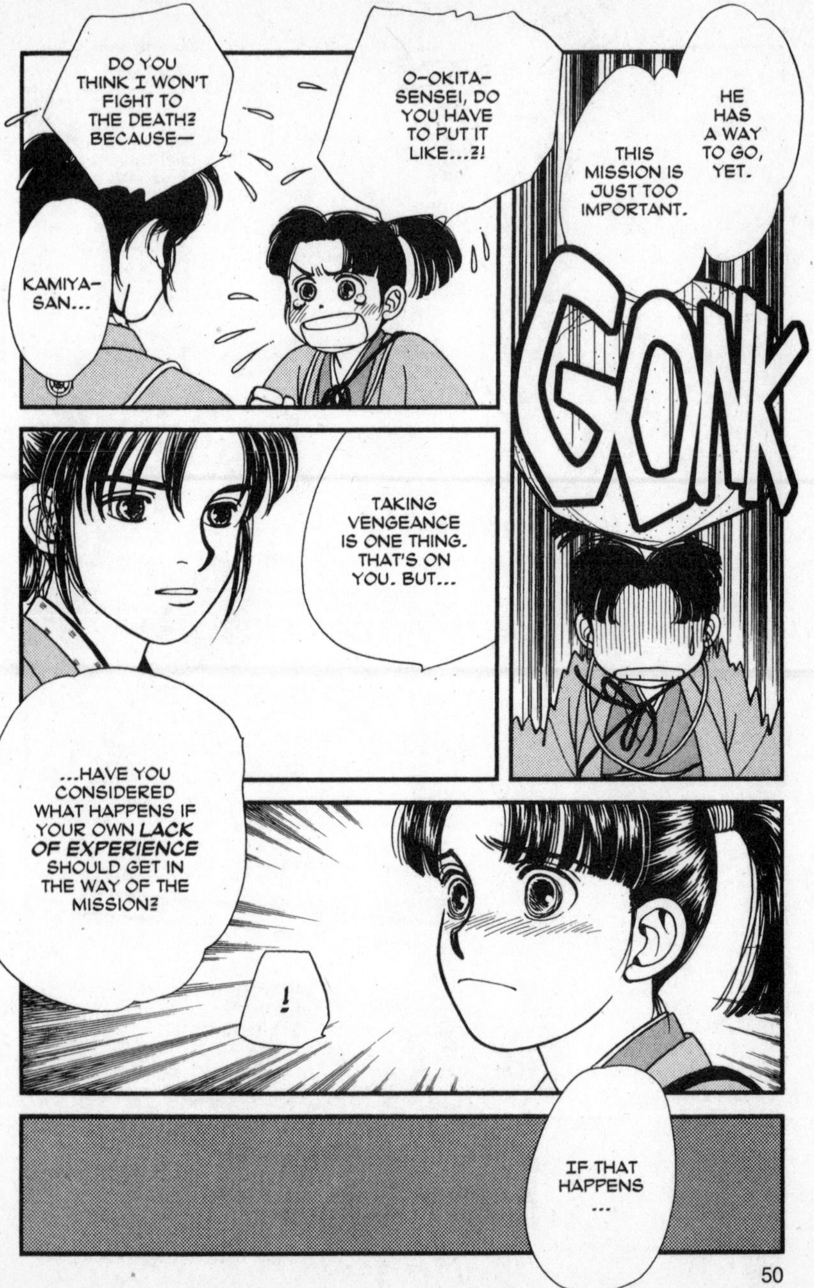
HE HAS A WAY TO GO, YET.
THIS MISSION IS JUST TOO IMPORTANT.
GONK
O-OKITA-SENSEI, DO YOU HAVE TO PUT IT LIKE...?!
DO YOU THINK I WON'T FIGHT TO THE DEATH? BECAUSE—
KAMIYA-SAN...
TAKING VENGEANCE IS ONE THING. THAT'S ON YOU. BUT...
...HAVE YOU CONSIDERED WHAT HAPPENS IF YOUR OWN *LACK OF EXPERIENCE* SHOULD GET IN THE WAY OF THE MISSION?
!
IF THAT HAPPENS ...

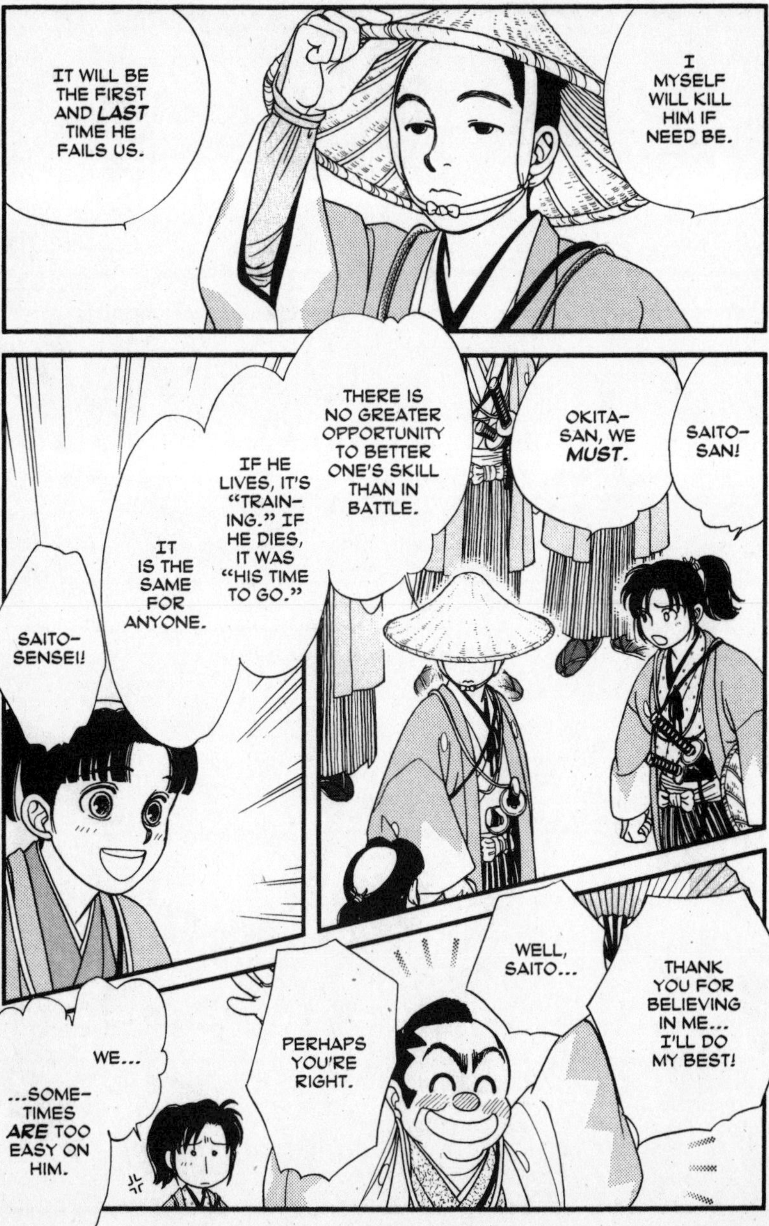

I MYSELF WILL KILL HIM IF NEED BE.
IT WILL BE THE FIRST AND LAST TIME HE FAILS US.
SAITO-SAN!
OKITA-SAN, WE MUST.
THERE IS NO GREATER OPPORTUNITY TO BETTER ONE'S SKILL THAN IN BATTLE.
IF HE LIVES, IT'S "TRAINING." IF HE DIES, IT WAS "HIS TIME TO GO."
IT IS THE SAME FOR ANYONE.
SAITO-SENSEI!
THANK YOU FOR BELIEVING IN ME... I'LL DO MY BEST!
WELL, SAITO...
PERHAPS YOU'RE RIGHT.
WE...
...SOMETIMES ARE TOO EASY ON HIM.

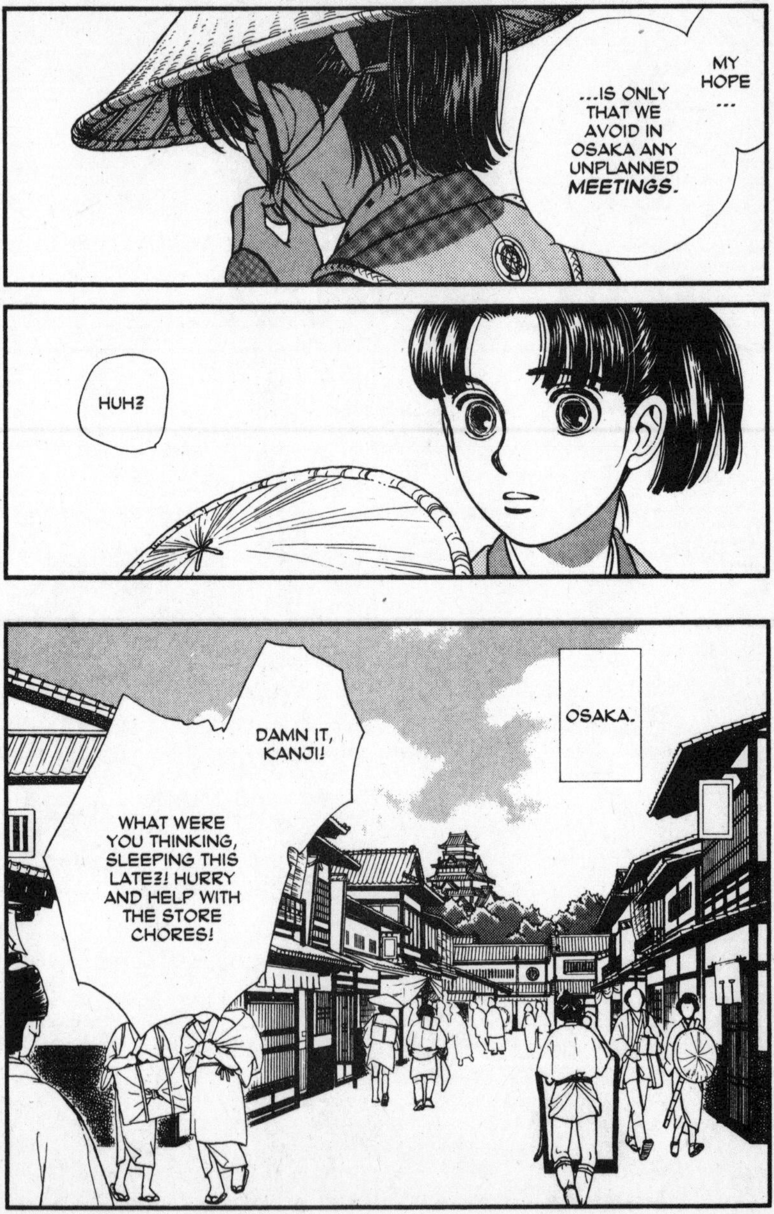
MY HOPE ...
...IS ONLY THAT WE AVOID IN OSAKA ANY UNPLANNED MEETINGS.
HUH?
OSAKA.
DAMN IT, KANJI!
WHAT WERE YOU THINKING, SLEEPING THIS LATE?! HURRY AND HELP WITH THE STORE CHORES!

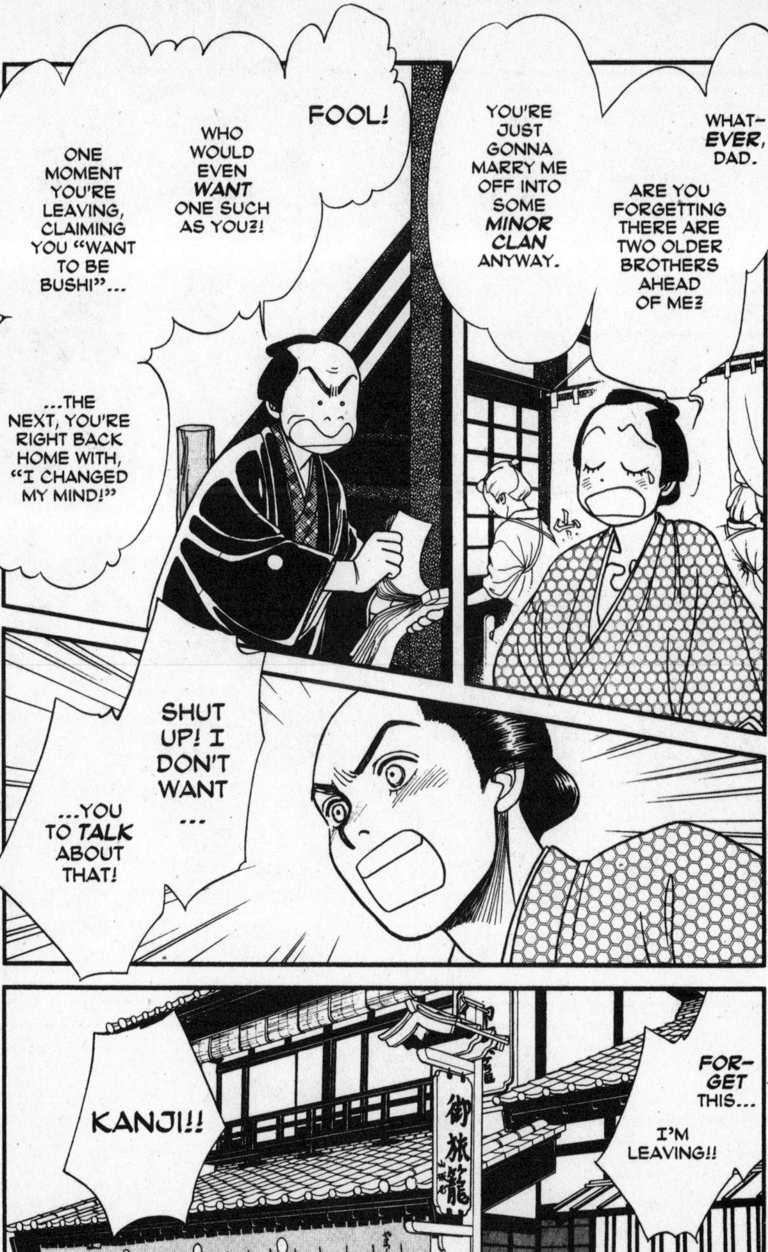
WHAT-EVER, DAD.
ARE YOU FORGETTING THERE ARE TWO OLDER BROTHERS AHEAD OF ME?
YOU'RE JUST GONNA MARRY ME OFF INTO SOME MINOR CLAN ANYWAY.
FOOL!
WHO WOULD EVEN WANT ONE SUCH AS YOU?!
ONE MOMENT YOU'RE LEAVING, CLAIMING YOU "WANT TO BE BUSHI"...
...THE NEXT, YOU'RE RIGHT BACK HOME WITH, "I CHANGED MY MIND!"
SHUT UP! I DON'T WANT ...
...YOU TO TALK ABOUT THAT!
FOR-GET THIS...
I'M LEAVING!!
KANJI!!

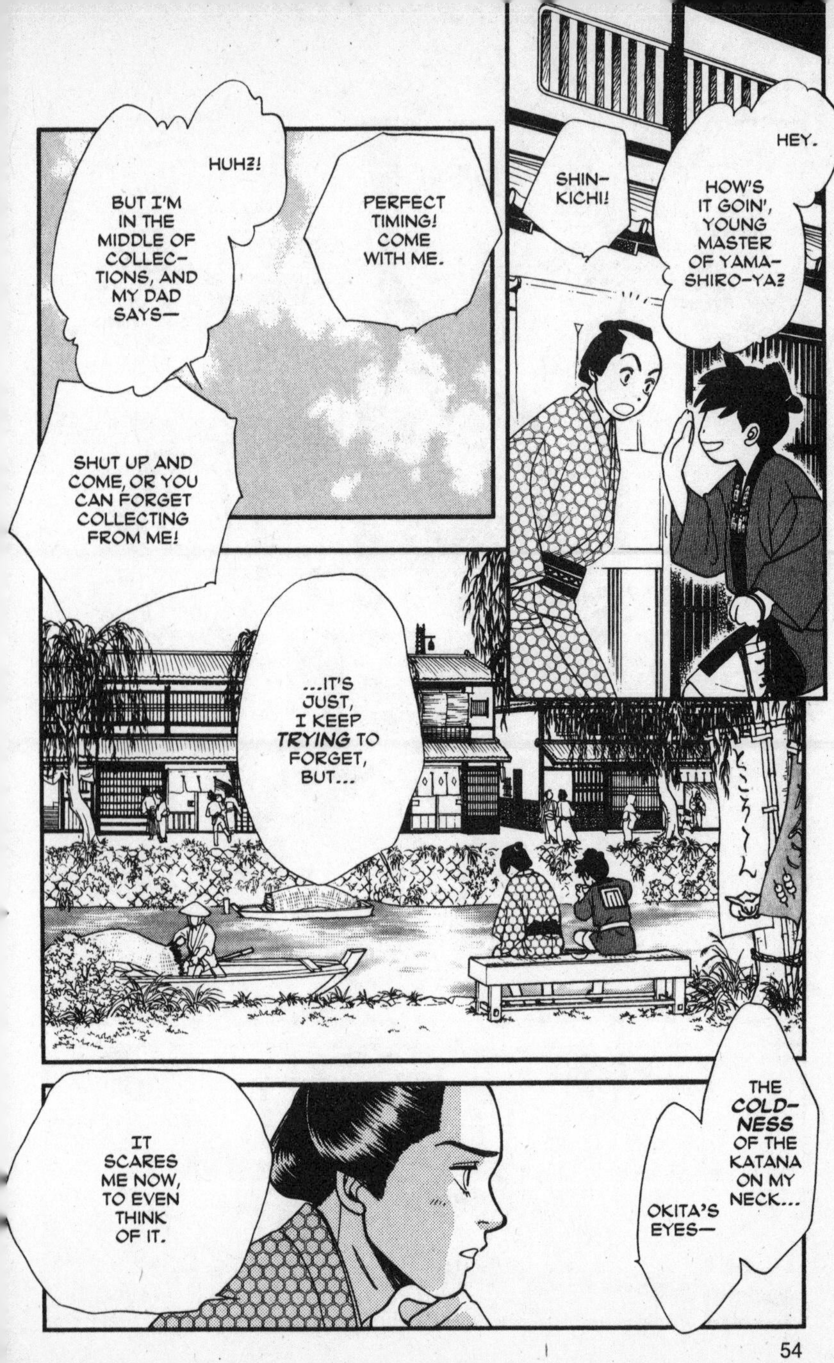
HEY. HOW'S IT GOIN', YOUNG MASTER OF YAMA-SHIRO-YA?
SHIN-KICHI!
PERFECT TIMING! COME WITH ME.
HUH?! BUT I'M IN THE MIDDLE OF COLLEC-TIONS, AND MY DAD SAYS—
SHUT UP AND COME, OR YOU CAN FORGET COLLECTING FROM ME!
...IT'S JUST, I KEEP *TRYING* TO FORGET, BUT...
THE *COLD-NESS* OF THE KATANA ON MY NECK...
OKITA'S EYES—
IT SCARES ME NOW, TO EVEN THINK OF IT.

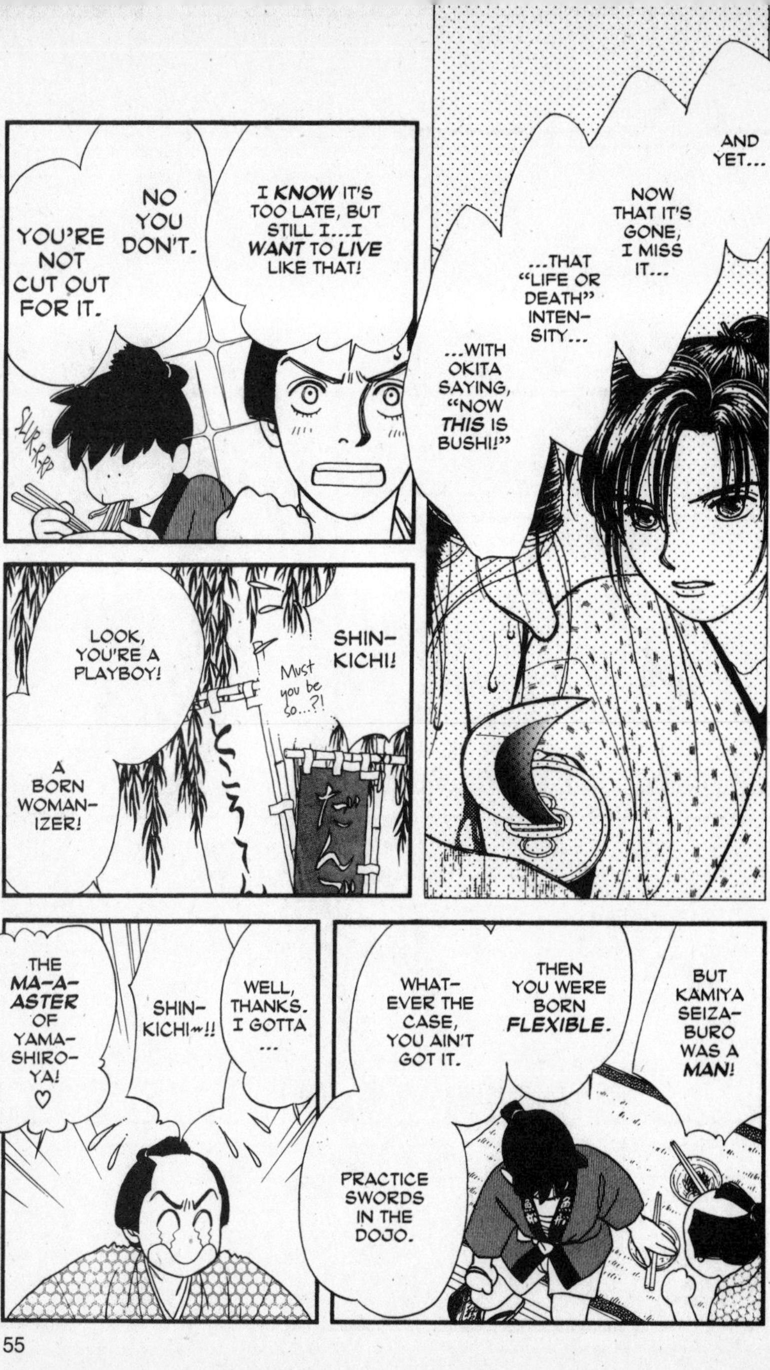
AND YET...
NOW THAT IT'S GONE, I MISS IT...
...THAT "LIFE OR DEATH" INTENSITY...
...WITH OKITA SAYING, "NOW THIS IS BUSHI!"
I KNOW IT'S TOO LATE, BUT STILL I...I WANT TO LIVE LIKE THAT!
NO YOU DON'T.
YOU'RE NOT CUT OUT FOR IT.
SLUR-R-RP
SHIN-KICHI!
Must you be so...?!
LOOK, YOU'RE A PLAYBOY!
A BORN WOMANIZER!
BUT KAMIYA SEIZABURO WAS A MAN!
THEN YOU WERE BORN FLEXIBLE.
WHATEVER THE CASE, YOU AIN'T GOT IT.
PRACTICE SWORDS IN THE DOJO.
WELL, THANKS. I GOTTA ...
SHIN-KICHI~!!
THE MA-A-ASTER OF YAMASHIROYA! ♡

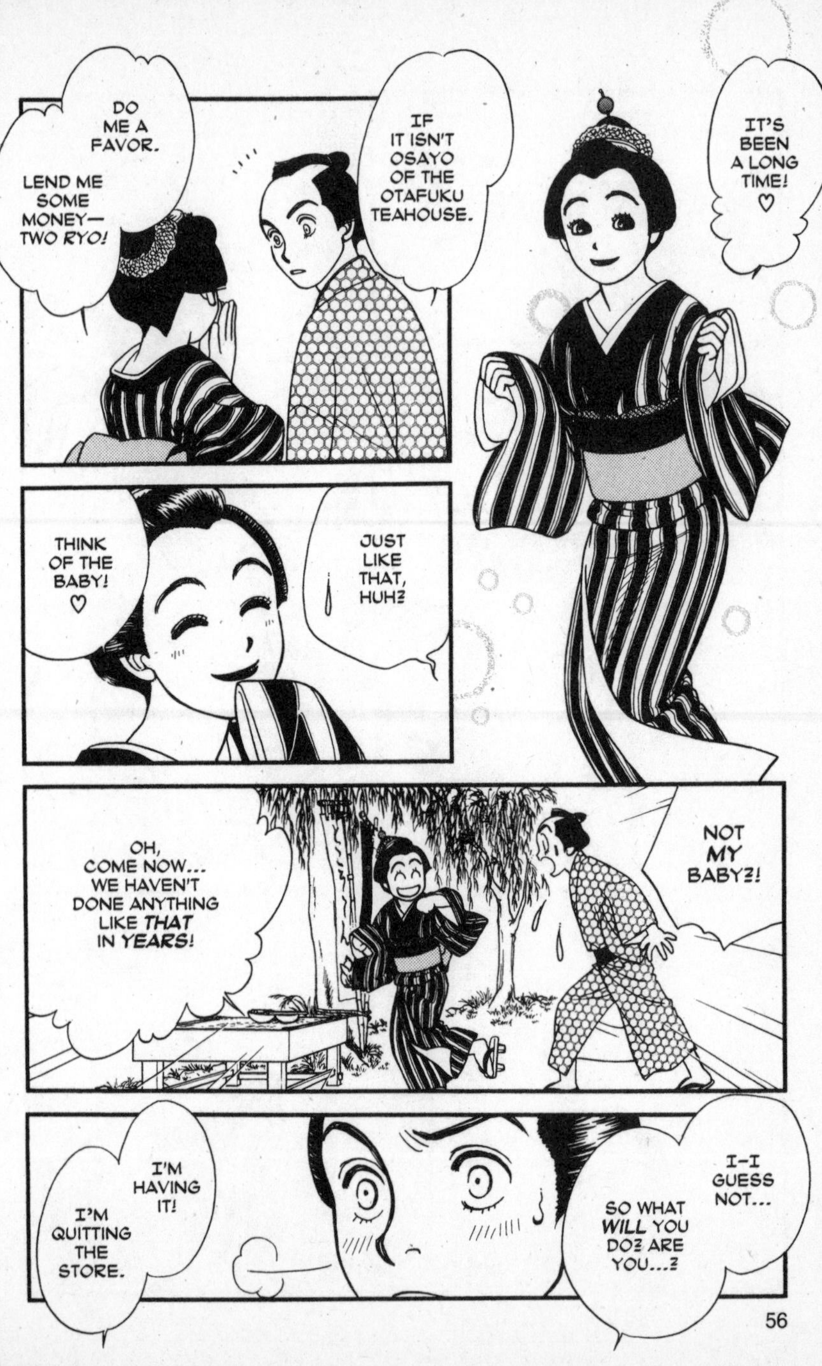
IT'S BEEN A LONG TIME! ♡
IF IT ISN'T OSAYO OF THE OTAFUKU TEAHOUSE.
DO ME A FAVOR.
LEND ME SOME MONEY— TWO *RYO!*
JUST LIKE THAT, HUH?
THINK OF THE BABY! ♡
NOT **MY** BABY?!
OH, COME NOW... WE HAVEN'T DONE ANYTHING LIKE *THAT* IN *YEARS!*
I-I GUESS NOT...
SO WHAT **WILL** YOU DO? ARE YOU...?
I'M HAVING IT!
I'M QUITTING THE STORE.

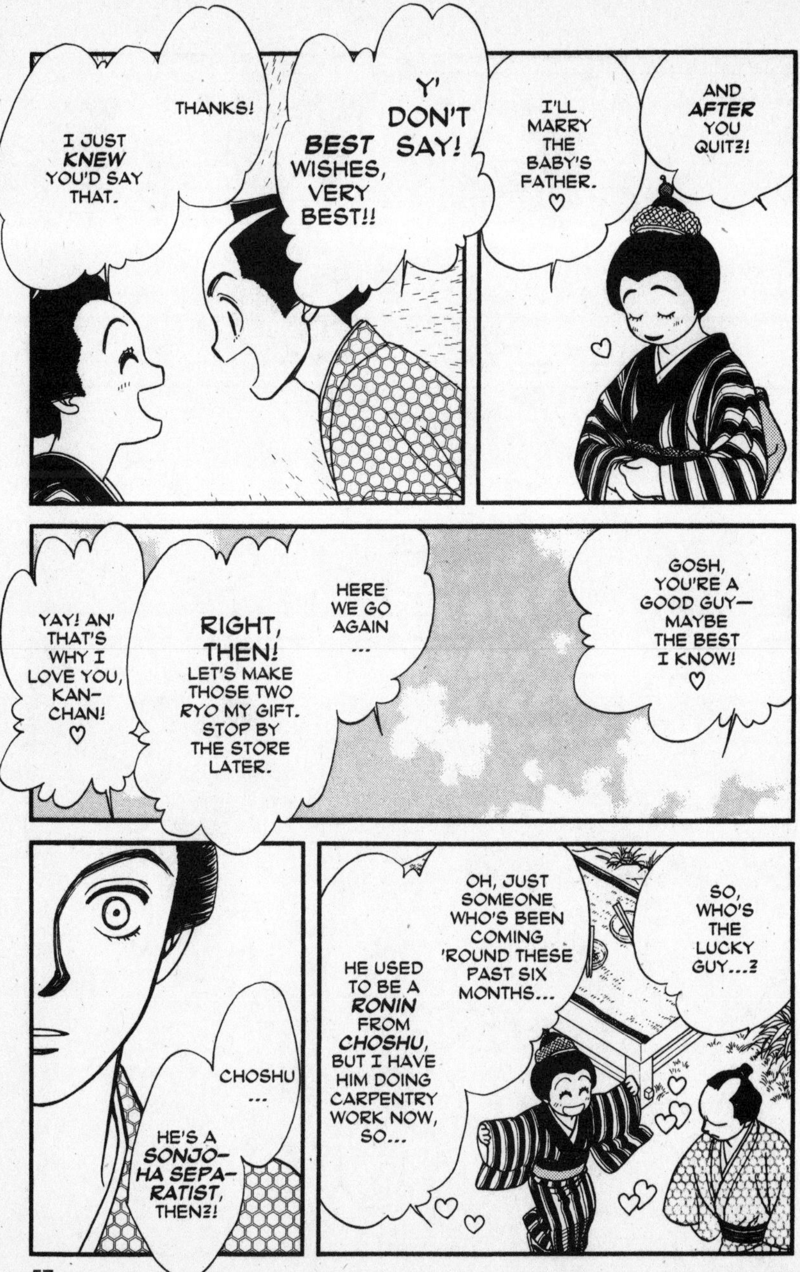
AND AFTER YOU QUIT?!
I'LL MARRY THE BABY'S FATHER. ♡
Y' DON'T SAY!
BEST WISHES, VERY BEST!!
THANKS!
I JUST KNEW YOU'D SAY THAT.
GOSH, YOU'RE A GOOD GUY— MAYBE THE BEST I KNOW! ♡
HERE WE GO AGAIN ...
RIGHT, THEN! LET'S MAKE THOSE TWO RYO MY GIFT. STOP BY THE STORE LATER.
YAY! AN' THAT'S WHY I LOVE YOU, KAN-CHAN! ♡
SO, WHO'S THE LUCKY GUY...?
OH, JUST SOMEONE WHO'S BEEN COMING 'ROUND THESE PAST SIX MONTHS...
HE USED TO BE A RONIN FROM CHOSHU, BUT I HAVE HIM DOING CARPENTRY WORK NOW, SO...
CHOSHU ...
HE'S A SONJO-HA SEPARATIST, THEN?!

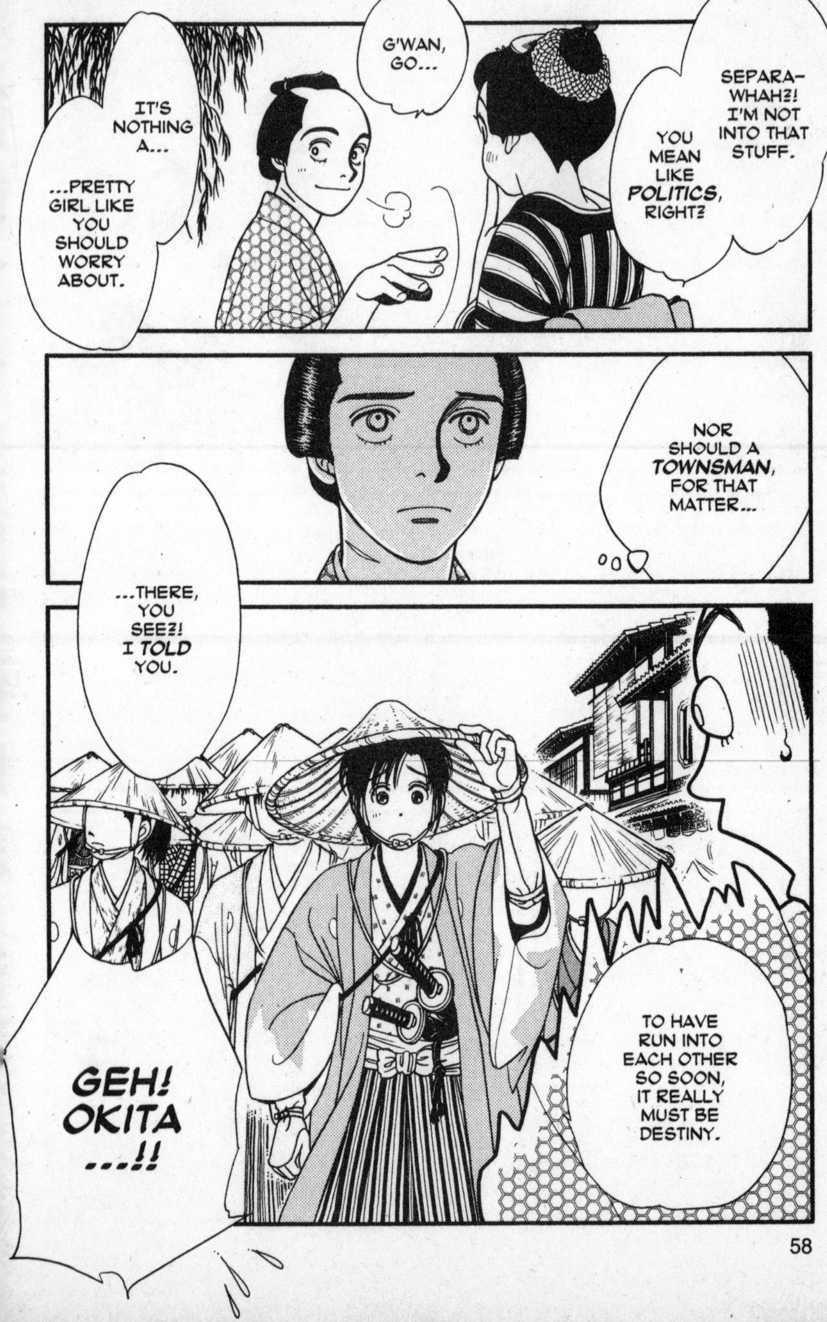
SEPARA-WHAH?! I'M NOT INTO THAT STUFF.
YOU MEAN LIKE *POLITICS*, RIGHT?
G'WAN, GO...
IT'S NOTHING A...
...PRETTY GIRL LIKE YOU SHOULD WORRY ABOUT.
NOR SHOULD A *TOWNSMAN*, FOR THAT MATTER...
TO HAVE RUN INTO EACH OTHER SO SOON, IT REALLY MUST BE DESTINY.
...THERE, YOU SEE?! I *TOLD* YOU.
GEH! OKITA ...!!

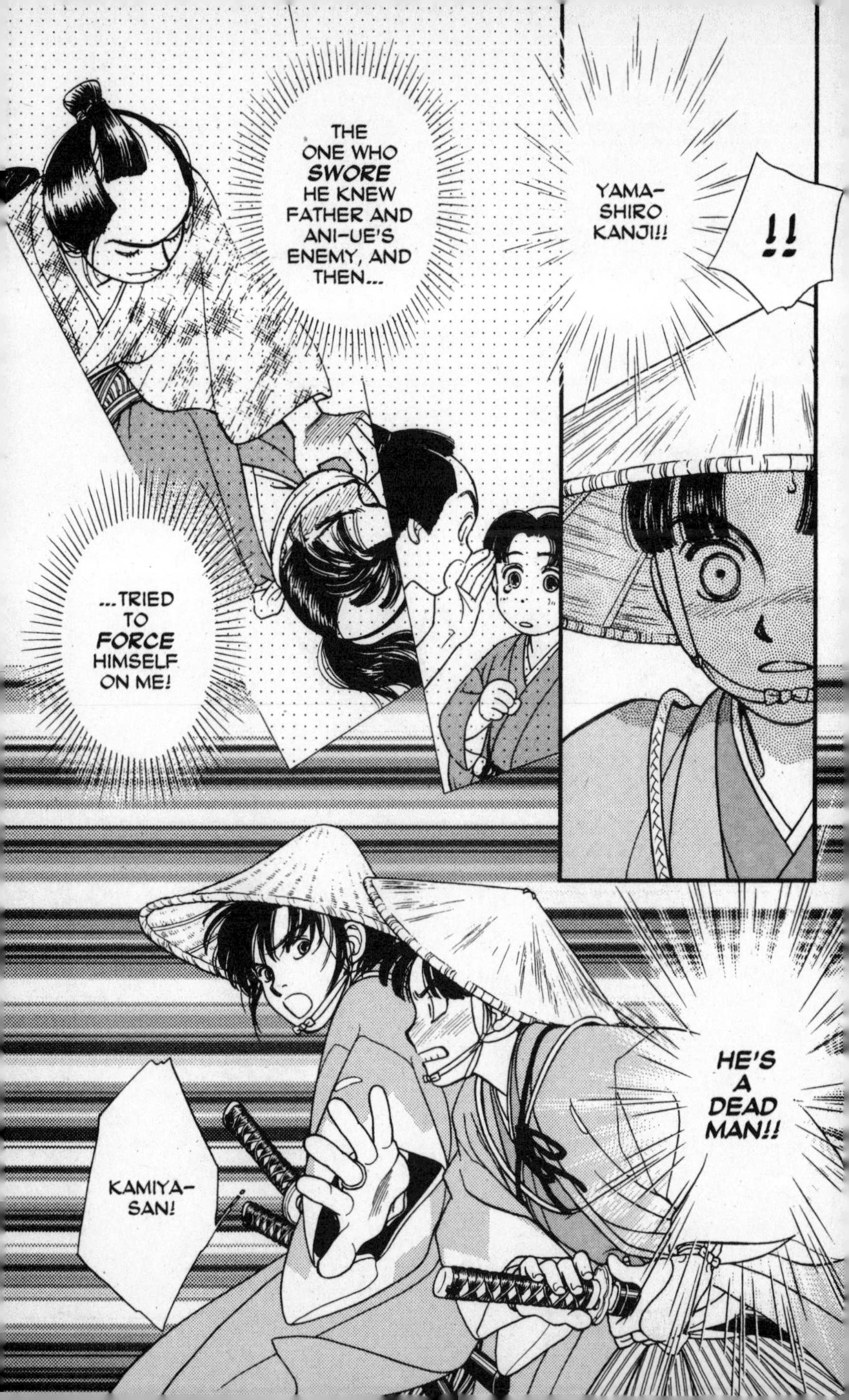
!!
YAMA-SHIRO KANJI!!
THE ONE WHO SWORE HE KNEW FATHER AND ANI-UE'S ENEMY, AND THEN...
...TRIED TO FORCE HIMSELF ON ME!
HE'S A DEAD MAN!!
KAMIYA-SAN!

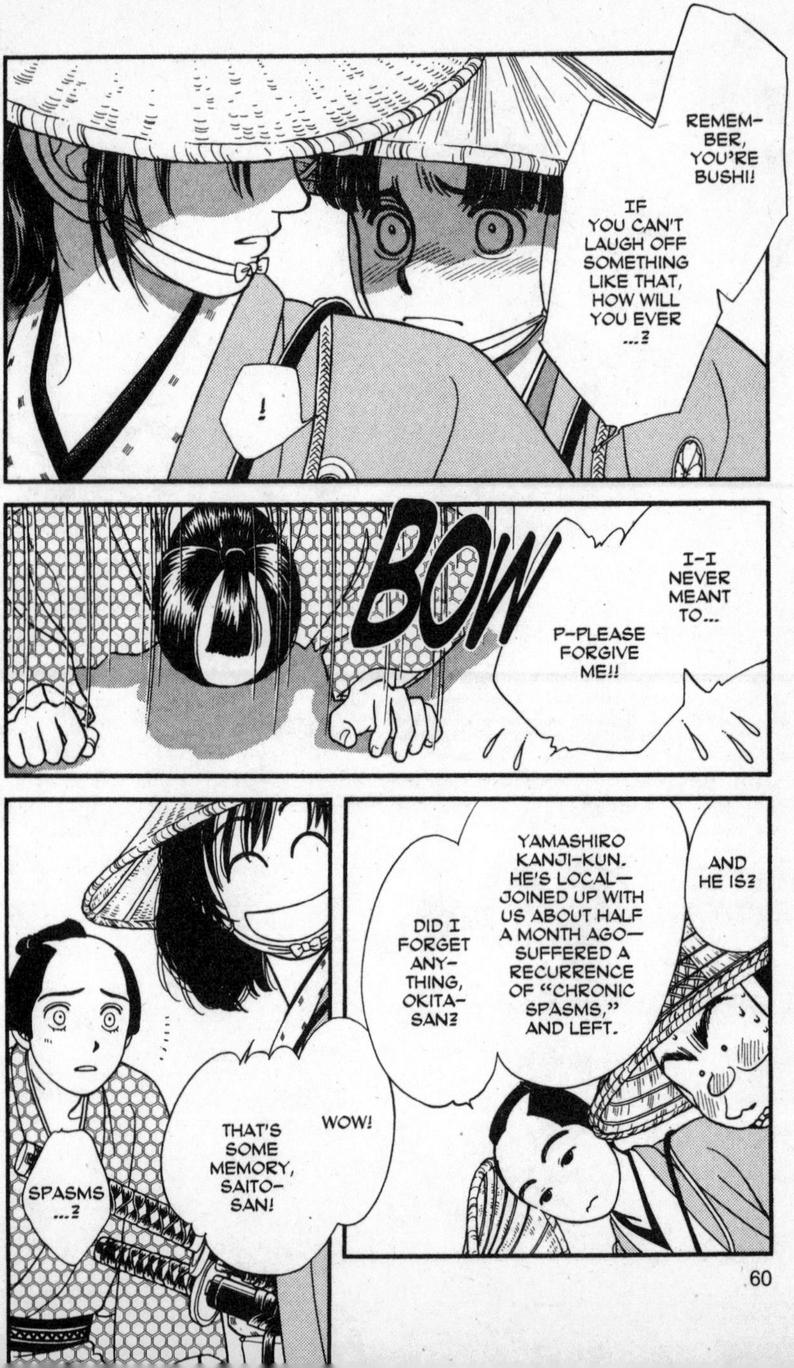
REMEMBER, YOU'RE BUSHI!
IF YOU CAN'T LAUGH OFF SOMETHING LIKE THAT, HOW WILL YOU EVER ...?
!
BOW
I-I NEVER MEANT TO...
P-PLEASE FORGIVE ME!!
AND HE IS?
YAMASHIRO KANJI-KUN. HE'S LOCAL—JOINED UP WITH US ABOUT HALF A MONTH AGO—SUFFERED A RECURRENCE OF "CHRONIC SPASMS," AND LEFT.
DID I FORGET ANYTHING, OKITA-SAN?
WOW!
THAT'S SOME MEMORY, SAITO-SAN!
SPASMS ...?

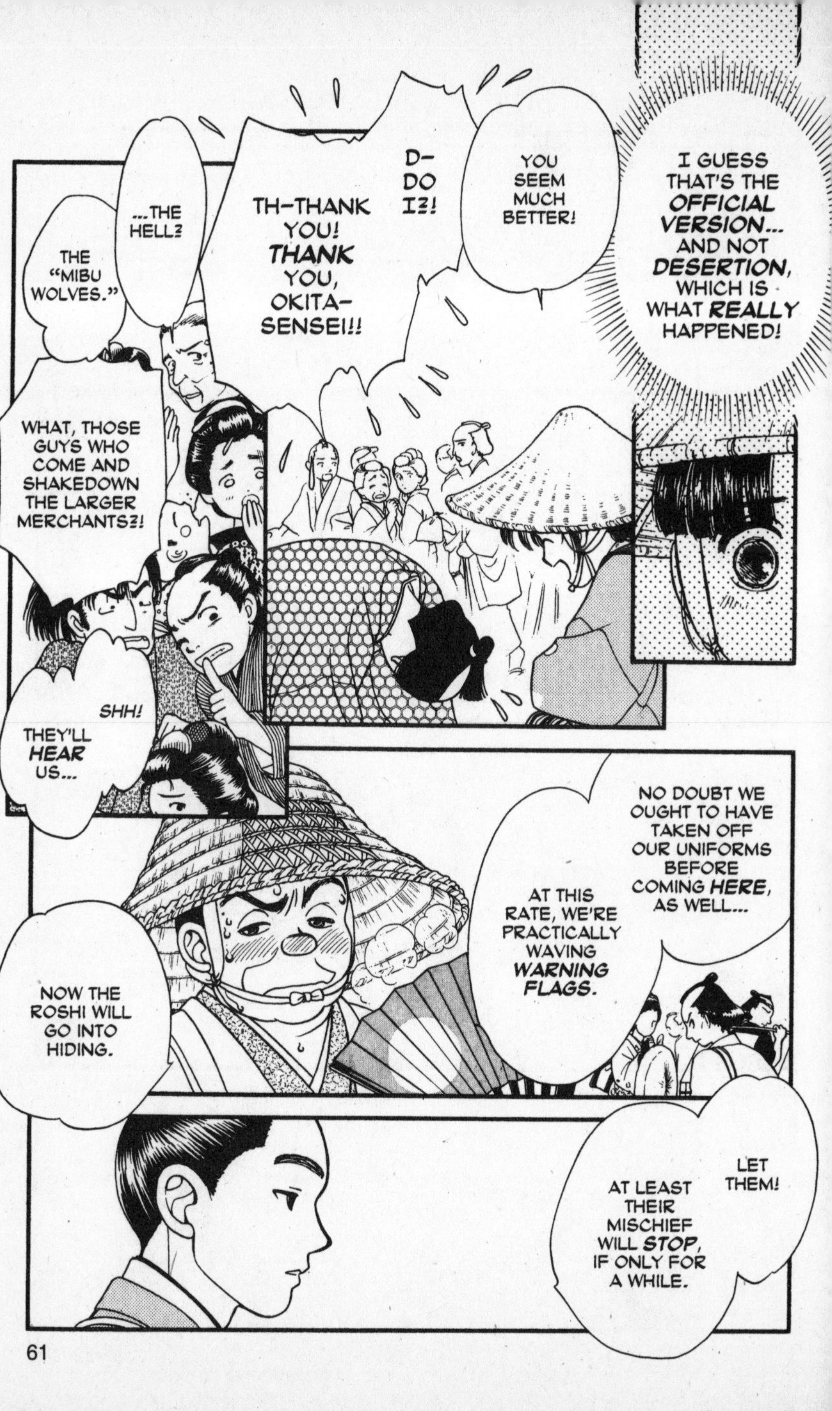
I GUESS THAT'S THE *OFFICIAL VERSION...* AND NOT *DESERTION*, WHICH IS WHAT *REALLY* HAPPENED!
YOU SEEM MUCH BETTER!
D-DO I?!
TH-THANK YOU! *THANK* YOU, OKITA-SENSEI!!
...THE HELL?
THE "MIBU WOLVES."
WHAT, THOSE GUYS WHO COME AND SHAKEDOWN THE LARGER MERCHANTS?!
SHH!
THEY'LL *HEAR* US...
NO DOUBT WE OUGHT TO HAVE TAKEN OFF OUR UNIFORMS BEFORE COMING *HERE*, AS WELL...
AT THIS RATE, WE'RE PRACTICALLY WAVING *WARNING FLAGS.*
NOW THE ROSHI WILL GO INTO HIDING.
LET THEM!
AT LEAST THEIR MISCHIEF WILL *STOP*, IF ONLY FOR A WHILE.

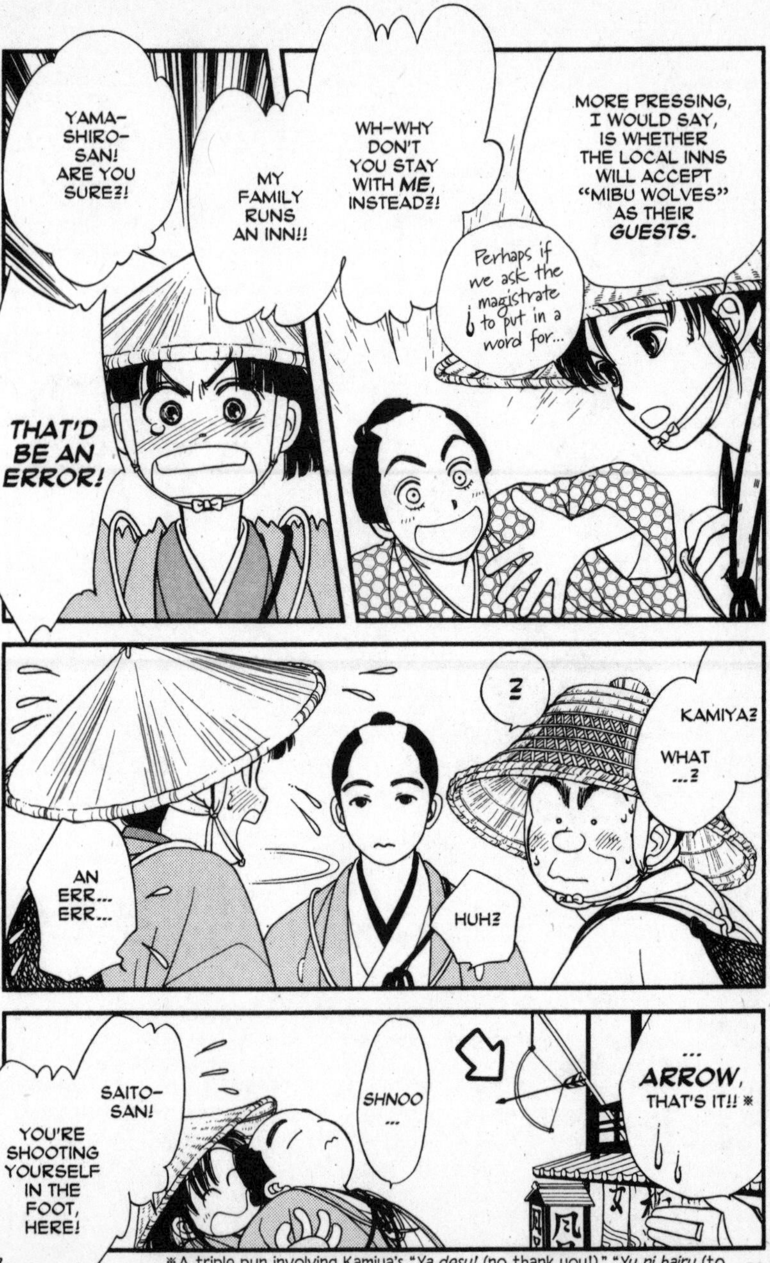
MORE PRESSING, I WOULD SAY, IS WHETHER THE LOCAL INNS WILL ACCEPT "MIBU WOLVES" AS THEIR GUESTS.
Perhaps if we ask the magistrate to put in a word for...
WH-WHY DON'T YOU STAY WITH ME, INSTEAD?!
MY FAMILY RUNS AN INN!!
YAMA-SHIRO-SAN! ARE YOU SURE?!
THAT'D BE AN ERROR!
KAMIYA?
WHAT ...?
?
HUH?
AN ERR... ERR...
... ARROW, THAT'S IT!! ※
SHNOO ...
SAITO-SAN!
YOU'RE SHOOTING YOURSELF IN THE FOOT, HERE!

※A triple pun involving Kamiya's "*Ya desu!* (no thank you!)," "*Yu ni hairu* (to take a bath)," and "*Yumi iru* (to shoot a bow)." "*Yu ni hairu*" and "*Yumi iru*" sound alike, thus the arrow on the public-bathhouse nameboard.

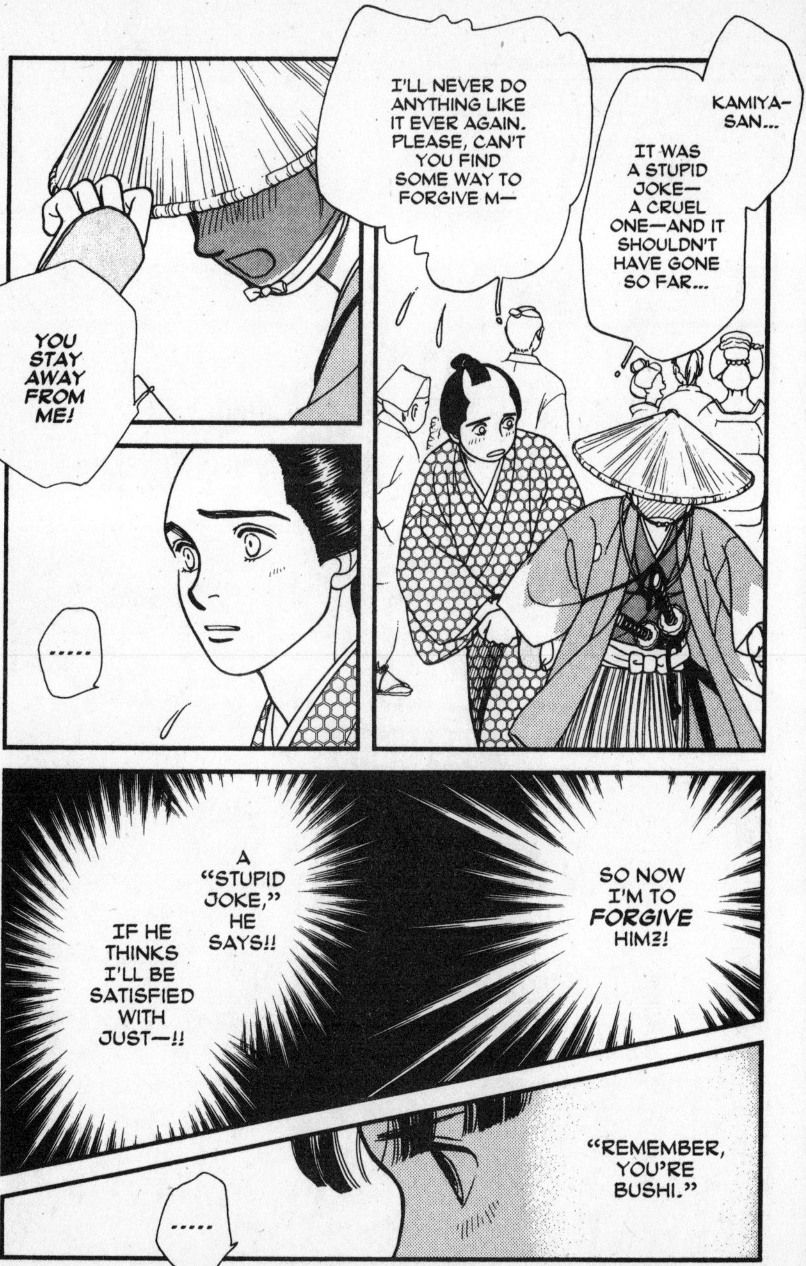
KAMIYA-SAN...
IT WAS A STUPID JOKE—A CRUEL ONE—AND IT SHOULDN'T HAVE GONE SO FAR...
I'LL NEVER DO ANYTHING LIKE IT EVER AGAIN. PLEASE, CAN'T YOU FIND SOME WAY TO FORGIVE M—
YOU STAY AWAY FROM ME!
.....
SO NOW I'M TO **FORGIVE** HIM?!
A "STUPID JOKE," HE SAYS!!
IF HE THINKS I'LL BE SATISFIED WITH JUST—!!
"REMEMBER, YOU'RE BUSHI."
.....

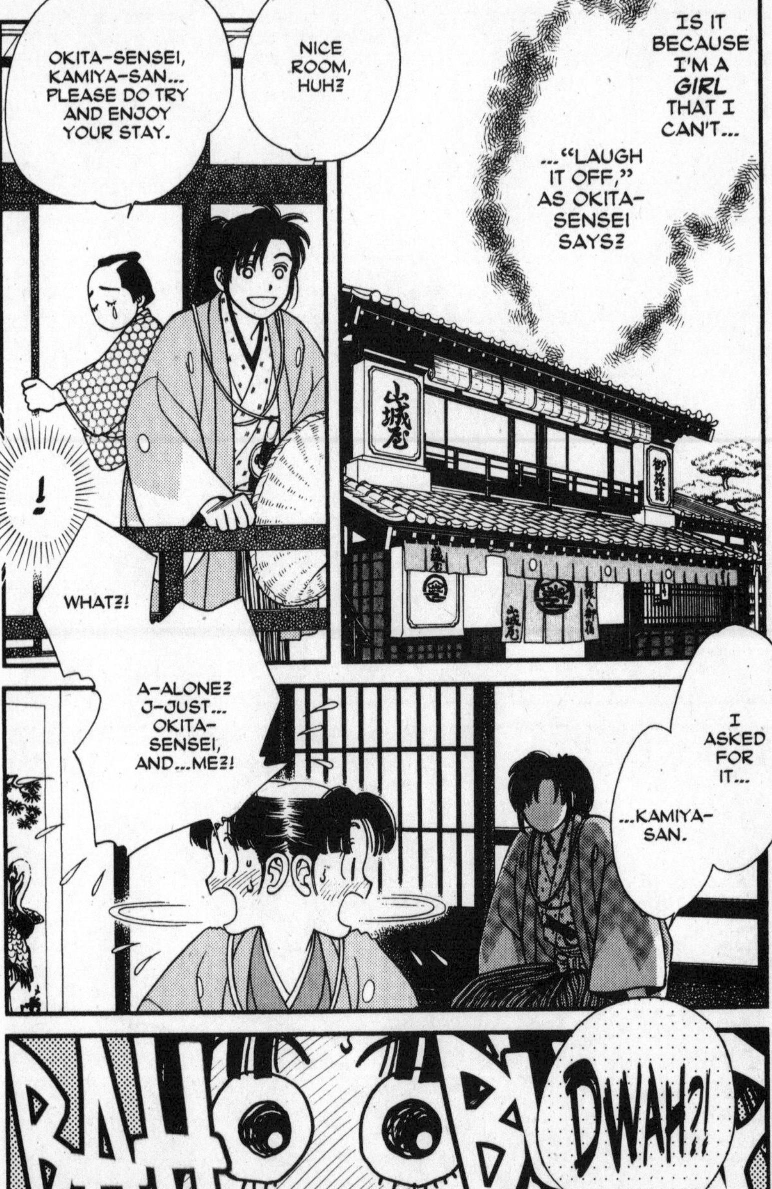
IS IT BECAUSE I'M A GIRL THAT I CAN'T...
..."LAUGH IT OFF," AS OKITA-SENSEI SAYS?
NICE ROOM, HUH?
OKITA-SENSEI, KAMIYA-SAN... PLEASE DO TRY AND ENJOY YOUR STAY.
!
WHAT?!
I ASKED FOR IT...
...KAMIYA-SAN.
A-ALONE? J-JUST... OKITA-SENSEI, AND...ME?!
DWAH?!

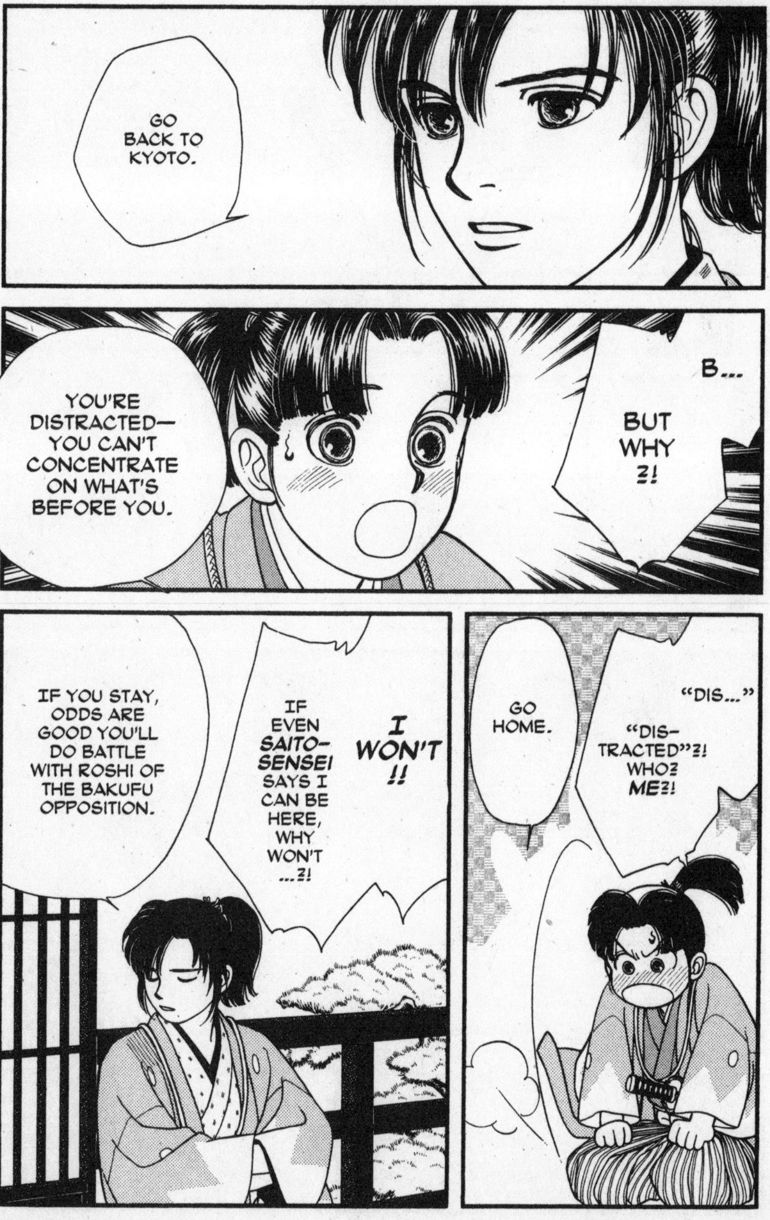
GO BACK TO KYOTO.
B...
BUT WHY ?!
YOU'RE DISTRACTED— YOU CAN'T CONCENTRATE ON WHAT'S BEFORE YOU.
"DIS..."
"DIS-TRACTED"?! WHO? ME?!
GO HOME.
I WON'T !!
IF EVEN SAITO-SENSEI SAYS I CAN BE HERE, WHY WON'T ...?!
IF YOU STAY, ODDS ARE GOOD YOU'LL DO BATTLE WITH ROSHI OF THE BAKUFU OPPOSITION.

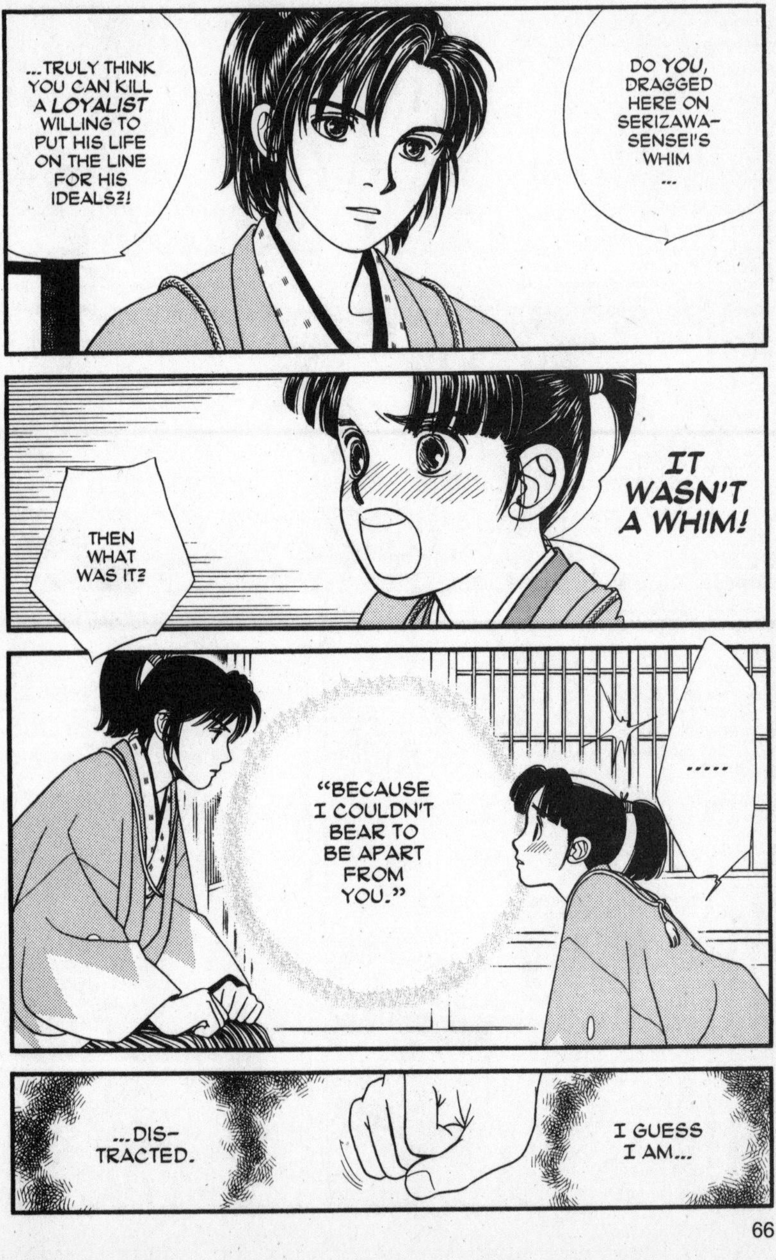
DO YOU, DRAGGED HERE ON SERIZAWA-SENSEI'S WHIM ...
...TRULY THINK YOU CAN KILL A LOYALIST WILLING TO PUT HIS LIFE ON THE LINE FOR HIS IDEALS?!
IT WASN'T A WHIM!
THEN WHAT WAS IT?
.....
"BECAUSE I COULDN'T BEAR TO BE APART FROM YOU."
I GUESS I AM...
...DIS-TRACTED.

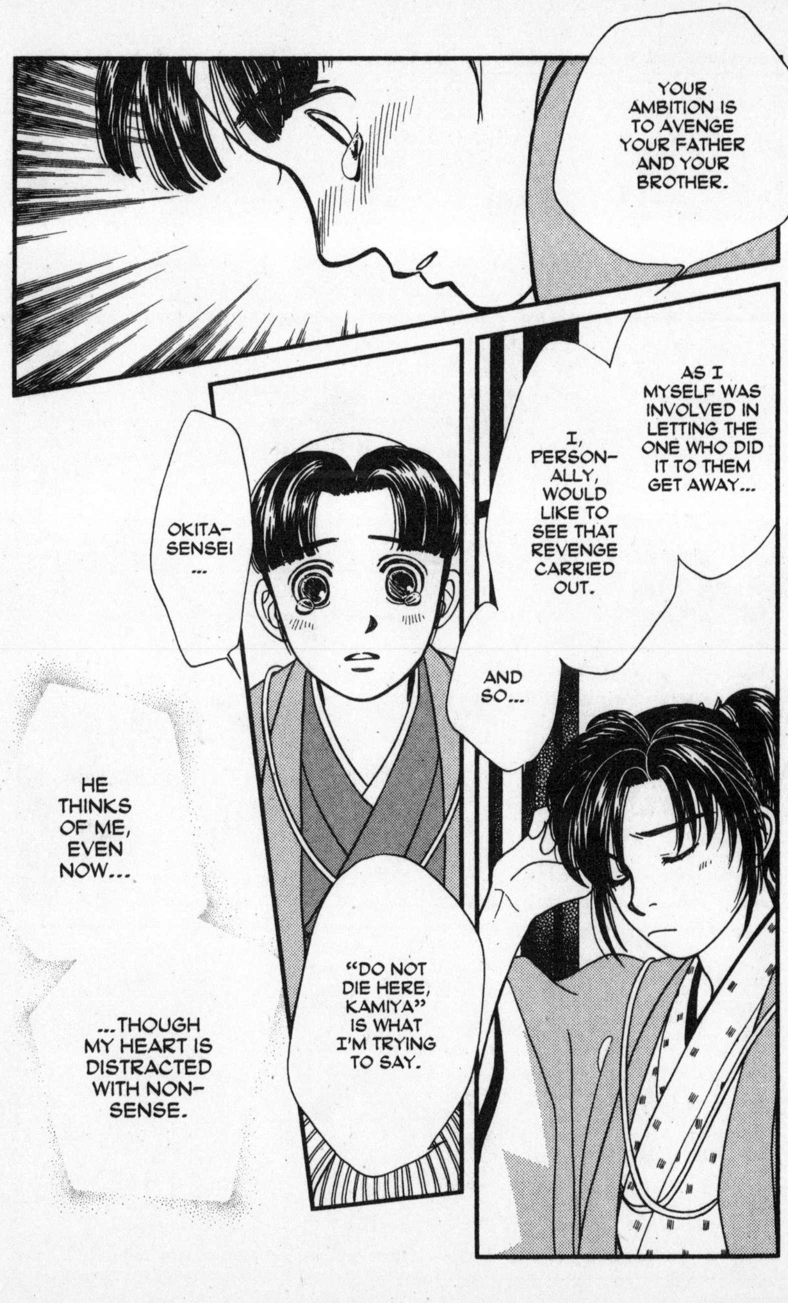
YOUR AMBITION IS TO AVENGE YOUR FATHER AND YOUR BROTHER.
AS I MYSELF WAS INVOLVED IN LETTING THE ONE WHO DID IT TO THEM GET AWAY...
I, PERSON-ALLY, WOULD LIKE TO SEE THAT REVENGE CARRIED OUT.
AND SO...
“DO NOT DIE HERE, KAMIYA” IS WHAT I'M TRYING TO SAY.
OKITA-SENSEI ...
HE THINKS OF ME, EVEN NOW...
...THOUGH MY HEART IS DISTRACTED WITH NON-SENSE.

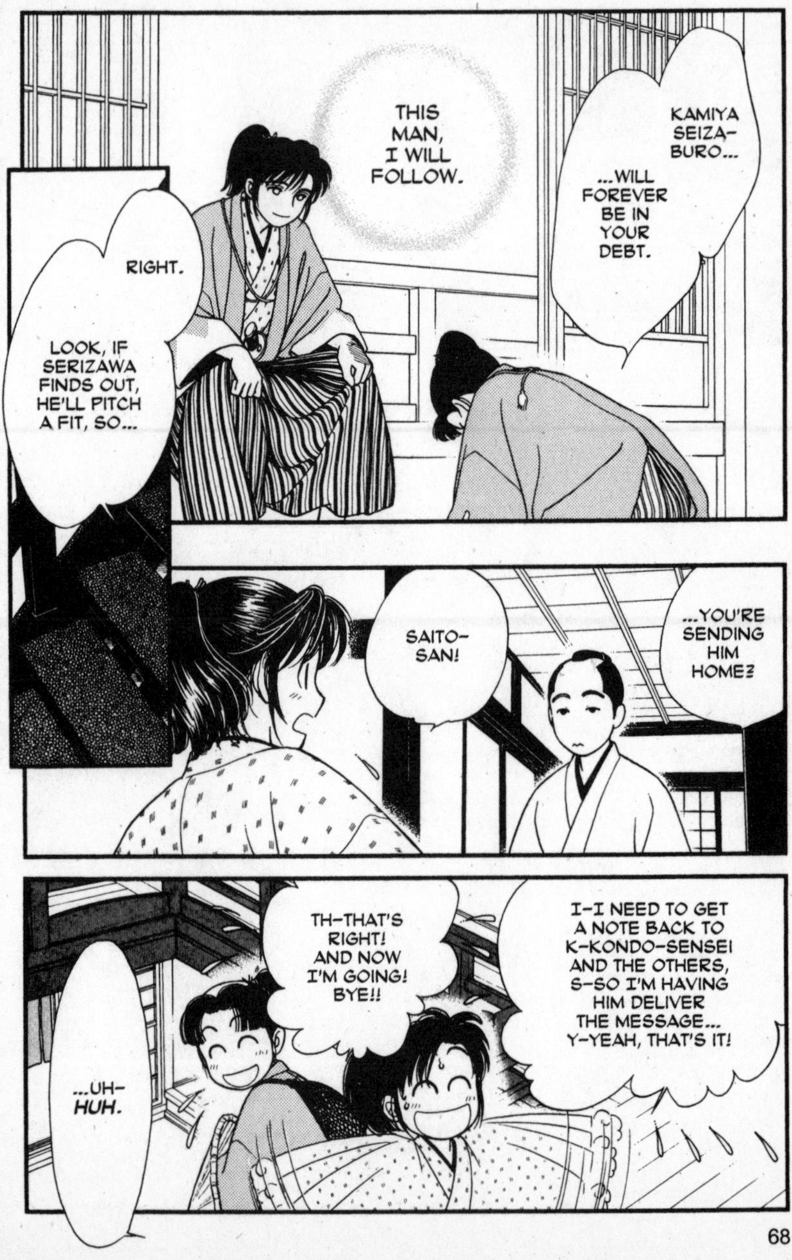
KAMIYA SEIZABURO...
...WILL FOREVER BE IN YOUR DEBT.
THIS MAN, I WILL FOLLOW.
RIGHT.
LOOK, IF SERIZAWA FINDS OUT, HE'LL PITCH A FIT, SO...
...YOU'RE SENDING HIM HOME?
SAITO-SAN!
I-I NEED TO GET A NOTE BACK TO K-KONDO-SENSEI AND THE OTHERS, S-SO I'M HAVING HIM DELIVER THE MESSAGE... Y-YEAH, THAT'S IT!
TH-THAT'S RIGHT! AND NOW I'M GOING! BYE!!
...UH-HUH.

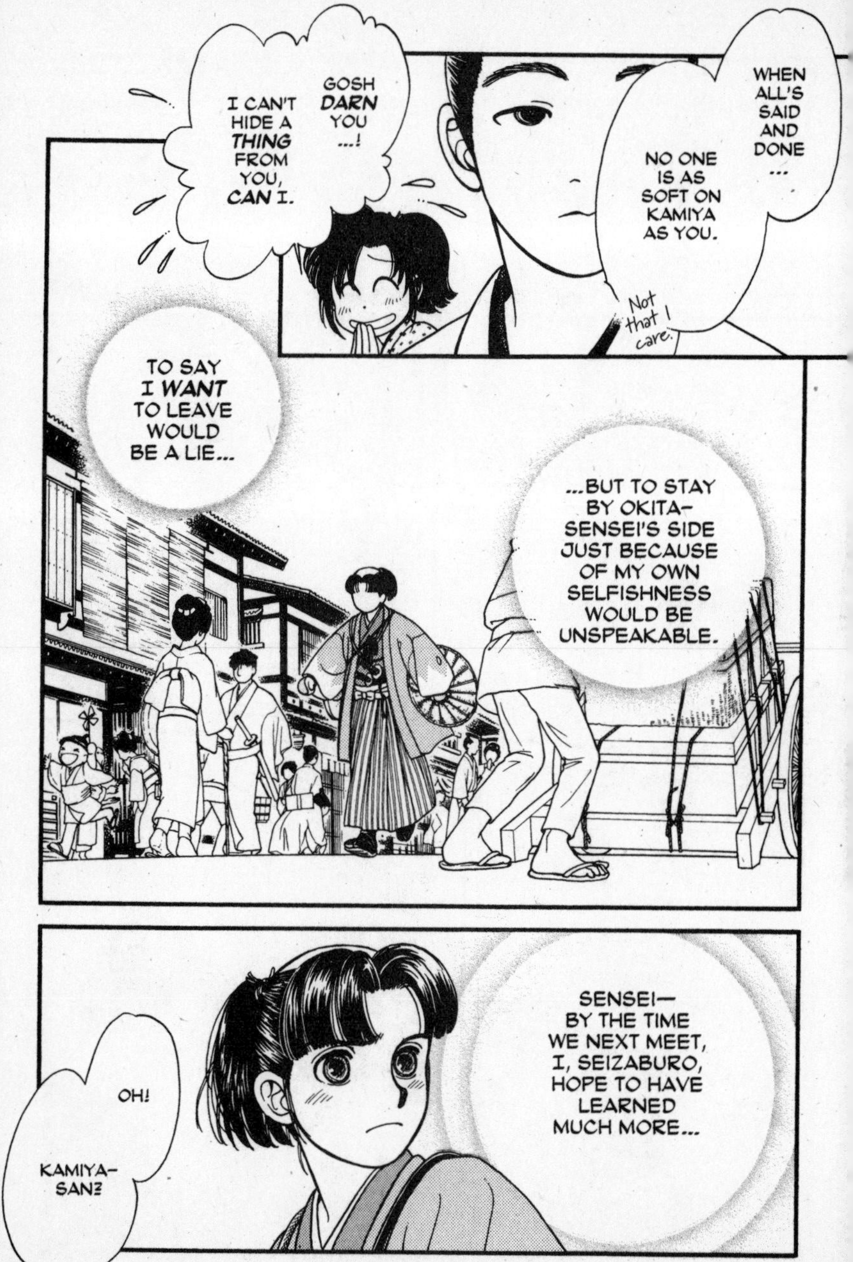
WHEN ALL'S SAID AND DONE ...
NO ONE IS AS SOFT ON KAMIYA AS YOU.
Not that I care.
GOSH DARN YOU ...!
I CAN'T HIDE A THING FROM YOU, CAN I.
TO SAY I WANT TO LEAVE WOULD BE A LIE...
...BUT TO STAY BY OKITA-SENSEI'S SIDE JUST BECAUSE OF MY OWN SELFISHNESS WOULD BE UNSPEAKABLE.
SENSEI— BY THE TIME WE NEXT MEET, I, SEIZABURO, HOPE TO HAVE LEARNED MUCH MORE...
OH!
KAMIYA-SAN?

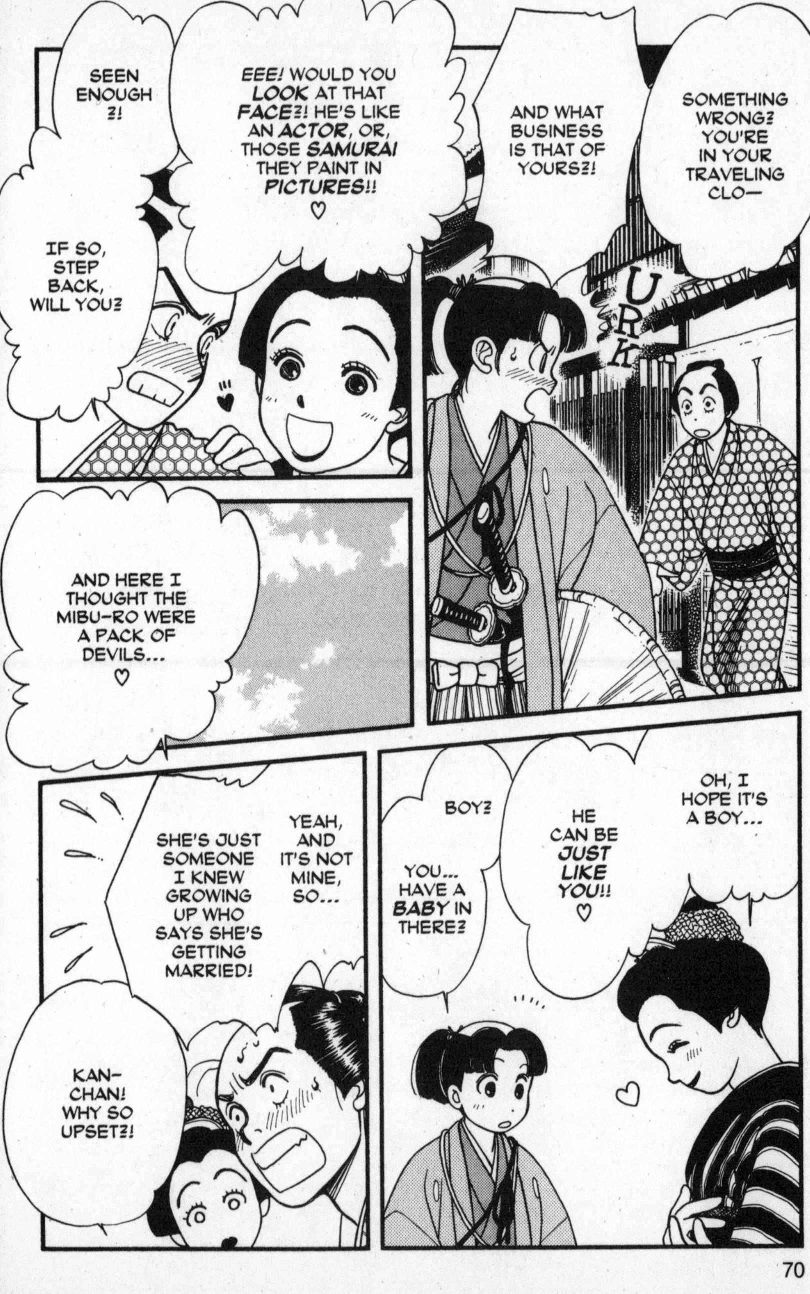

SOMETHING WRONG? YOU'RE IN YOUR TRAVELING CLO—
AND WHAT BUSINESS IS THAT OF YOURS?!
URK
EEE! WOULD YOU LOOK AT THAT FACE?! HE'S LIKE AN ACTOR, OR, THOSE SAMURAI THEY PAINT IN PICTURES!! ♡
SEEN ENOUGH?!
IF SO, STEP BACK, WILL YOU?
AND HERE I THOUGHT THE MIBU-RO WERE A PACK OF DEVILS... ♡
OH, I HOPE IT'S A BOY...
HE CAN BE JUST LIKE YOU!! ♡
BOY?
YOU... HAVE A BABY IN THERE?
YEAH, AND IT'S NOT MINE, SO...
SHE'S JUST SOMEONE I KNEW GROWING UP WHO SAYS SHE'S GETTING MARRIED!
KAN-CHAN! WHY SO UPSET?!

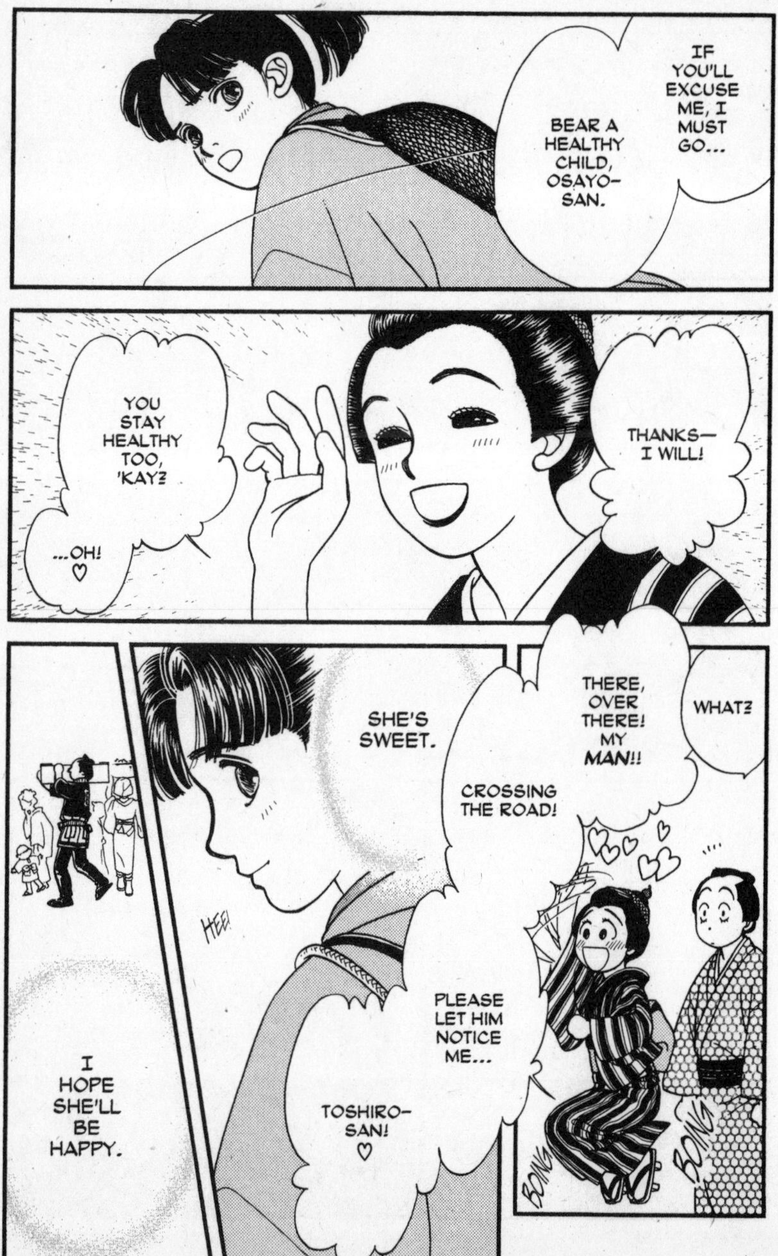
IF YOU'LL EXCUSE ME, I MUST GO...
BEAR A HEALTHY CHILD, OSAYO-SAN.
THANKS— I WILL!
YOU STAY HEALTHY TOO, 'KAY?
...OH! ♡
WHAT?
THERE, OVER THERE! MY MAN!!
CROSSING THE ROAD!
....
PLEASE LET HIM NOTICE ME...
TOSHIRO-SAN! ♡
BOING
BOING
SHE'S SWEET.
HEE!
I HOPE SHE'LL BE HAPPY.

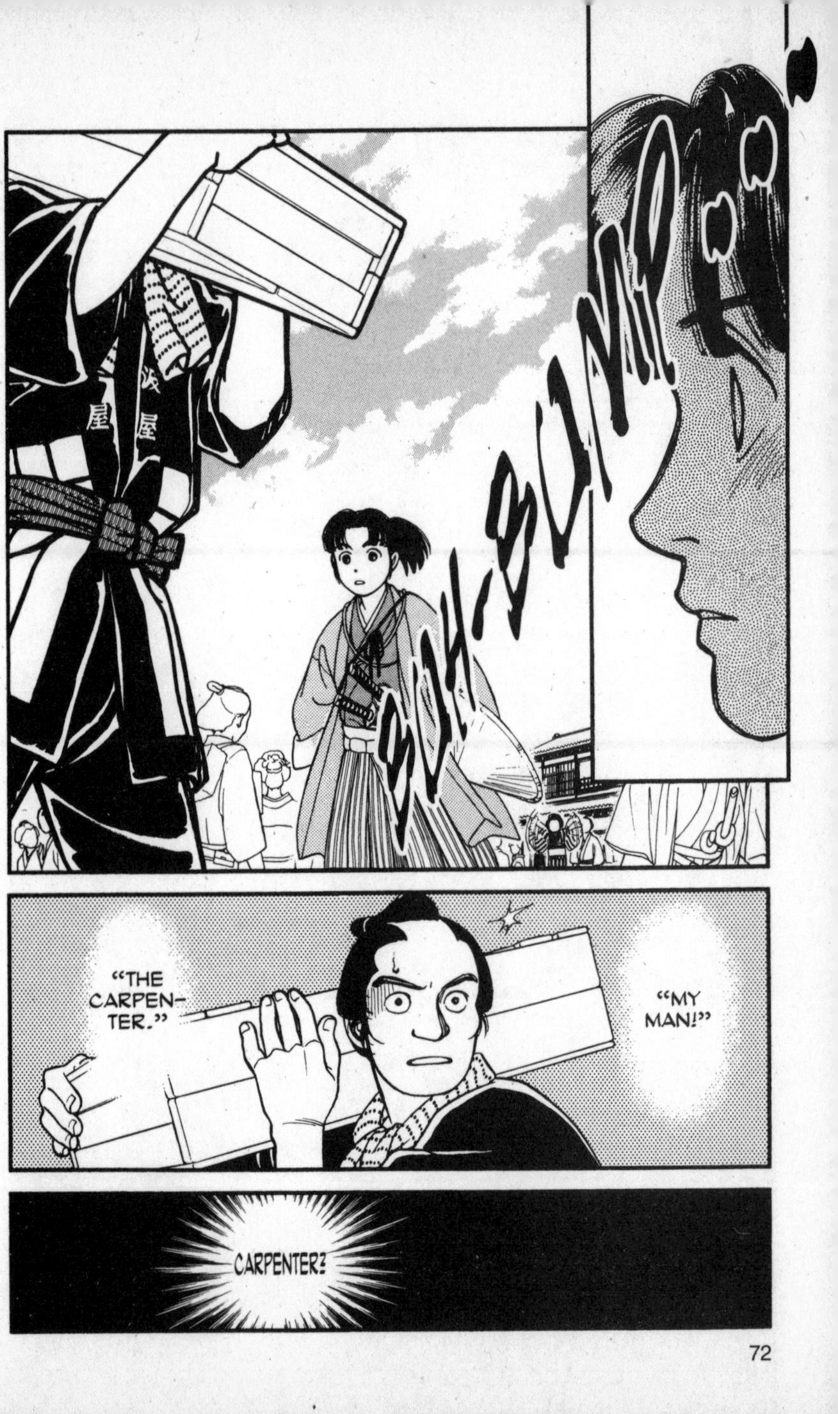
SOH-SUMP...
"MY MAN!"
"THE CARPENTER."
CARPENTER?

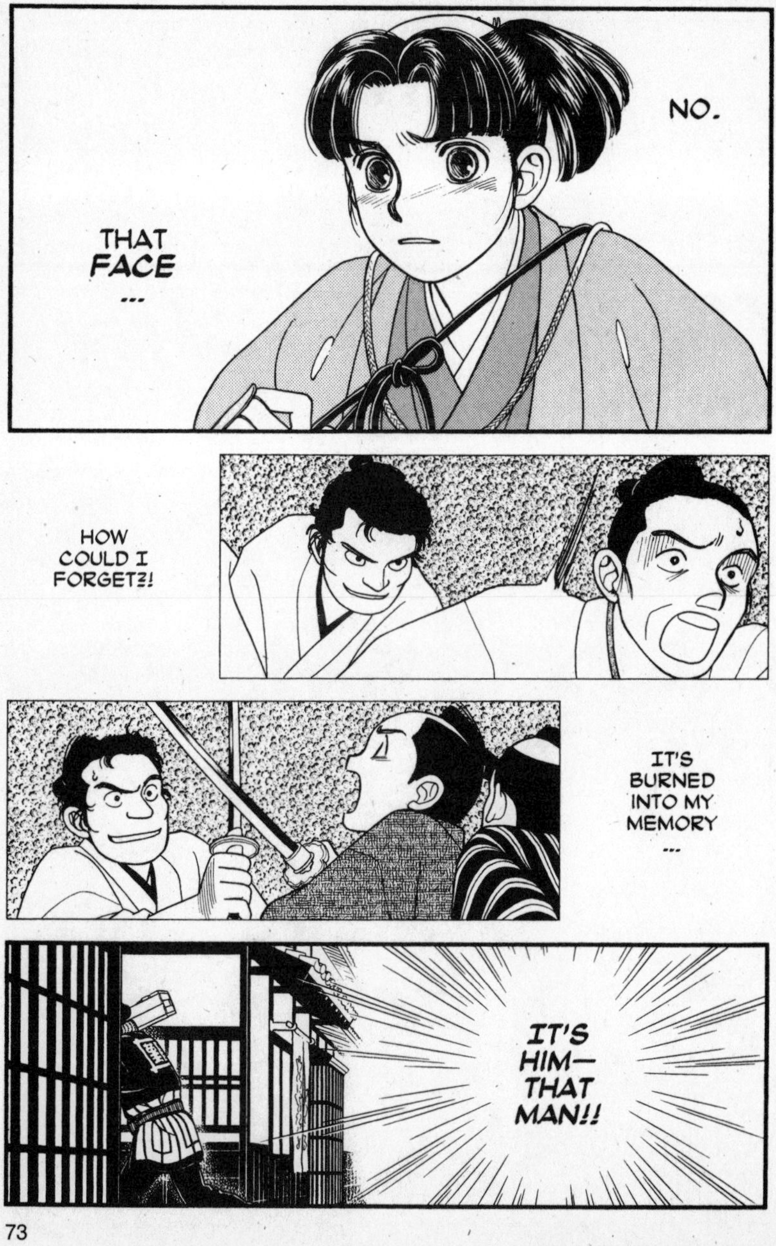
NO.
THAT FACE ...
HOW COULD I FORGET?!
IT'S BURNED INTO MY MEMORY ...
IT'S HIM— THAT MAN!!

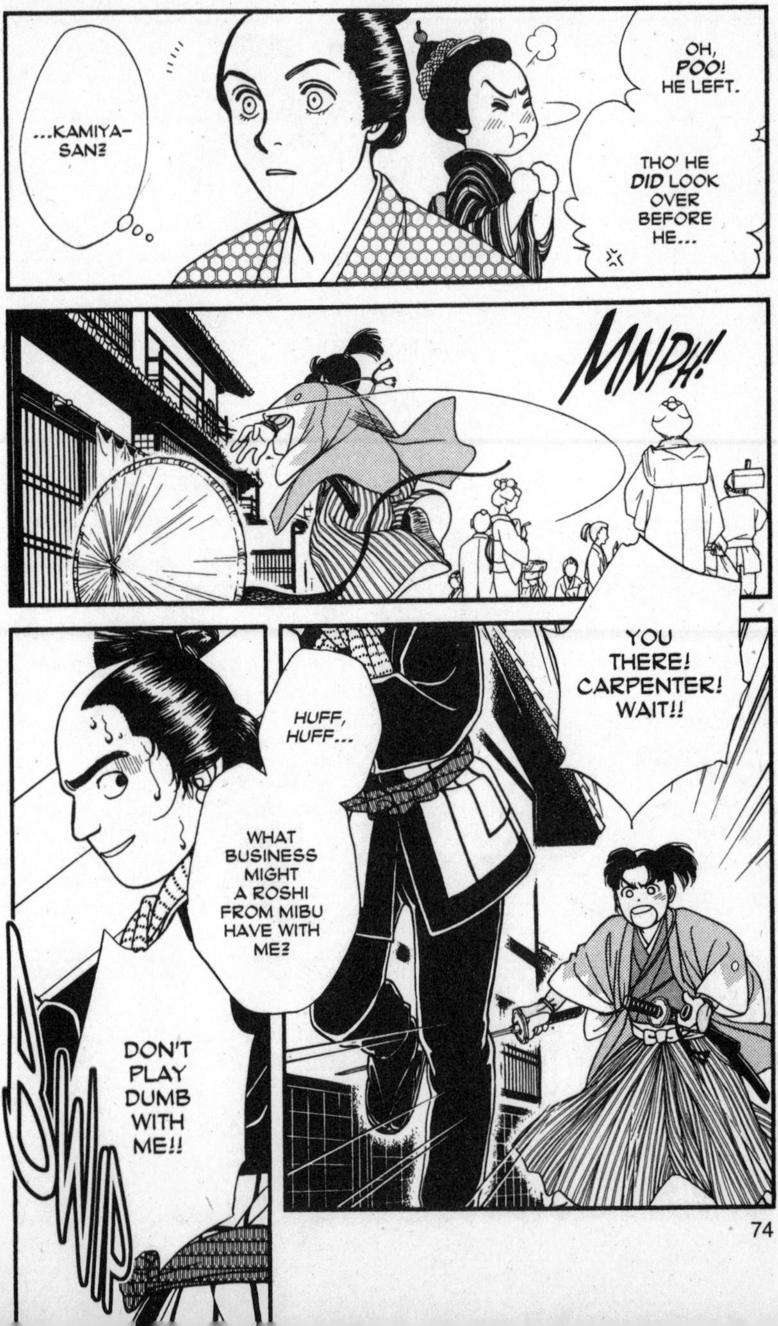
OH, POO! HE LEFT.
THO' HE DID LOOK OVER BEFORE HE...
...KAMIYA-SAN?
MNPH!
YOU THERE! CARPENTER! WAIT!!
HUFF, HUFF...
WHAT BUSINESS MIGHT A ROSHI FROM MIBU HAVE WITH ME?
DON'T PLAY DUMB WITH ME!!

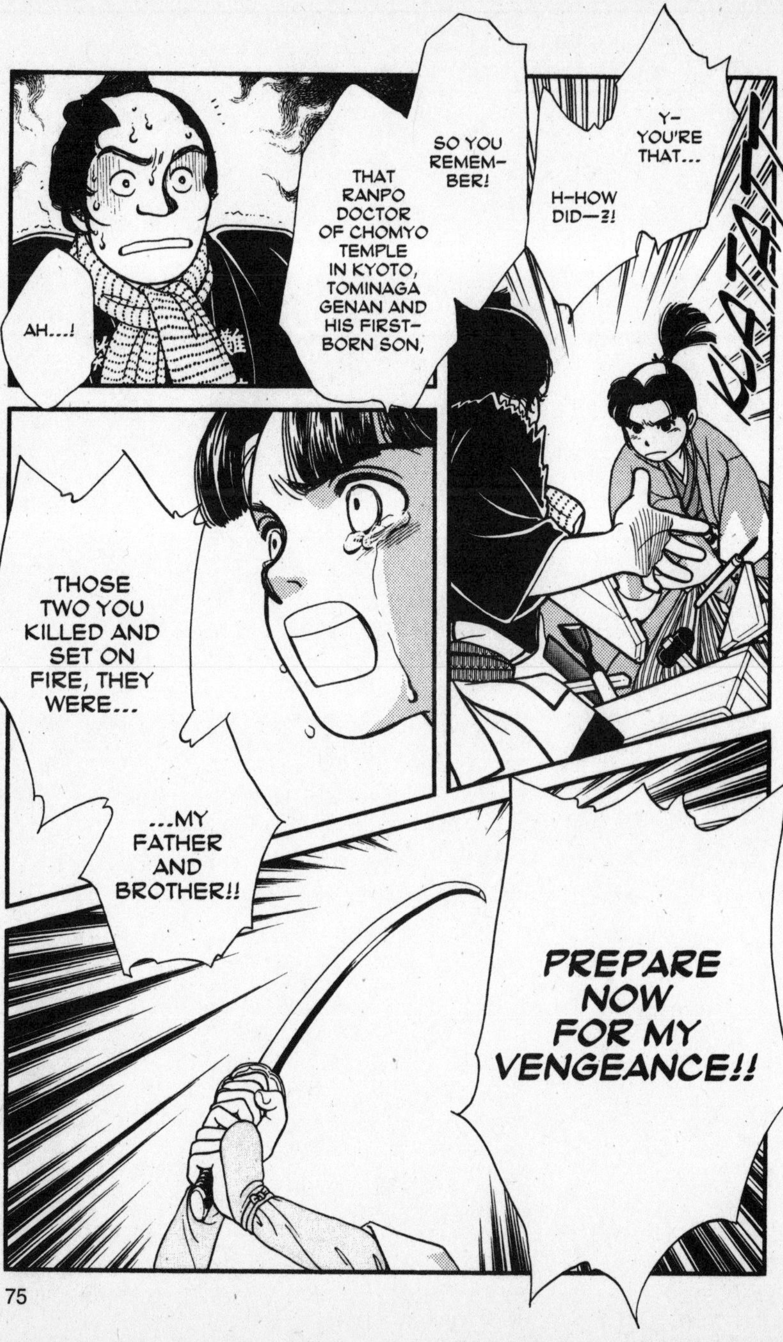

KATATT
Y- YOU'RE THAT...
H-HOW DID—?!
SO YOU REMEMBER!
THAT RANPO DOCTOR OF CHOMYO TEMPLE IN KYOTO, TOMINAGA GENAN AND HIS FIRST-BORN SON,
AH...!
THOSE TWO YOU KILLED AND SET ON FIRE, THEY WERE...
...MY FATHER AND BROTHER!!
PREPARE NOW FOR MY VENGEANCE!!

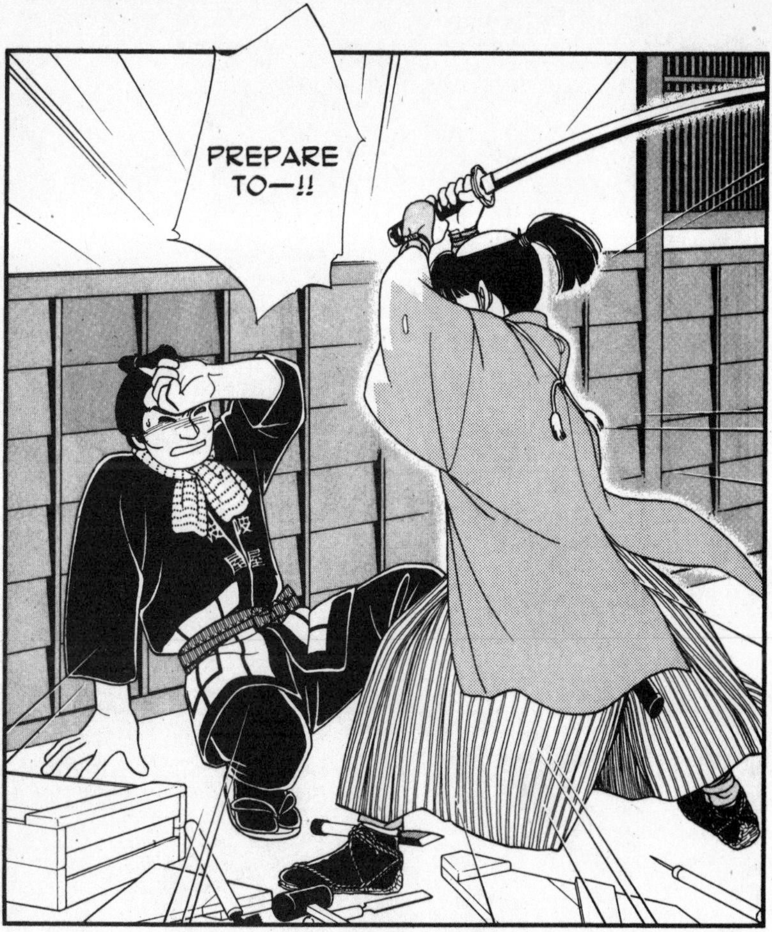
PREPARE TO—!!

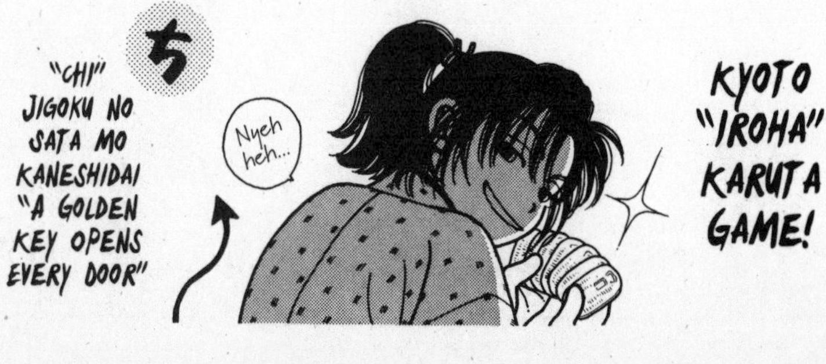
KYOTO "IROHA" KARUTA GAME!
Nyeh heh...
ち
"CHI" JIGOKU NO SATA MO KANESHIDAI "A GOLDEN KEY OPENS EVERY DOOR"

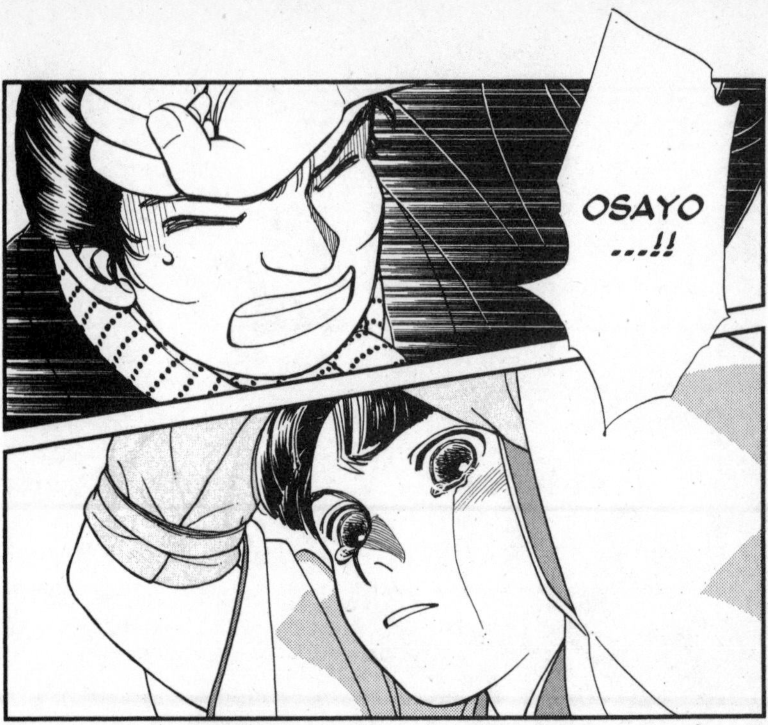
OSAYO ...!!

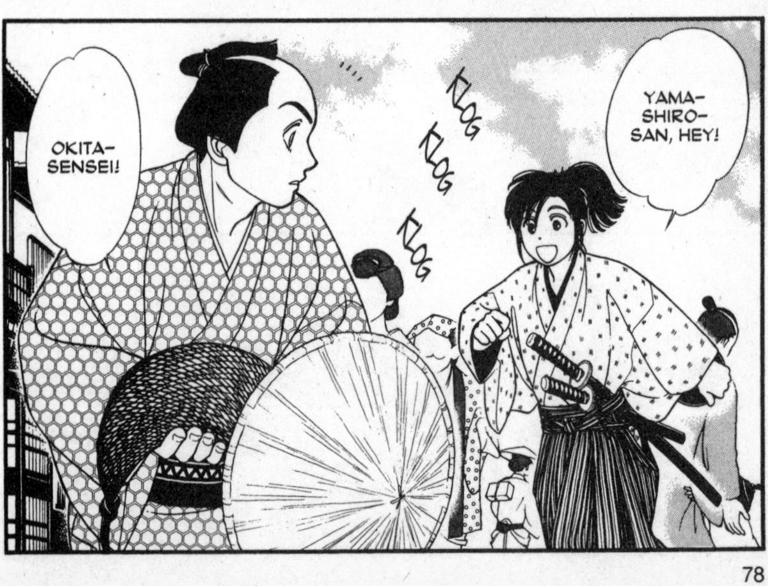
YAMA-SHIRO-SAN, HEY!
KLOG
KLOG
KLOG
OKITA-SENSEI!

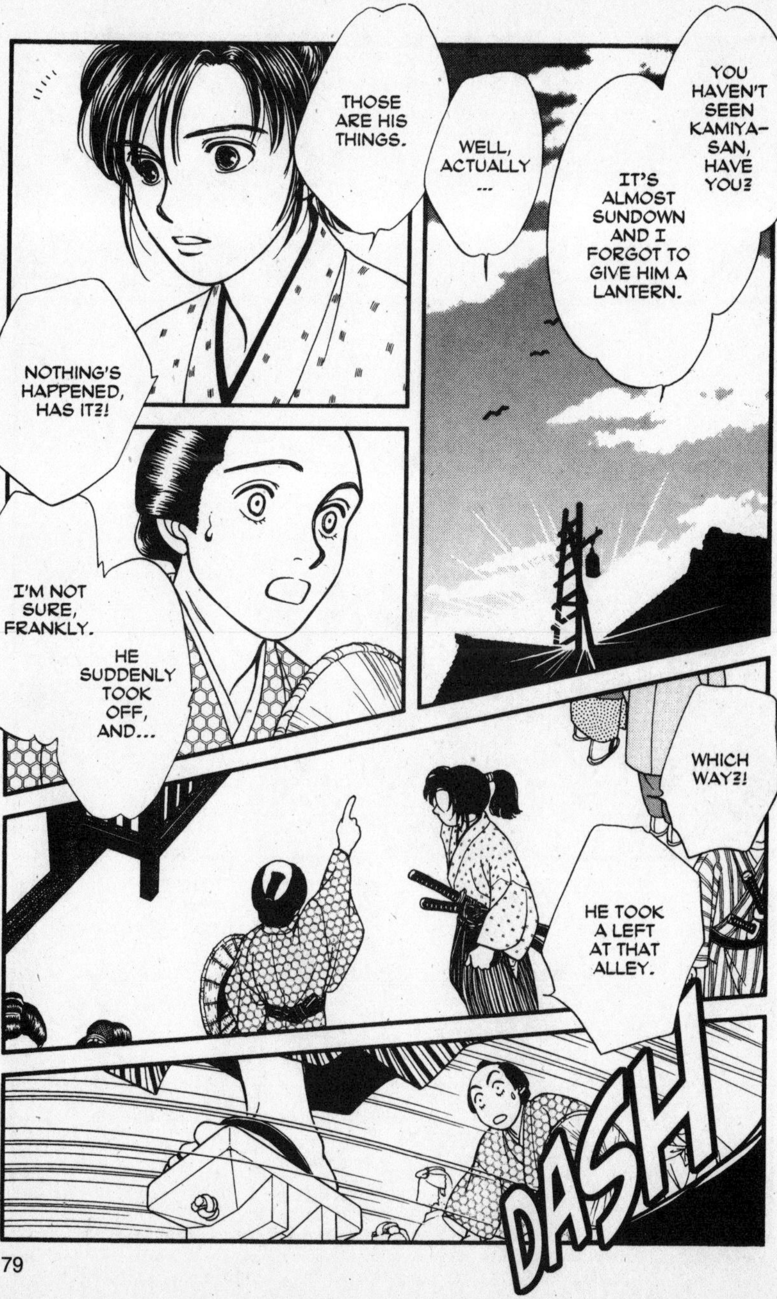
YOU HAVEN'T SEEN KAMIYA-SAN, HAVE YOU?
IT'S ALMOST SUNDOWN AND I FORGOT TO GIVE HIM A LANTERN.
WELL, ACTUALLY ...
THOSE ARE HIS THINGS.
NOTHING'S HAPPENED, HAS IT?!
I'M NOT SURE, FRANKLY.
HE SUDDENLY TOOK OFF, AND...
WHICH WAY?!
HE TOOK A LEFT AT THAT ALLEY.
DASH

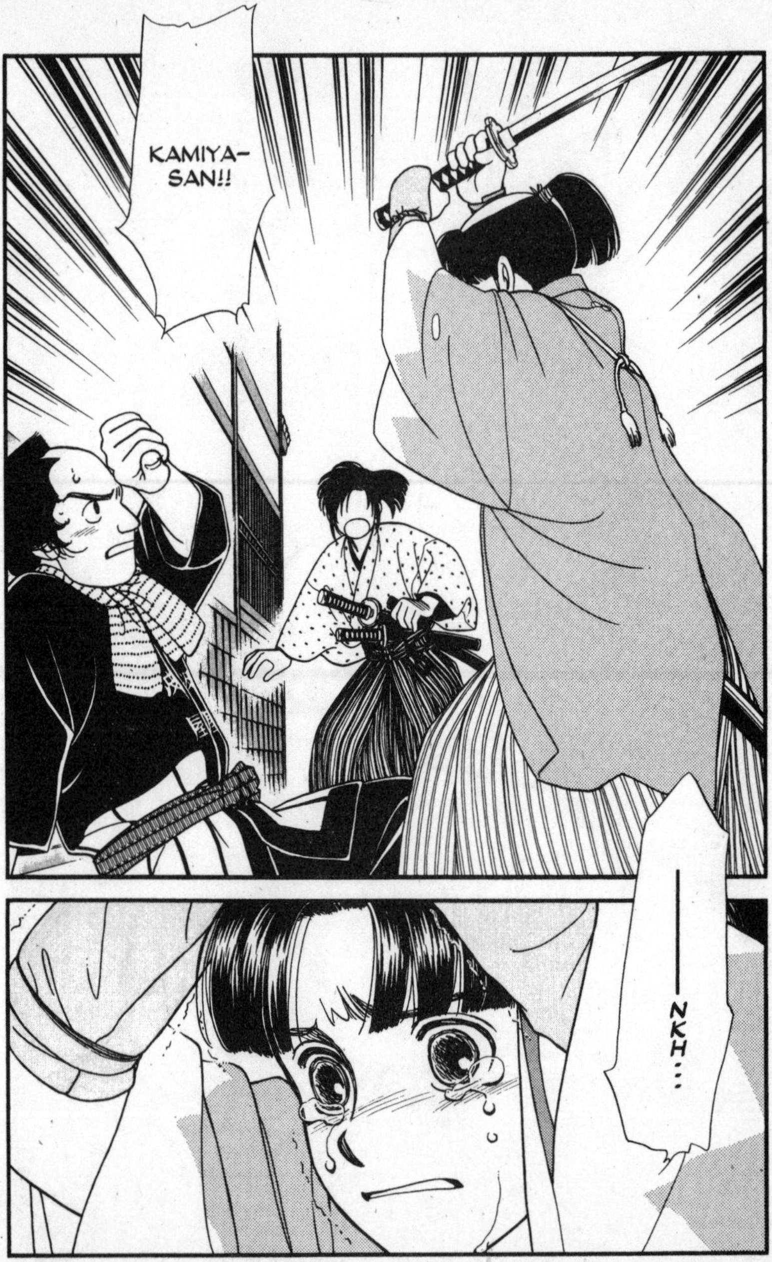
KAMIYA-SAN!!
——NKH...

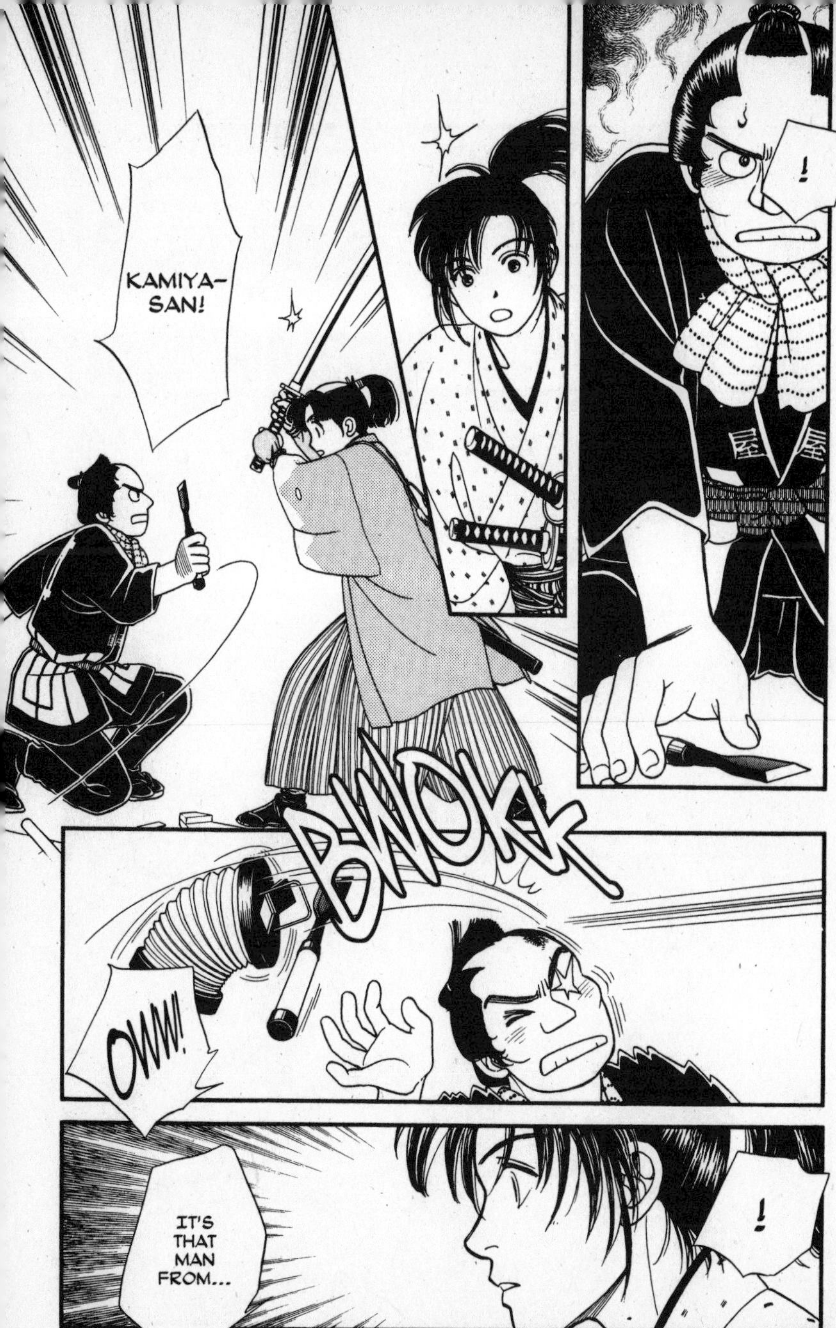
!
KAMIYA-SAN!
BWOKK
OWW!
!
IT'S THAT MAN FROM...

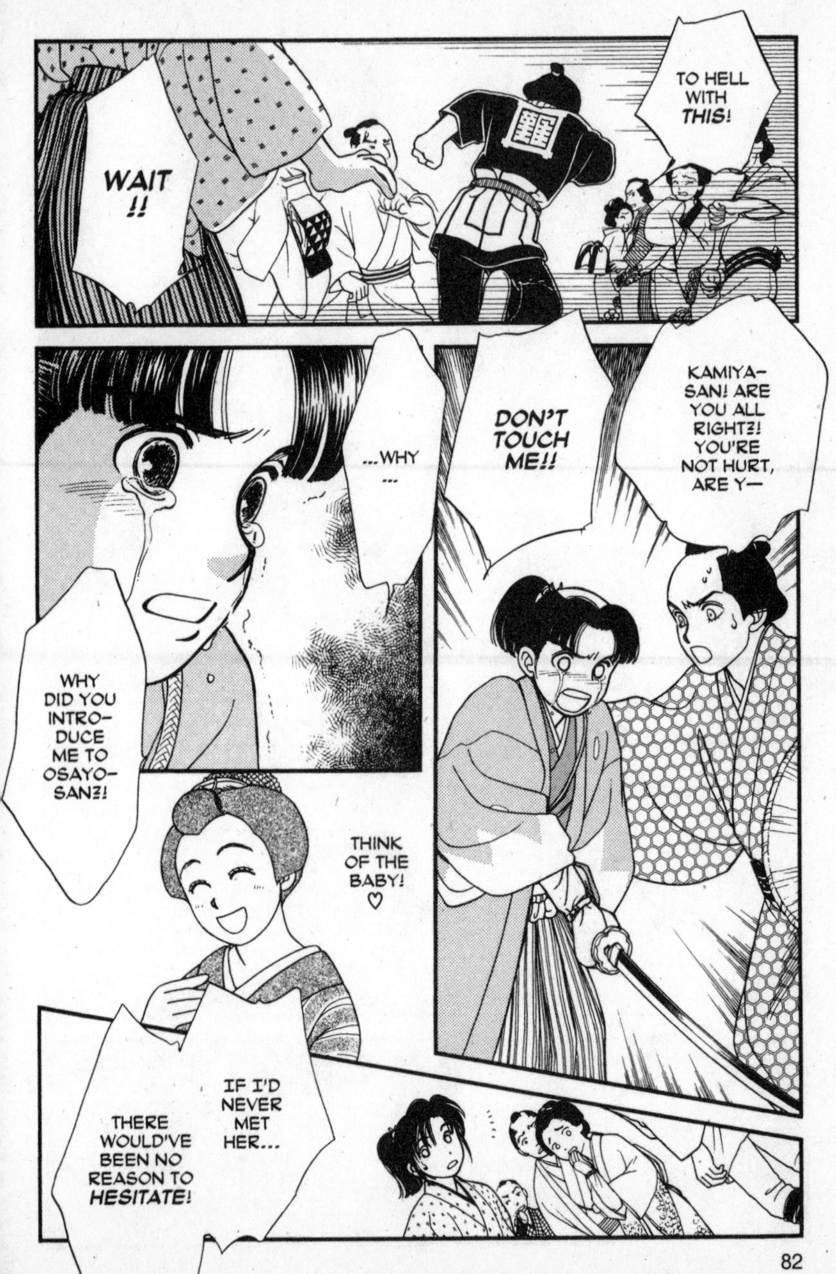
TO HELL WITH THIS!
WAIT !!
KAMIYA-SAN! ARE YOU ALL RIGHT?! YOU'RE NOT HURT, ARE Y—
DON'T TOUCH ME!!
...WHY ...
WHY DID YOU INTRO-DUCE ME TO OSAYO-SAN?!
THINK OF THE BABY! ♡
IF I'D NEVER MET HER...
THERE WOULD'VE BEEN NO REASON TO HESITATE!

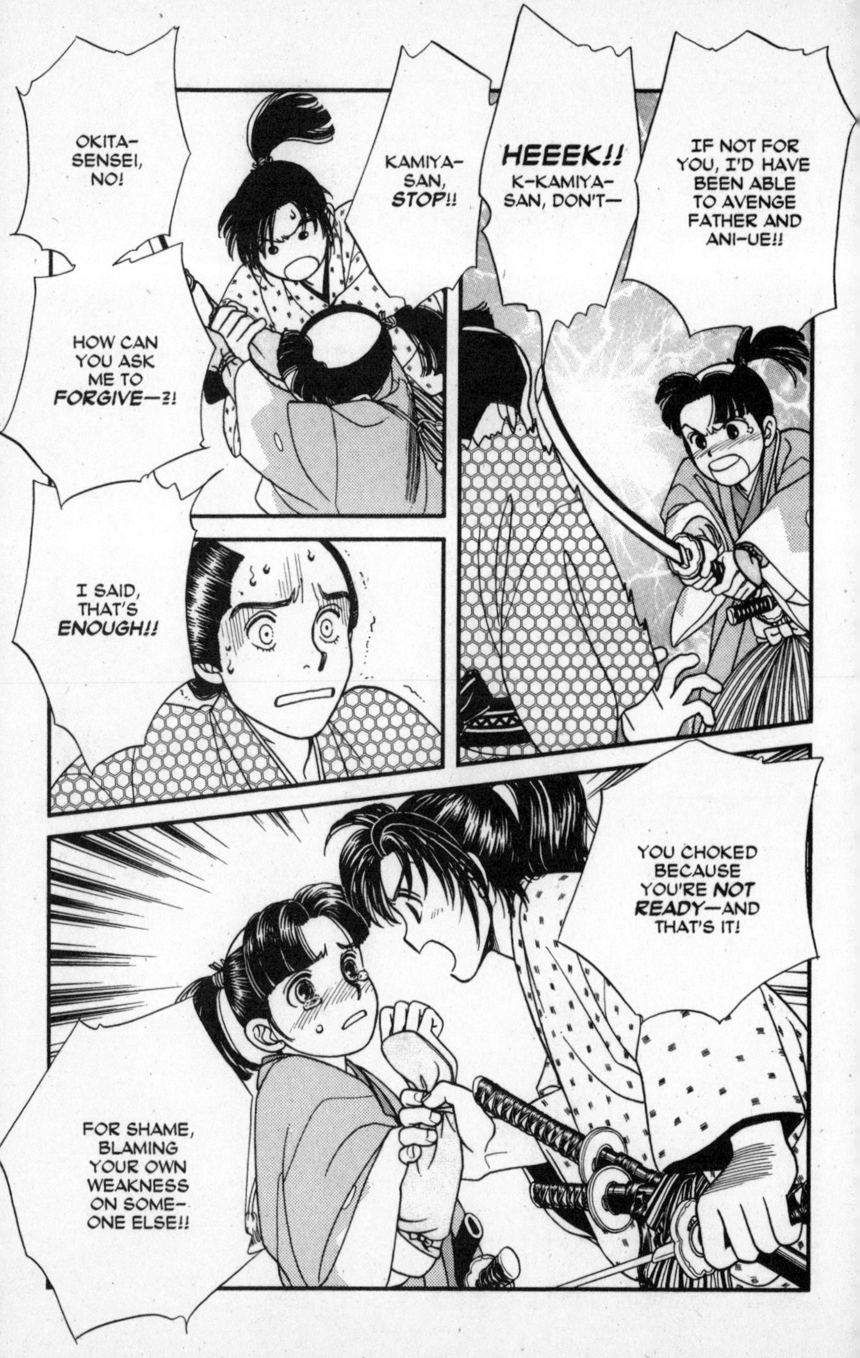
IF NOT FOR YOU, I'D HAVE BEEN ABLE TO AVENGE FATHER AND ANI-UE!!
HEEEK!! K-KAMIYA-SAN, DON'T—
KAMIYA-SAN, STOP!!
OKITA-SENSEI, NO!
HOW CAN YOU ASK ME TO FORGIVE—?!
I SAID, THAT'S ENOUGH!!
YOU CHOKED BECAUSE YOU'RE NOT READY—AND THAT'S IT!
FOR SHAME, BLAMING YOUR OWN WEAKNESS ON SOME-ONE ELSE!!

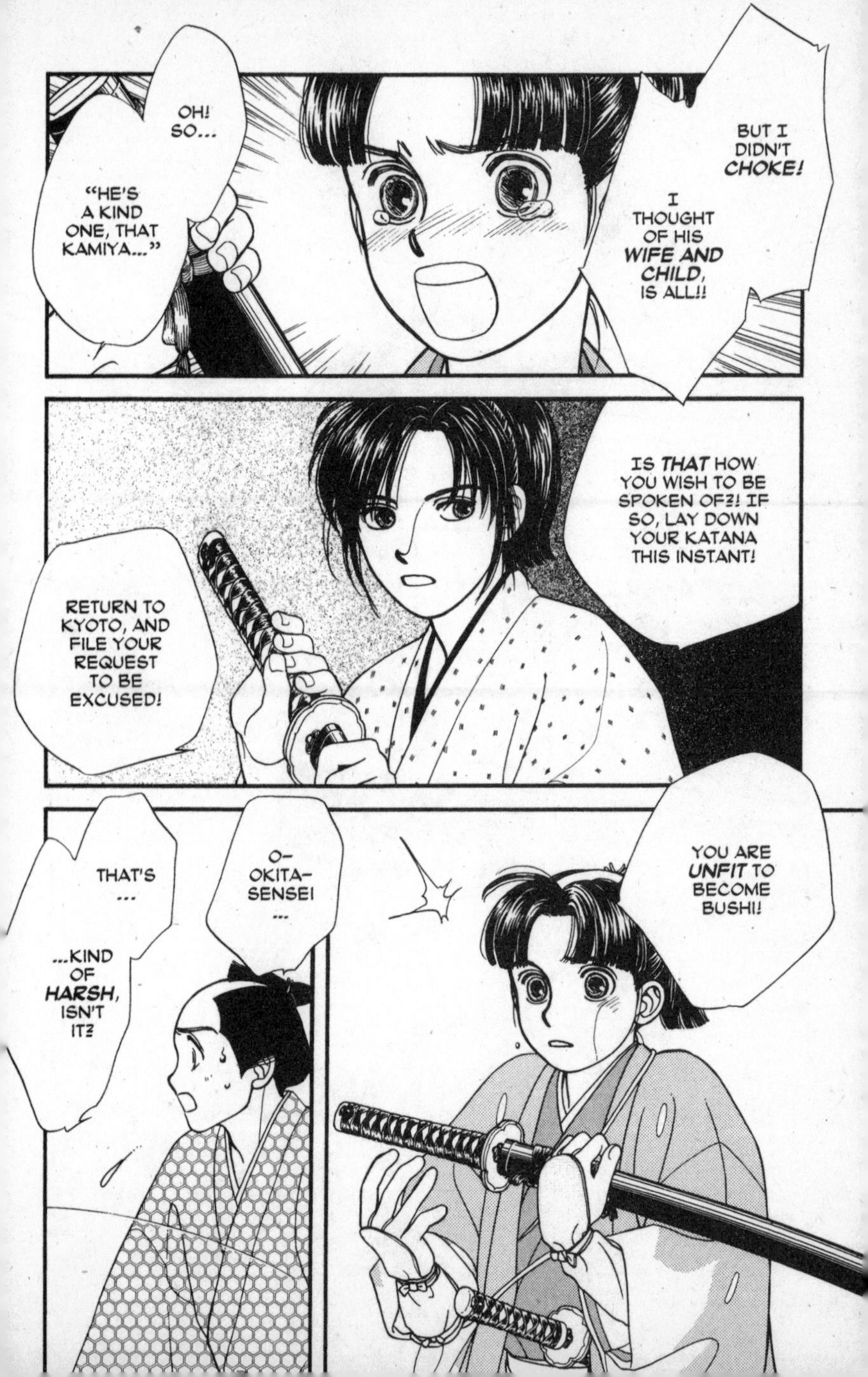
BUT I DIDN'T CHOKE!
I THOUGHT OF HIS WIFE AND CHILD, IS ALL!!
OH! SO...
"HE'S A KIND ONE, THAT KAMIYA..."
IS THAT HOW YOU WISH TO BE SPOKEN OF?! IF SO, LAY DOWN YOUR KATANA THIS INSTANT!
RETURN TO KYOTO, AND FILE YOUR REQUEST TO BE EXCUSED!
YOU ARE UNFIT TO BECOME BUSHI!
O-OKITA-SENSEI...
THAT'S...
...KIND OF HARSH, ISN'T IT?

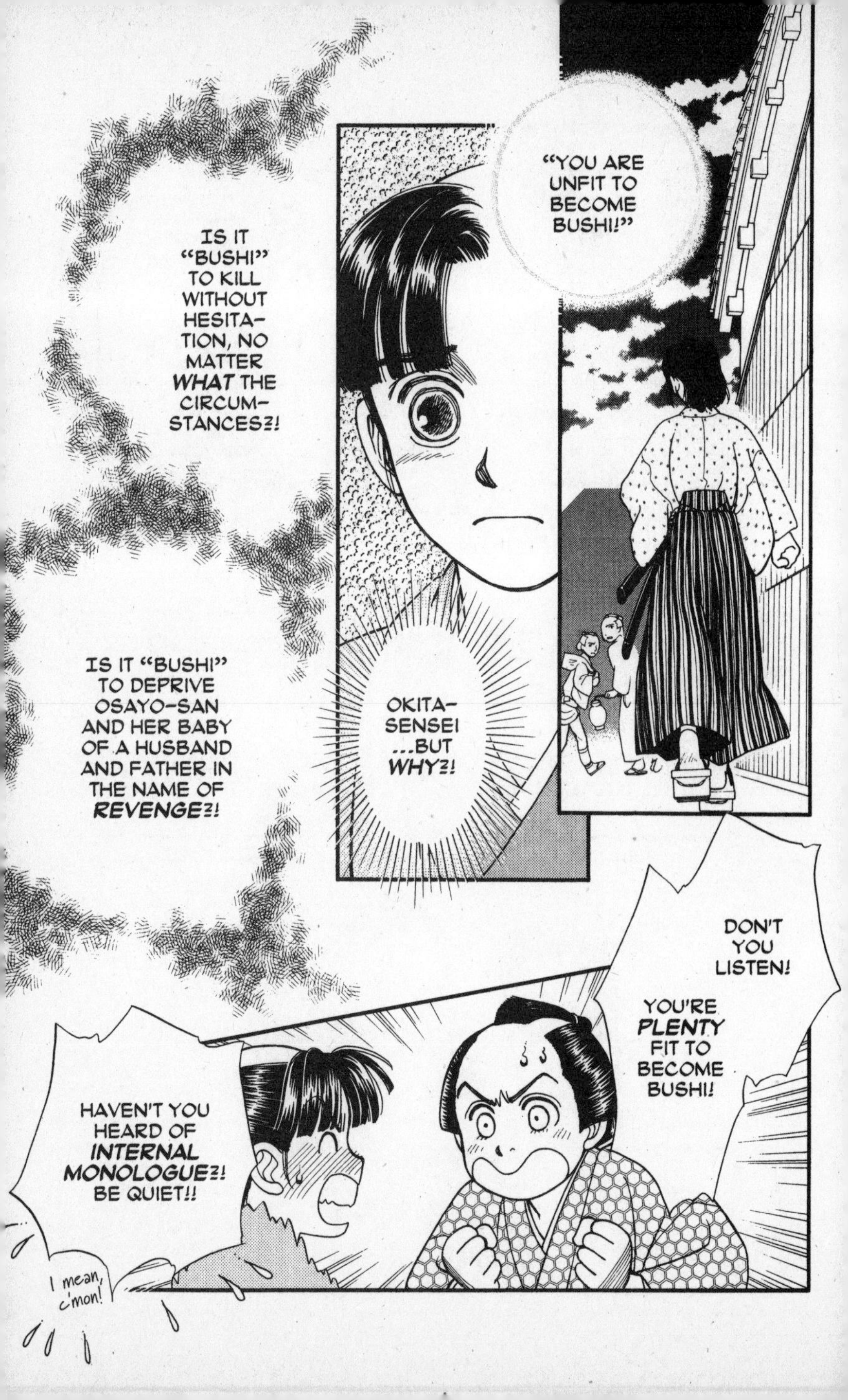
"YOU ARE UNFIT TO BECOME BUSHI!"
OKITA-SENSEI ...BUT WHY?!
IS IT "BUSHI" TO KILL WITHOUT HESITATION, NO MATTER WHAT THE CIRCUMSTANCES?!
IS IT "BUSHI" TO DEPRIVE OSAYO-SAN AND HER BABY OF A HUSBAND AND FATHER IN THE NAME OF REVENGE?!
DON'T YOU LISTEN!
YOU'RE PLENTY FIT TO BECOME BUSHI!
HAVEN'T YOU HEARD OF INTERNAL MONOLOGUE?! BE QUIET!!
I mean, c'mon!

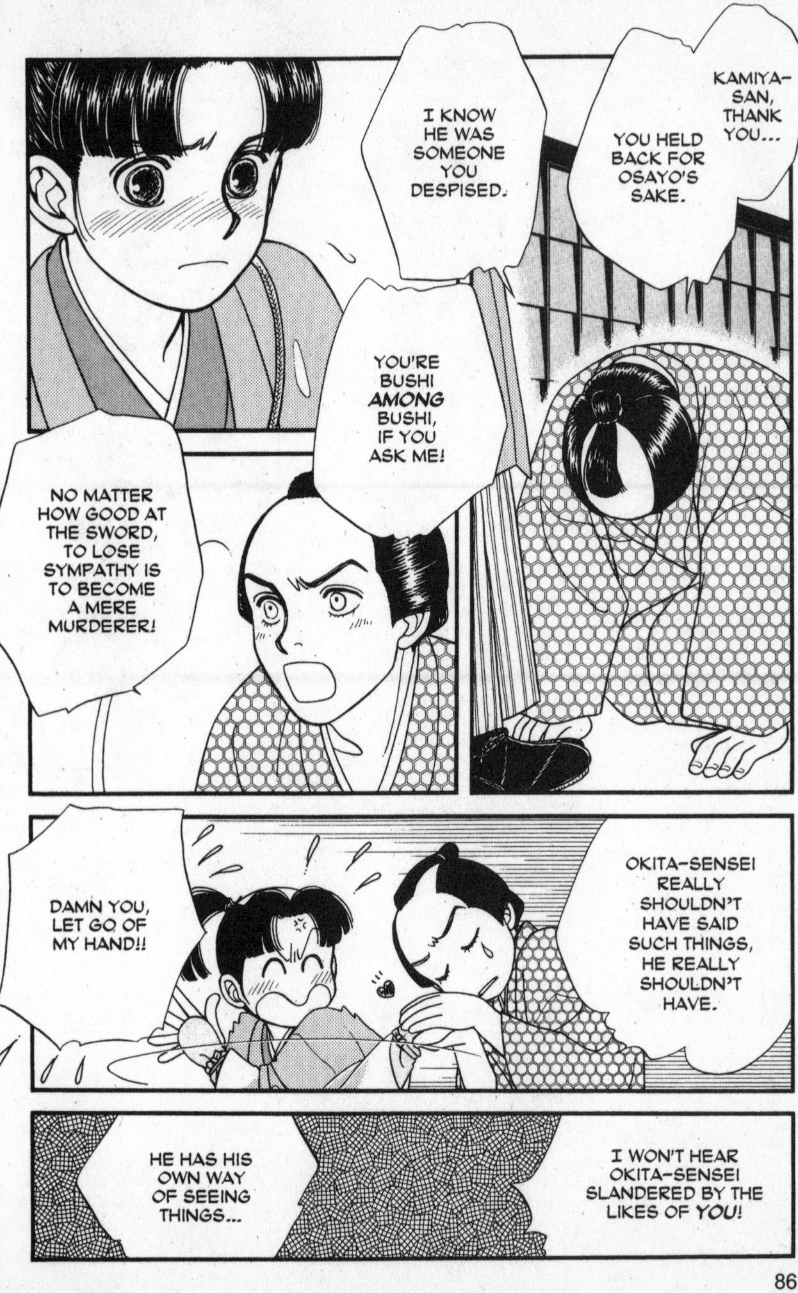
KAMIYA-SAN, THANK YOU...
YOU HELD BACK FOR OSAYO'S SAKE.
I KNOW HE WAS SOMEONE YOU DESPISED.
YOU'RE BUSHI ***AMONG*** BUSHI, IF YOU ASK ME!
NO MATTER HOW GOOD AT THE SWORD, TO LOSE SYMPATHY IS TO BECOME A MERE MURDERER!
OKITA-SENSEI REALLY SHOULDN'T HAVE SAID SUCH THINGS, HE REALLY SHOULDN'T HAVE.
DAMN YOU, LET GO OF MY HAND!!
I WON'T HEAR OKITA-SENSEI SLANDERED BY THE LIKES OF ***YOU***!
HE HAS HIS OWN WAY OF SEEING THINGS...

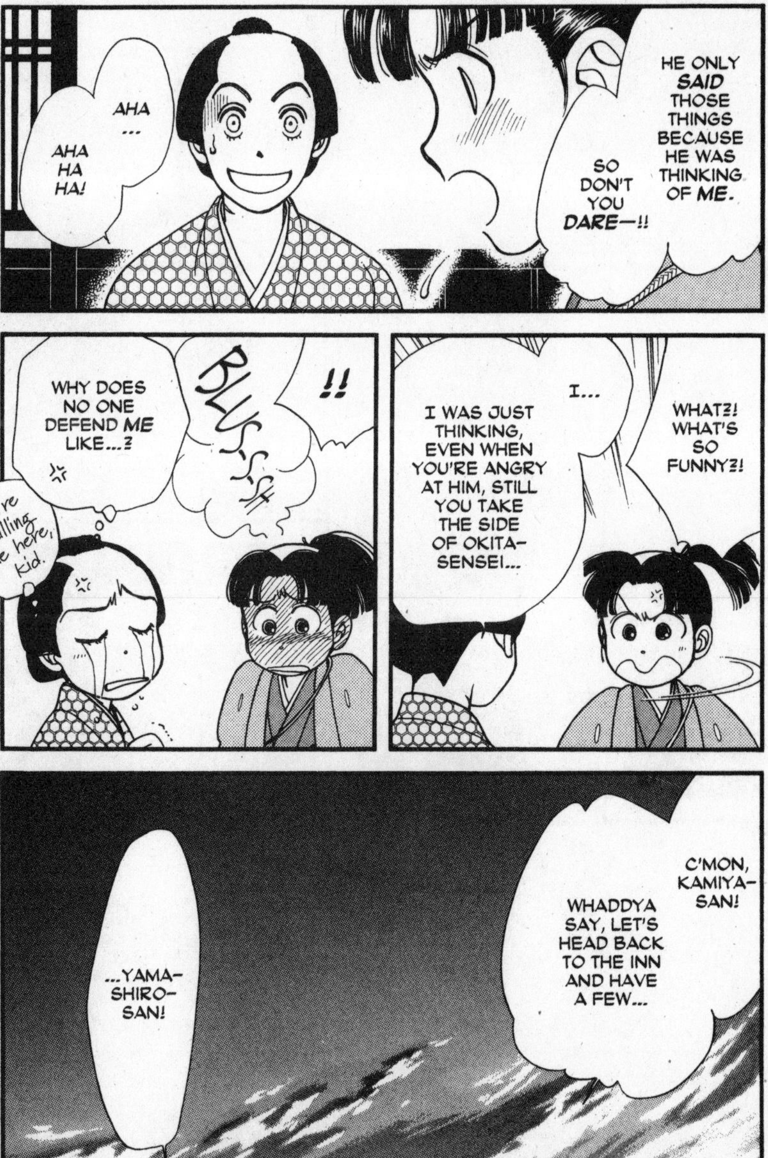
HE ONLY SAID THOSE THINGS BECAUSE HE WAS THINKING OF ME.
SO DON'T YOU DARE—!!
AHA...
AHA HA HA!
WHAT?! WHAT'S SO FUNNY?!
I...
I WAS JUST THINKING, EVEN WHEN YOU'RE ANGRY AT HIM, STILL YOU TAKE THE SIDE OF OKITA-SENSEI...
!!
BLUSSSH
WHY DOES NO ONE DEFEND ME LIKE...?
You're killing me here, kid.
C'MON, KAMIYA-SAN!
WHADDYA SAY, LET'S HEAD BACK TO THE INN AND HAVE A FEW...
...YAMA-SHIRO-SAN!

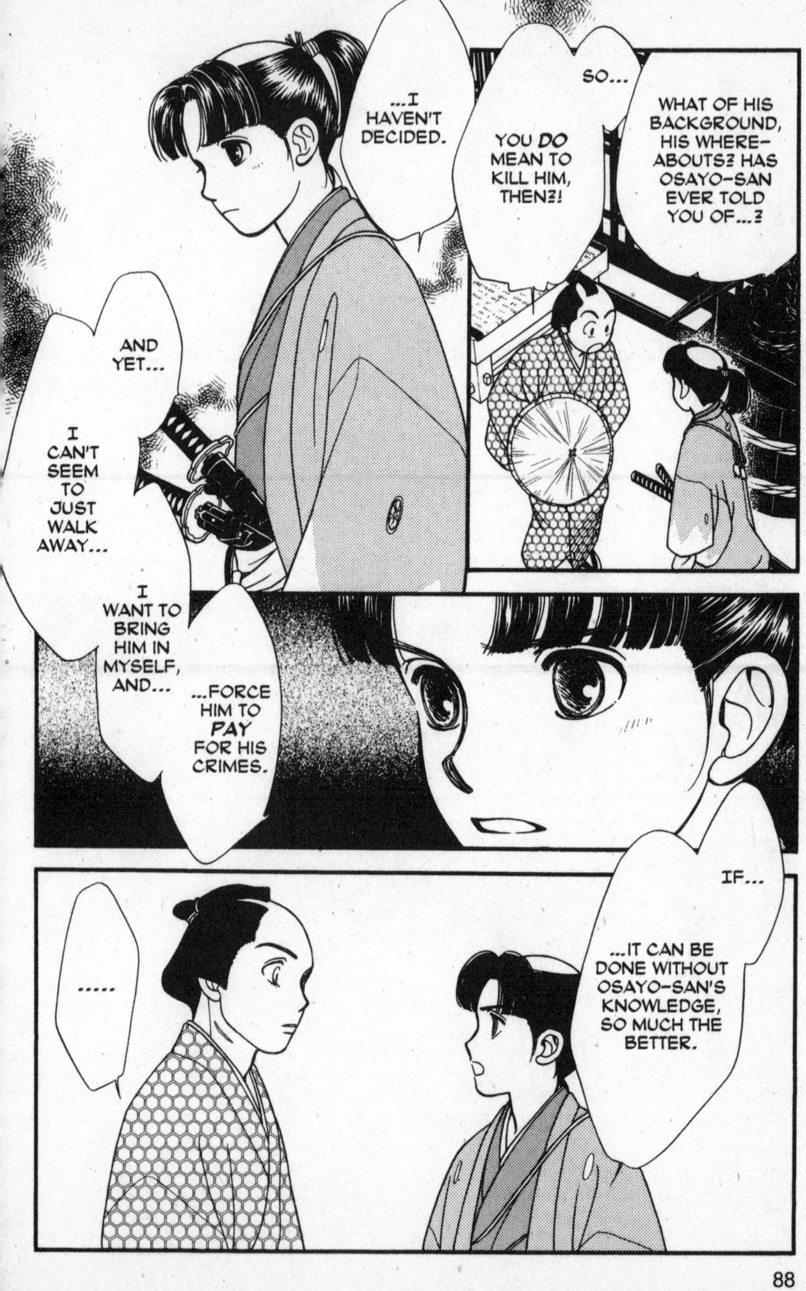
WHAT OF HIS BACKGROUND, HIS WHERE-ABOUTS? HAS OSAYO-SAN EVER TOLD YOU OF...?
SO...
YOU *DO* MEAN TO KILL HIM, THEN?!
...I HAVEN'T DECIDED.
AND YET...
I CAN'T SEEM TO JUST WALK AWAY...
I WANT TO BRING HIM IN MYSELF, AND...
...FORCE HIM TO *PAY* FOR HIS CRIMES.
IF...
...IT CAN BE DONE WITHOUT OSAYO-SAN'S KNOWLEDGE, SO MUCH THE BETTER.
.....

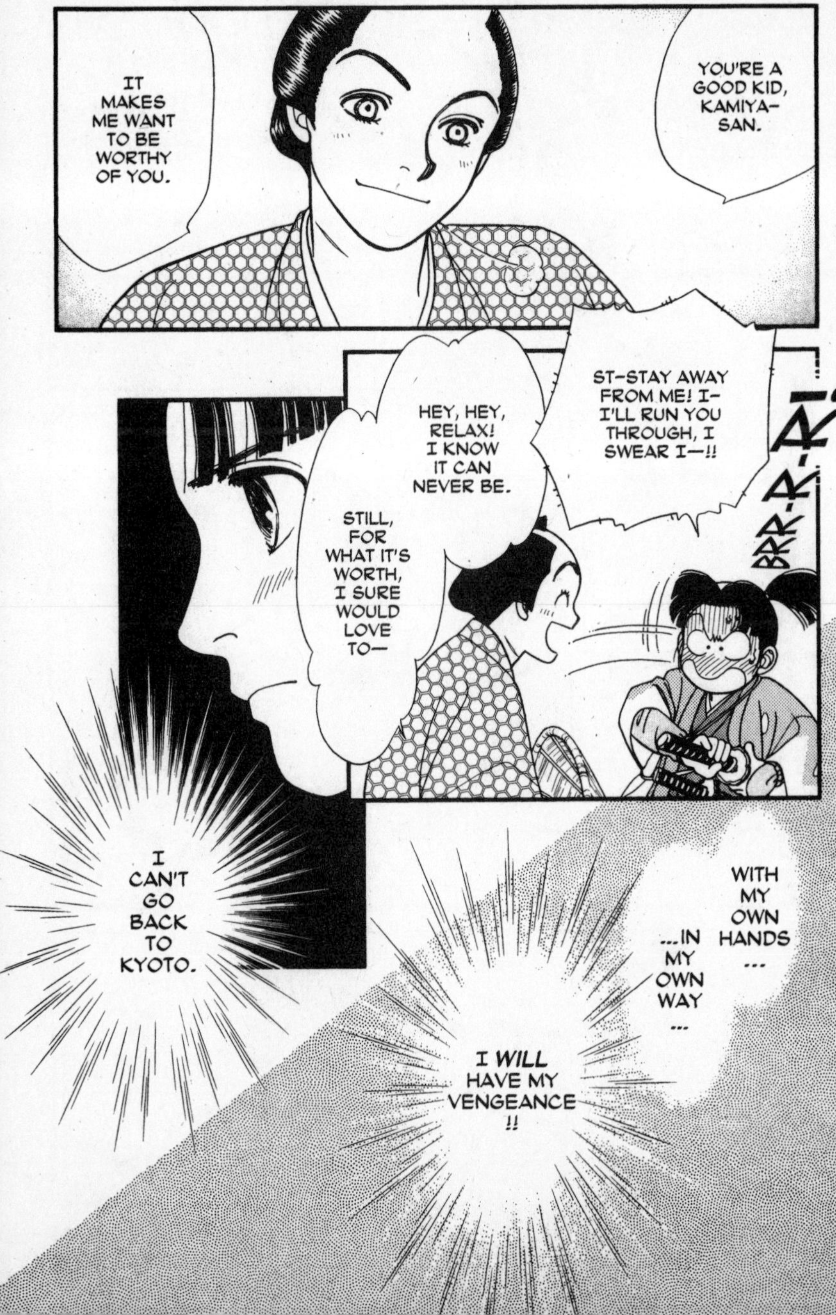
YOU'RE A GOOD KID, KAMIYA-SAN.
IT MAKES ME WANT TO BE WORTHY OF YOU.
ST-STAY AWAY FROM ME! I-I'LL RUN YOU THROUGH, I SWEAR I—!!
HEY, HEY, RELAX! I KNOW IT CAN NEVER BE.
STILL, FOR WHAT IT'S WORTH, I SURE WOULD LOVE TO—
I CAN'T GO BACK TO KYOTO.
WITH MY OWN HANDS...
...IN MY OWN WAY...
I *WILL* HAVE MY VENGEANCE!!

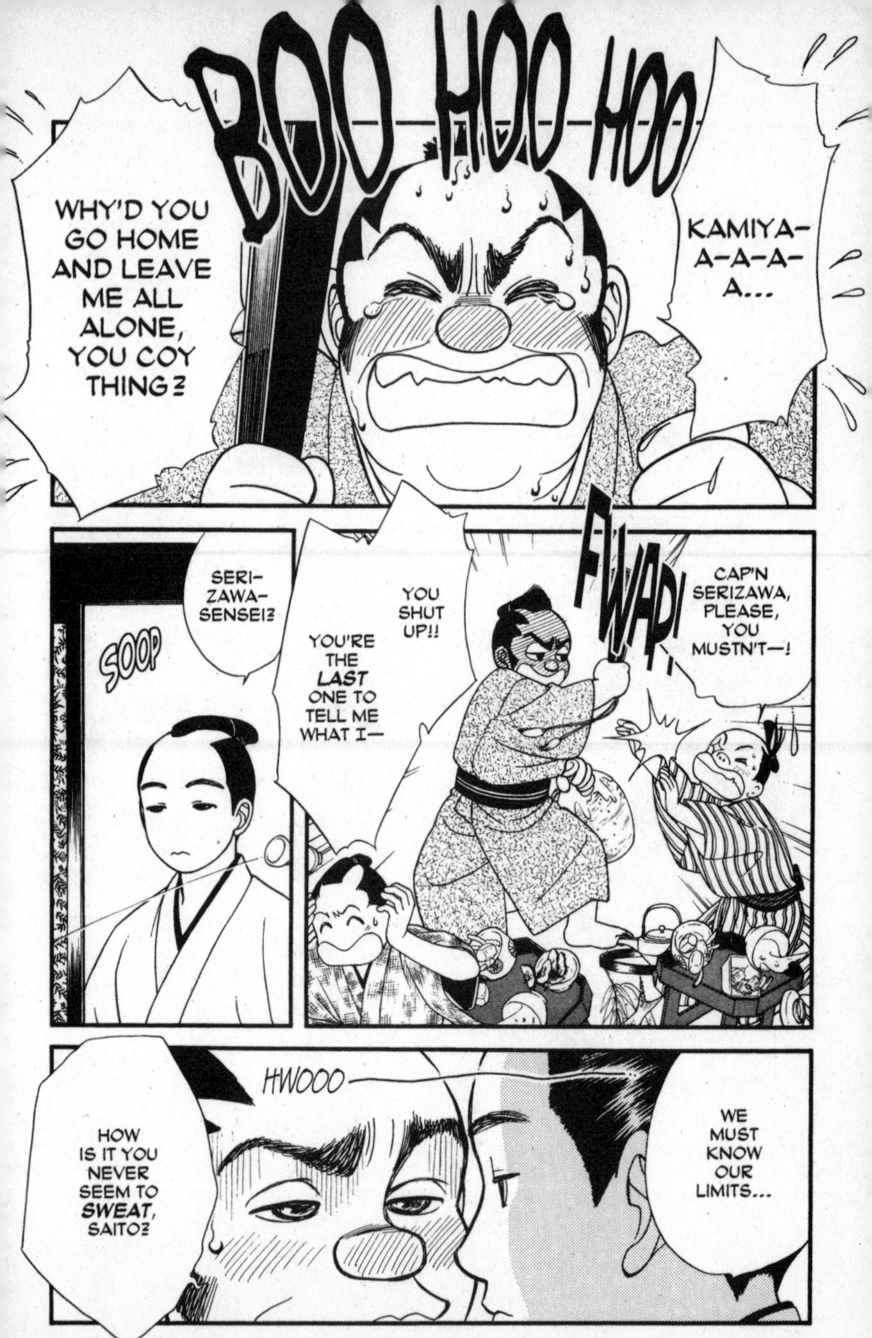
BOO HOO HOO
KAMIYA-A-A-A-A...
WHY'D YOU GO HOME AND LEAVE ME ALL ALONE, YOU COY THING?!
FWAP!
CAP'N SERIZAWA, PLEASE, YOU MUSTN'T—!
YOU SHUT UP!!
YOU'RE THE LAST ONE TO TELL ME WHAT I—
SERI-ZAWA-SENSEI?!
SOOP
WE MUST KNOW OUR LIMITS...
HWOOO
HOW IS IT YOU NEVER SEEM TO SWEAT, SAITO?!

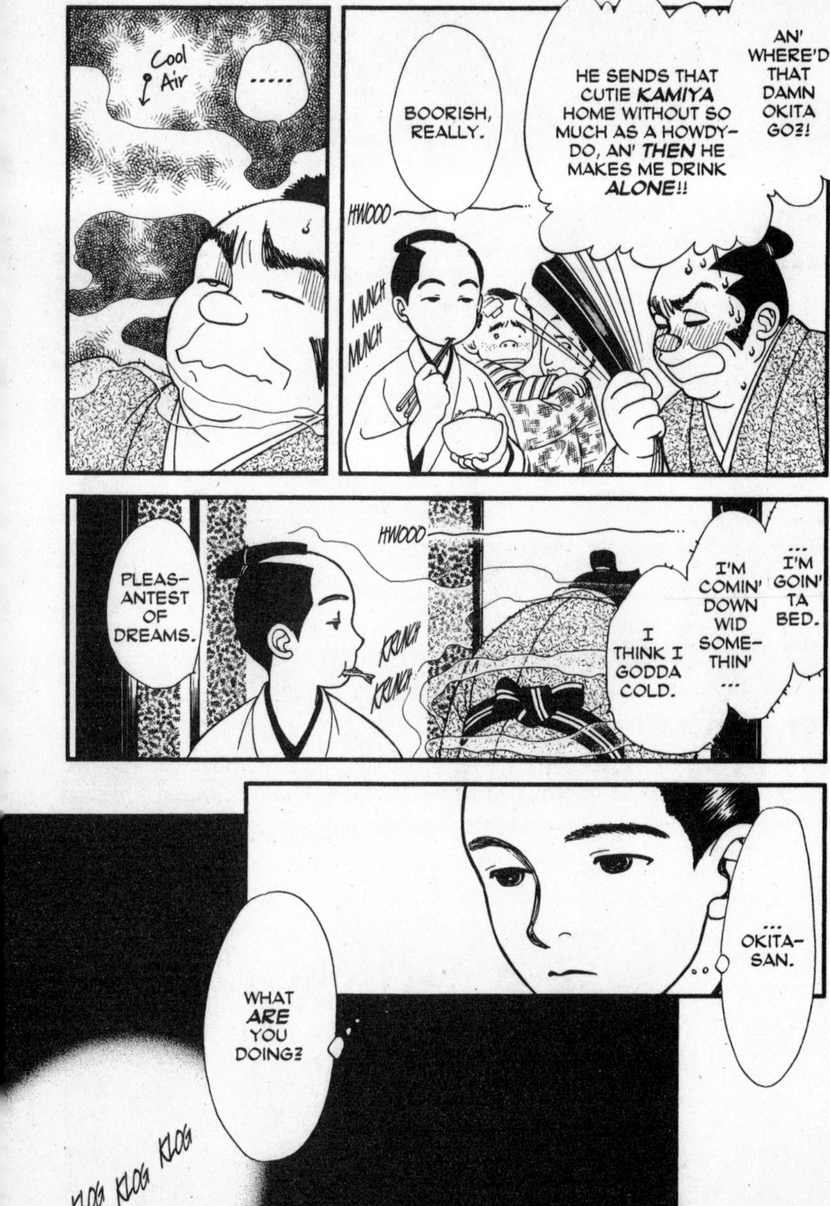
AN' WHERE'D THAT DAMN OKITA GO?!
HE SENDS THAT CUTIE KAMIYA HOME WITHOUT SO MUCH AS A HOWDY-DO, AN' THEN HE MAKES ME DRINK ALONE!!
BOORISH, REALLY.
HWOOO
MUNCH MUNCH
......
Cool Air
... I'M GOIN' TA BED.
I'M COMIN' DOWN WID SOMETHIN' ...
I THINK I GODDA COLD.
HWOOO
KRUNCH KRUNCH
PLEAS-ANTEST OF DREAMS.
... OKITA-SAN.
WHAT ARE YOU DOING?
KLOG KLOG KLOG

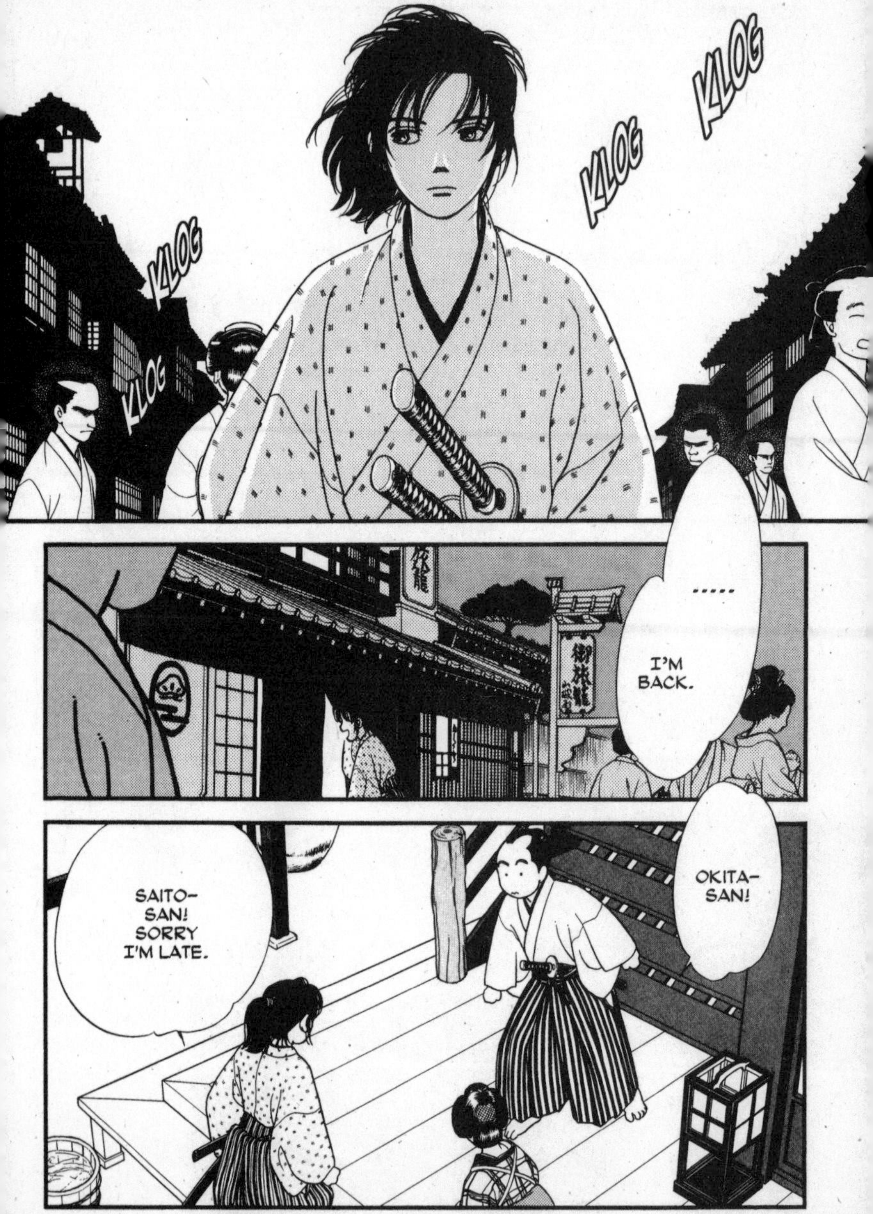
KLOG
KLOG
KLOG
KLOG
.....
I'M BACK.
OKITA-SAN!
SAITO-SAN! SORRY I'M LATE.

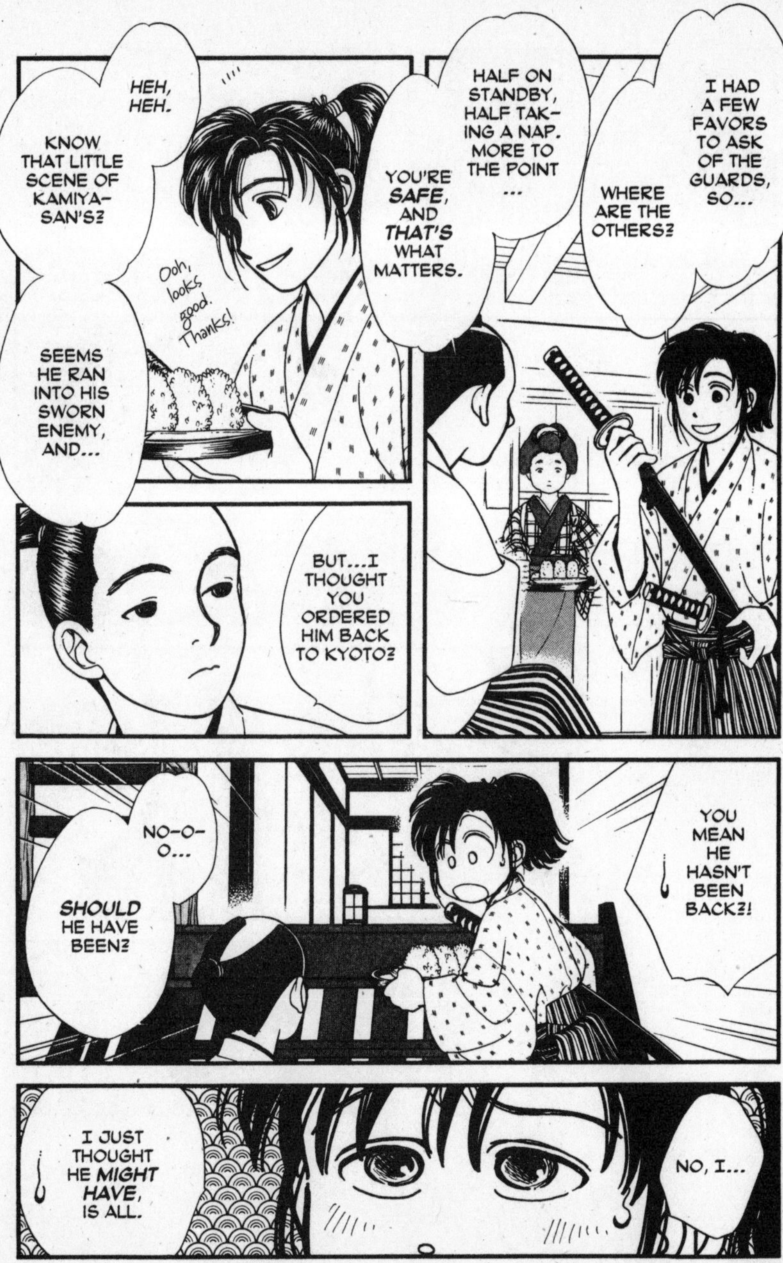
I HAD A FEW FAVORS TO ASK OF THE GUARDS, SO...
WHERE ARE THE OTHERS?
HALF ON STANDBY, HALF TAKING A NAP. MORE TO THE POINT...
YOU'RE *SAFE*, AND *THAT'S* WHAT MATTERS.
HEH, HEH.
KNOW THAT LITTLE SCENE OF KAMIYA-SAN'S?
Ooh, looks good. Thanks!
SEEMS HE RAN INTO HIS SWORN ENEMY, AND...
BUT...I THOUGHT YOU ORDERED HIM BACK TO KYOTO?
YOU MEAN HE HASN'T BEEN BACK?!
NO-O-O...
SHOULD HE HAVE BEEN?
NO, I...
I JUST THOUGHT HE *MIGHT HAVE*, IS ALL.

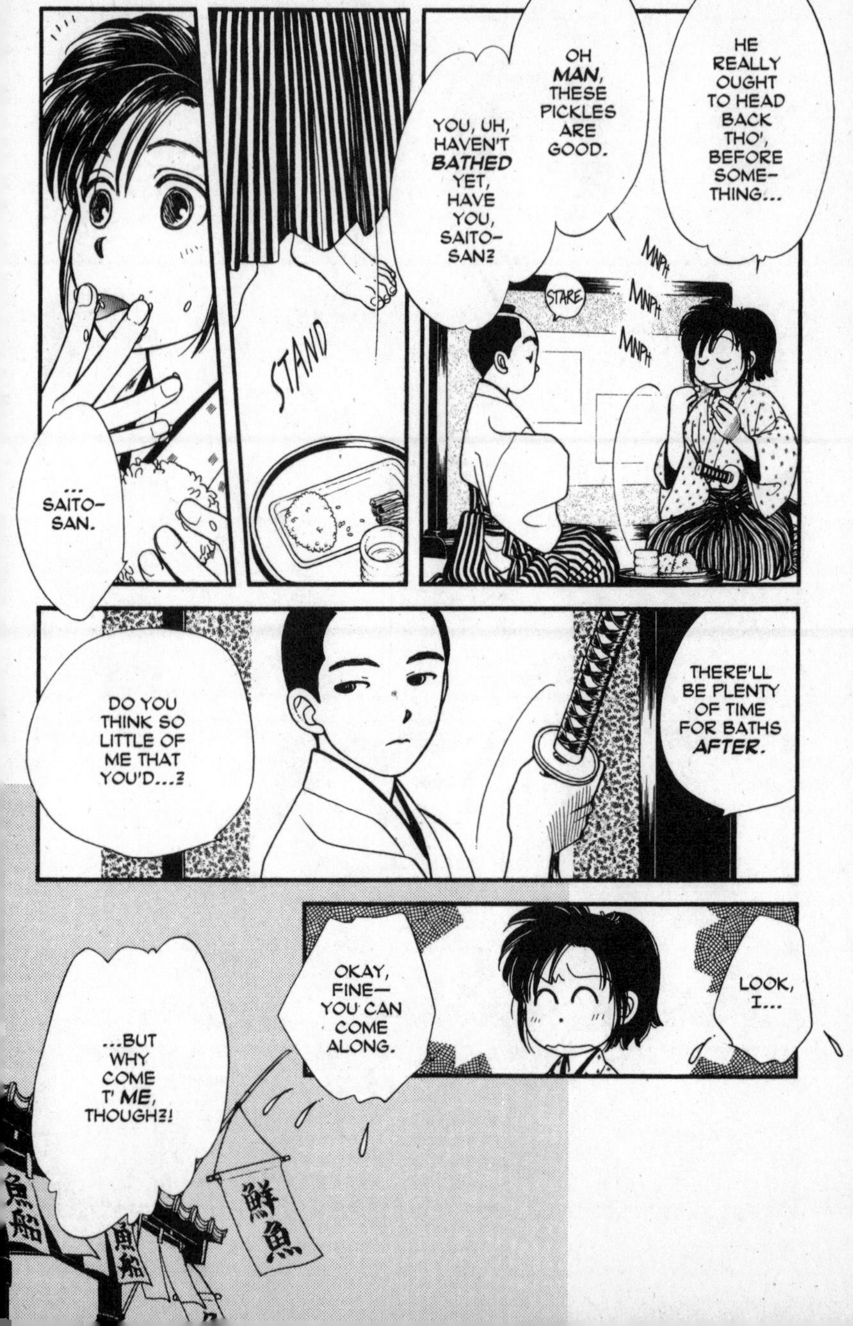
HE REALLY OUGHT TO HEAD BACK THO', BEFORE SOME-THING...
OH MAN, THESE PICKLES ARE GOOD.
YOU, UH, HAVEN'T BATHED YET, HAVE YOU, SAITO-SAN?
MNPH MNPH MNPH
STARE
STAND
...SAITO-SAN.
THERE'LL BE PLENTY OF TIME FOR BATHS AFTER.
DO YOU THINK SO LITTLE OF ME THAT YOU'D...?
LOOK, I...
OKAY, FINE—YOU CAN COME ALONG.
...BUT WHY COME T' ME, THOUGH?!
鮮魚
魚船

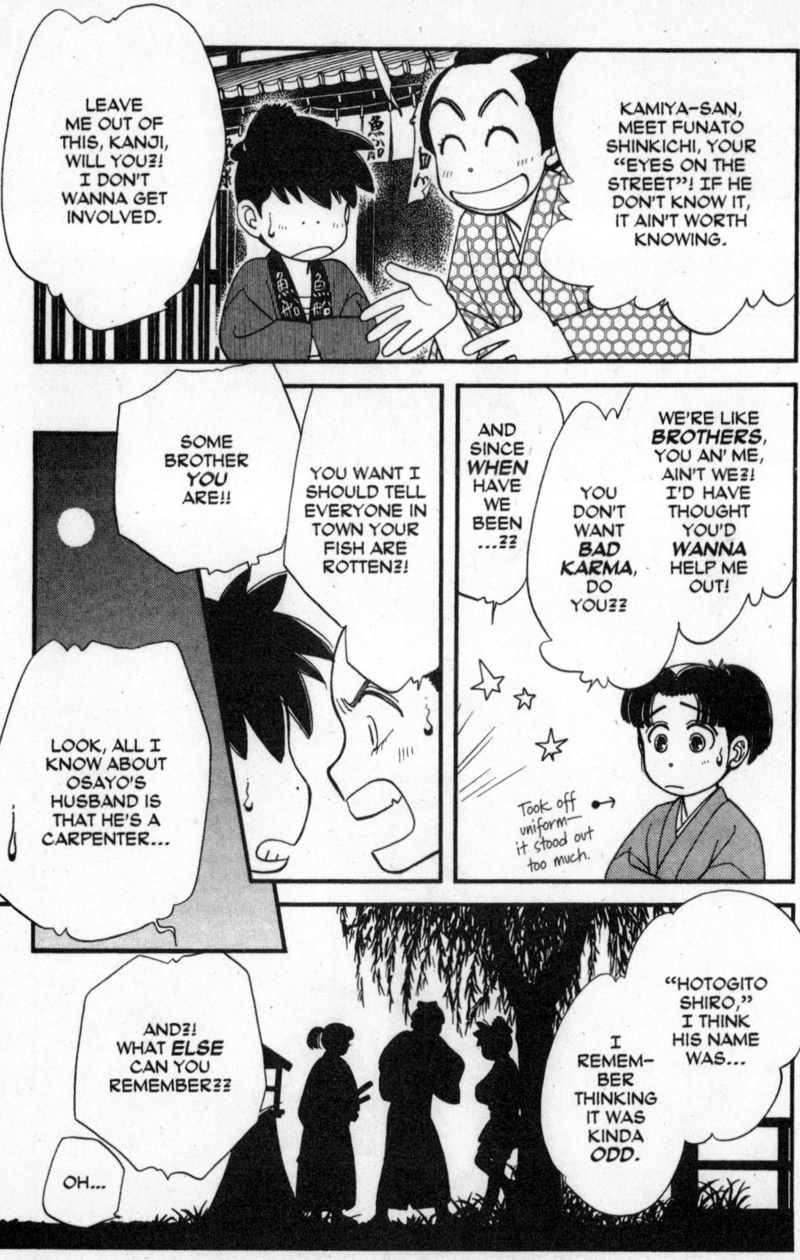
KAMIYA-SAN, MEET FUNATO SHINKICHI, YOUR "EYES ON THE STREET"! IF HE DON'T KNOW IT, IT AIN'T WORTH KNOWING.
LEAVE ME OUT OF THIS, KANJI, WILL YOU?! I DON'T WANNA GET INVOLVED.
WE'RE LIKE BROTHERS, YOU AN' ME, AIN'T WE?! I'D HAVE THOUGHT YOU'D WANNA HELP ME OUT!
YOU DON'T WANT BAD KARMA, DO YOU??
AND SINCE WHEN HAVE WE BEEN...??
Took off uniform— it stood out too much.
YOU WANT I SHOULD TELL EVERYONE IN TOWN YOUR FISH ARE ROTTEN?!
SOME BROTHER YOU ARE!!
LOOK, ALL I KNOW ABOUT OSAYO'S HUSBAND IS THAT HE'S A CARPENTER...
"HOTOGITO SHIRO," I THINK HIS NAME WAS...
I REMEMBER THINKING IT WAS KINDA ODD.
AND?! WHAT ELSE CAN YOU REMEMBER??
OH...

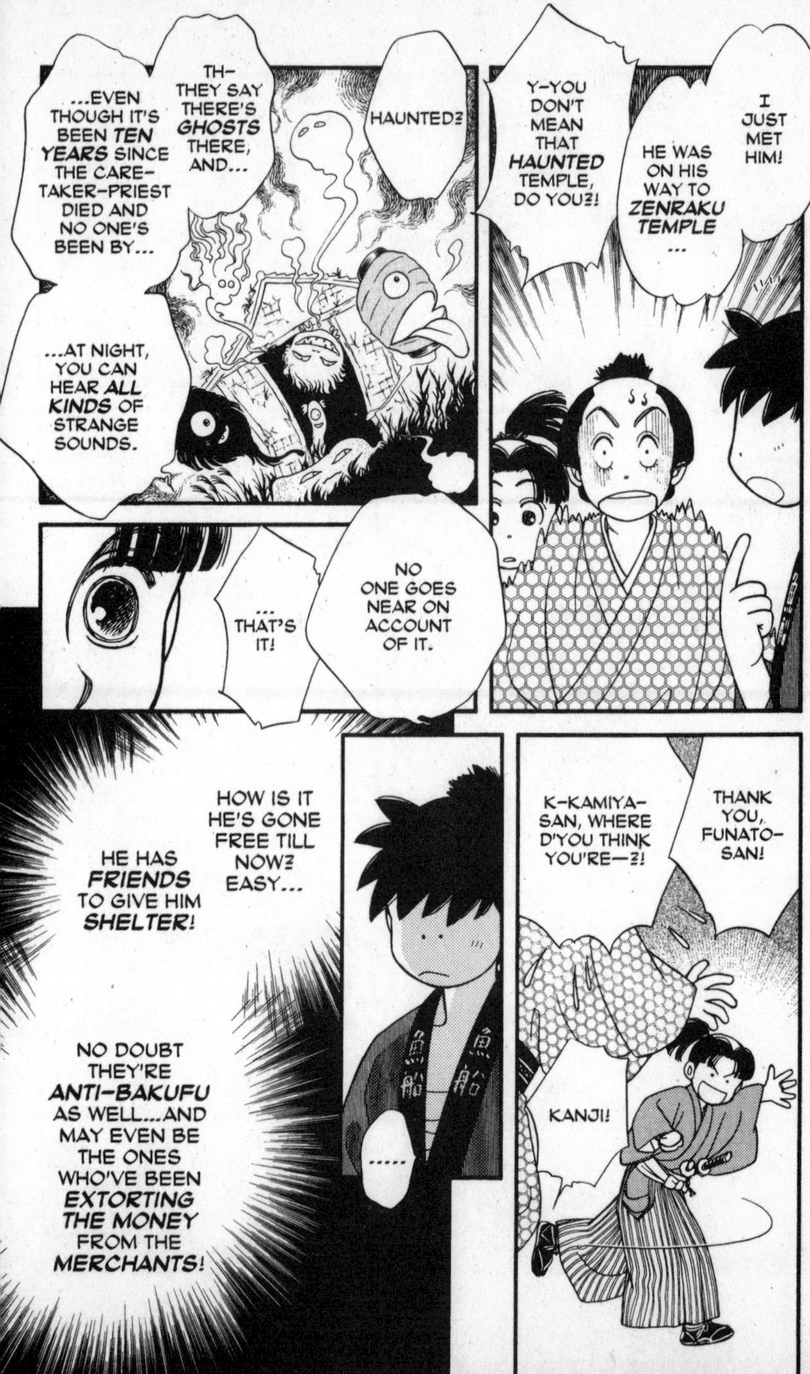
I JUST MET HIM!
HE WAS ON HIS WAY TO ZENRAKU TEMPLE ...
Y-YOU DON'T MEAN THAT HAUNTED TEMPLE, DO YOU?!
HAUNTED?
TH- THEY SAY THERE'S GHOSTS THERE, AND...
...EVEN THOUGH IT'S BEEN TEN YEARS SINCE THE CARE-TAKER-PRIEST DIED AND NO ONE'S BEEN BY...
...AT NIGHT, YOU CAN HEAR ALL KINDS OF STRANGE SOUNDS.
NO ONE GOES NEAR ON ACCOUNT OF IT.
... THAT'S IT!
THANK YOU, FUNATO-SAN!
K-KAMIYA-SAN, WHERE D'YOU THINK YOU'RE—?!
KANJI!
HOW IS IT HE'S GONE FREE TILL NOW? EASY...
.....
HE HAS FRIENDS TO GIVE HIM SHELTER!
NO DOUBT THEY'RE ANTI-BAKUFU AS WELL...AND MAY EVEN BE THE ONES WHO'VE BEEN EXTORTING THE MONEY FROM THE MERCHANTS!

FWIP?? FWIP?? K-BOOM!

WE'LL WANNA GO THIS WAY, THEN.

OF COURSE! IT'S SO *OBVIOUS!!*

WHAT BETTER PLACE THAN SOME SO-CALLED "HAUNTED TEMPLE" FOR THEIR GATHERING PLACE?!

REAL GHOSTS?! NO THANKS! *FAKE*, THOUGH...!

WHY DIDN'T YOU *SAY* THAT BEFORE?!

...HEADING OUT? THEN TAKE THESE TAGS WITH YOU.

OF COURSE. THANK YOU.

SHOW THEM TO THE GUARD AT THE MAIN GATE...※

THAT'S HOW HE'LL KNOW YOU'RE A GUEST HERE.

※ Serving the purpose of both fire and crime prevention, the massive wooden doors of a town's main gate are ceremonially opened and closed each day, with all strangers subject to inspection.

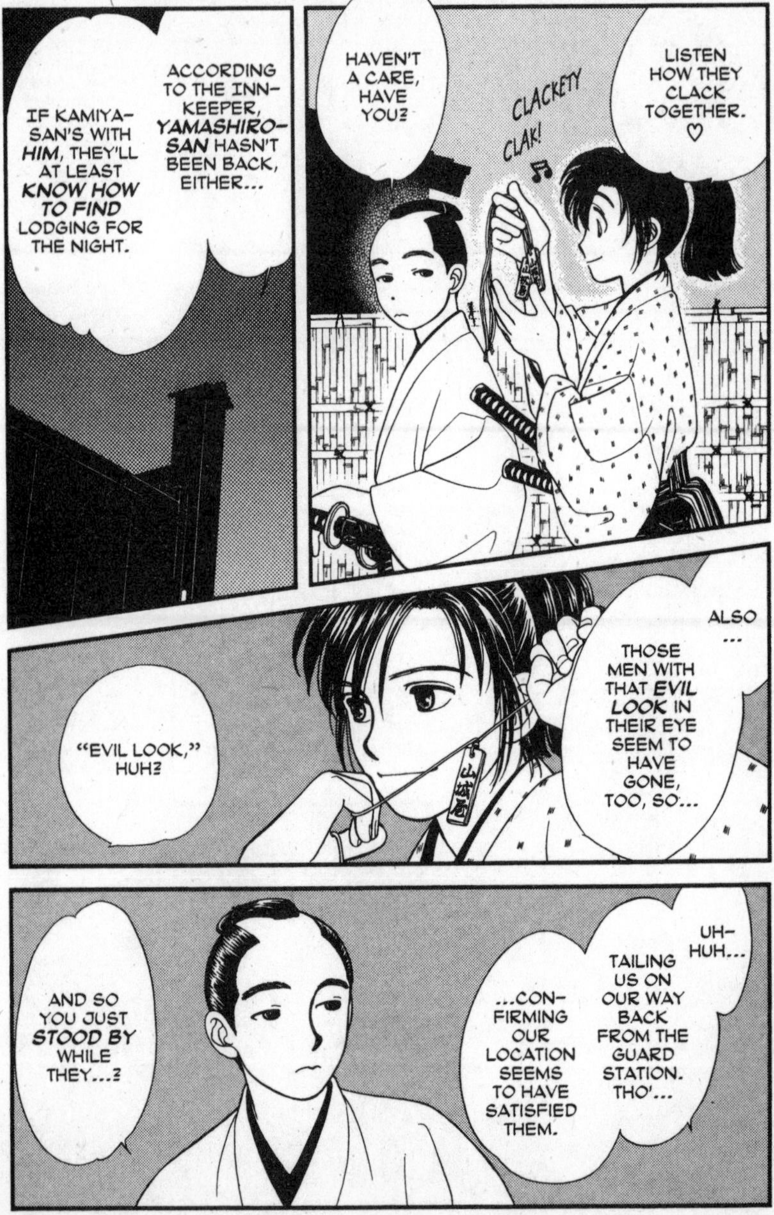
LISTEN HOW THEY CLACK TOGETHER. ♡
CLACKETY CLAK!
HAVEN'T A CARE, HAVE YOU?
ACCORDING TO THE INN-KEEPER, YAMASHIRO-SAN HASN'T BEEN BACK, EITHER...
IF KAMIYA-SAN'S WITH HIM, THEY'LL AT LEAST KNOW HOW TO FIND LODGING FOR THE NIGHT.
ALSO...
THOSE MEN WITH THAT EVIL LOOK IN THEIR EYE SEEM TO HAVE GONE, TOO, SO...
"EVIL LOOK," HUH?
UH-HUH...
TAILING US ON OUR WAY BACK FROM THE GUARD STATION. THO'...
...CON-FIRMING OUR LOCATION SEEMS TO HAVE SATISFIED THEM.
AND SO YOU JUST STOOD BY WHILE THEY...?

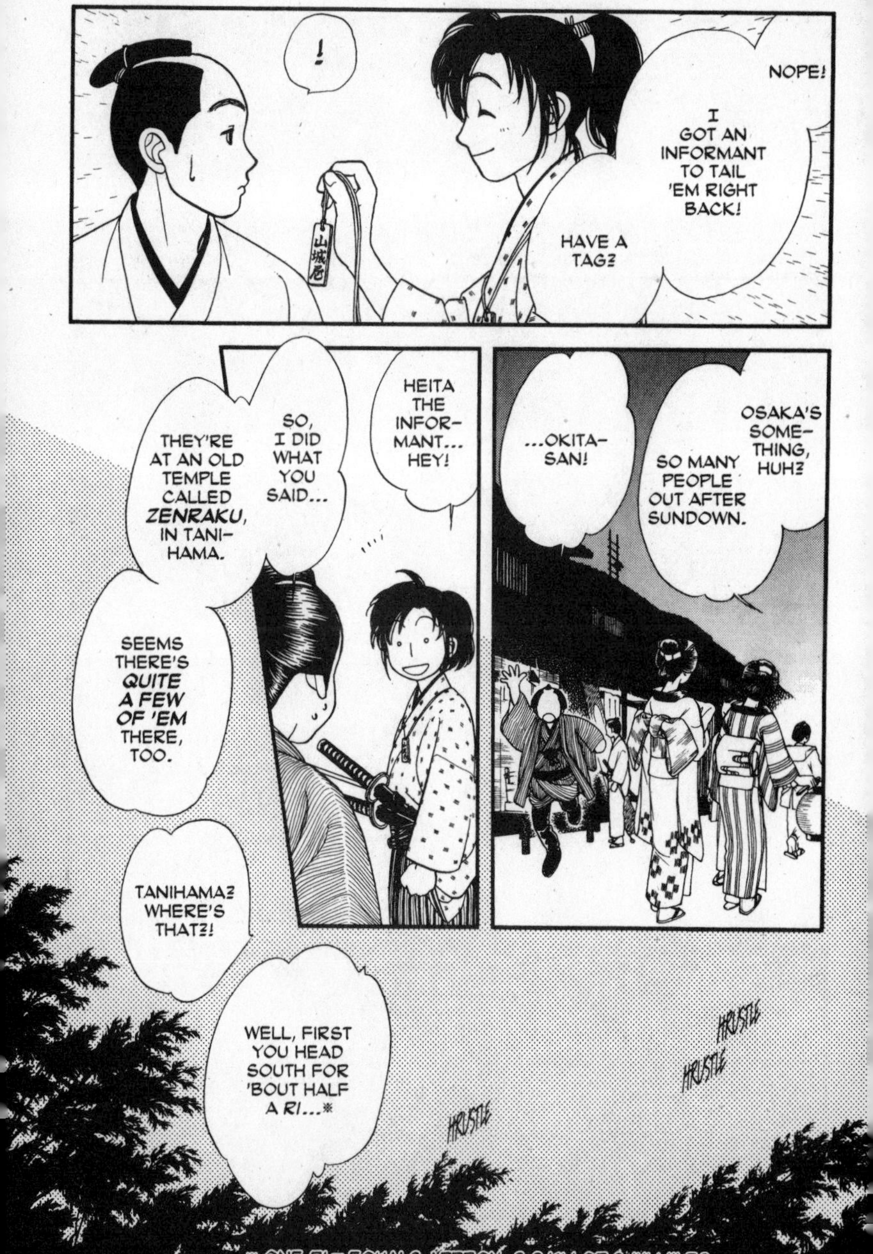
NOPE!
I GOT AN INFORMANT TO TAIL 'EM RIGHT BACK!
HAVE A TAG?
!
OSAKA'S SOMETHING, HUH?
SO MANY PEOPLE OUT AFTER SUNDOWN.
...OKITA-SAN!
HEITA THE INFORMANT... HEY!
SO, I DID WHAT YOU SAID...
THEY'RE AT AN OLD TEMPLE CALLED ZENRAKU, IN TANIHAMA.
SEEMS THERE'S QUITE A FEW OF 'EM THERE, TOO.
TANIHAMA? WHERE'S THAT?!
WELL, FIRST YOU HEAD SOUTH FOR 'BOUT HALF A RI...※
HRUSTLE
HRUSTLE
HRUSTLE

※ ONE RI EQUALS APPROX. 3.9 KM OR 2.44 MILES

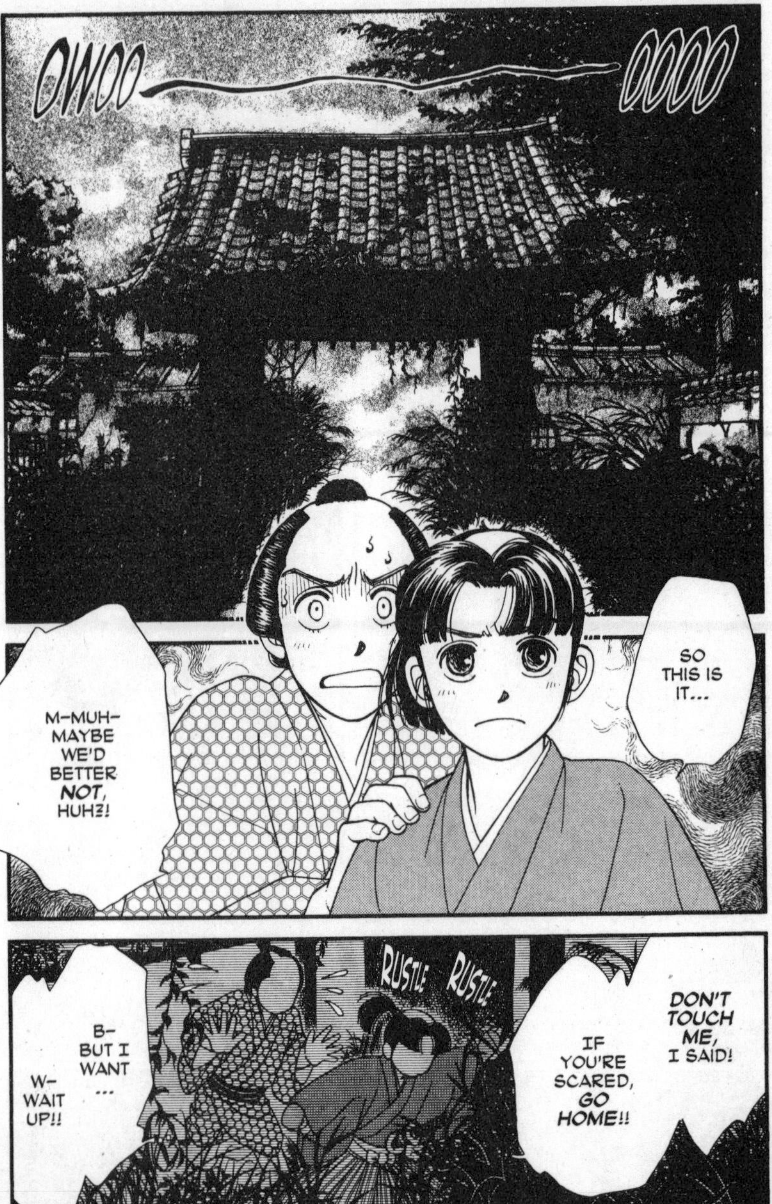
OWOO—OOOO
SO THIS IS IT...
M-MUH-MAYBE WE'D BETTER **NOT**, HUH?!
DON'T TOUCH ME, I SAID!
IF YOU'RE SCARED, **GO HOME!!**
RUSTLE RUSTLE
B-BUT I WANT ...
W-WAIT UP!!

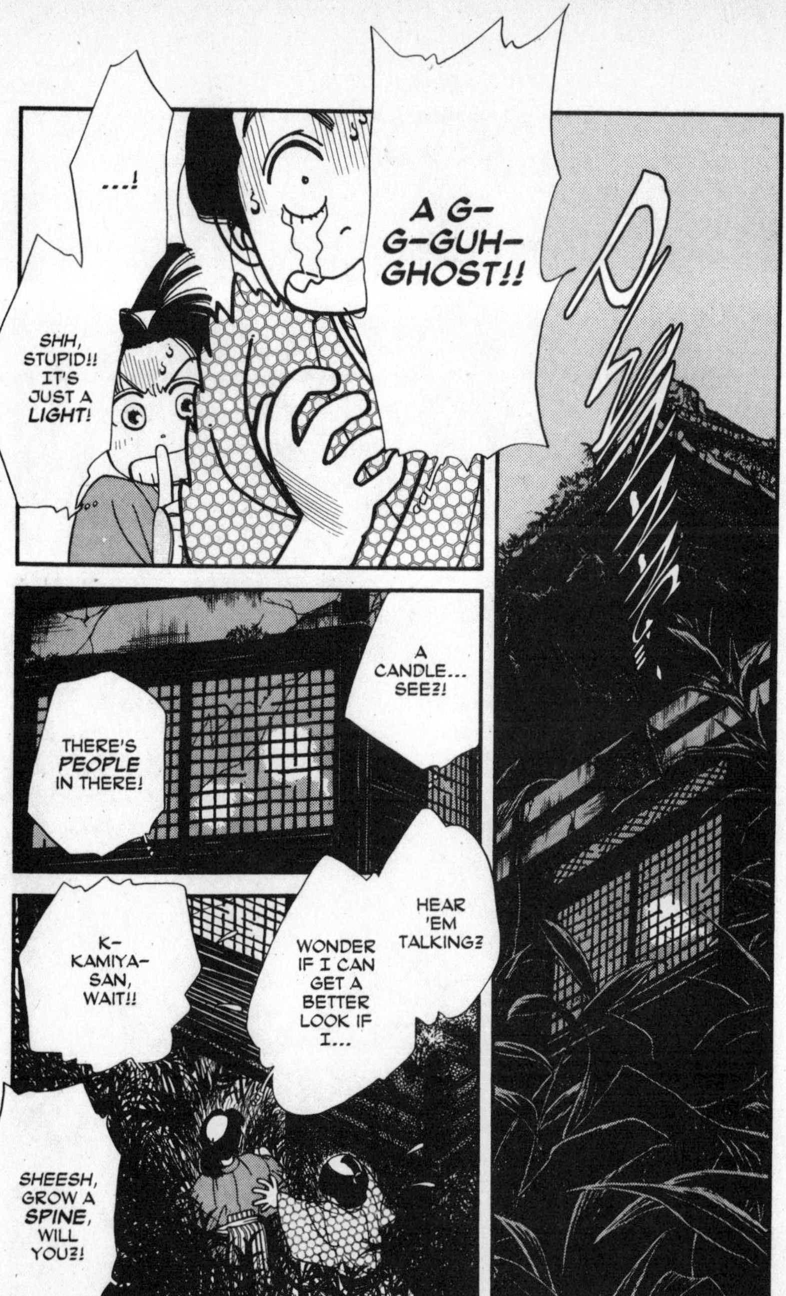
A G-G-GUH-GHOST!!
...!
SHH, STUPID!! IT'S JUST A LIGHT!
A CANDLE... SEE?!
THERE'S PEOPLE IN THERE!
HEAR 'EM TALKING?
WONDER IF I CAN GET A BETTER LOOK IF I...
K-KAMIYA-SAN, WAIT!!
SHEESH, GROW A SPINE, WILL YOU?!

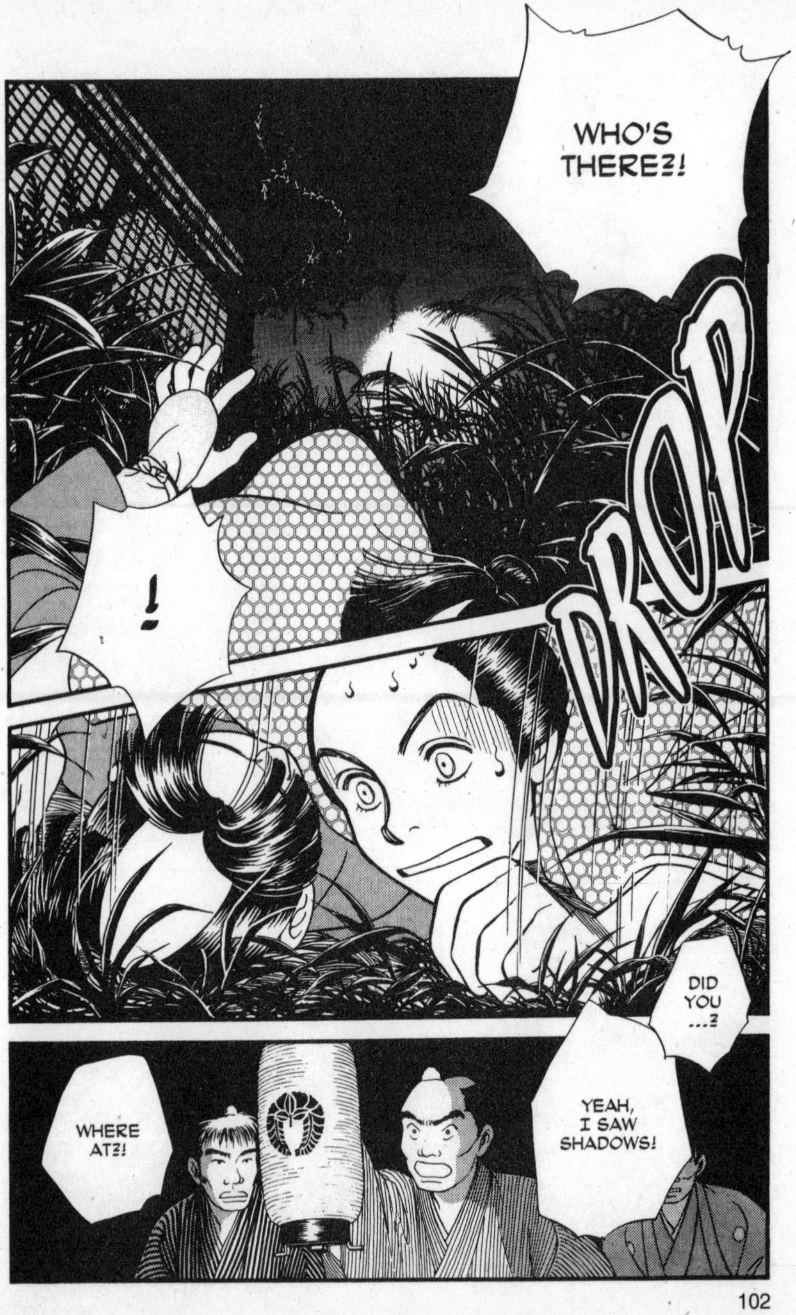
WHO'S THERE?!
DROP
!
DID YOU ...?
YEAH, I SAW SHADOWS!
WHERE AT?!

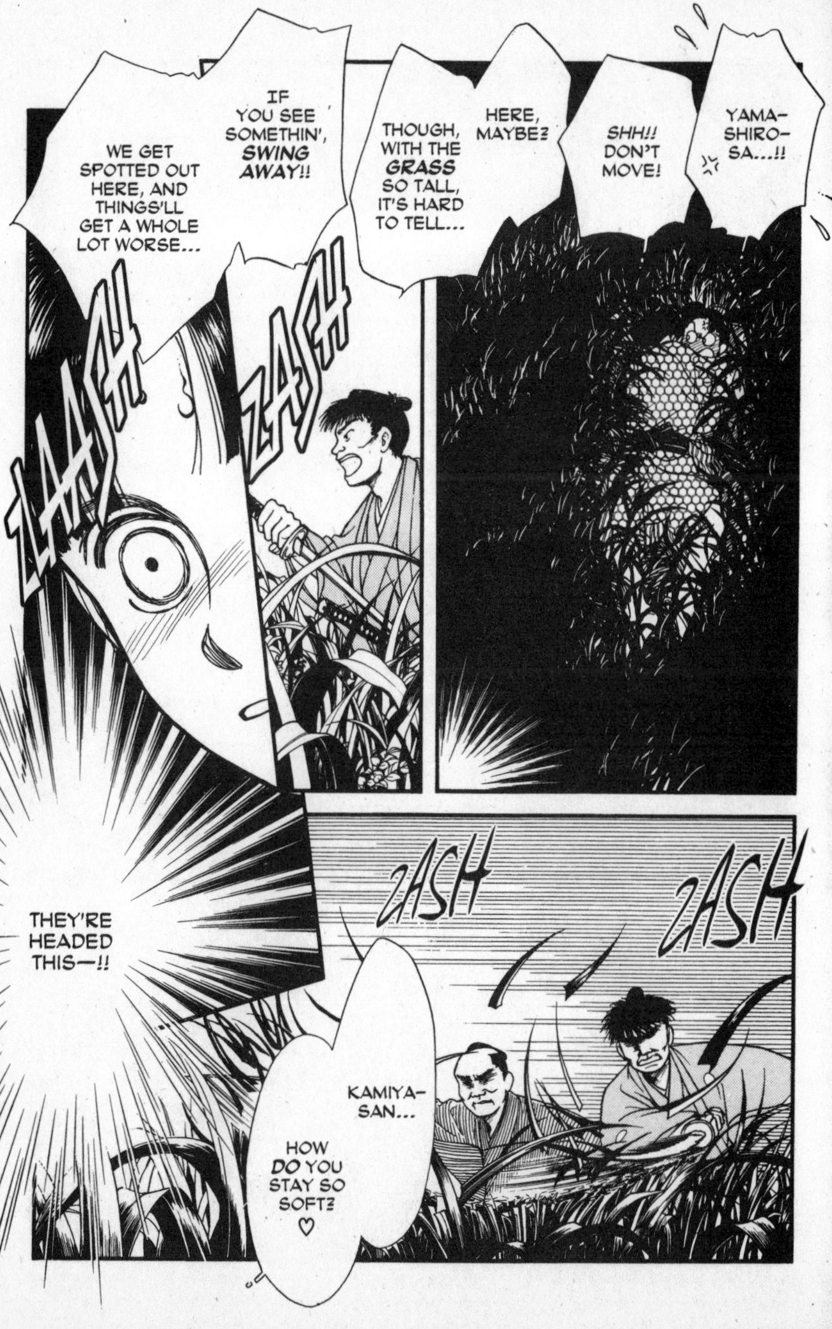
YAMA-SHIRO-SA...!!
SHH!! DON'T MOVE!
HERE, MAYBE?
THOUGH, WITH THE GRASS SO TALL, IT'S HARD TO TELL...
IF YOU SEE SOMETHIN', SWING AWAY!!
WE GET SPOTTED OUT HERE, AND THINGS'LL GET A WHOLE LOT WORSE...
ZASH
ZASH
THEY'RE HEADED THIS—!!
ZASH
ZASH
KAMIYA-SAN...
HOW DO YOU STAY SO SOFT? ♡

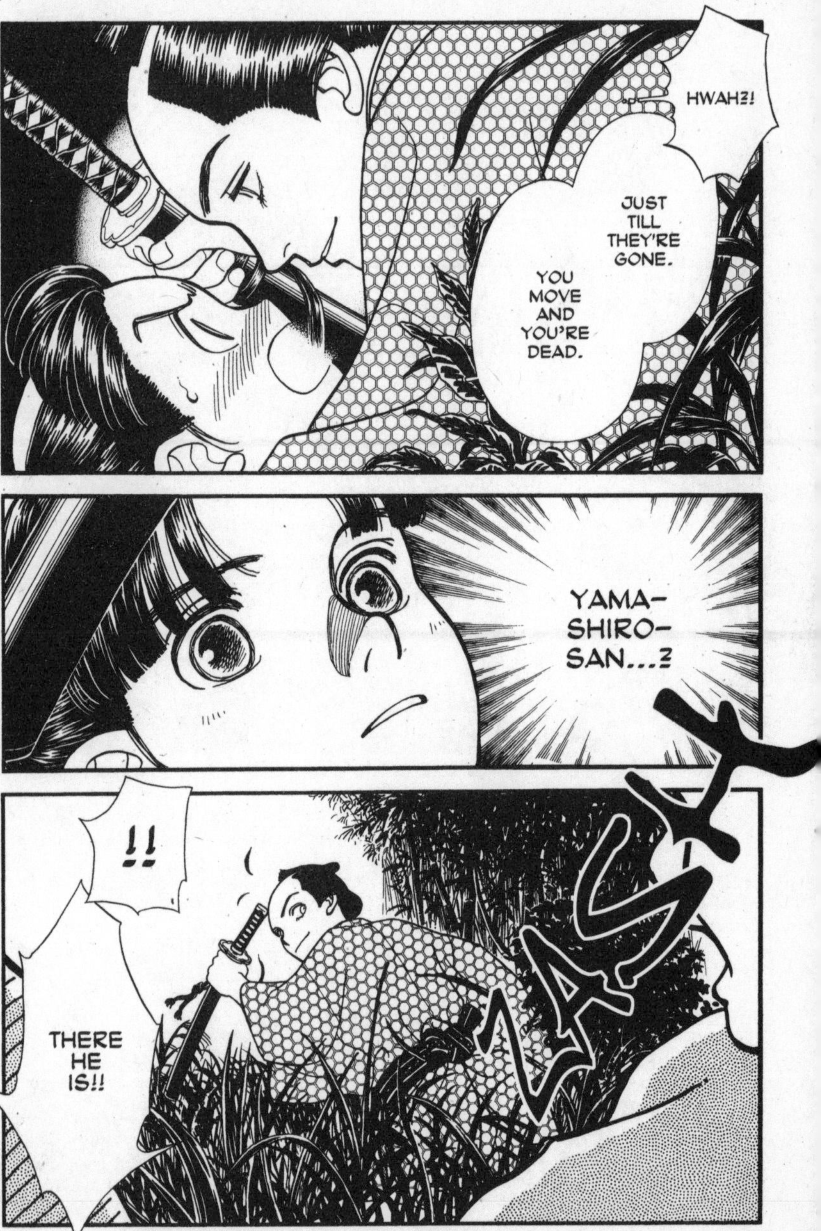
HWAH?!
JUST TILL THEY'RE GONE.
YOU MOVE AND YOU'RE DEAD.
YAMA-SHIRO-SAN...?
ZASH
!!
THERE HE IS!!

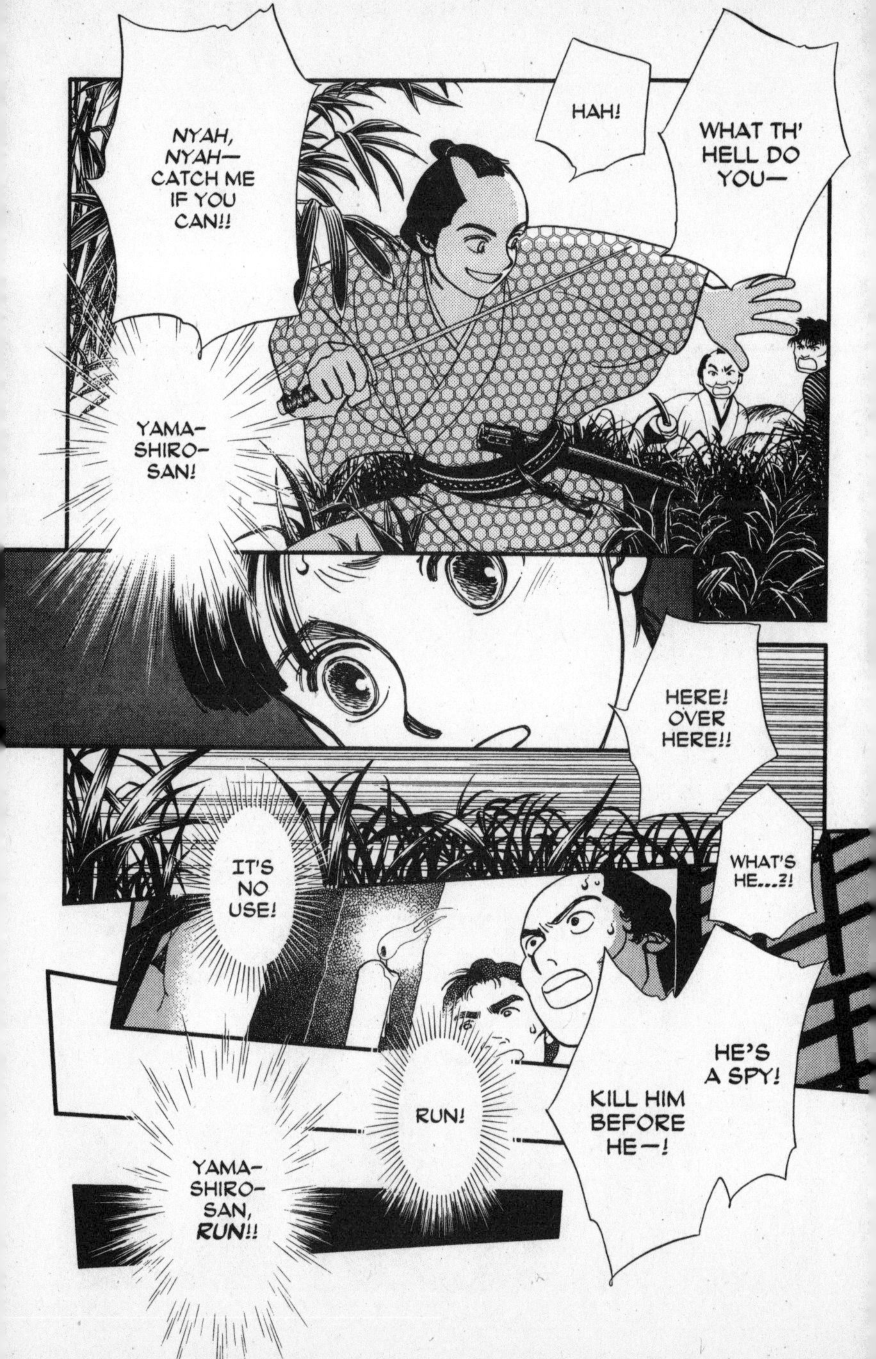
WHAT TH' HELL DO YOU—
HAH!
NYAH, NYAH—CATCH ME IF YOU CAN!!
YAMA-SHIRO-SAN!
HERE! OVER HERE!!
WHAT'S HE...?!
IT'S NO USE!
HE'S A SPY!
KILL HIM BEFORE HE—!
RUN!
YAMA-SHIRO-SAN, RUN!!

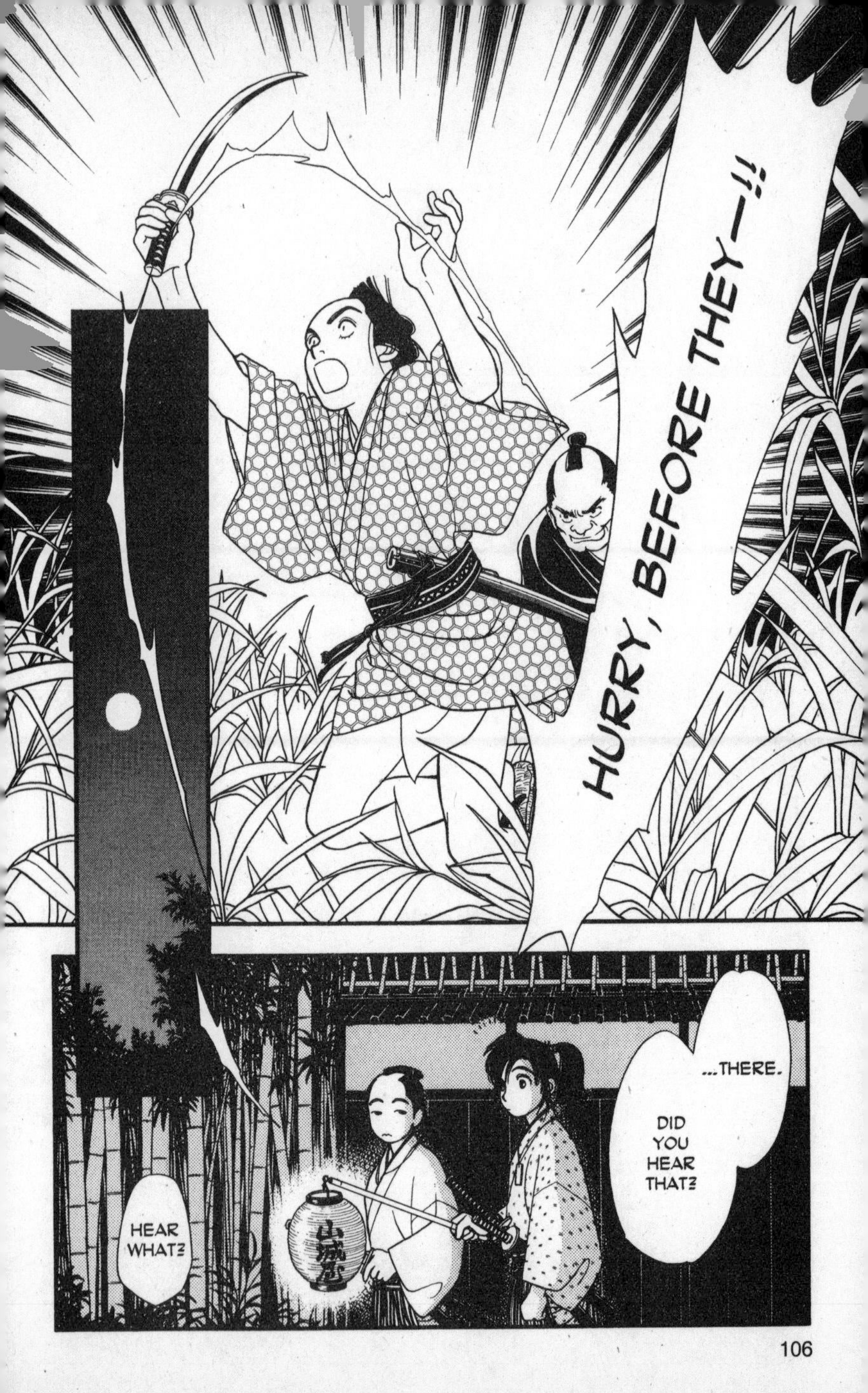
HURRY, BEFORE THEY—!!
...THERE.
DID YOU HEAR THAT?
HEAR WHAT?

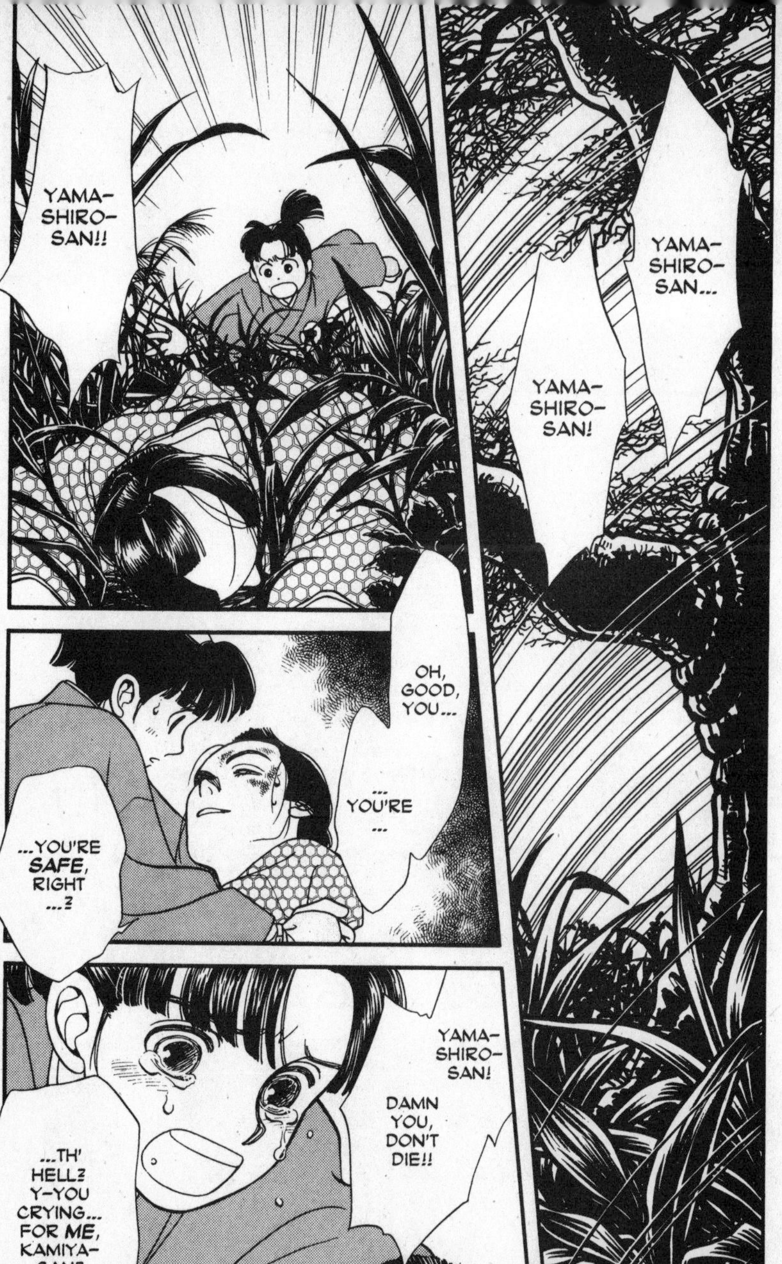
YAMA-SHIRO-SAN...
YAMA-SHIRO-SAN!
YAMA-SHIRO-SAN!!
OH, GOOD, YOU...
... YOU'RE ...
...YOU'RE SAFE, RIGHT ...?
YAMA-SHIRO-SAN!
DAMN YOU, DON'T DIE!!
...TH' HELL? Y-YOU CRYING... FOR ME, KAMIYA-SAN?

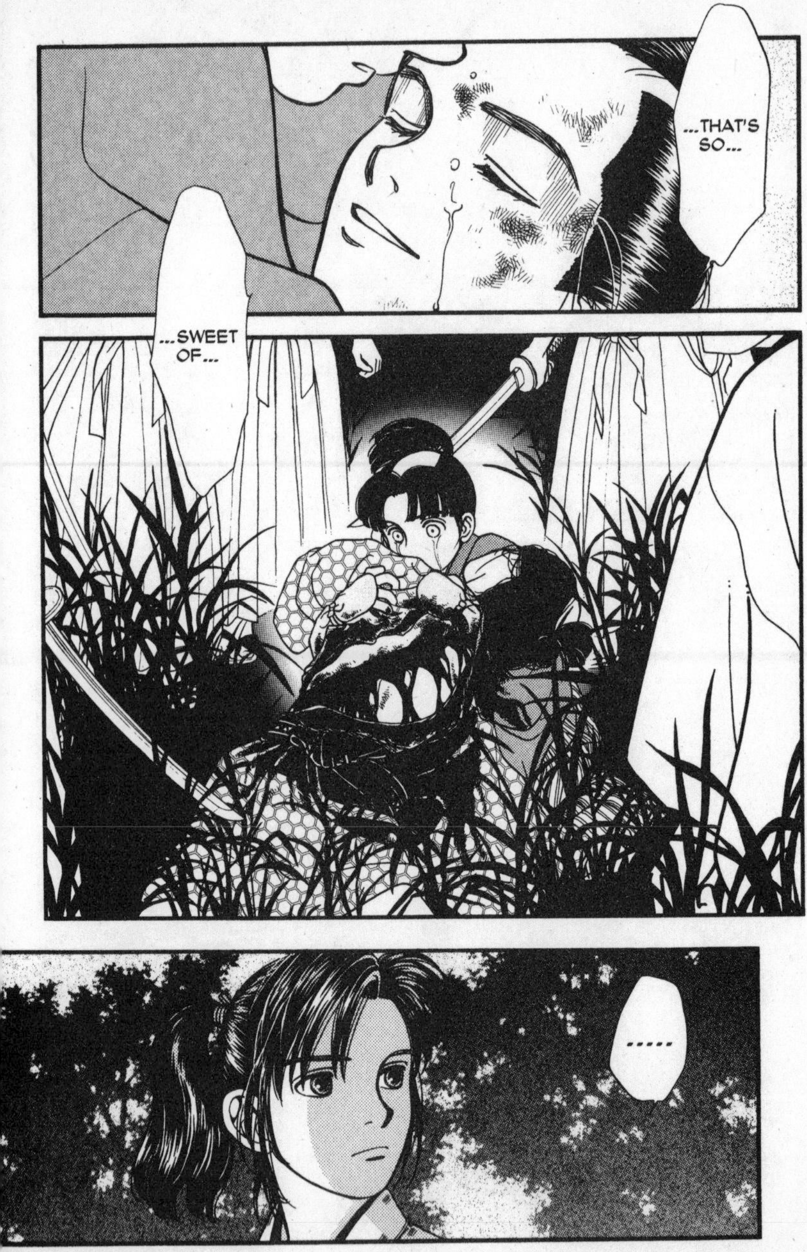
...THAT'S SO...
...SWEET OF...
.....

KYOTO "IROHA" KARUTA GAME!

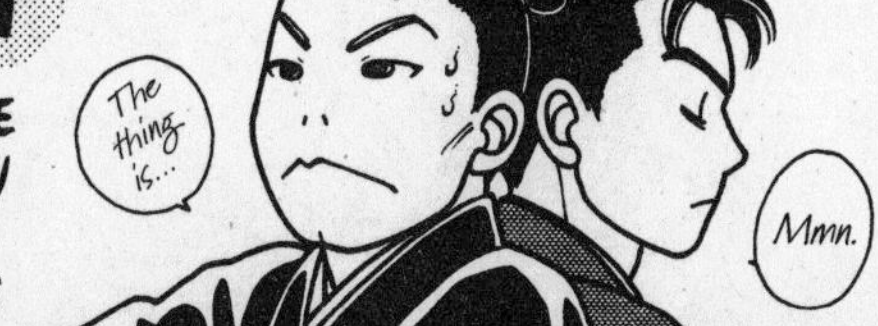
Mmn.
The thing is...

り

"RI"
RINGEN ASE NO GOTOSHI
"A WORD SPOKEN IS AN ARROW LET FLY"

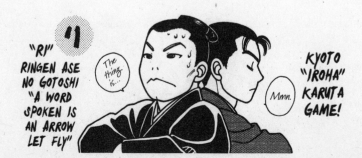

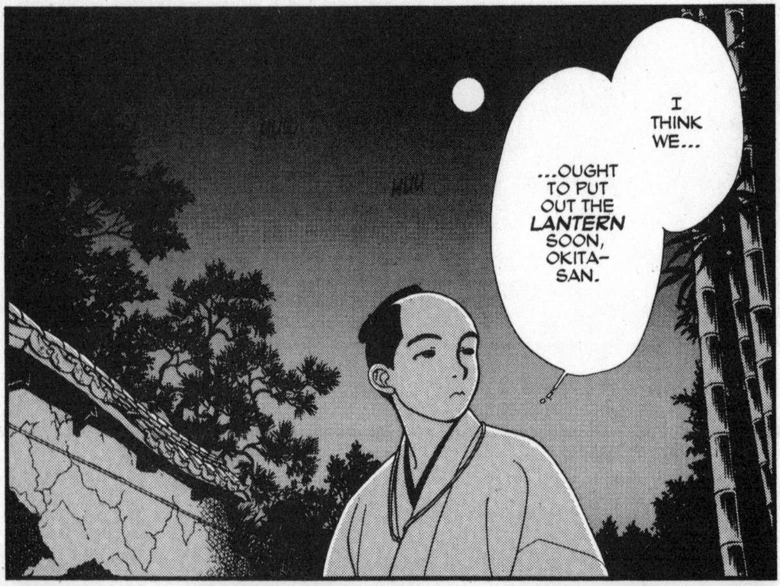
I THINK WE...
...OUGHT TO PUT OUT THE LANTERN SOON, OKITA-SAN.
HUU
HUU

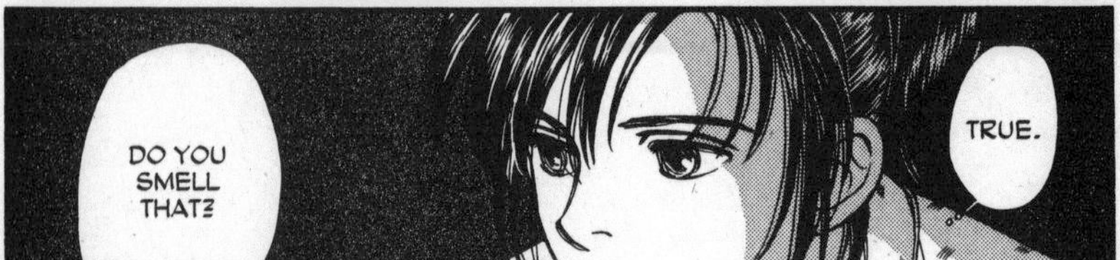
TRUE.
DO YOU SMELL THAT?

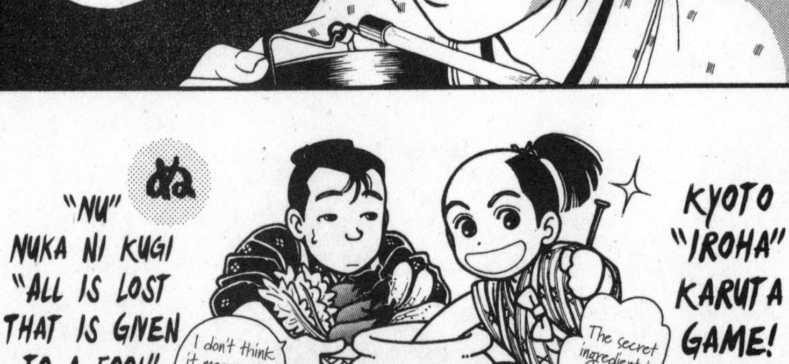
KYOTO "IROHA" KARUTA GAME!
The secret ingredient in nukazuke!
I don't think it means what you think it means.
ぬ
"NU"
NUKA NI KUGI
"ALL IS LOST THAT IS GIVEN TO A FOOL"

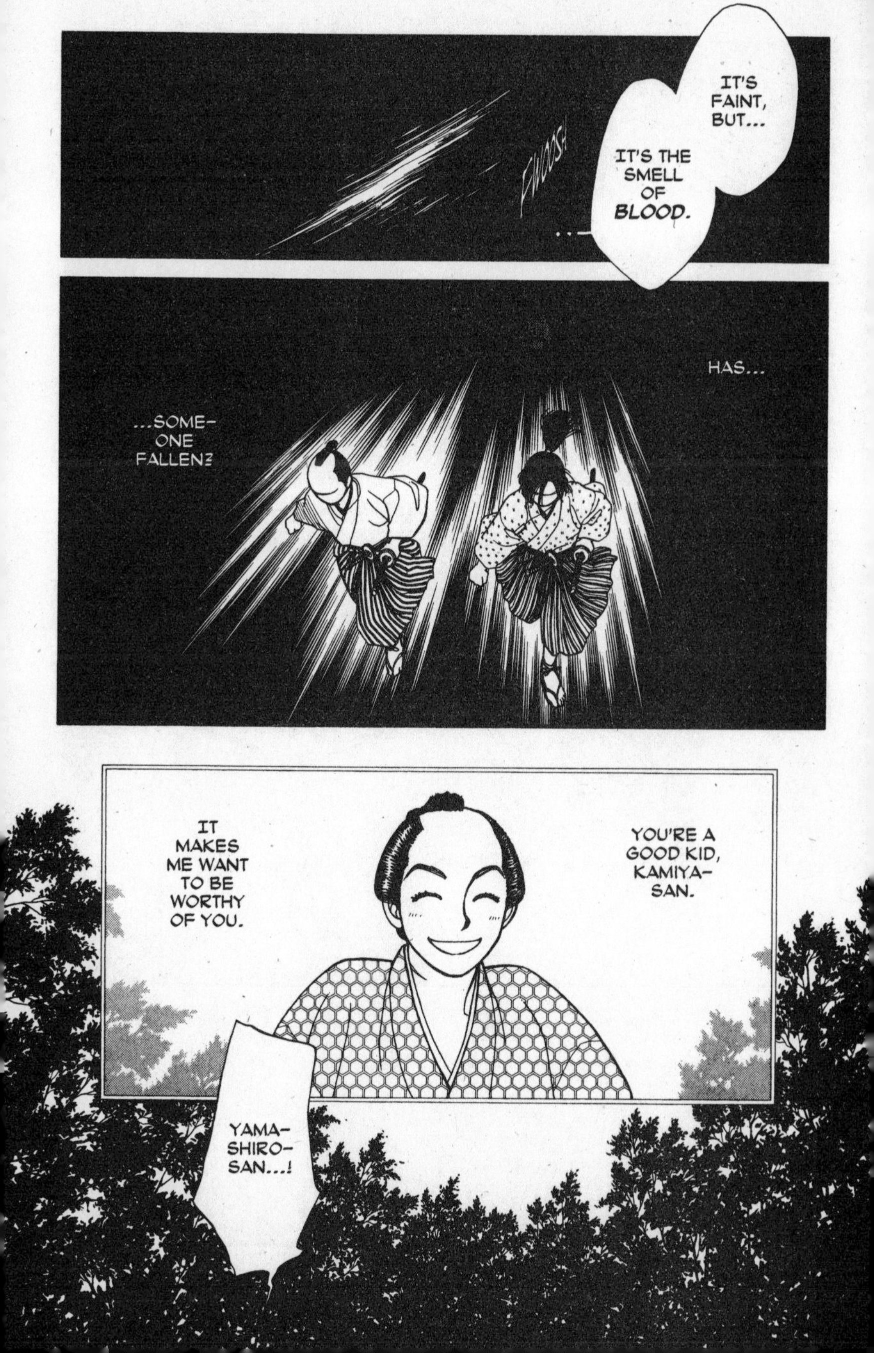
IT'S FAINT, BUT...
IT'S THE SMELL OF BLOOD.
FWOOSH
HAS...
...SOME-ONE FALLEN?
YOU'RE A GOOD KID, KAMIYA-SAN.
IT MAKES ME WANT TO BE WORTHY OF YOU.
YAMA-SHIRO-SAN...!

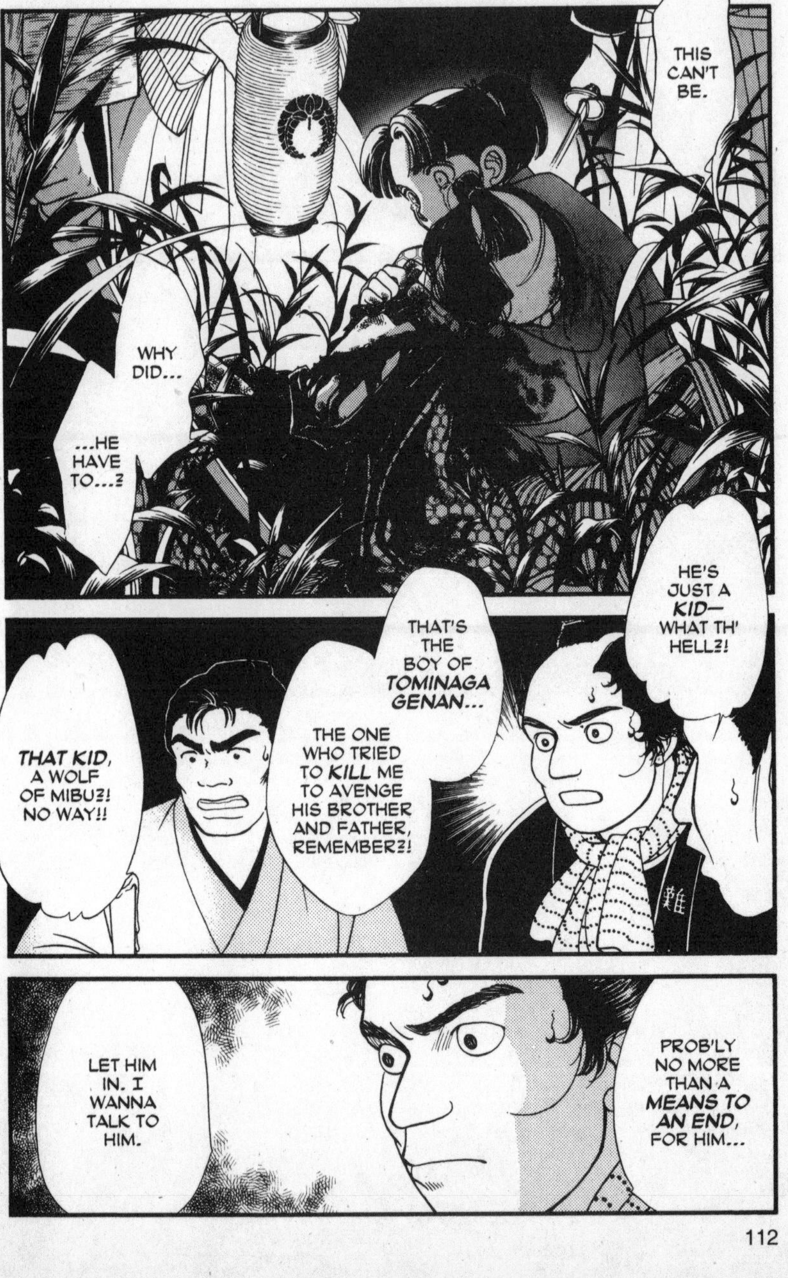
THIS CAN'T BE.
WHY DID...
...HE HAVE TO...?
HE'S JUST A KID— WHAT TH' HELL?!
THAT'S THE BOY OF TOMINAGA GENAN...
THE ONE WHO TRIED TO KILL ME TO AVENGE HIS BROTHER AND FATHER, REMEMBER?!
THAT KID, A WOLF OF MIBU?! NO WAY!!
PROB'LY NO MORE THAN A MEANS TO AN END, FOR HIM...
LET HIM IN. I WANNA TALK TO HIM.

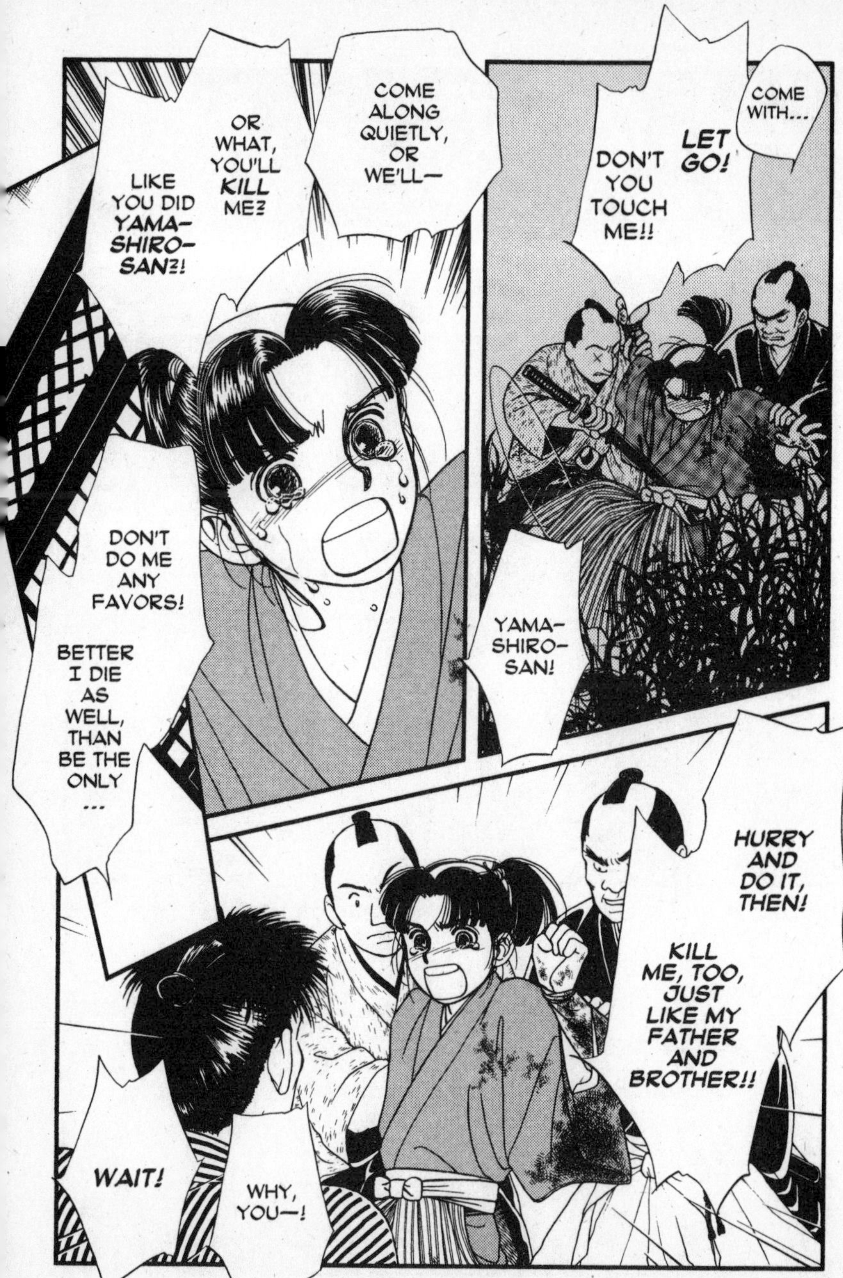
COME WITH...
LET GO!
DON'T YOU TOUCH ME!!
YAMA-SHIRO-SAN!
COME ALONG QUIETLY, OR WE'LL—
OR WHAT, YOU'LL KILL ME?
LIKE YOU DID YAMA-SHIRO-SAN?!
DON'T DO ME ANY FAVORS!
BETTER I DIE AS WELL, THAN BE THE ONLY ...
HURRY AND DO IT, THEN!
KILL ME, TOO, JUST LIKE MY FATHER AND BROTHER!!
WHY, YOU—!
WAIT!

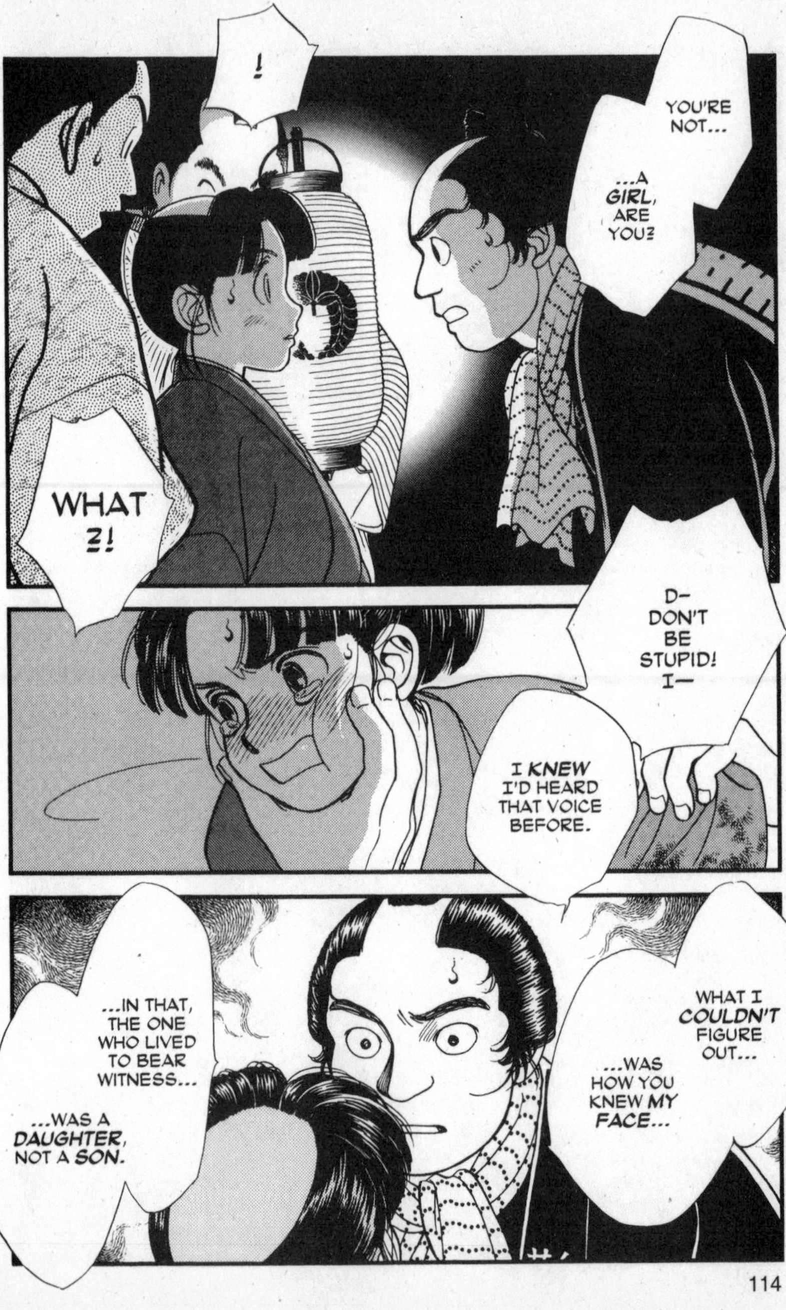
YOU'RE NOT...
...A GIRL, ARE YOU?
!
WHAT?!
D-DON'T BE STUPID! I—
I KNEW I'D HEARD THAT VOICE BEFORE.
WHAT I COULDN'T FIGURE OUT...
...WAS HOW YOU KNEW MY FACE...
...IN THAT, THE ONE WHO LIVED TO BEAR WITNESS...
...WAS A DAUGHTER, NOT A SON.

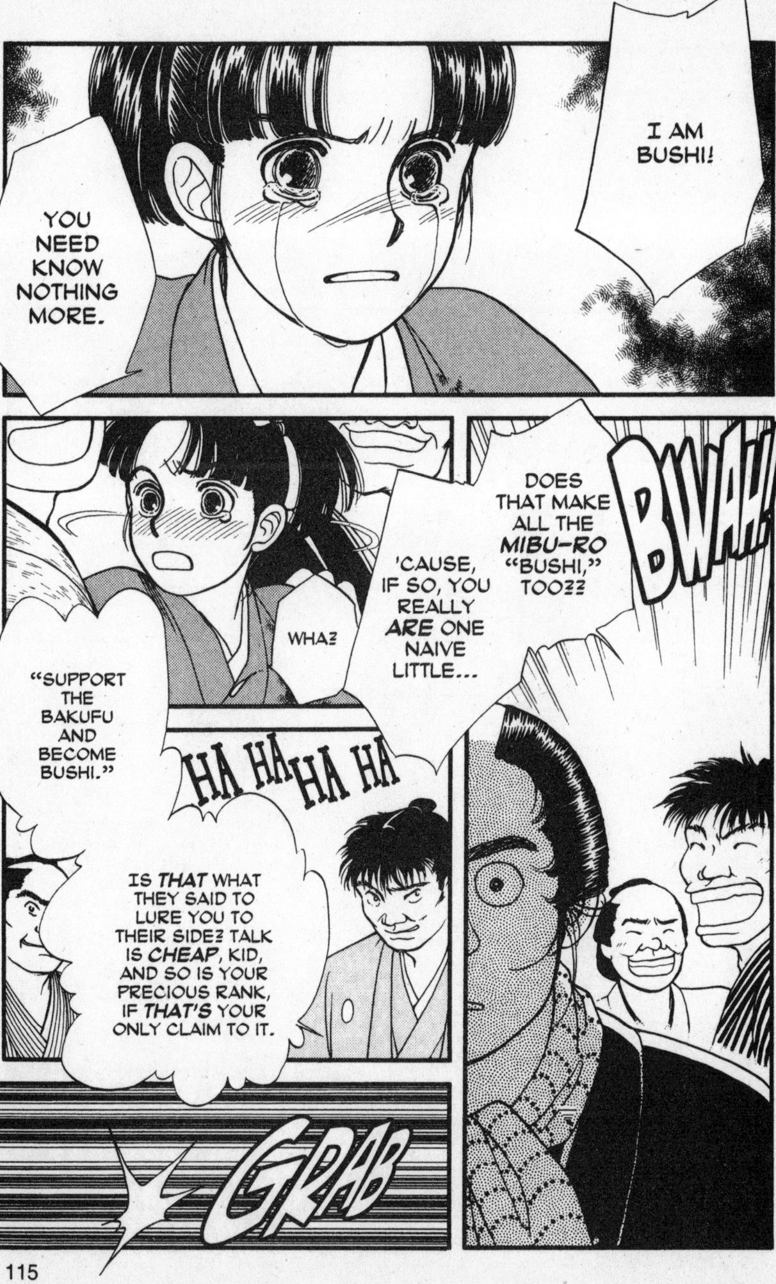
I AM BUSHI!
YOU NEED KNOW NOTHING MORE.
BWAH!
DOES THAT MAKE ALL THE *MIBU-RO* "BUSHI," TOO??
'CAUSE, IF SO, YOU REALLY **ARE** ONE NAIVE LITTLE...
WHA?
"SUPPORT THE BAKUFU AND BECOME BUSHI."
HA HA HA HA
IS *THAT* WHAT THEY SAID TO LURE YOU TO THEIR SIDE? TALK IS *CHEAP*, KID, AND SO IS YOUR PRECIOUS RANK, IF *THAT'S* YOUR ONLY CLAIM TO IT.
GRAB

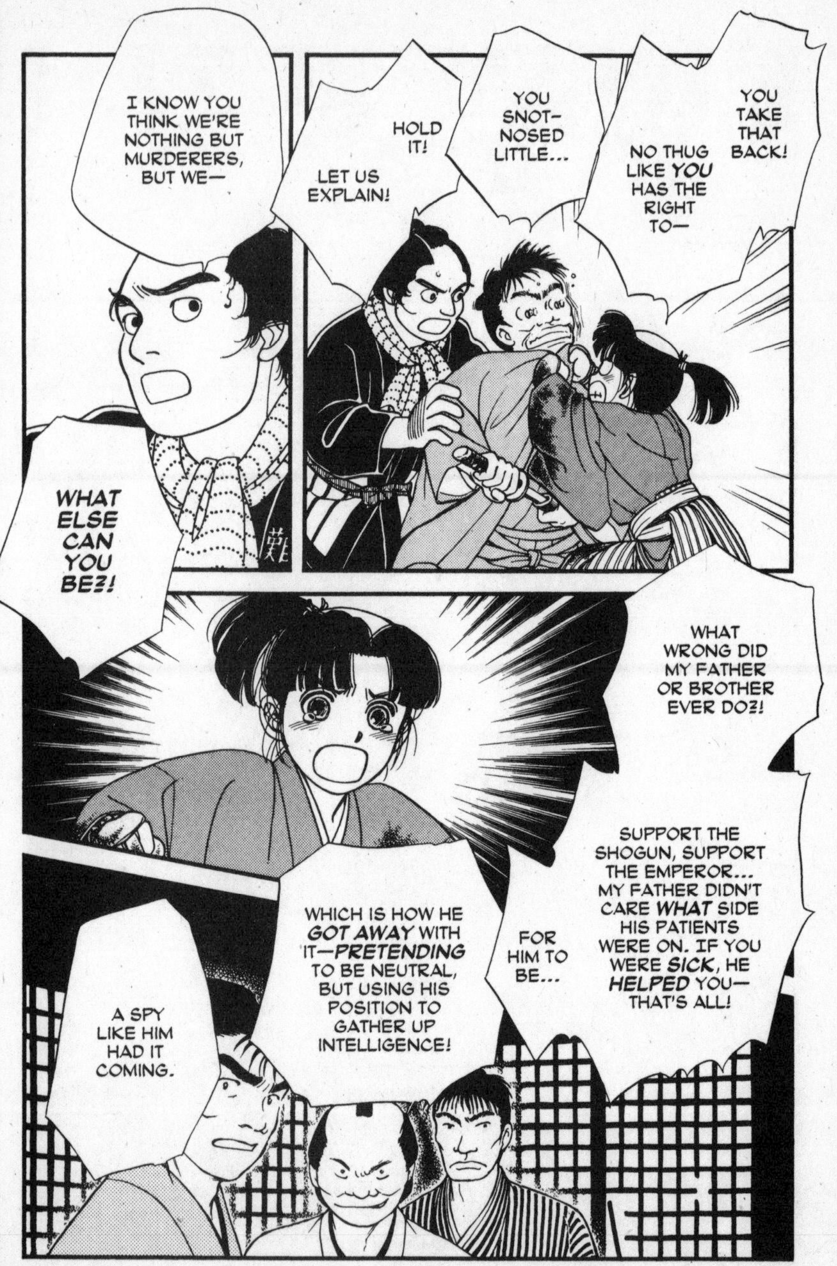
YOU TAKE THAT BACK!
NO THUG LIKE YOU HAS THE RIGHT TO—
YOU SNOT-NOSED LITTLE...
HOLD IT!
LET US EXPLAIN!
I KNOW YOU THINK WE'RE NOTHING BUT MURDERERS, BUT WE—
WHAT ELSE CAN YOU BE?!
WHAT WRONG DID MY FATHER OR BROTHER EVER DO?!
SUPPORT THE SHOGUN, SUPPORT THE EMPEROR... MY FATHER DIDN'T CARE WHAT SIDE HIS PATIENTS WERE ON. IF YOU WERE SICK, HE HELPED YOU—THAT'S ALL!
FOR HIM TO BE...
WHICH IS HOW HE GOT AWAY WITH IT—PRETENDING TO BE NEUTRAL, BUT USING HIS POSITION TO GATHER UP INTELLIGENCE!
A SPY LIKE HIM HAD IT COMING.

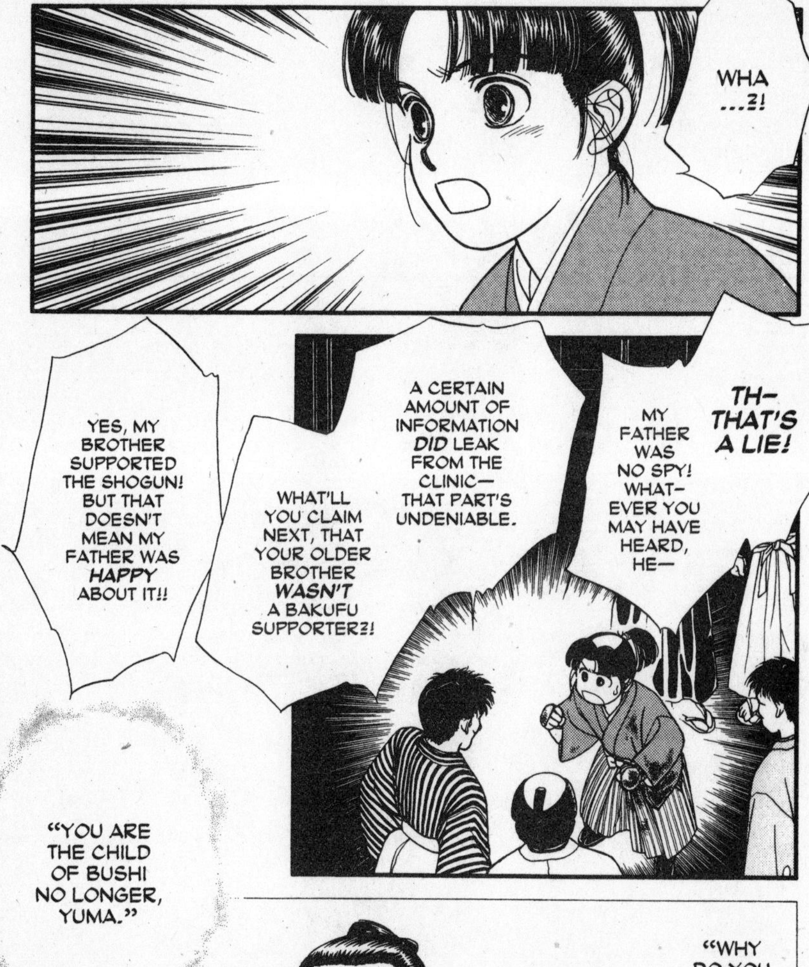
WHA ...?!
TH-THAT'S A LIE!
MY FATHER WAS NO SPY! WHAT-EVER YOU MAY HAVE HEARD, HE—
A CERTAIN AMOUNT OF INFORMATION DID LEAK FROM THE CLINIC—THAT PART'S UNDENIABLE.
WHAT'LL YOU CLAIM NEXT, THAT YOUR OLDER BROTHER WASN'T A BAKUFU SUPPORTER?!
YES, MY BROTHER SUPPORTED THE SHOGUN! BUT THAT DOESN'T MEAN MY FATHER WAS HAPPY ABOUT IT!!
"WHY DO YOU INSIST ON TAKING UP THE SWORD?"
"DO YOU NOT SEE THE FOOLISHNESS OF DEBATING IDEALS ON THE TIP OF A BLADE?"
"YOU ARE THE CHILD OF BUSHI NO LONGER, YUMA."

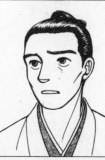

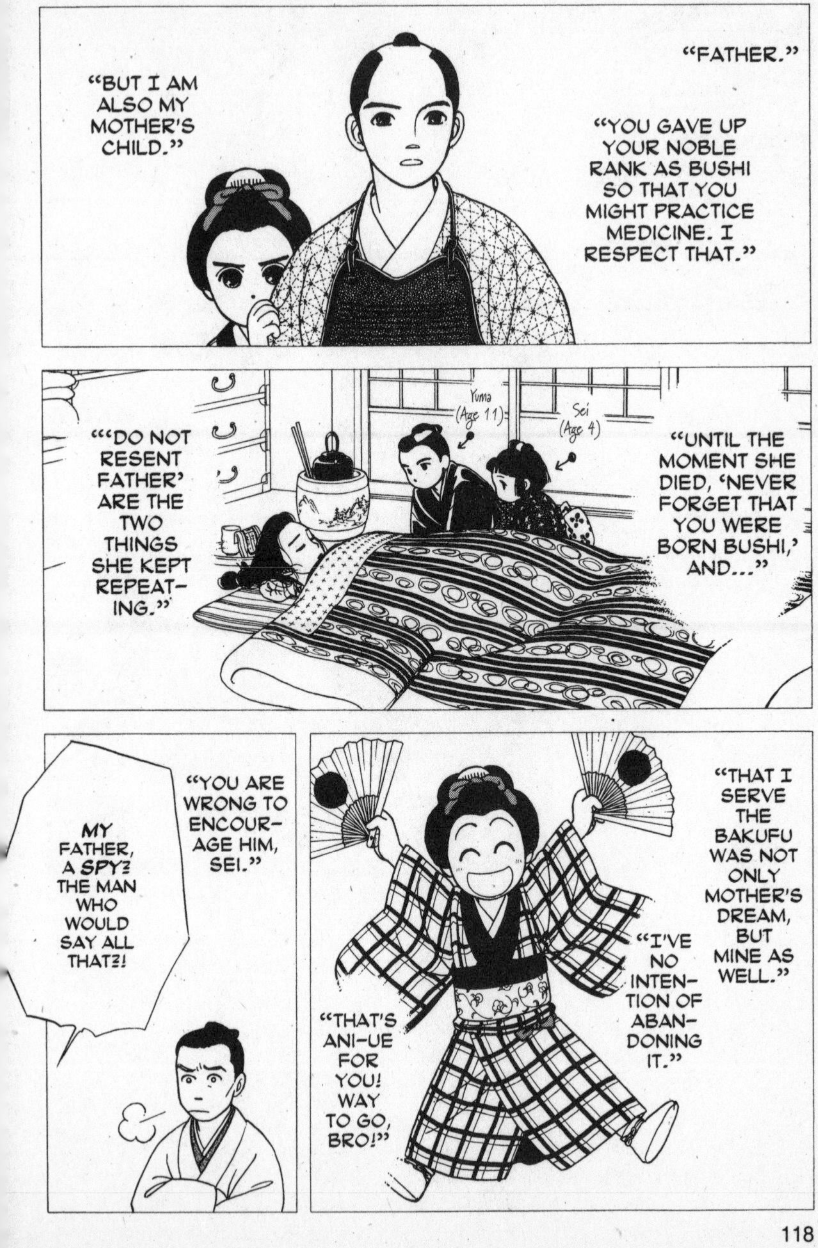
"FATHER."
"YOU GAVE UP YOUR NOBLE RANK AS BUSHI SO THAT YOU MIGHT PRACTICE MEDICINE. I RESPECT THAT."
"BUT I AM ALSO MY MOTHER'S CHILD."
"UNTIL THE MOMENT SHE DIED, 'NEVER FORGET THAT YOU WERE BORN BUSHI,' AND..."
Sei (Age 4)
Yuma (Age 11)
"'DO NOT RESENT FATHER' ARE THE TWO THINGS SHE KEPT REPEATING."
"THAT I SERVE THE BAKUFU WAS NOT ONLY MOTHER'S DREAM, BUT MINE AS WELL."
"I'VE NO INTENTION OF ABANDONING IT."
"THAT'S ANI-UE FOR YOU! WAY TO GO, BRO!"
"YOU ARE WRONG TO ENCOURAGE HIM, SEI."
MY FATHER, A SPY?! THE MAN WHO WOULD SAY ALL THAT?!

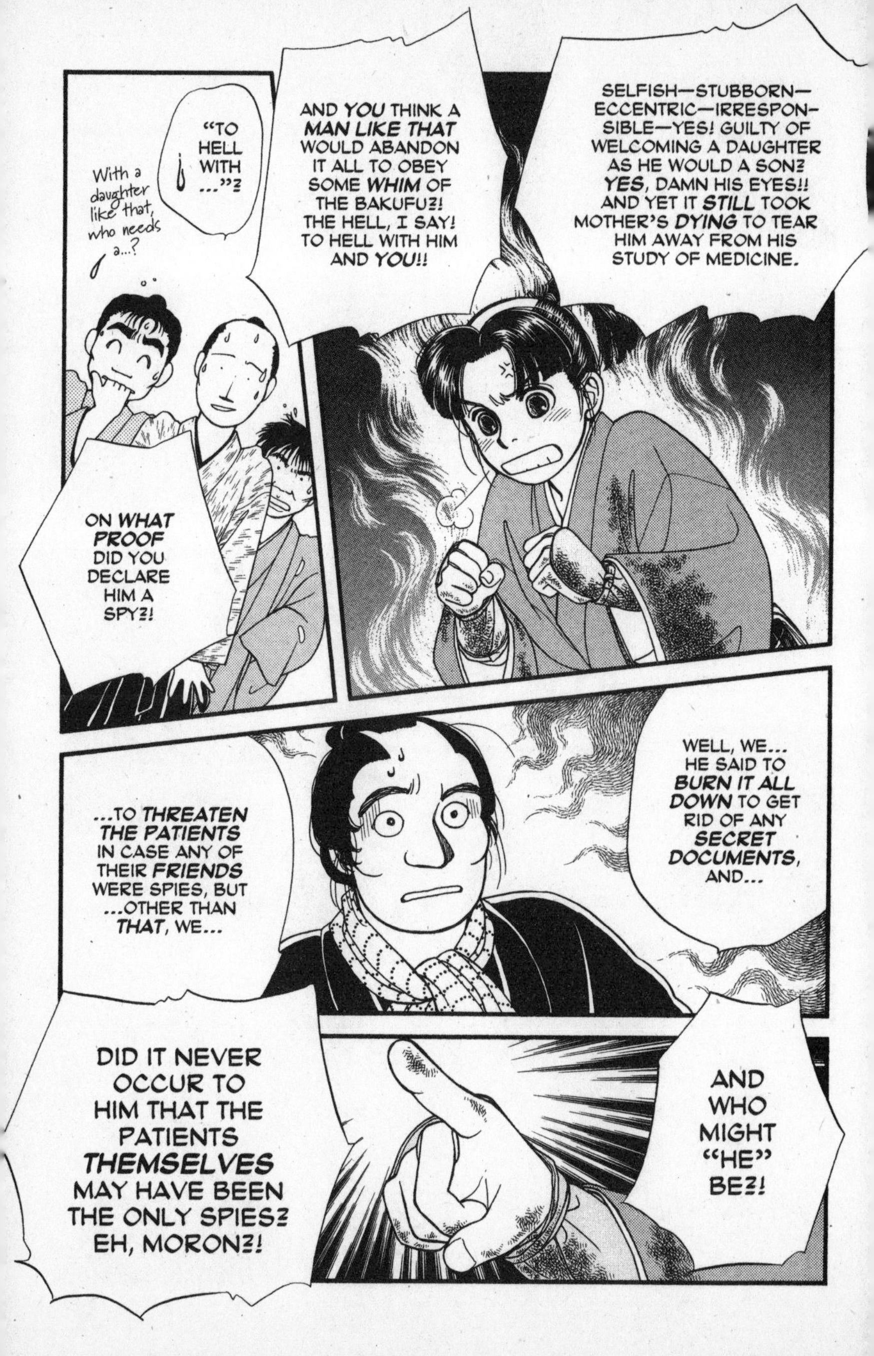
SELFISH—STUBBORN—ECCENTRIC—IRRESPONSIBLE—YES! GUILTY OF WELCOMING A DAUGHTER AS HE WOULD A SON? YES, DAMN HIS EYES!! AND YET IT STILL TOOK MOTHER'S DYING TO TEAR HIM AWAY FROM HIS STUDY OF MEDICINE.
AND YOU THINK A MAN LIKE THAT WOULD ABANDON IT ALL TO OBEY SOME WHIM OF THE BAKUFU?! THE HELL, I SAY! TO HELL WITH HIM AND YOU!!
"TO HELL WITH ..."?
With a daughter like that, who needs a...?
ON WHAT PROOF DID YOU DECLARE HIM A SPY?!
WELL, WE... HE SAID TO BURN IT ALL DOWN TO GET RID OF ANY SECRET DOCUMENTS, AND...
...TO THREATEN THE PATIENTS IN CASE ANY OF THEIR FRIENDS WERE SPIES, BUT ...OTHER THAN THAT, WE...
AND WHO MIGHT "HE" BE?!
DID IT NEVER OCCUR TO HIM THAT THE PATIENTS THEMSELVES MAY HAVE BEEN THE ONLY SPIES? EH, MORON?!

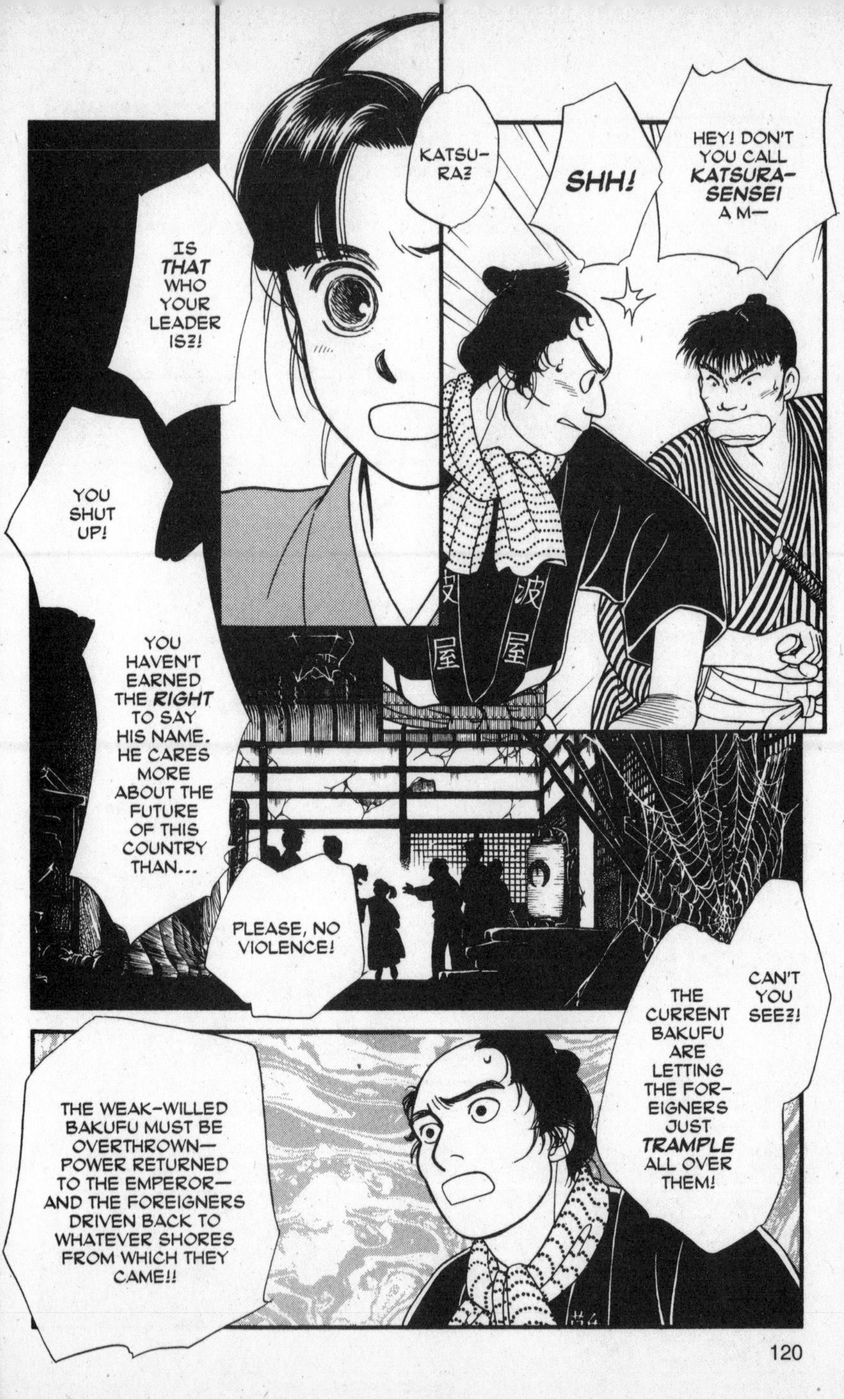
HEY! DON'T YOU CALL KATSURA-SENSEI A M—
SHH!
KATSURA?
IS THAT WHO YOUR LEADER IS?!
YOU SHUT UP!
YOU HAVEN'T EARNED THE RIGHT TO SAY HIS NAME. HE CARES MORE ABOUT THE FUTURE OF THIS COUNTRY THAN...
PLEASE, NO VIOLENCE!
CAN'T YOU SEE?!
THE CURRENT BAKUFU ARE LETTING THE FOREIGNERS JUST TRAMPLE ALL OVER THEM!
THE WEAK-WILLED BAKUFU MUST BE OVERTHROWN—POWER RETURNED TO THE EMPEROR—AND THE FOREIGNERS DRIVEN BACK TO WHATEVER SHORES FROM WHICH THEY CAME!!

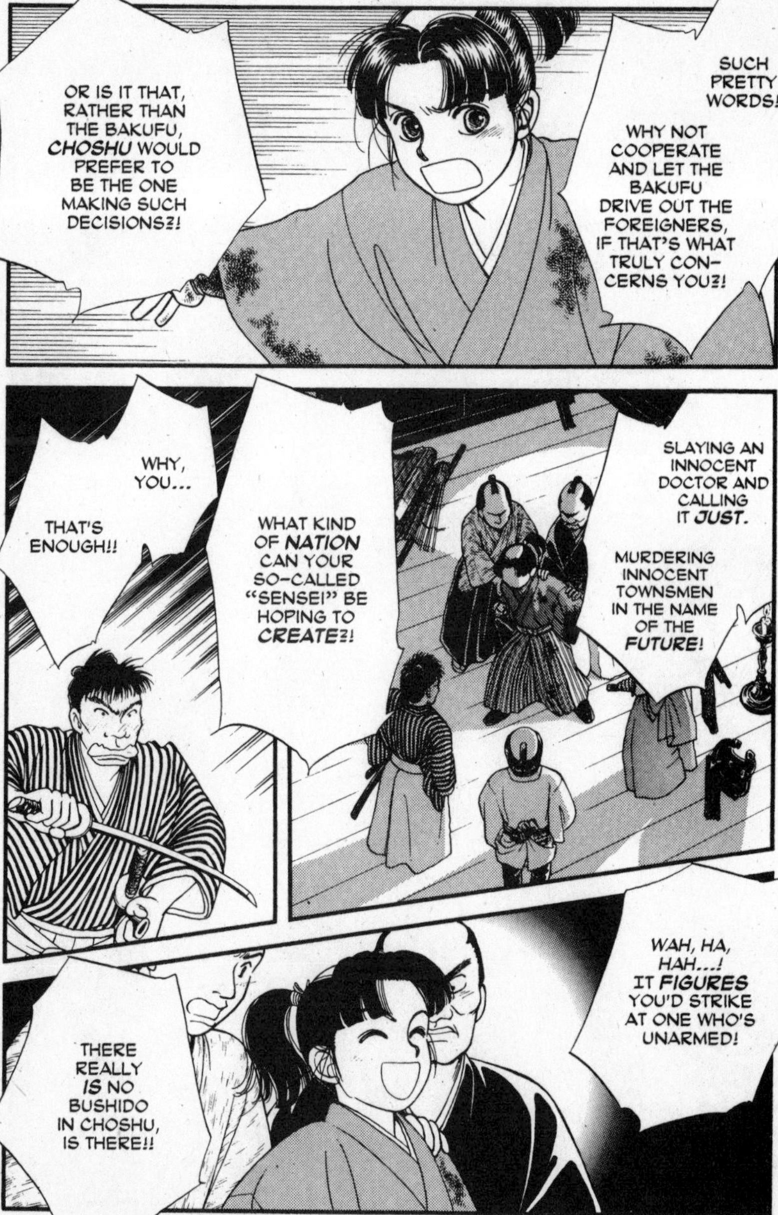
SUCH PRETTY WORDS!
WHY NOT COOPERATE AND LET THE BAKUFU DRIVE OUT THE FOREIGNERS, IF THAT'S WHAT TRULY CONCERNS YOU?!
OR IS IT THAT, RATHER THAN THE BAKUFU, *CHOSHU* WOULD PREFER TO BE THE ONE MAKING SUCH DECISIONS?!
SLAYING AN INNOCENT DOCTOR AND CALLING IT *JUST*.
MURDERING INNOCENT TOWNSMEN IN THE NAME OF THE *FUTURE*!
WHAT KIND OF *NATION* CAN YOUR SO-CALLED "SENSEI" BE HOPING TO *CREATE*?!
WHY, YOU...
THAT'S ENOUGH!!
WAH, HA, HAH...! IT FIGURES YOU'D STRIKE AT ONE WHO'S UNARMED!
THERE REALLY *IS* NO BUSHIDO IN CHOSHU, IS THERE!!

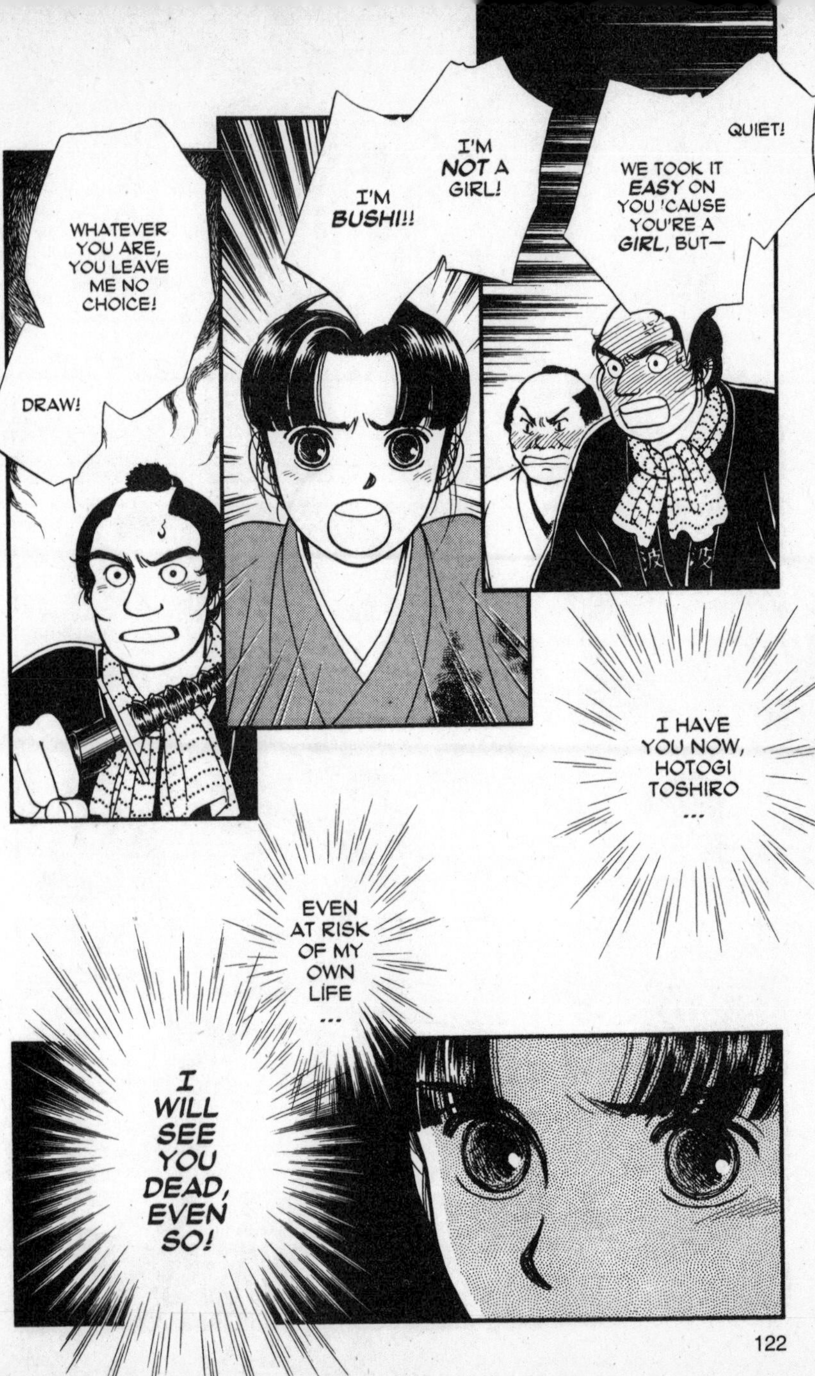
QUIET!
WE TOOK IT EASY ON YOU 'CAUSE YOU'RE A GIRL, BUT—
I'M NOT A GIRL!
I'M BUSHI!!
WHATEVER YOU ARE, YOU LEAVE ME NO CHOICE!
DRAW!
I HAVE YOU NOW, HOTOGI TOSHIRO ...
EVEN AT RISK OF MY OWN LIFE ...
I WILL SEE YOU DEAD, EVEN SO!

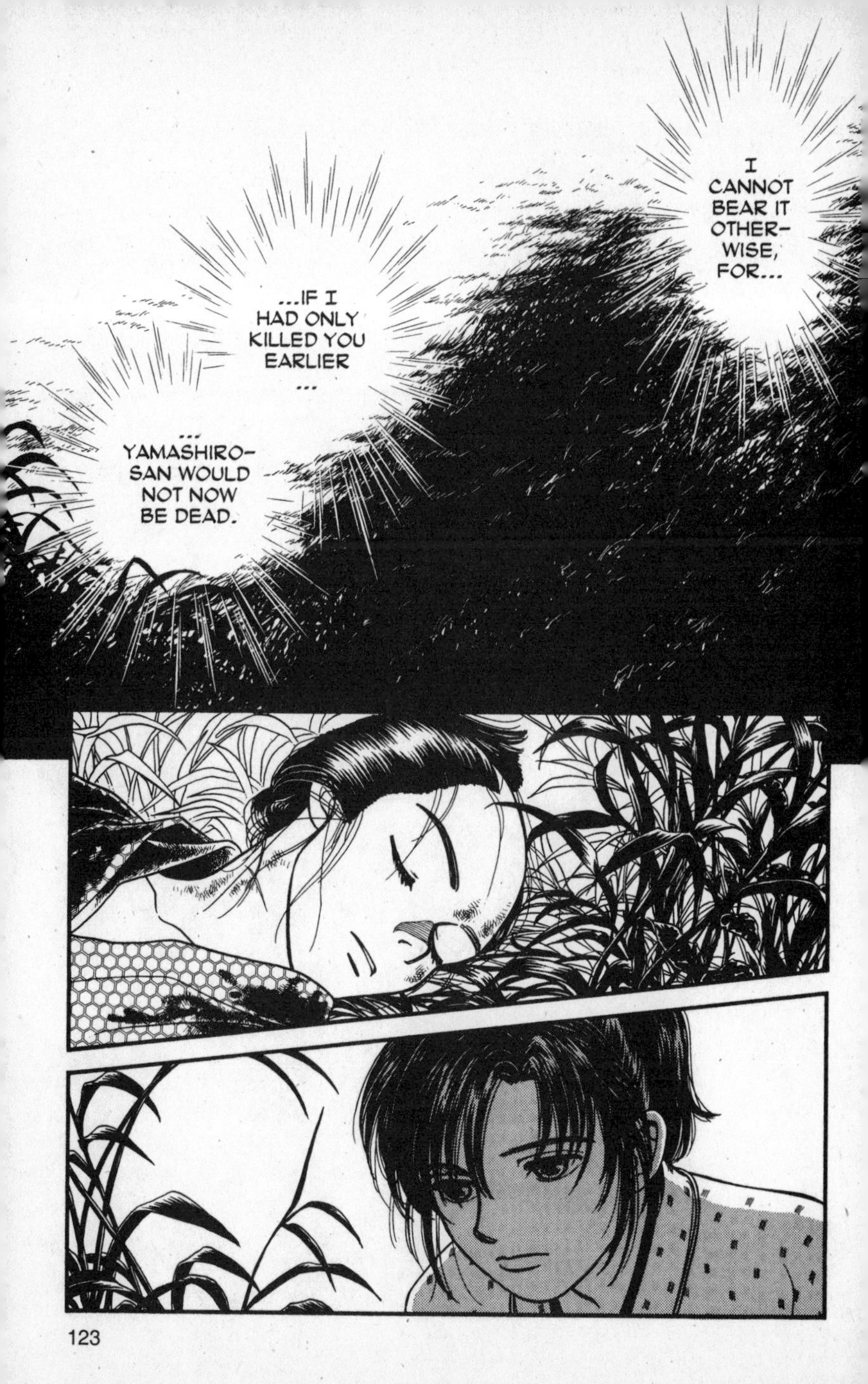
I CANNOT BEAR IT OTHER-WISE, FOR...
...IF I HAD ONLY KILLED YOU EARLIER ...
... YAMASHIRO-SAN WOULD NOT NOW BE DEAD.

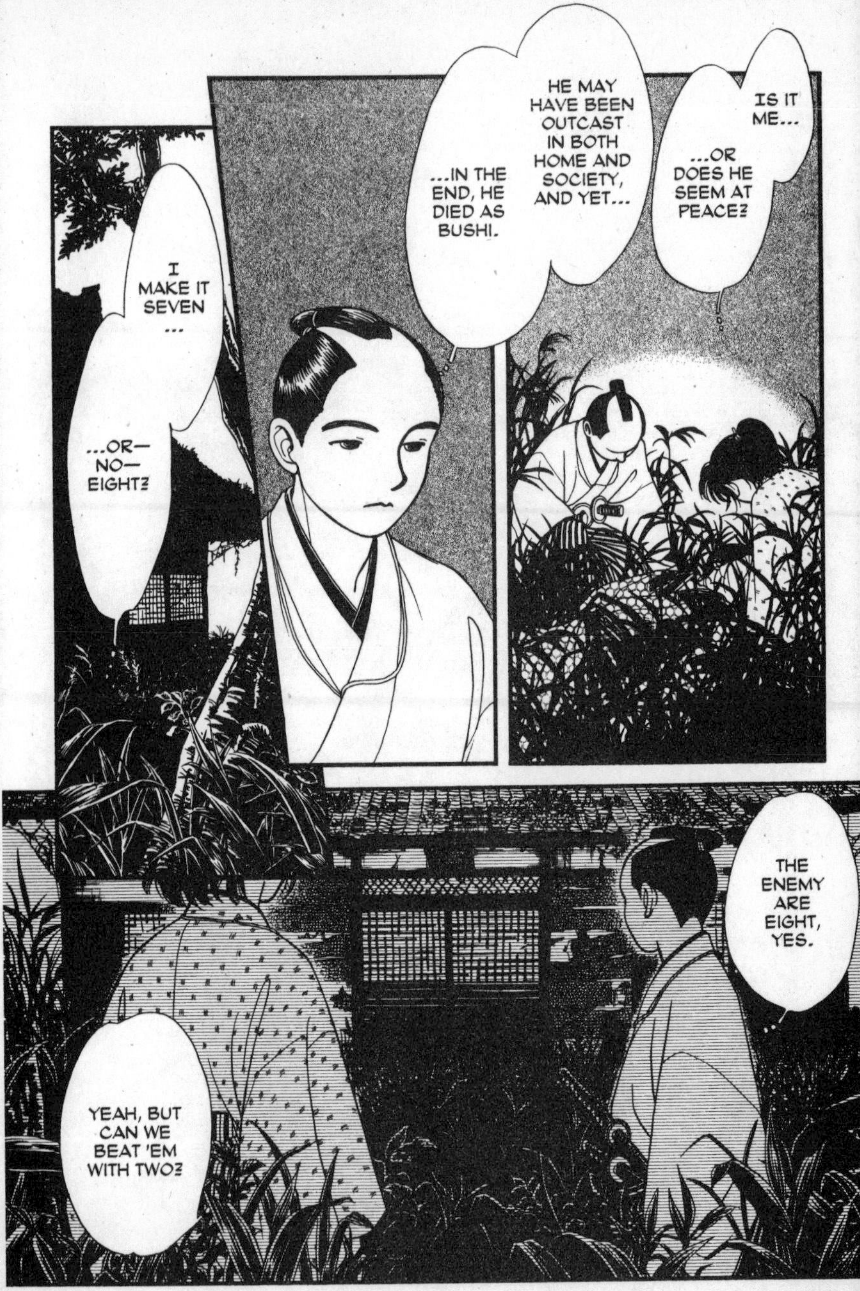
IS IT ME...
...OR DOES HE SEEM AT PEACE?
HE MAY HAVE BEEN OUTCAST IN BOTH HOME AND SOCIETY, AND YET...
...IN THE END, HE DIED AS BUSHI.
I MAKE IT SEVEN...
...OR— NO— EIGHT?
THE ENEMY ARE EIGHT, YES.
YEAH, BUT CAN WE BEAT 'EM WITH TWO?

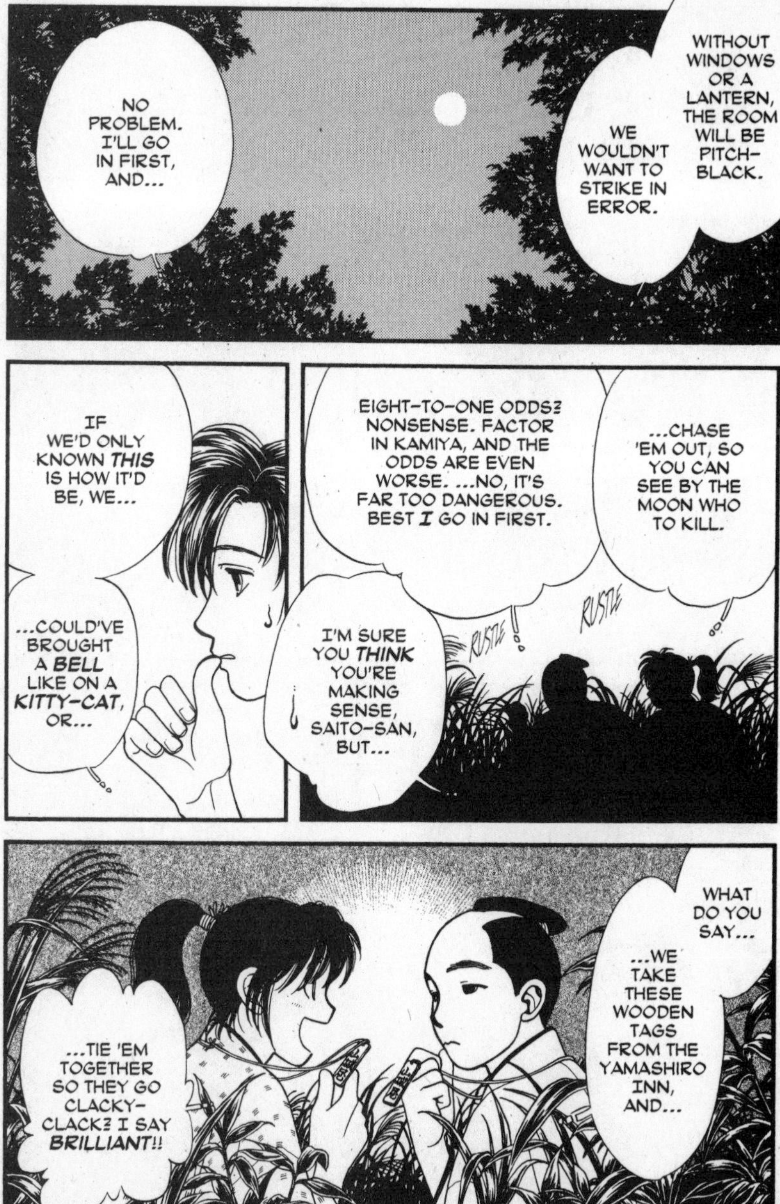
WITHOUT WINDOWS OR A LANTERN, THE ROOM WILL BE PITCH-BLACK.
WE WOULDN'T WANT TO STRIKE IN ERROR.
NO PROBLEM. I'LL GO IN FIRST, AND...
...CHASE 'EM OUT, SO YOU CAN SEE BY THE MOON WHO TO KILL.
EIGHT-TO-ONE ODDS? NONSENSE. FACTOR IN KAMIYA, AND THE ODDS ARE EVEN WORSE. ...NO, IT'S FAR TOO DANGEROUS. BEST *I* GO IN FIRST.
RUSTLE
RUSTLE
I'M SURE YOU *THINK* YOU'RE MAKING SENSE, SAITO-SAN, BUT...
IF WE'D ONLY KNOWN *THIS* IS HOW IT'D BE, WE...
...COULD'VE BROUGHT A *BELL* LIKE ON A *KITTY-CAT*, OR...
WHAT DO YOU SAY...
...WE TAKE THESE WOODEN TAGS FROM THE YAMASHIRO INN, AND...
...TIE 'EM TOGETHER SO THEY GO CLACKY-CLACK? I SAY *BRILLIANT*!!

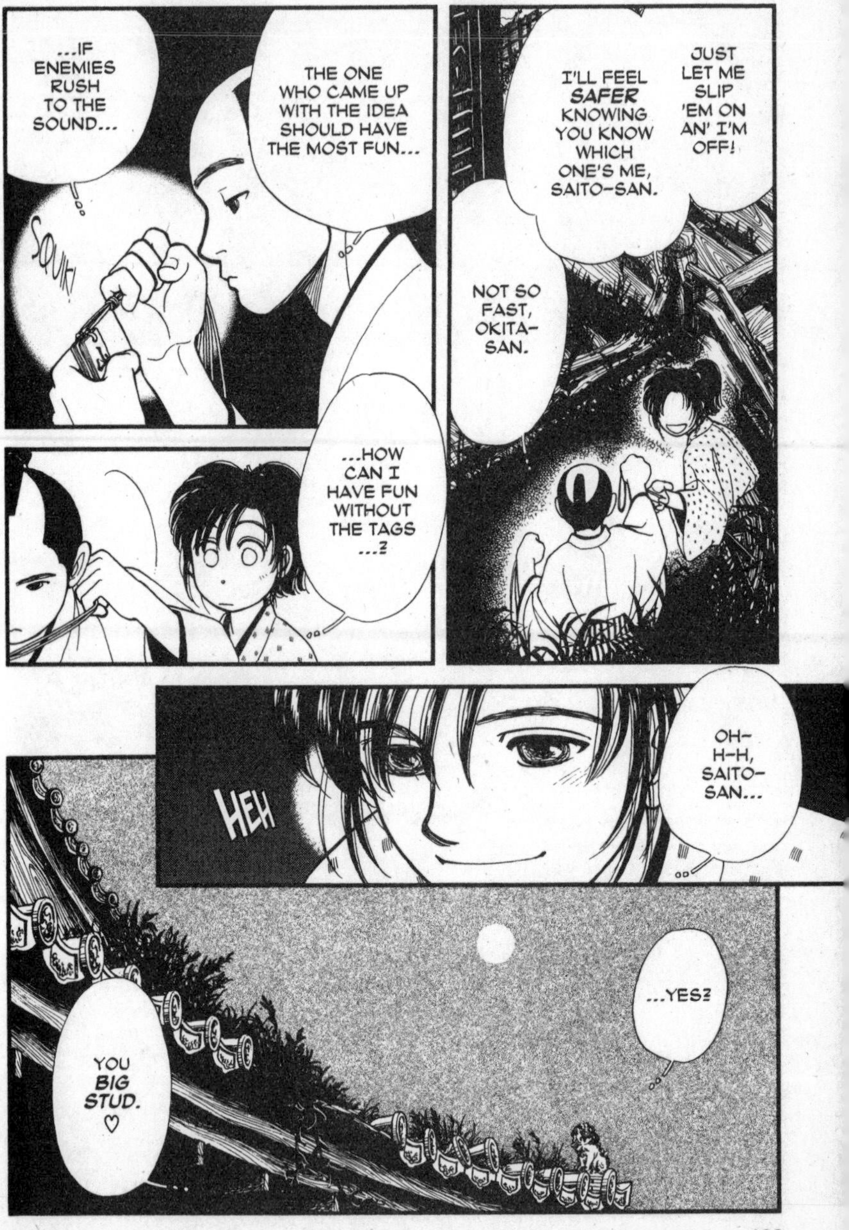
JUST LET ME SLIP 'EM ON AN' I'M OFF!
I'LL FEEL SAFER KNOWING YOU KNOW WHICH ONE'S ME, SAITO-SAN.
NOT SO FAST, OKITA-SAN.
THE ONE WHO CAME UP WITH THE IDEA SHOULD HAVE THE MOST FUN...
...IF ENEMIES RUSH TO THE SOUND...
SQUIK!
...HOW CAN I HAVE FUN WITHOUT THE TAGS...?
OH-H-H, SAITO-SAN...
HEH
...YES?
YOU BIG STUD. ♡

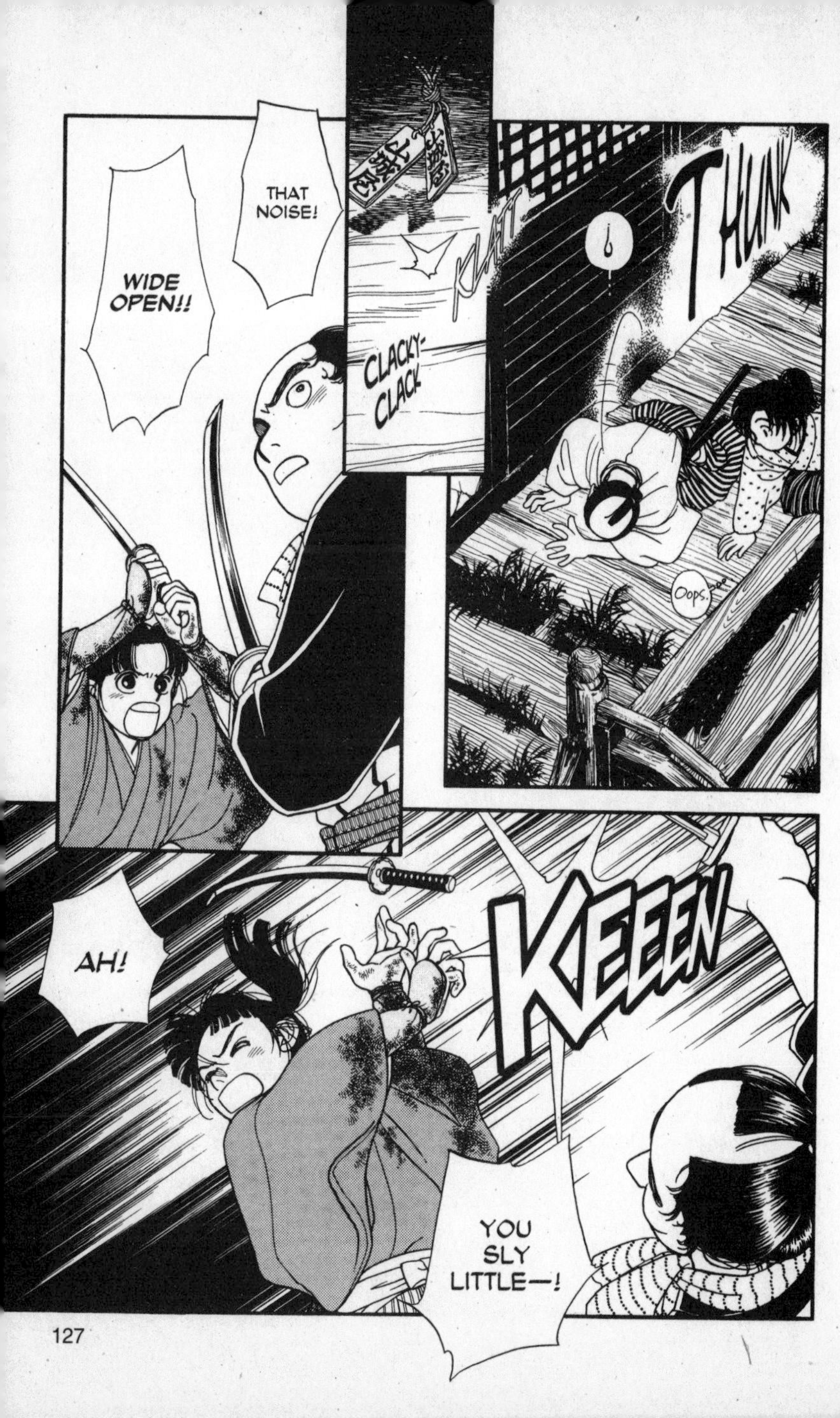
THUNK
Oops.
KLATT
CLACKY-CLACK
THAT NOISE!
WIDE OPEN!!
KEEEN
AH!
YOU SLY LITTLE—!

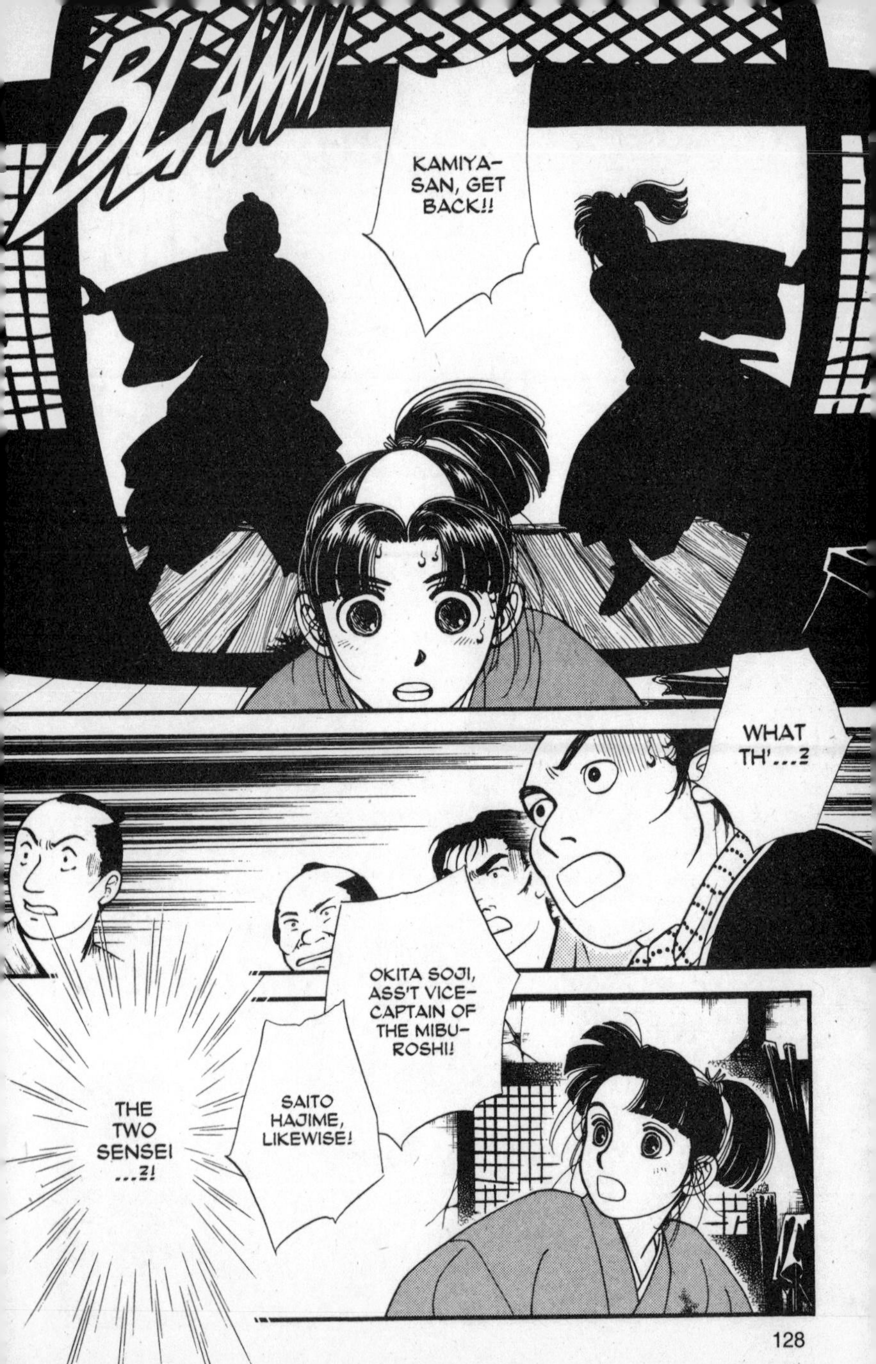
KAMIYA-SAN, GET BACK!!
BLAMM
WHAT TH'...?!
OKITA SOJI, ASS'T VICE-CAPTAIN OF THE MIBU-ROSHI!
SAITO HAJIME, LIKEWISE!
THE TWO SENSEI ...?!

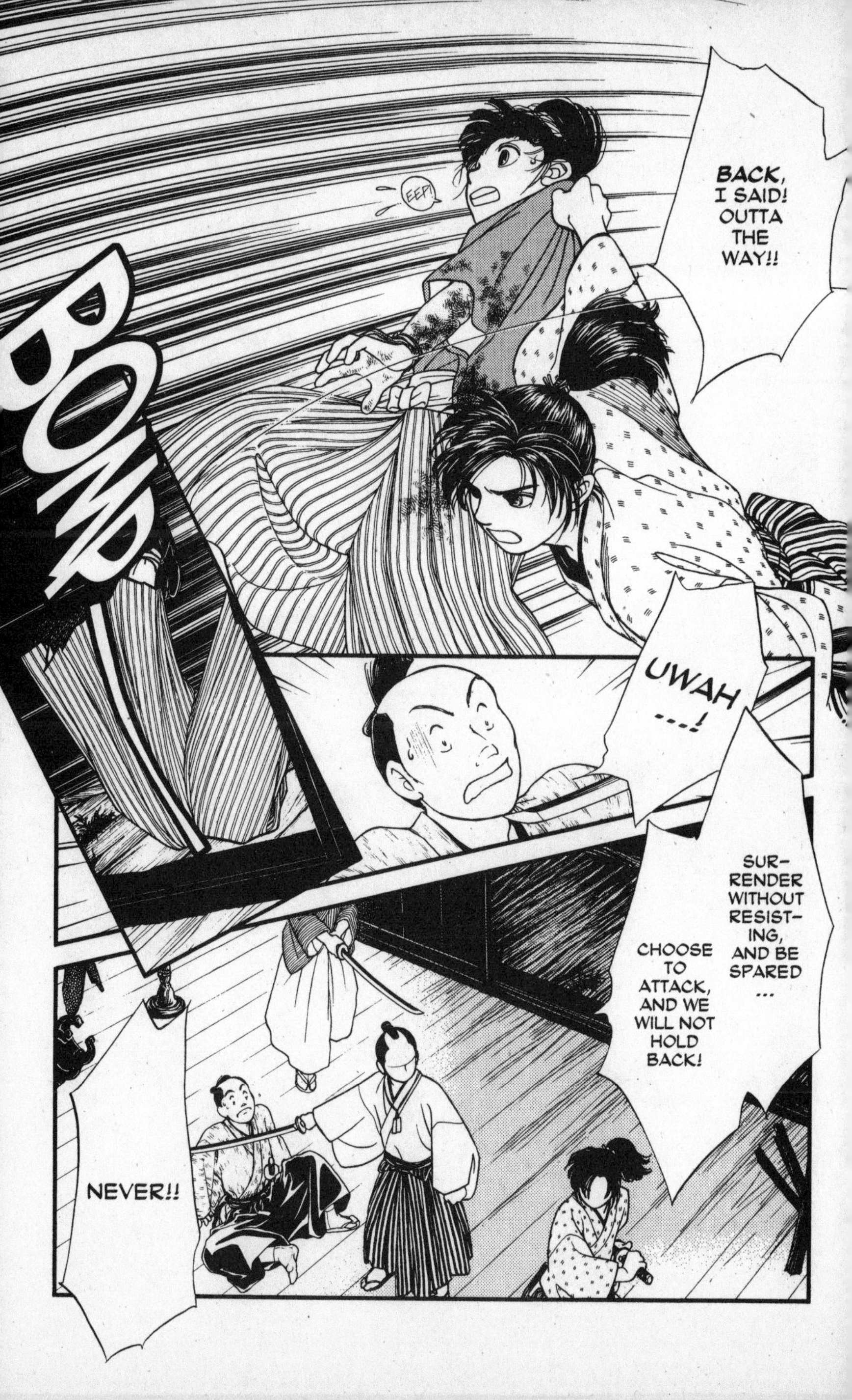
BACK, I SAID! OUTTA THE WAY!!
EEP!
BOMP
UWAH ...!
SURRENDER WITHOUT RESISTING, AND BE SPARED ...
CHOOSE TO ATTACK, AND WE WILL NOT HOLD BACK!
NEVER!!

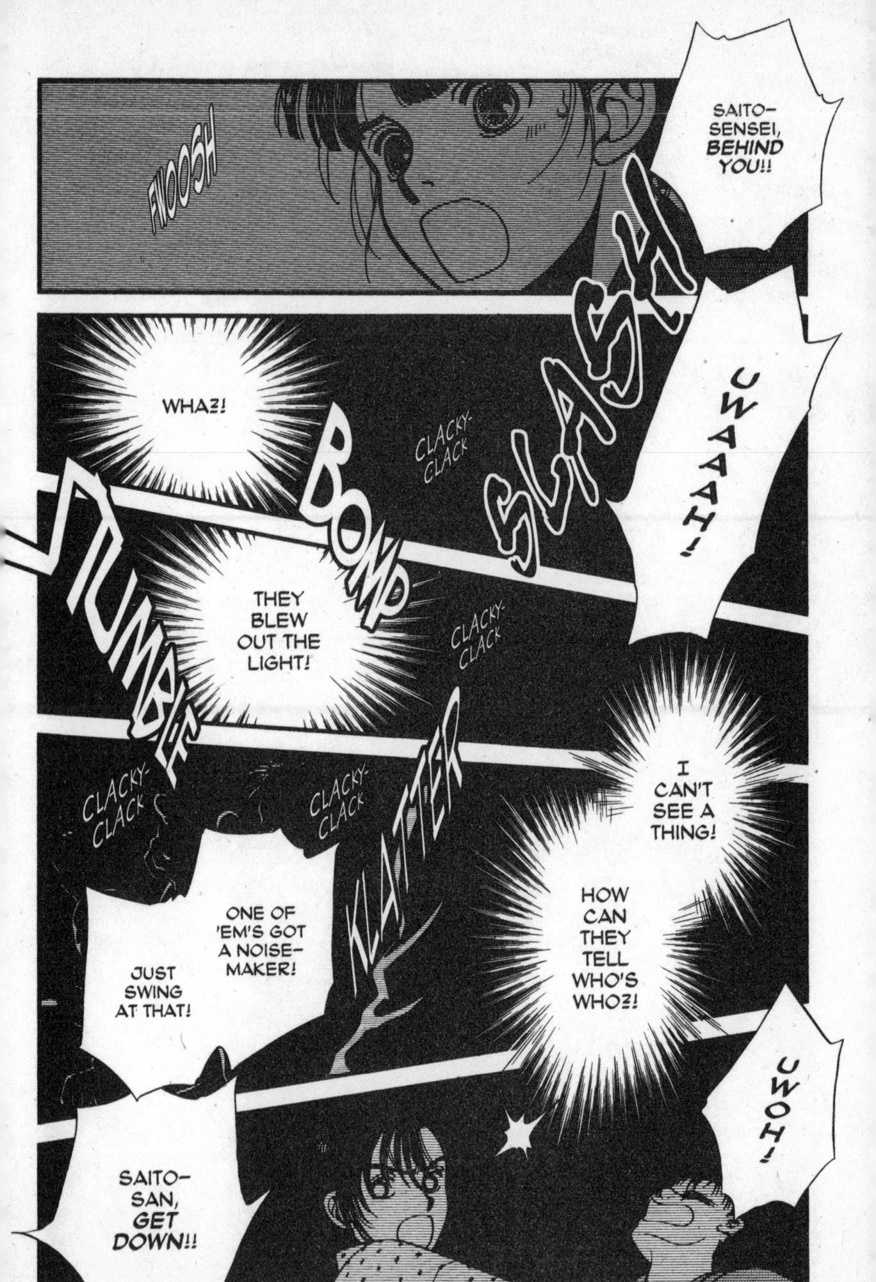
SAITO-SENSEI, BEHIND YOU!!
FWOOSH
UWAAAAH!
SLASH
CLACKY-CLACK
BOMP
WHA?!
STUMBLE
CLACKY-CLACK
THEY BLEW OUT THE LIGHT!
I CAN'T SEE A THING!
HOW CAN THEY TELL WHO'S WHO?!
KLATTER
CLACKY-CLACK
ONE OF 'EM'S GOT A NOISE-MAKER!
CLACKY-CLACK
JUST SWING AT THAT!
UWOH!
SAITO-SAN, GET DOWN!!

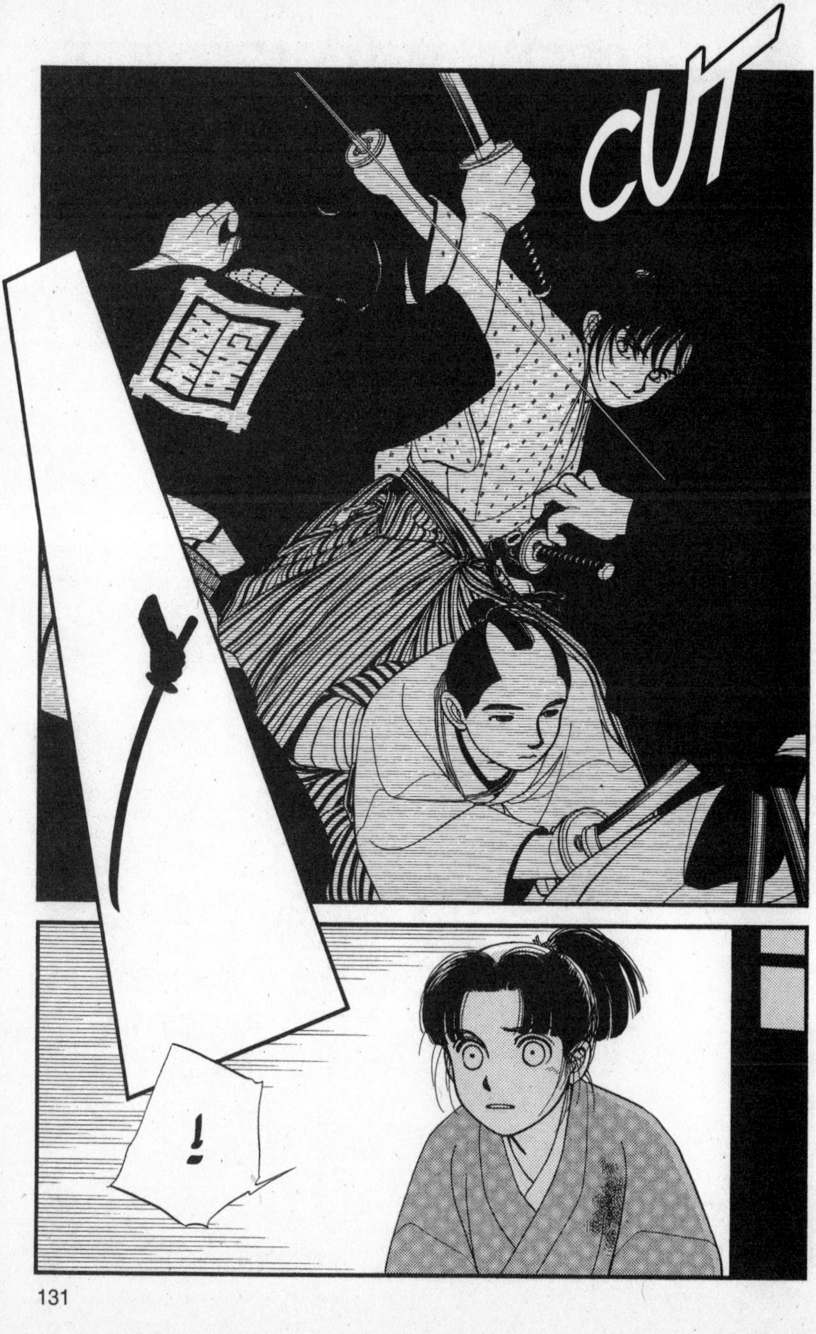
CUT
!

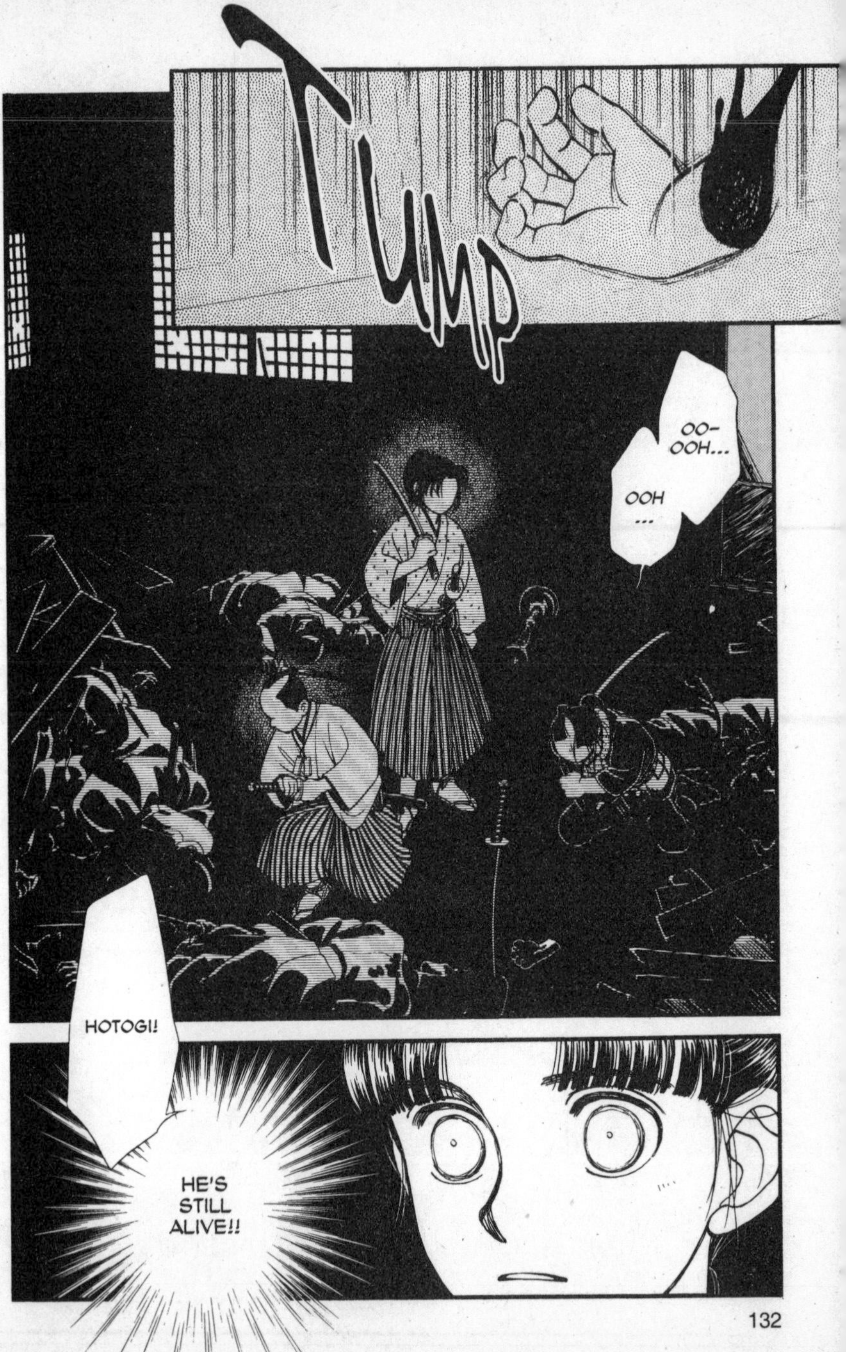
TUMP
OO-OOH...
OOH ...
HOTOGI!
HE'S STILL ALIVE!!

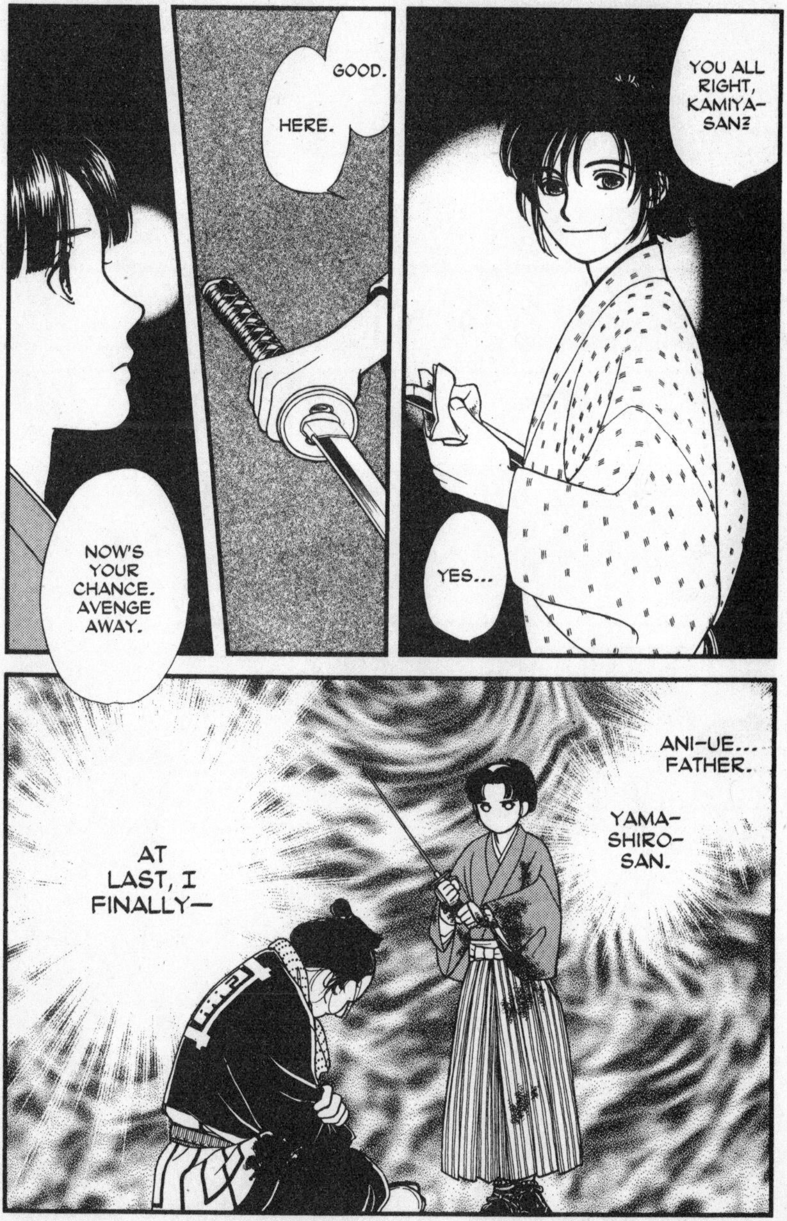
YOU ALL RIGHT, KAMIYA-SAN?
YES...
GOOD.
HERE.
NOW'S YOUR CHANCE. AVENGE AWAY.
ANI-UE... FATHER.
YAMA-SHIRO-SAN.
AT LAST, I FINALLY—

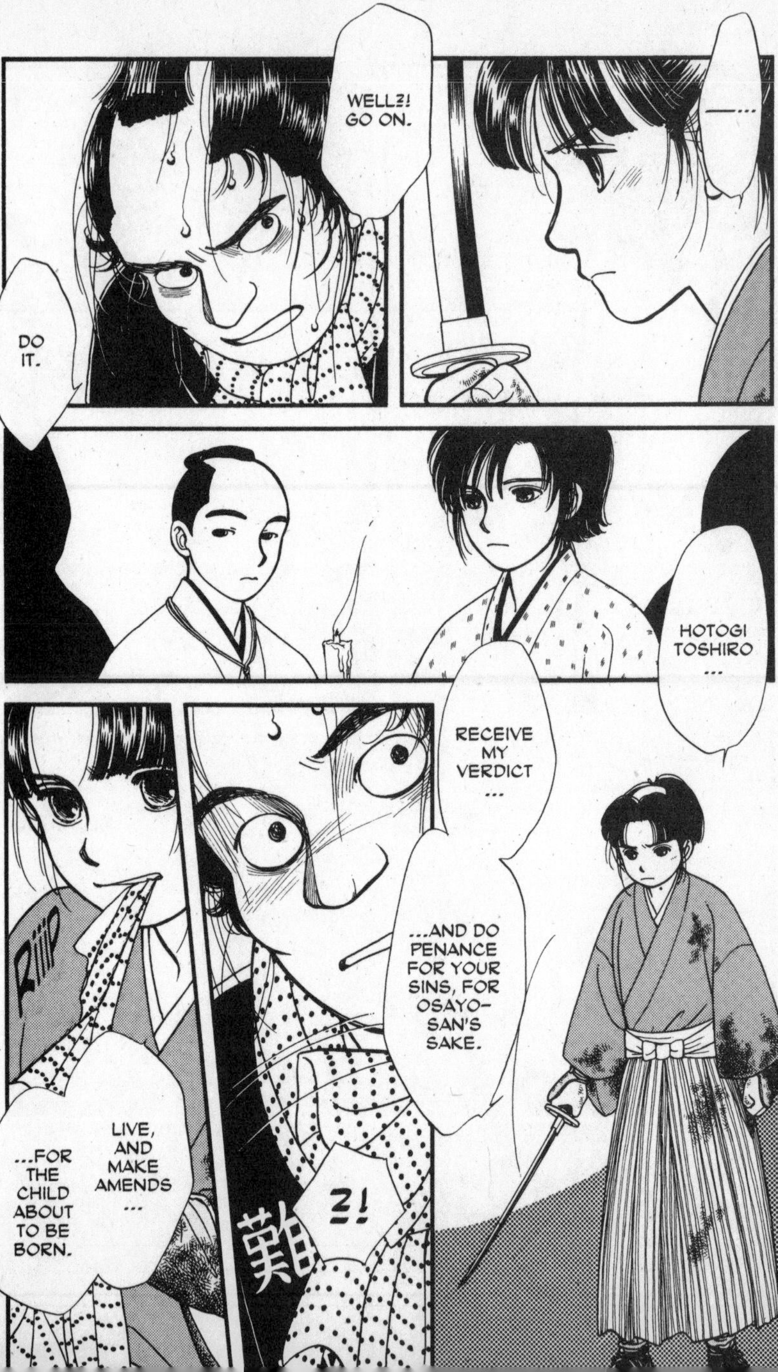
——...
WELL?! GO ON.
DO IT.
HOTOGI TOSHIRO ...
RECEIVE MY VERDICT ...
...AND DO PENANCE FOR YOUR SINS, FOR OSAYO-SAN'S SAKE.
?!
RIIIP
LIVE, AND MAKE AMENDS ...
...FOR THE CHILD ABOUT TO BE BORN.

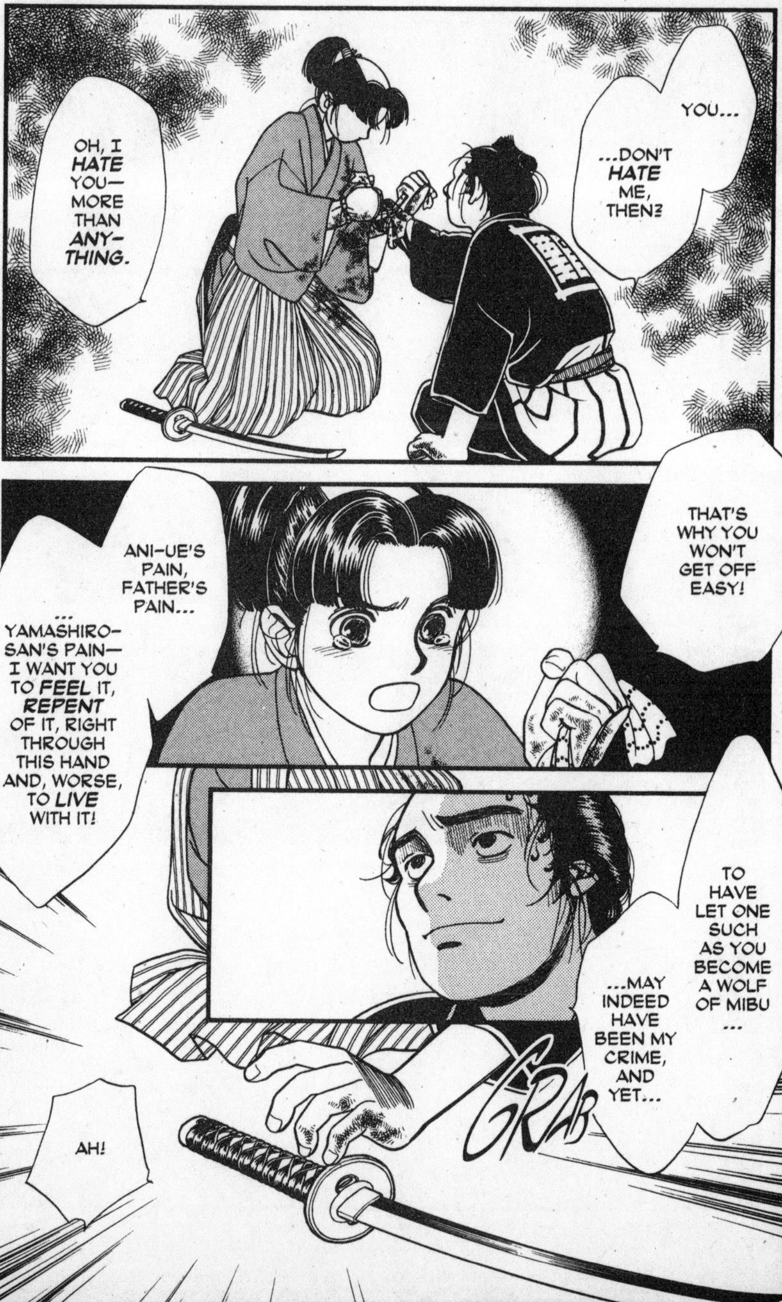
YOU...
...DON'T HATE ME, THEN?
OH, I HATE YOU—MORE THAN ANYTHING.
THAT'S WHY YOU WON'T GET OFF EASY!
ANI-UE'S PAIN, FATHER'S PAIN...
...YAMASHIRO-SAN'S PAIN—I WANT YOU TO FEEL IT, REPENT OF IT, RIGHT THROUGH THIS HAND AND, WORSE, TO LIVE WITH IT!
TO HAVE LET ONE SUCH AS YOU BECOME A WOLF OF MIBU...
...MAY INDEED HAVE BEEN MY CRIME, AND YET...
GRAB
AH!

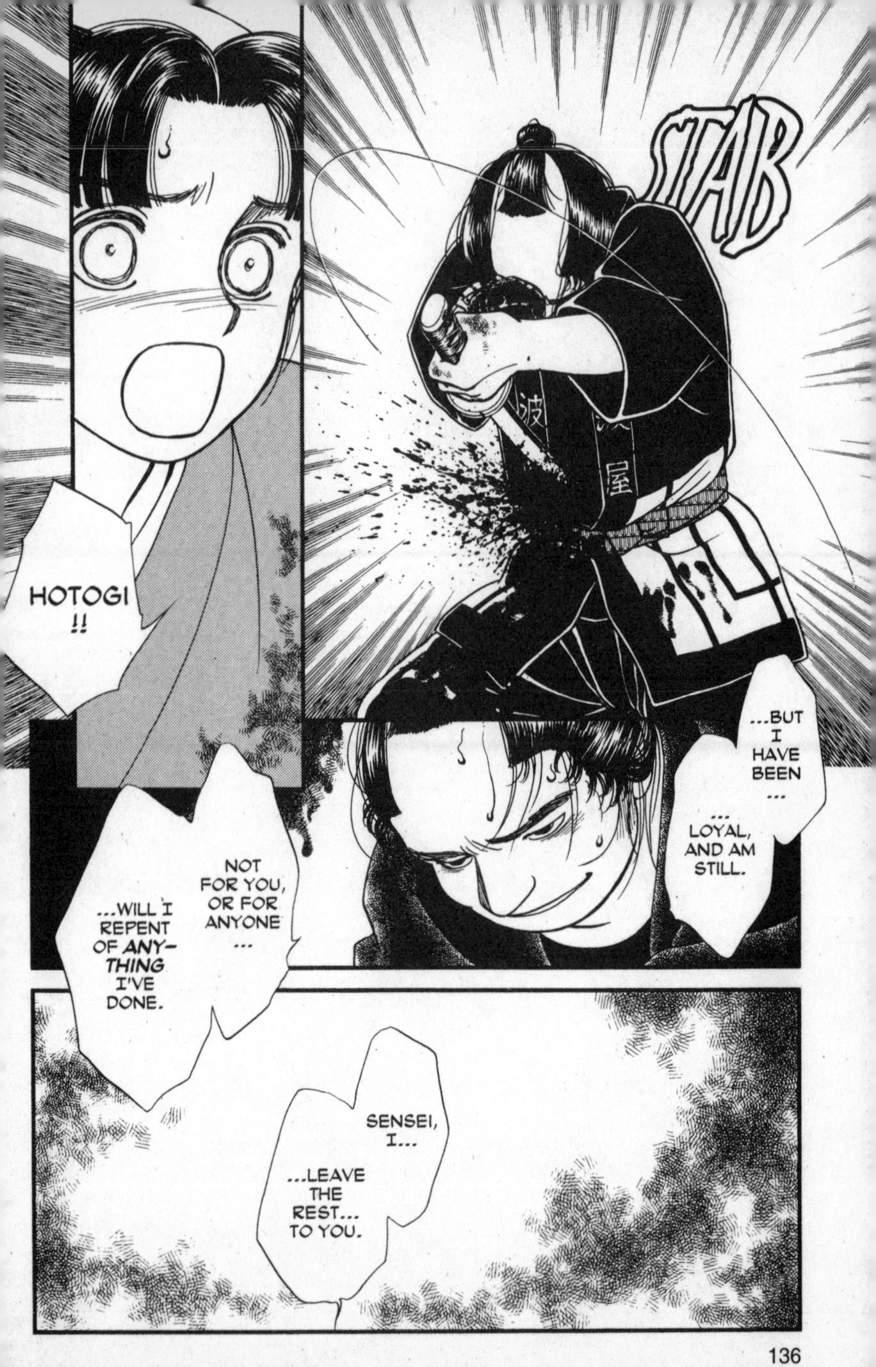
STAB
HOTOGI !!
...BUT I HAVE BEEN...
...LOYAL, AND AM STILL.
NOT FOR YOU, OR FOR ANYONE...
...WILL I REPENT OF ANYTHING I'VE DONE.
SENSEI, I...
...LEAVE THE REST... TO YOU.

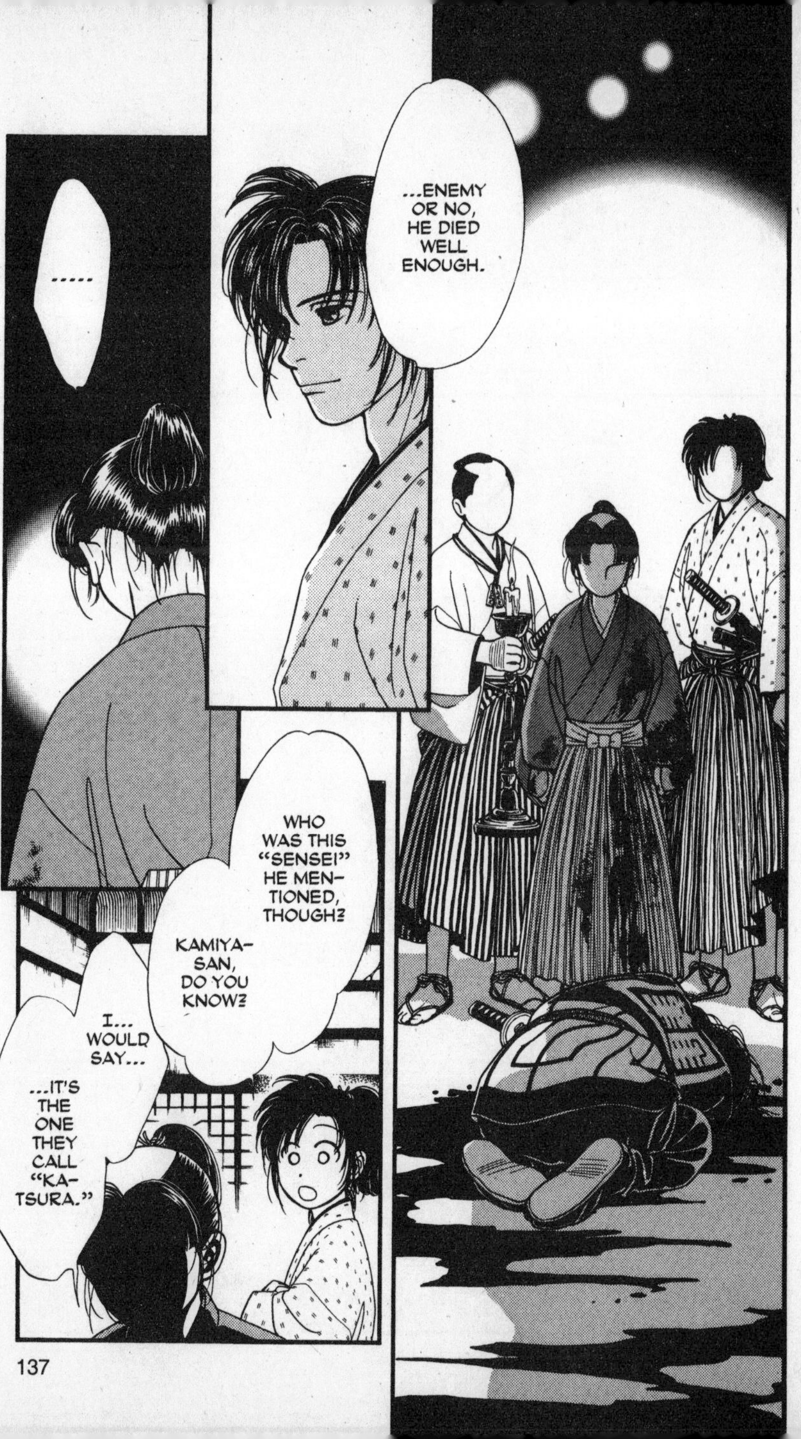
...ENEMY OR NO, HE DIED WELL ENOUGH.
......
WHO WAS THIS "SENSEI" HE MEN-TIONED, THOUGH?
KAMIYA-SAN, DO YOU KNOW?
I... WOULD SAY...
...IT'S THE ONE THEY CALL "KA-TSURA."

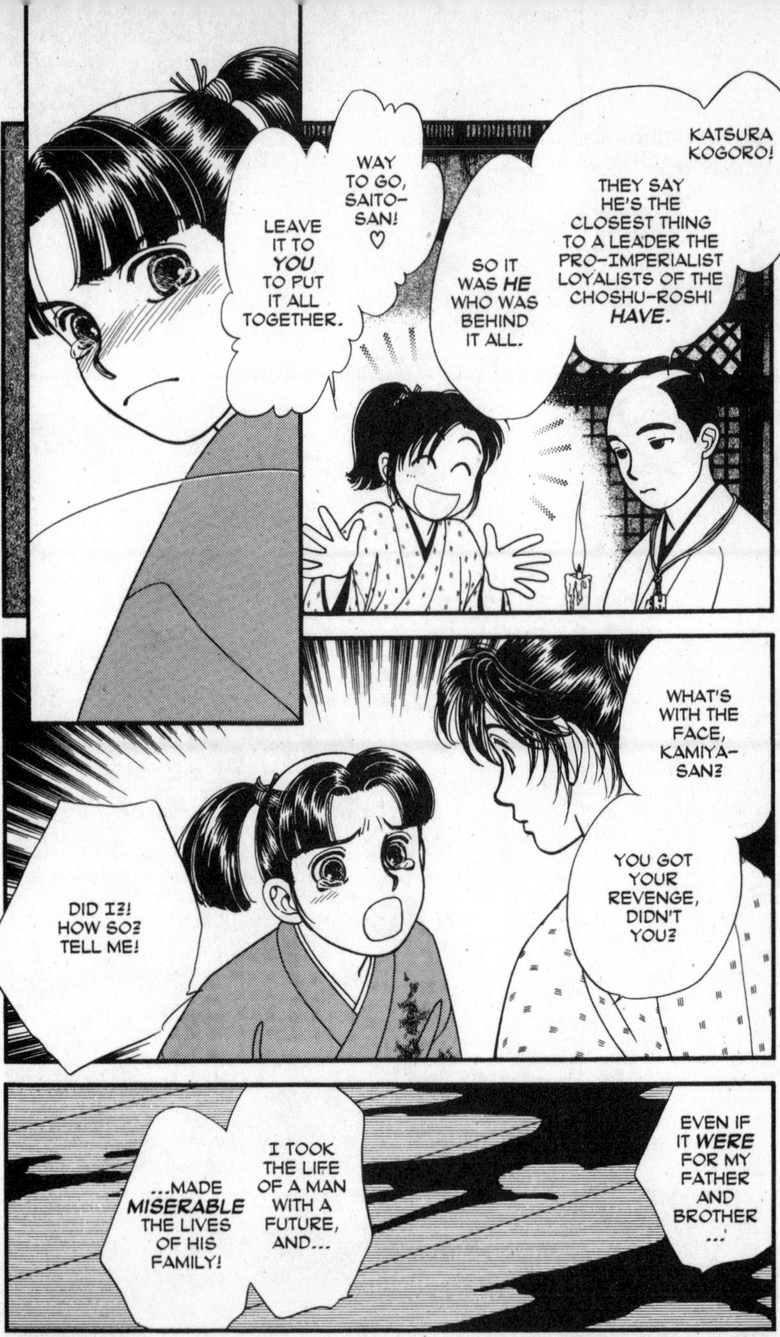
KATSURA KOGORO!
THEY SAY HE'S THE CLOSEST THING TO A LEADER THE PRO-IMPERIALIST LOYALISTS OF THE CHOSHU-ROSHI HAVE.
SO IT WAS HE WHO WAS BEHIND IT ALL.
WAY TO GO, SAITO-SAN! ♡
LEAVE IT TO YOU TO PUT IT ALL TOGETHER.
WHAT'S WITH THE FACE, KAMIYA-SAN?
YOU GOT YOUR REVENGE, DIDN'T YOU?
DID I?! HOW SO? TELL ME!
EVEN IF IT WERE FOR MY FATHER AND BROTHER...
I TOOK THE LIFE OF A MAN WITH A FUTURE, AND...
...MADE MISERABLE THE LIVES OF HIS FAMILY!

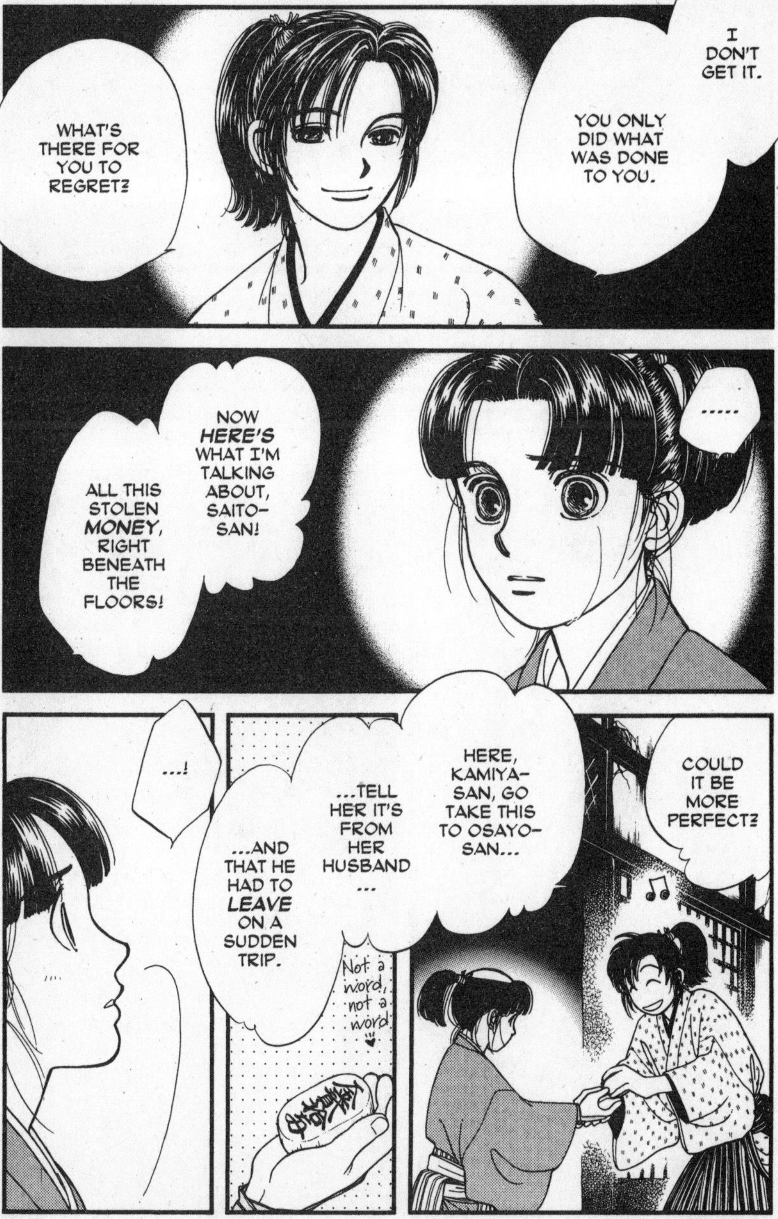
I DON'T GET IT.
YOU ONLY DID WHAT WAS DONE TO YOU.
WHAT'S THERE FOR YOU TO REGRET?
.....
NOW *HERE'S* WHAT I'M TALKING ABOUT, SAITO-SAN!
ALL THIS STOLEN *MONEY*, RIGHT BENEATH THE FLOORS!
COULD IT BE MORE PERFECT?
HERE, KAMIYA-SAN, GO TAKE THIS TO OSAYO-SAN...
...TELL HER IT'S FROM HER HUSBAND...
...AND THAT HE HAD TO *LEAVE* ON A SUDDEN TRIP.
Not a word, not a word
...!

BUT OKITA-SENSEI, HOW CAN YOU *LAUGH?*

HOW *CAN* YOU, KNOWING HOW BADLY POOR OSAYO-SAN IS GOING TO BE HURT?!

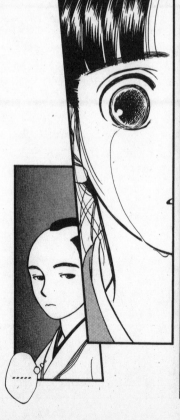

.....

I...

...AM BUSHI, *THAT'S* WHY.

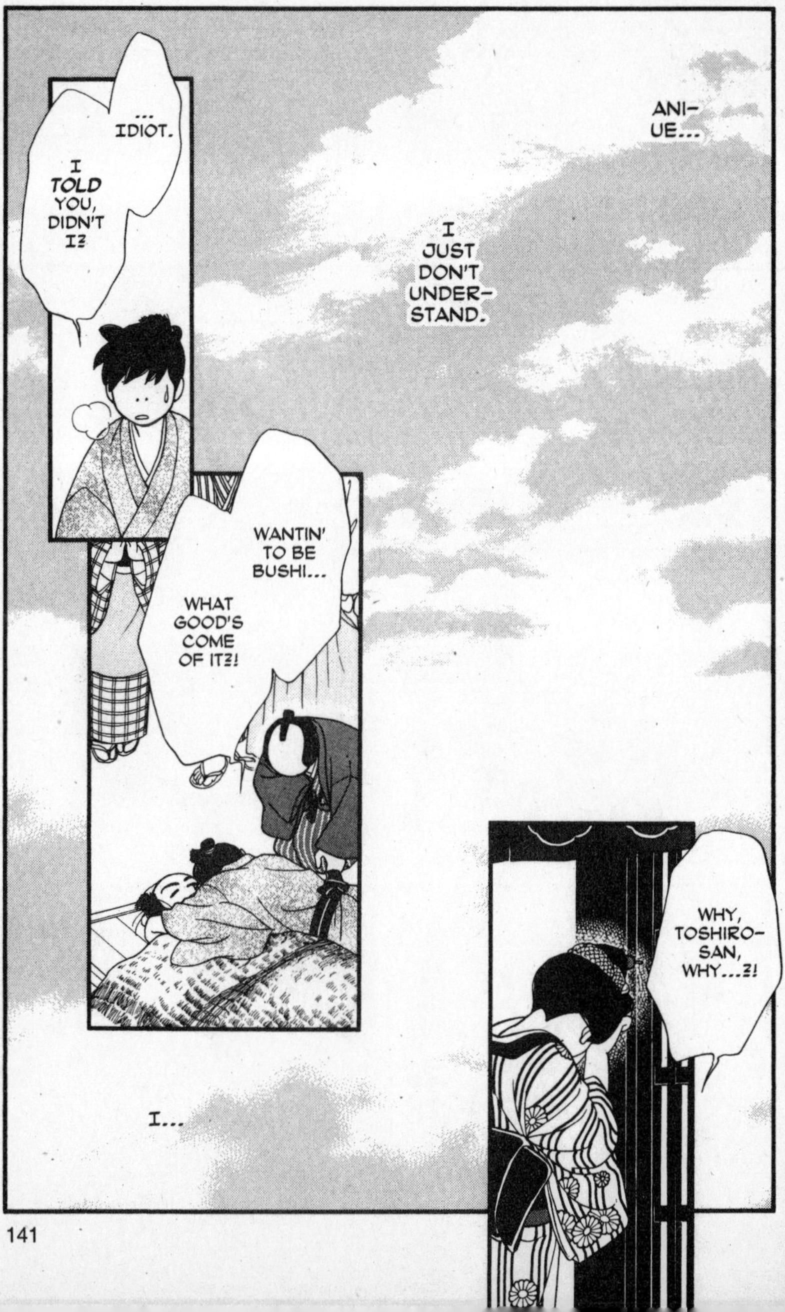
ANI-UE...
I JUST DON'T UNDERSTAND.
...IDIOT.
I *TOLD* YOU, DIDN'T I?
WANTIN' TO BE BUSHI...
WHAT GOOD'S COME OF IT?!
WHY, TOSHIRO-SAN, WHY...?!
I...

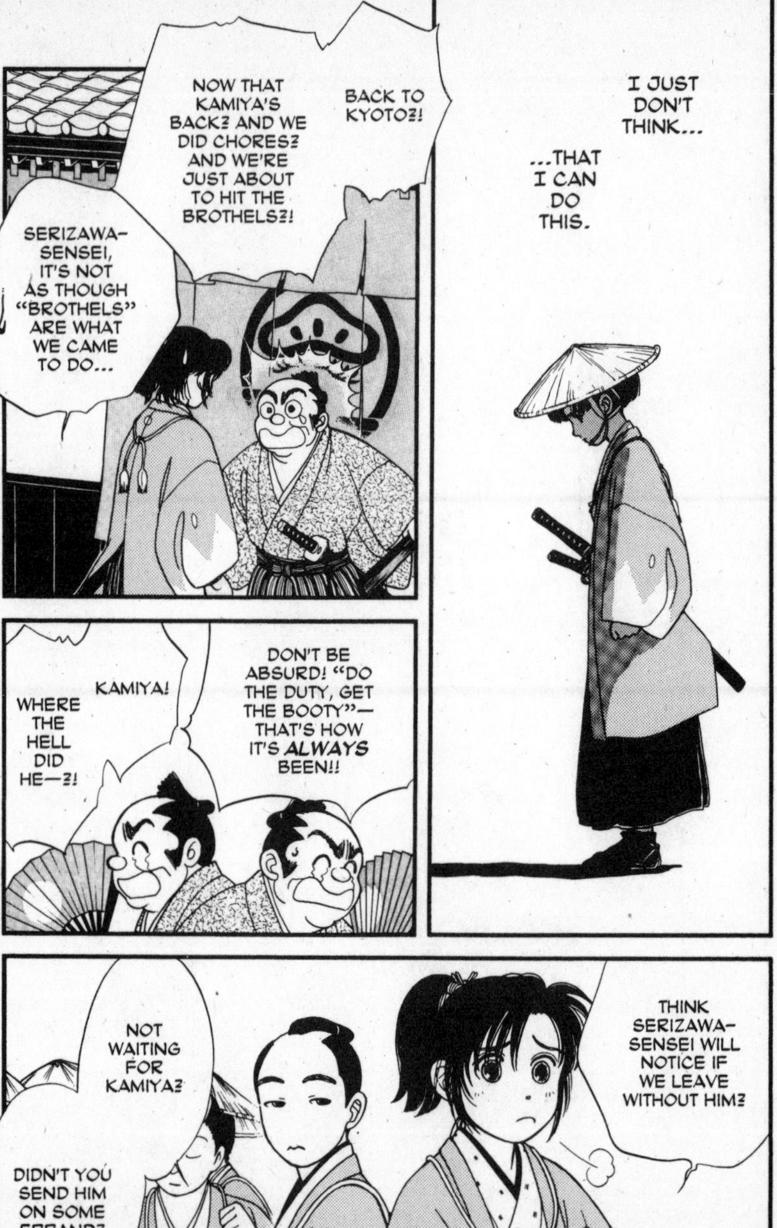
I JUST DON'T THINK...
...THAT I CAN DO THIS.
BACK TO KYOTO?!
NOW THAT KAMIYA'S BACK? AND WE DID CHORES? AND WE'RE JUST ABOUT TO HIT THE BROTHELS?!
SERIZAWA-SENSEI, IT'S NOT AS THOUGH "BROTHELS" ARE WHAT WE CAME TO DO...
DON'T BE ABSURD! "DO THE DUTY, GET THE BOOTY"—THAT'S HOW IT'S *ALWAYS* BEEN!!
KAMIYA!
WHERE THE HELL DID HE—?!
THINK SERIZAWA-SENSEI WILL NOTICE IF WE LEAVE WITHOUT HIM?
NOT WAITING FOR KAMIYA?
DIDN'T YOU SEND HIM ON SOME ERRAND?

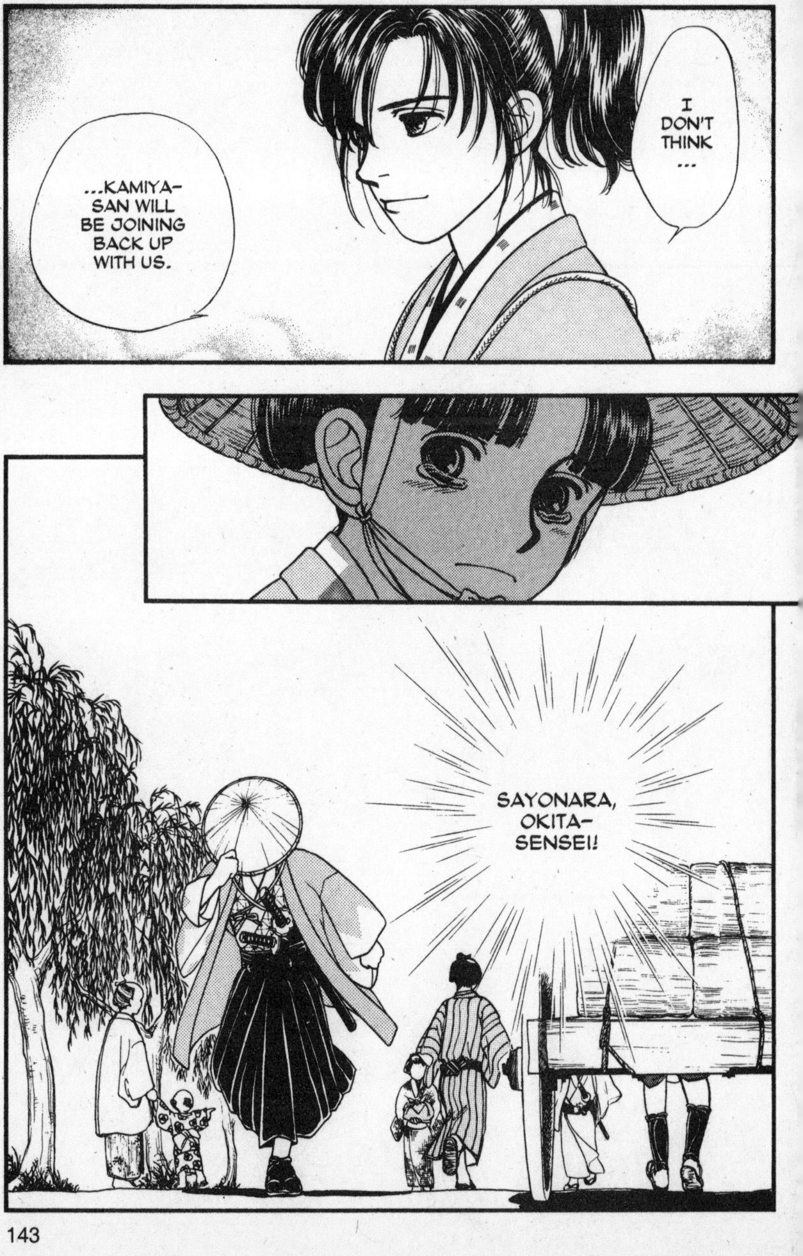
I DON'T THINK ...
...KAMIYA-SAN WILL BE JOINING BACK UP WITH US.
SAYONARA, OKITA-SENSEI!

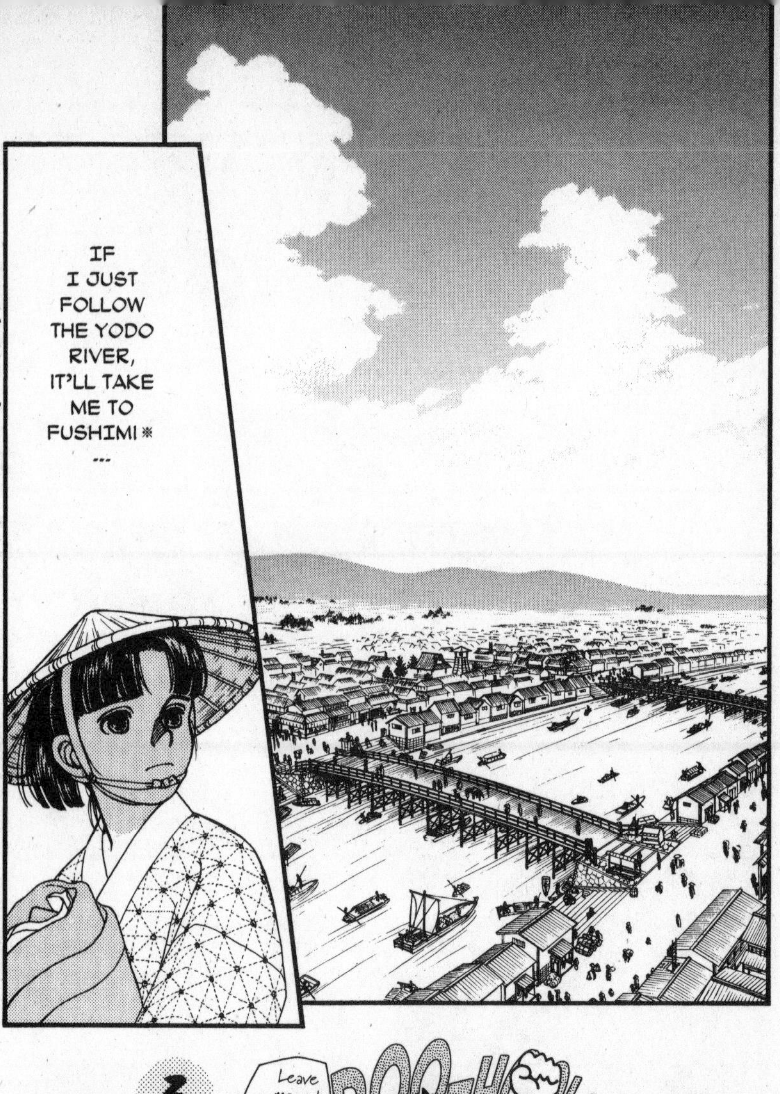
IF I JUST FOLLOW THE YODO RIVER, IT'LL TAKE ME TO FUSHIMI※ ...

※Kyoto's *Fushimi* (on the Yodo River) and Osaka's *Hakkenya* are both major shipping ports.

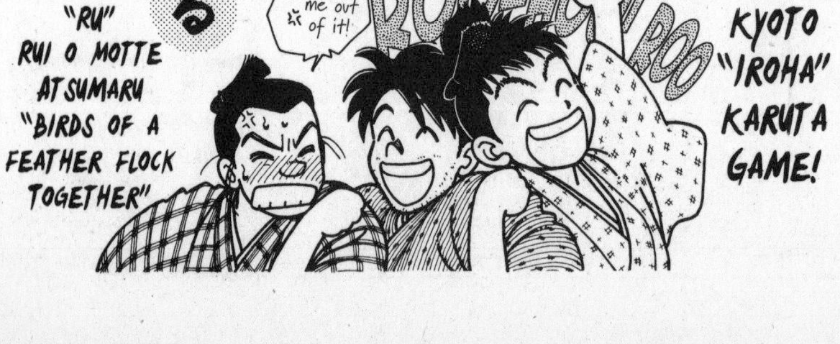
KYOTO "IROHA" KARUTA GAME!
Leave me out of it!
る
"RU"
RUI O MOTTE ATSUMARU
"BIRDS OF A FEATHER FLOCK TOGETHER"

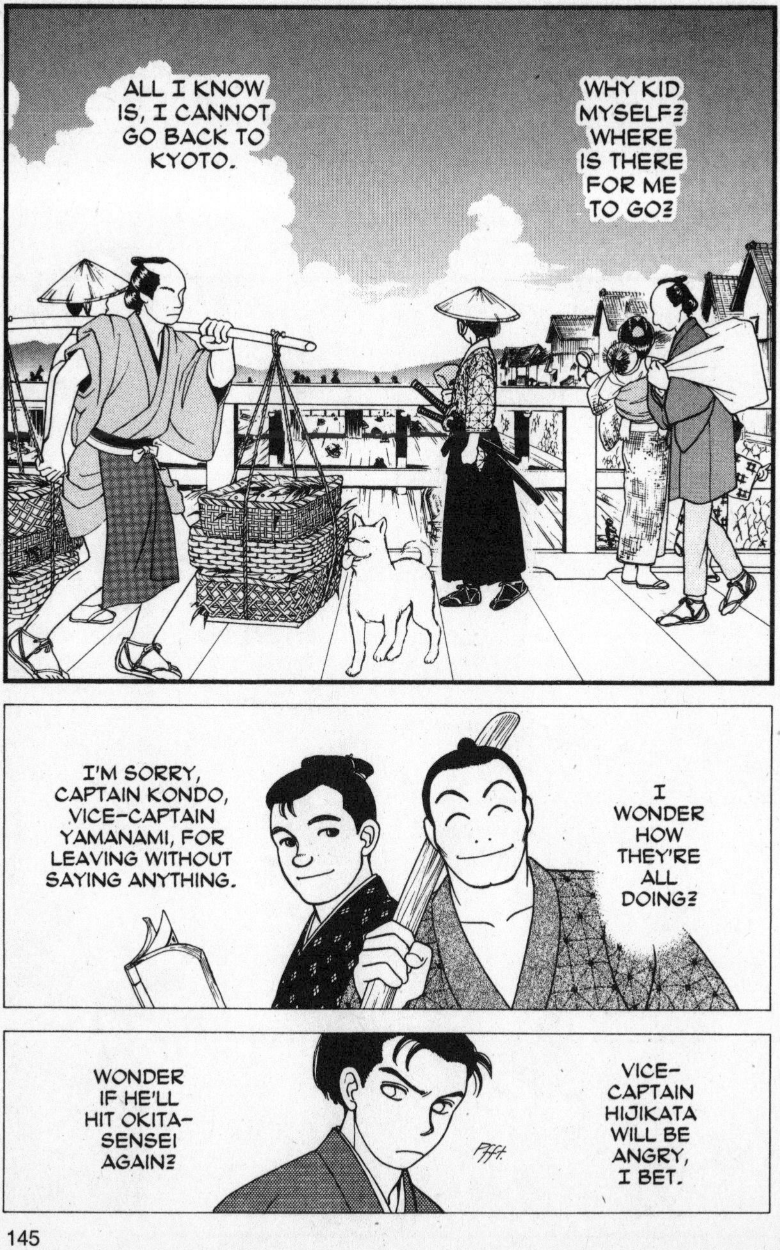
WHY KID MYSELF? WHERE IS THERE FOR ME TO GO?
ALL I KNOW IS, I CANNOT GO BACK TO KYOTO.
I WONDER HOW THEY'RE ALL DOING?
I'M SORRY, CAPTAIN KONDO, VICE-CAPTAIN YAMANAMI, FOR LEAVING WITHOUT SAYING ANYTHING.
VICE-CAPTAIN HIJIKATA WILL BE ANGRY, I BET.
PFFT
WONDER IF HE'LL HIT OKITA-SENSEI AGAIN?

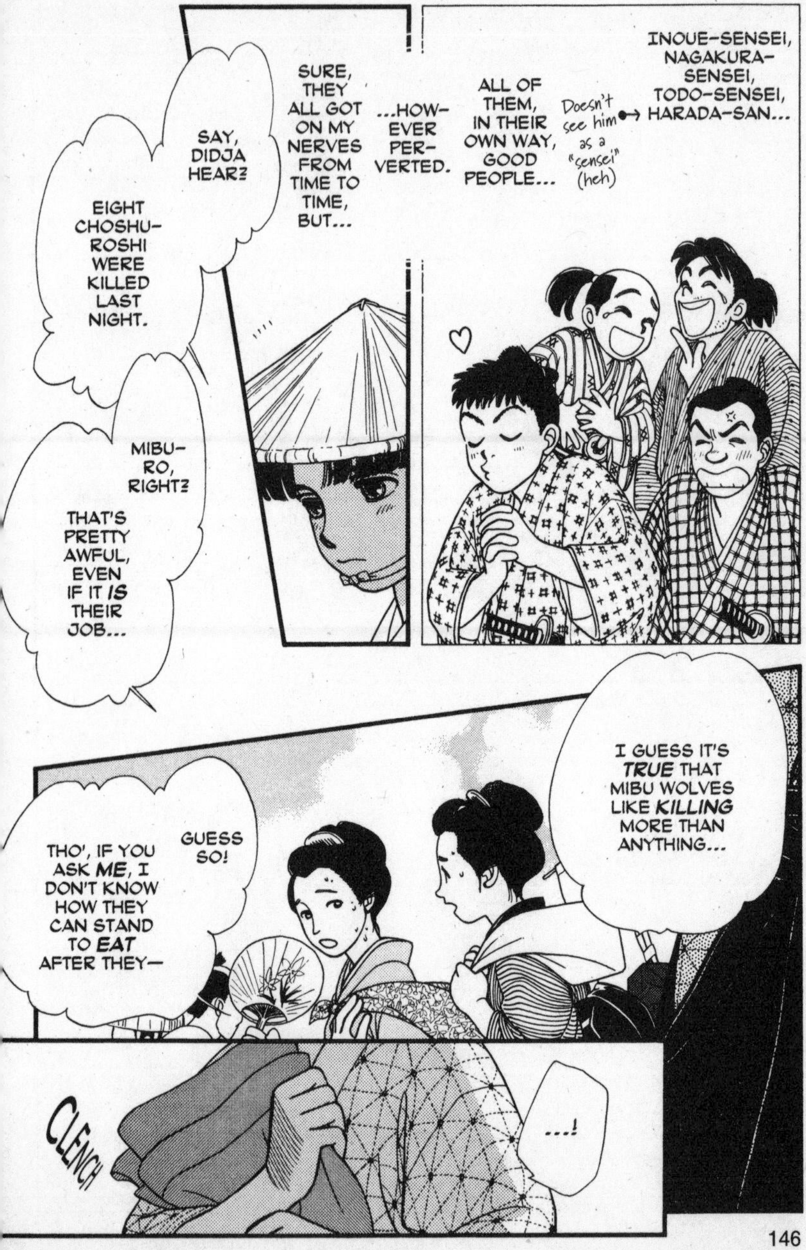
INOUE-SENSEI, NAGAKURA-SENSEI, TODO-SENSEI, HARADA-SAN...
Doesn't see him as a "sensei" (heh)
ALL OF THEM, IN THEIR OWN WAY, GOOD PEOPLE...
...HOWEVER PERVERTED.
SURE, THEY ALL GOT ON MY NERVES FROM TIME TO TIME, BUT...
SAY, DIDJA HEAR?
EIGHT CHOSHU-ROSHI WERE KILLED LAST NIGHT.
MIBURO, RIGHT?
THAT'S PRETTY AWFUL, EVEN IF IT *IS* THEIR JOB...
I GUESS IT'S *TRUE* THAT MIBU WOLVES LIKE *KILLING* MORE THAN ANYTHING...
GUESS SO!
THO', IF YOU ASK *ME*, I DON'T KNOW HOW THEY CAN STAND TO *EAT* AFTER THEY—
...!
CLENCH

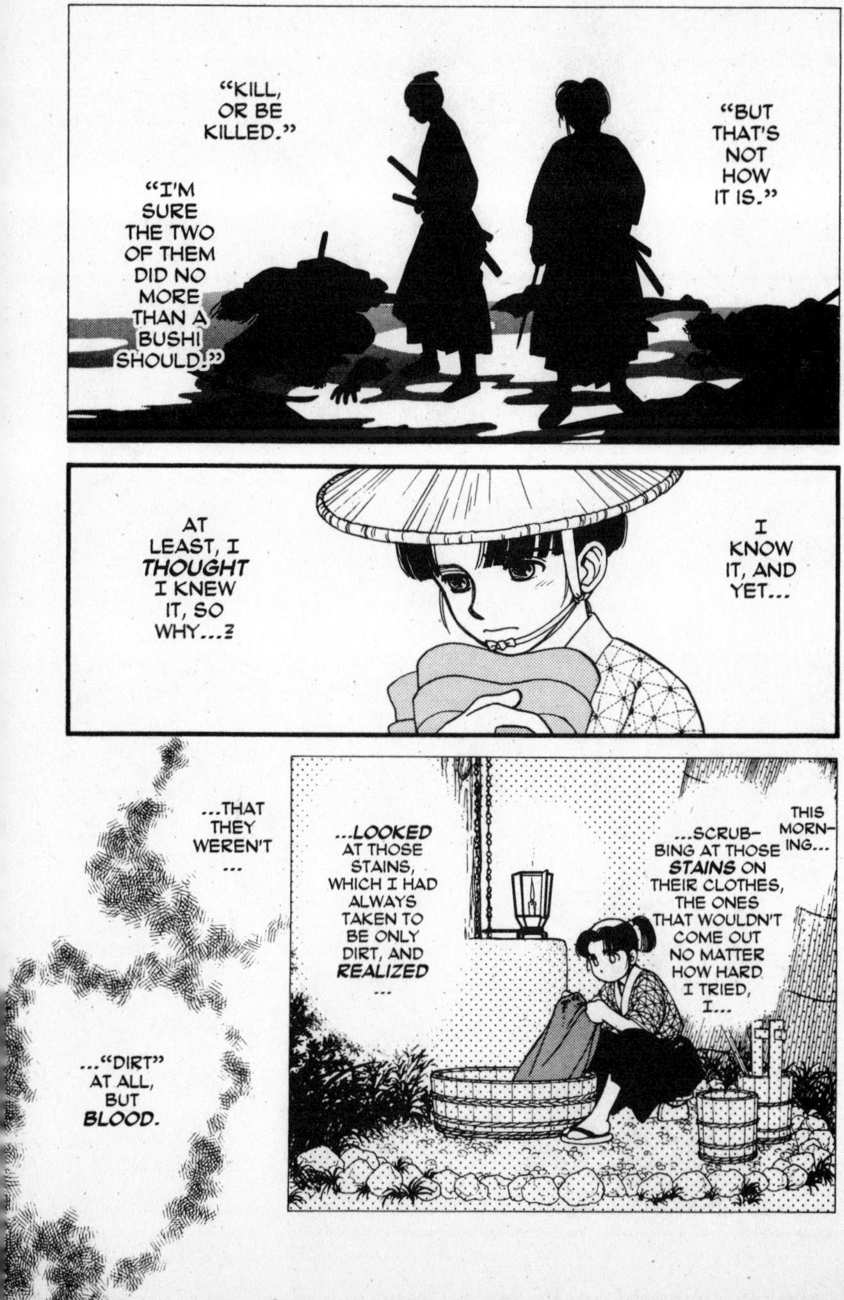
"BUT THAT'S NOT HOW IT IS."
"KILL, OR BE KILLED."
"I'M SURE THE TWO OF THEM DID NO MORE THAN A BUSHI SHOULD."
I KNOW IT, AND YET...
AT LEAST, I *THOUGHT* I KNEW IT, SO WHY...?
THIS MORNING...
...SCRUBBING AT THOSE *STAINS* ON THEIR CLOTHES, THE ONES THAT WOULDN'T COME OUT NO MATTER HOW HARD I TRIED, I...
...*LOOKED* AT THOSE STAINS, WHICH I HAD ALWAYS TAKEN TO BE ONLY DIRT, AND *REALIZED*...
...THAT THEY WEREN'T...
..."DIRT" AT ALL, BUT *BLOOD*.

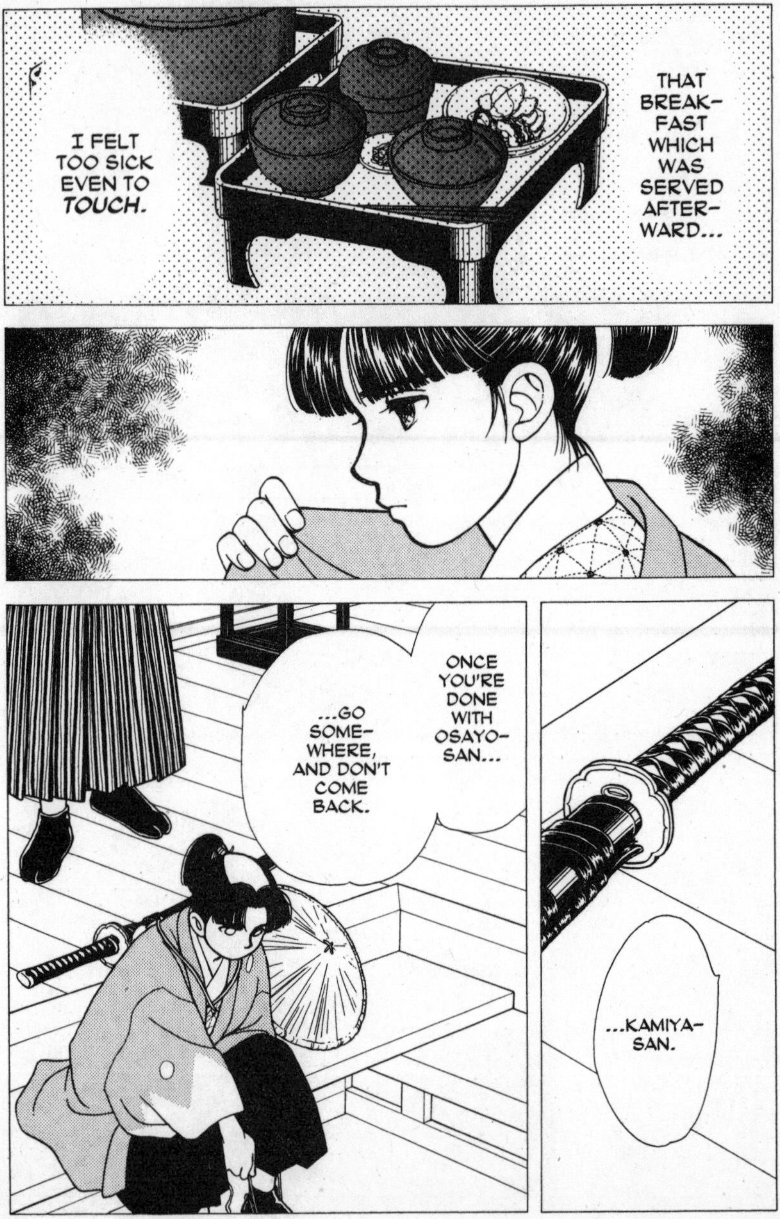
THAT BREAK-FAST WHICH WAS SERVED AFTER-WARD...
I FELT TOO SICK EVEN TO *TOUCH*.
...KAMIYA-SAN.
ONCE YOU'RE DONE WITH OSAYO-SAN...
...GO SOME-WHERE, AND DON'T COME BACK.

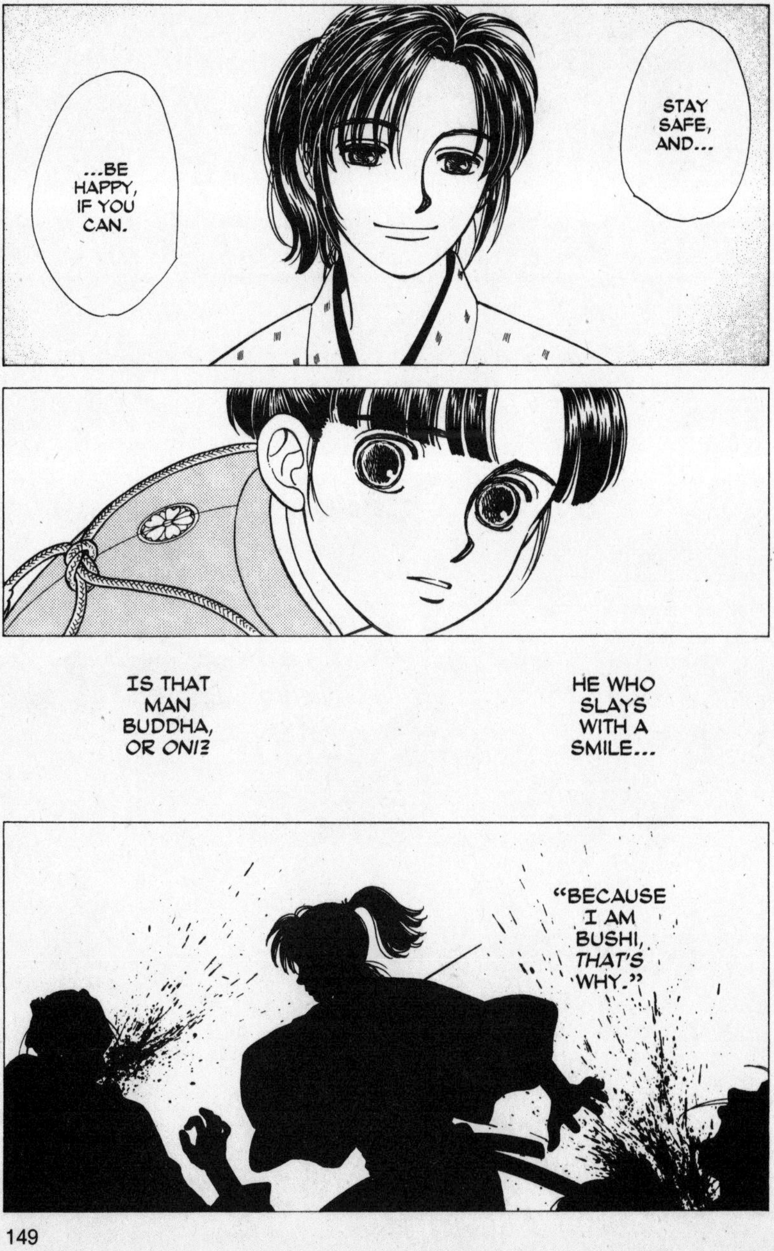
STAY SAFE, AND...
...BE HAPPY, IF YOU CAN.
HE WHO SLAYS WITH A SMILE...
IS THAT MAN BUDDHA, OR *ONI*?
"BECAUSE I AM BUSHI, *THAT'S* WHY."

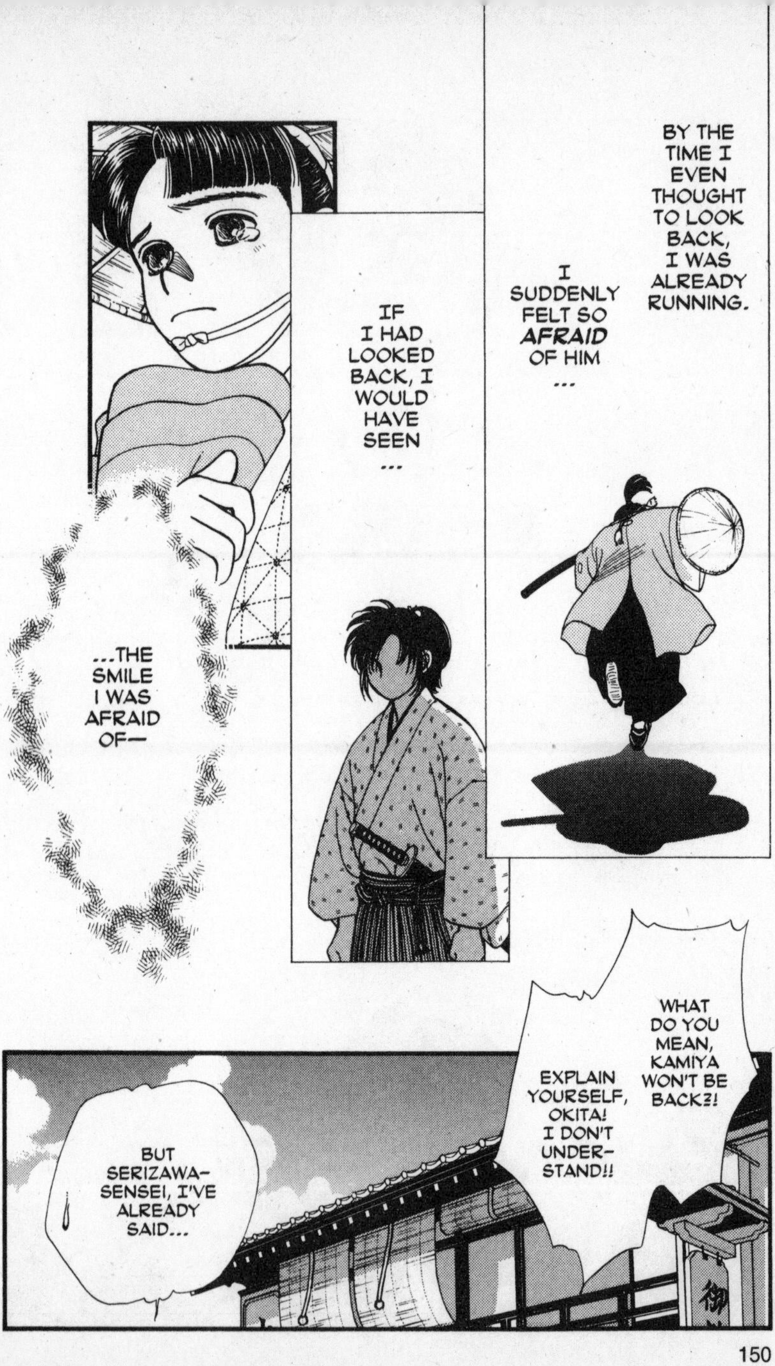
BY THE TIME I EVEN THOUGHT TO LOOK BACK, I WAS ALREADY RUNNING.
I SUDDENLY FELT SO AFRAID OF HIM...
IF I HAD LOOKED BACK, I WOULD HAVE SEEN...
...THE SMILE I WAS AFRAID OF—
WHAT DO YOU MEAN, KAMIYA WON'T BE BACK?!
EXPLAIN YOURSELF, OKITA! I DON'T UNDERSTAND!!
BUT SERIZAWA-SENSEI, I'VE ALREADY SAID...

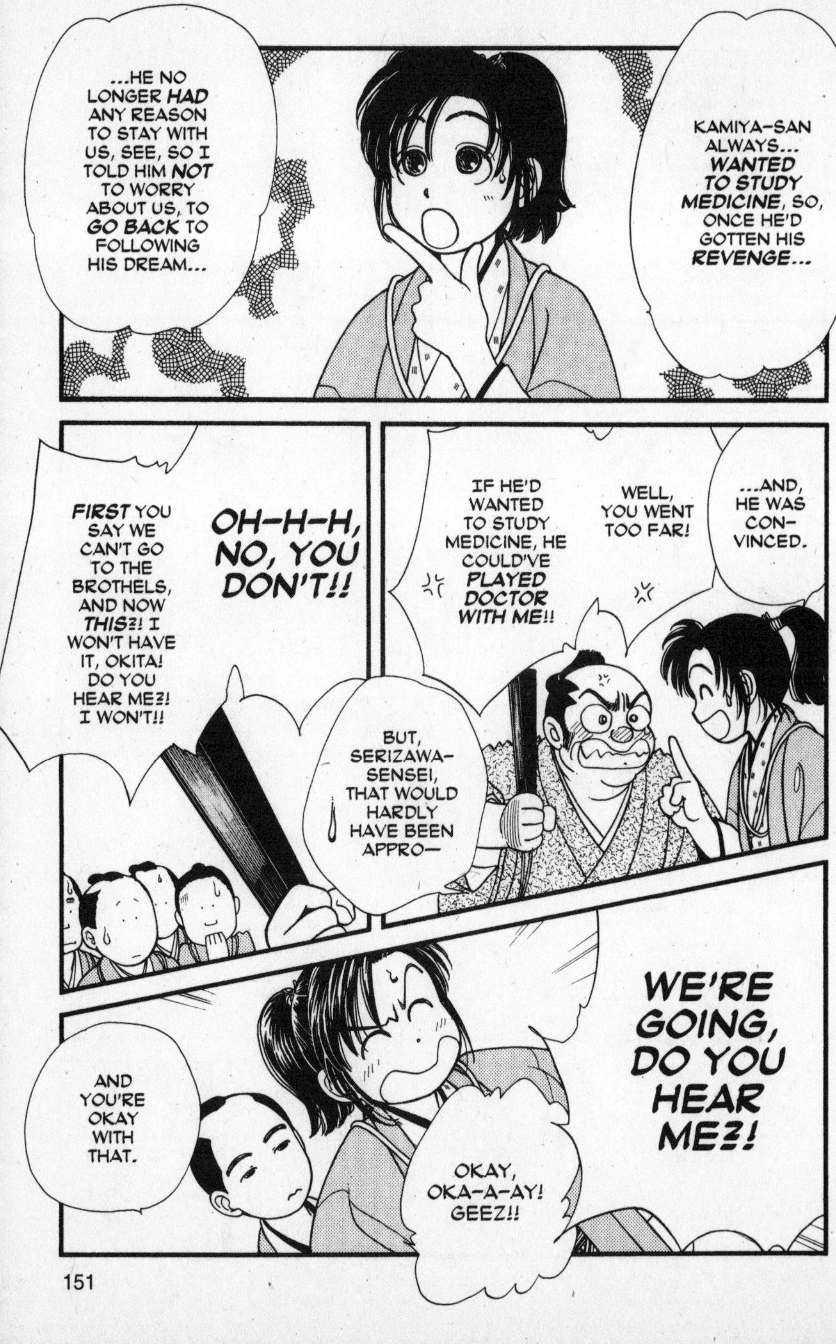
KAMIYA-SAN ALWAYS... WANTED TO STUDY MEDICINE, SO, ONCE HE'D GOTTEN HIS REVENGE...
...HE NO LONGER HAD ANY REASON TO STAY WITH US, SEE, SO I TOLD HIM NOT TO WORRY ABOUT US, TO GO BACK TO FOLLOWING HIS DREAM...
...AND, HE WAS CON-VINCED.
WELL, YOU WENT TOO FAR!
IF HE'D WANTED TO STUDY MEDICINE, HE COULD'VE PLAYED DOCTOR WITH ME!!
BUT, SERIZAWA-SENSEI, THAT WOULD HARDLY HAVE BEEN APPRO—
OH-H-H, NO, YOU DON'T!!
FIRST YOU SAY WE CAN'T GO TO THE BROTHELS, AND NOW THIS?! I WON'T HAVE IT, OKITA! DO YOU HEAR ME?! I WON'T!!
WE'RE GOING, DO YOU HEAR ME?!
OKAY, OKA-A-AY! GEEZ!!
AND YOU'RE OKAY WITH THAT.

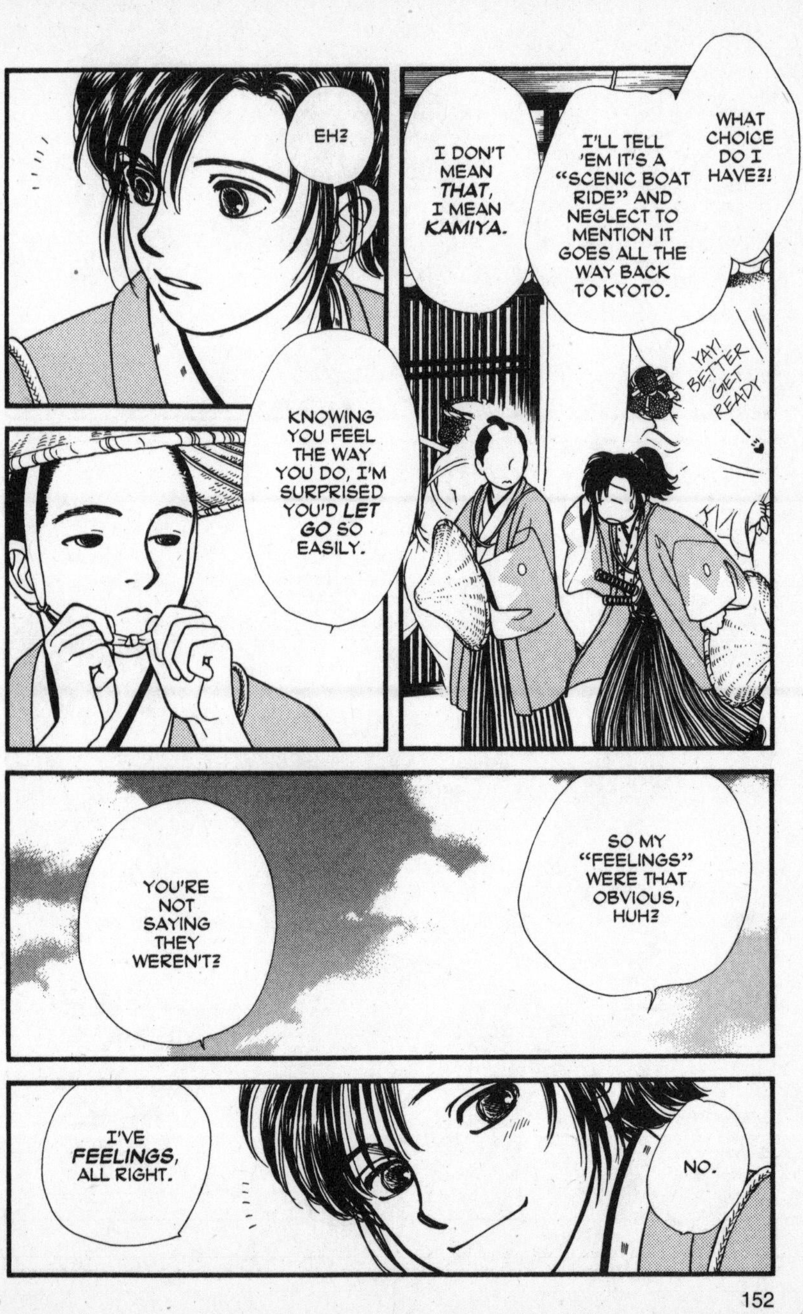

WHAT CHOICE DO I HAVE?!
I'LL TELL 'EM IT'S A "SCENIC BOAT RIDE" AND NEGLECT TO MENTION IT GOES ALL THE WAY BACK TO KYOTO.
YAY! BETTER GET READY
I DON'T MEAN *THAT*, I MEAN *KAMIYA*.
EH?
KNOWING YOU FEEL THE WAY YOU DO, I'M SURPRISED YOU'D *LET GO* SO EASILY.
SO MY "FEELINGS" WERE THAT OBVIOUS, HUH?
YOU'RE NOT SAYING THEY WEREN'T?
NO.
I'VE *FEELINGS*, ALL RIGHT.

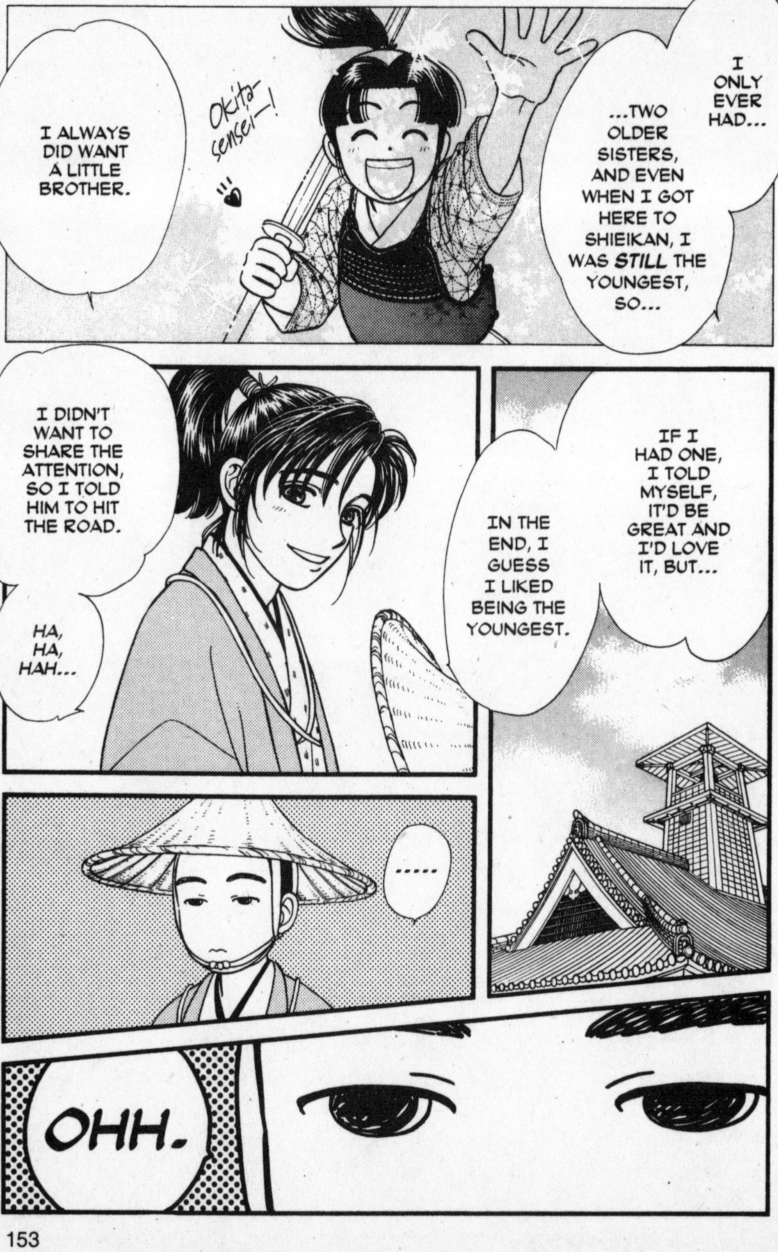
I ONLY EVER HAD...
...TWO OLDER SISTERS, AND EVEN WHEN I GOT HERE TO SHIEIKAN, I WAS STILL THE YOUNGEST, SO...
Okita-sensei—!
I ALWAYS DID WANT A LITTLE BROTHER.
IF I HAD ONE, I TOLD MYSELF, IT'D BE GREAT AND I'D LOVE IT, BUT...
IN THE END, I GUESS I LIKED BEING THE YOUNGEST.
I DIDN'T WANT TO SHARE THE ATTENTION, SO I TOLD HIM TO HIT THE ROAD.
HA, HA, HAH...
......
OHH.

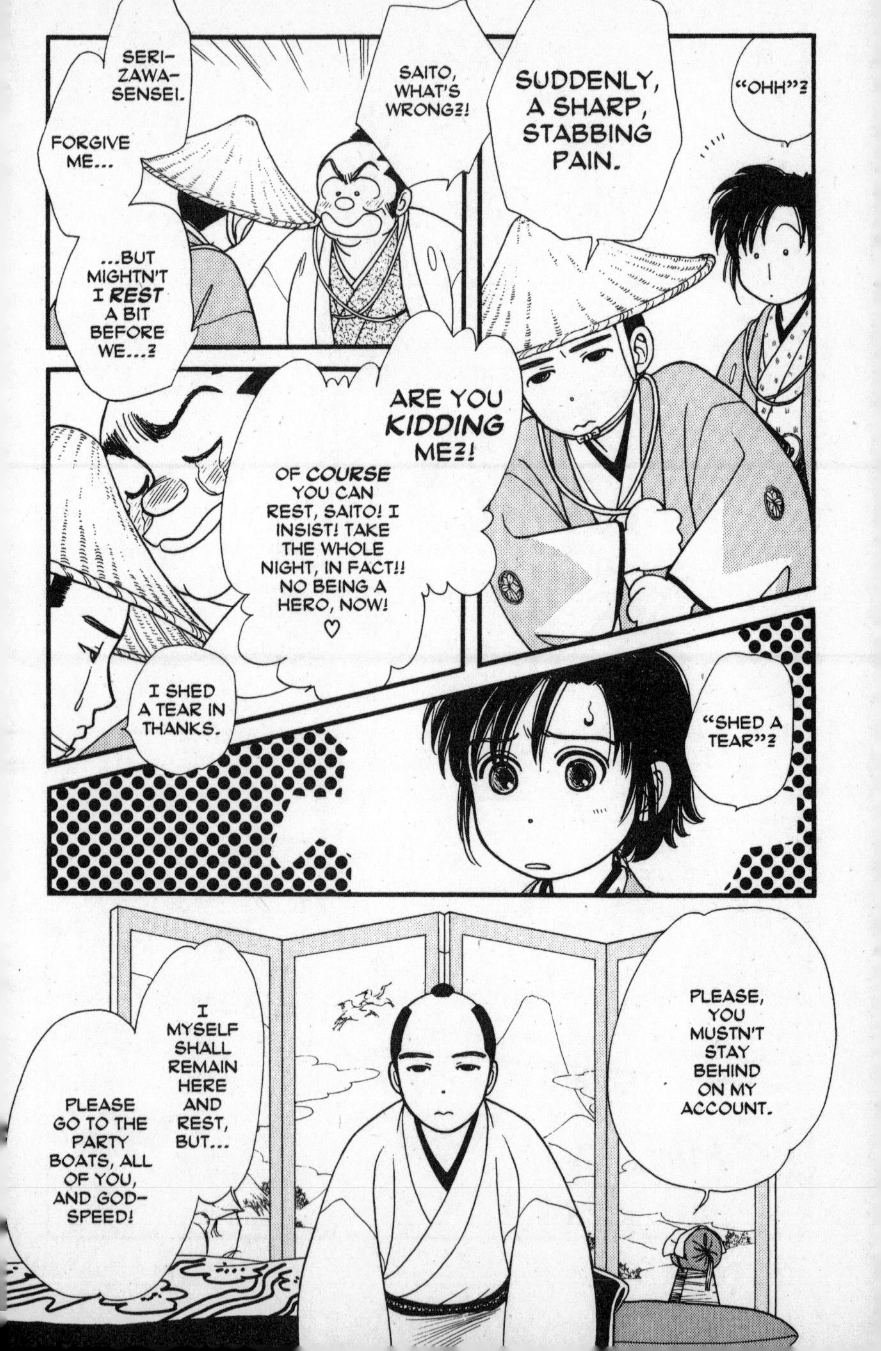
SERI-ZAWA-SENSEI.
FORGIVE ME...
...BUT MIGHTN'T I *REST* A BIT BEFORE WE...?
SAITO, WHAT'S WRONG?!
SUDDENLY, A SHARP, STABBING PAIN.
"OHH"?
ARE YOU *KIDDING* ME?!
OF *COURSE* YOU CAN REST, SAITO! I INSIST! TAKE THE WHOLE NIGHT, IN FACT!! NO BEING A HERO, NOW! ♡
I SHED A TEAR IN THANKS.
"SHED A TEAR"?
PLEASE, YOU MUSTN'T STAY BEHIND ON MY ACCOUNT.
I MYSELF SHALL REMAIN HERE AND REST, BUT...
PLEASE GO TO THE PARTY BOATS, ALL OF YOU, AND GOD-SPEED!

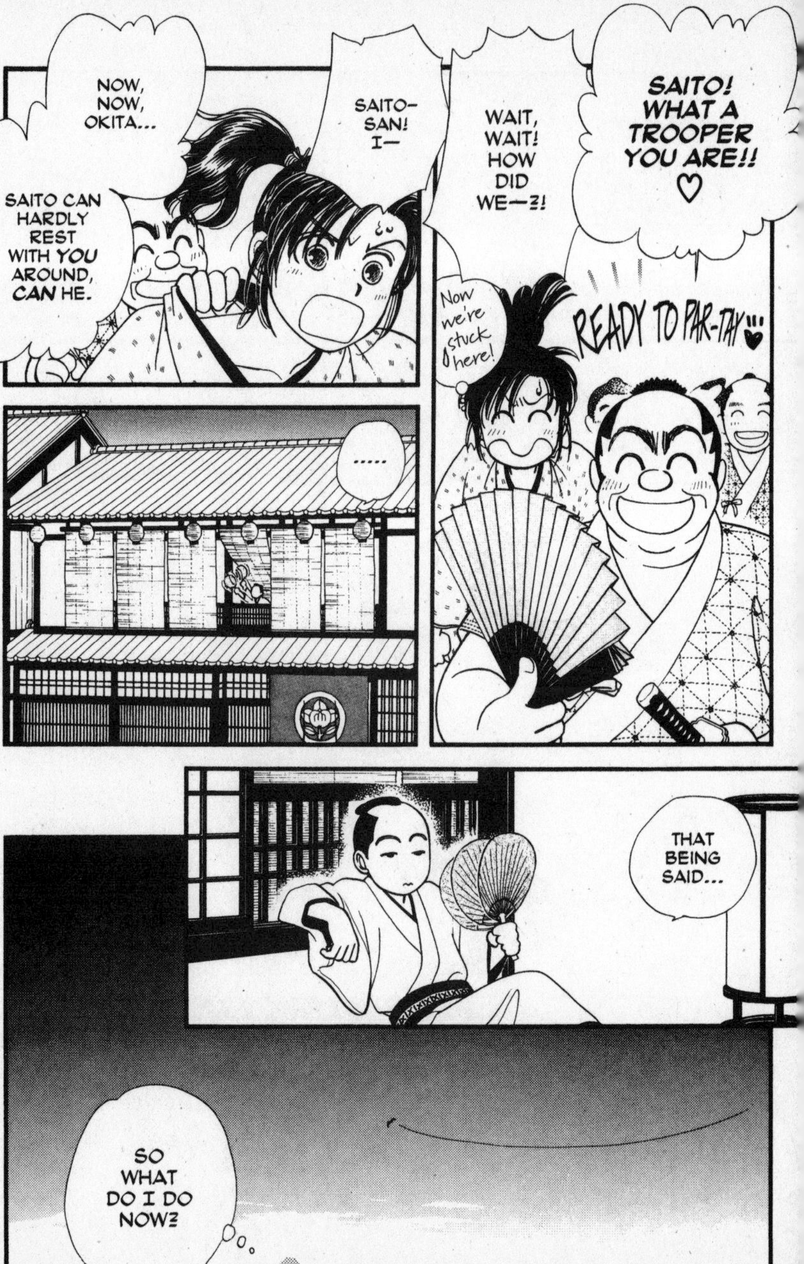
SAITO! WHAT A TROOPER YOU ARE!! ♡
WAIT, WAIT! HOW DID WE—?!
READY TO PAR-TAY!!♥
Now we're stuck here!
SAITO-SAN! I—
NOW, NOW, OKITA...
SAITO CAN HARDLY REST WITH **YOU** AROUND, **CAN** HE.
......
THAT BEING SAID...
SO WHAT DO I DO NOW?

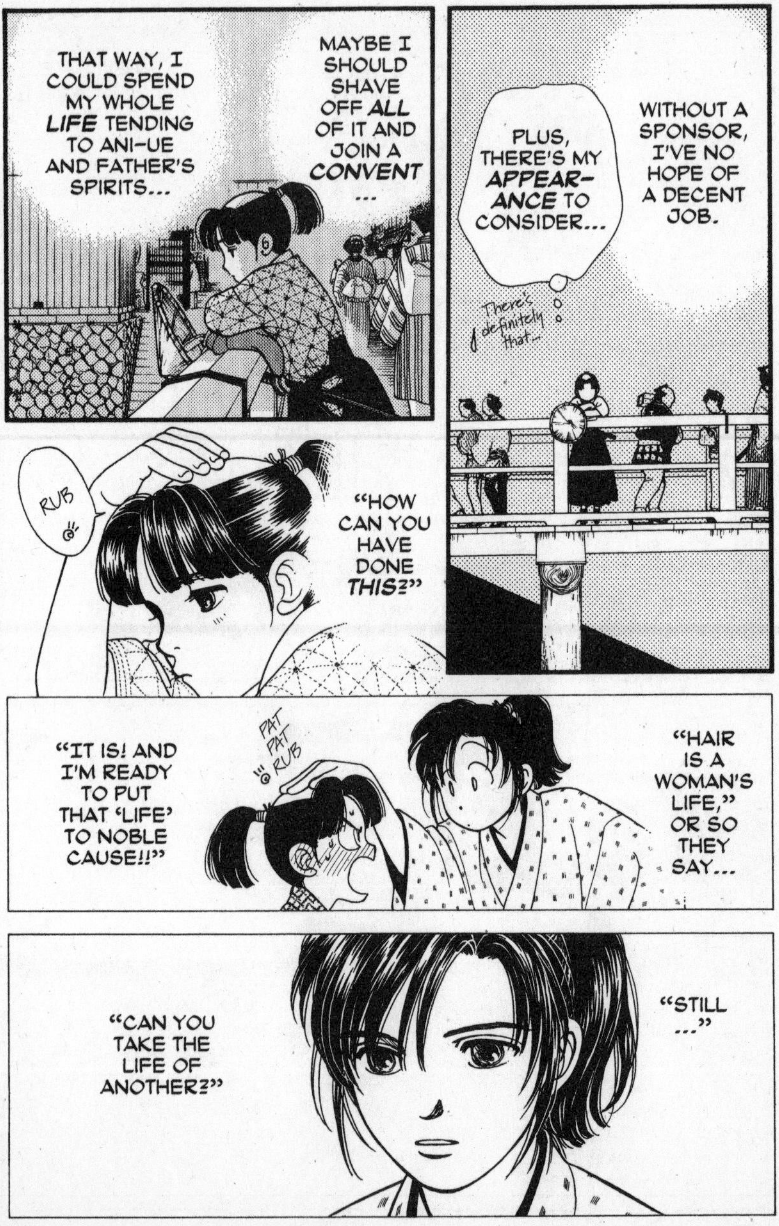
WITHOUT A SPONSOR, I'VE NO HOPE OF A DECENT JOB.
PLUS, THERE'S MY APPEARANCE TO CONSIDER...
There's definitely that...
MAYBE I SHOULD SHAVE OFF ALL OF IT AND JOIN A CONVENT...
THAT WAY, I COULD SPEND MY WHOLE LIFE TENDING TO ANI-UE AND FATHER'S SPIRITS...
"HOW CAN YOU HAVE DONE THIS?"
RUB
"HAIR IS A WOMAN'S LIFE," OR SO THEY SAY...
PAT PAT RUB
"IT IS! AND I'M READY TO PUT THAT 'LIFE' TO NOBLE CAUSE!!"
"STILL..."
"CAN YOU TAKE THE LIFE OF ANOTHER?"

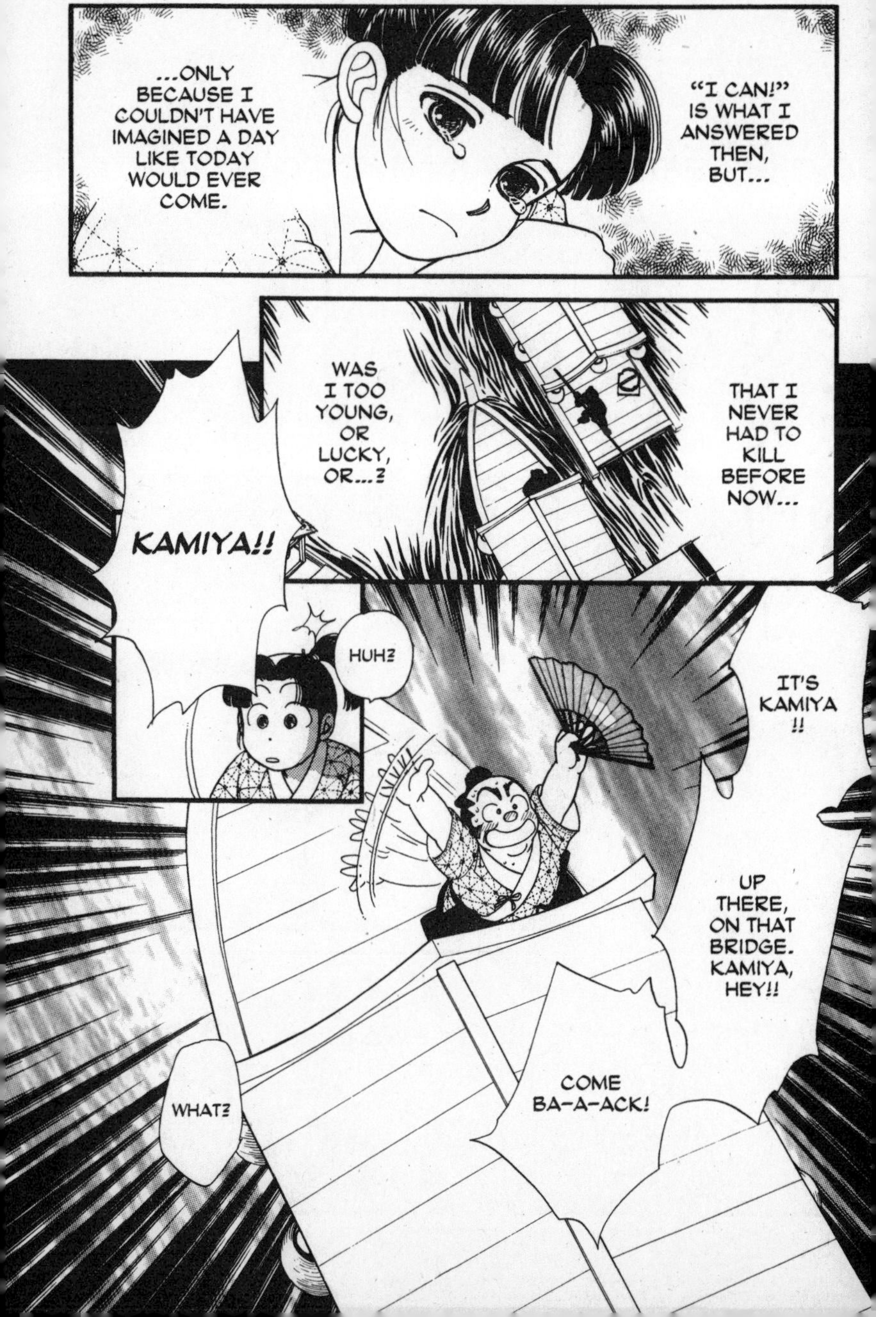
"I CAN!" IS WHAT I ANSWERED THEN, BUT...
...ONLY BECAUSE I COULDN'T HAVE IMAGINED A DAY LIKE TODAY WOULD EVER COME.
THAT I NEVER HAD TO KILL BEFORE NOW...
WAS I TOO YOUNG, OR LUCKY, OR...?
IT'S KAMIYA !!
UP THERE, ON THAT BRIDGE. KAMIYA, HEY!!
COME BA-A-ACK!
KAMIYA!!
HUH?
WHAT?

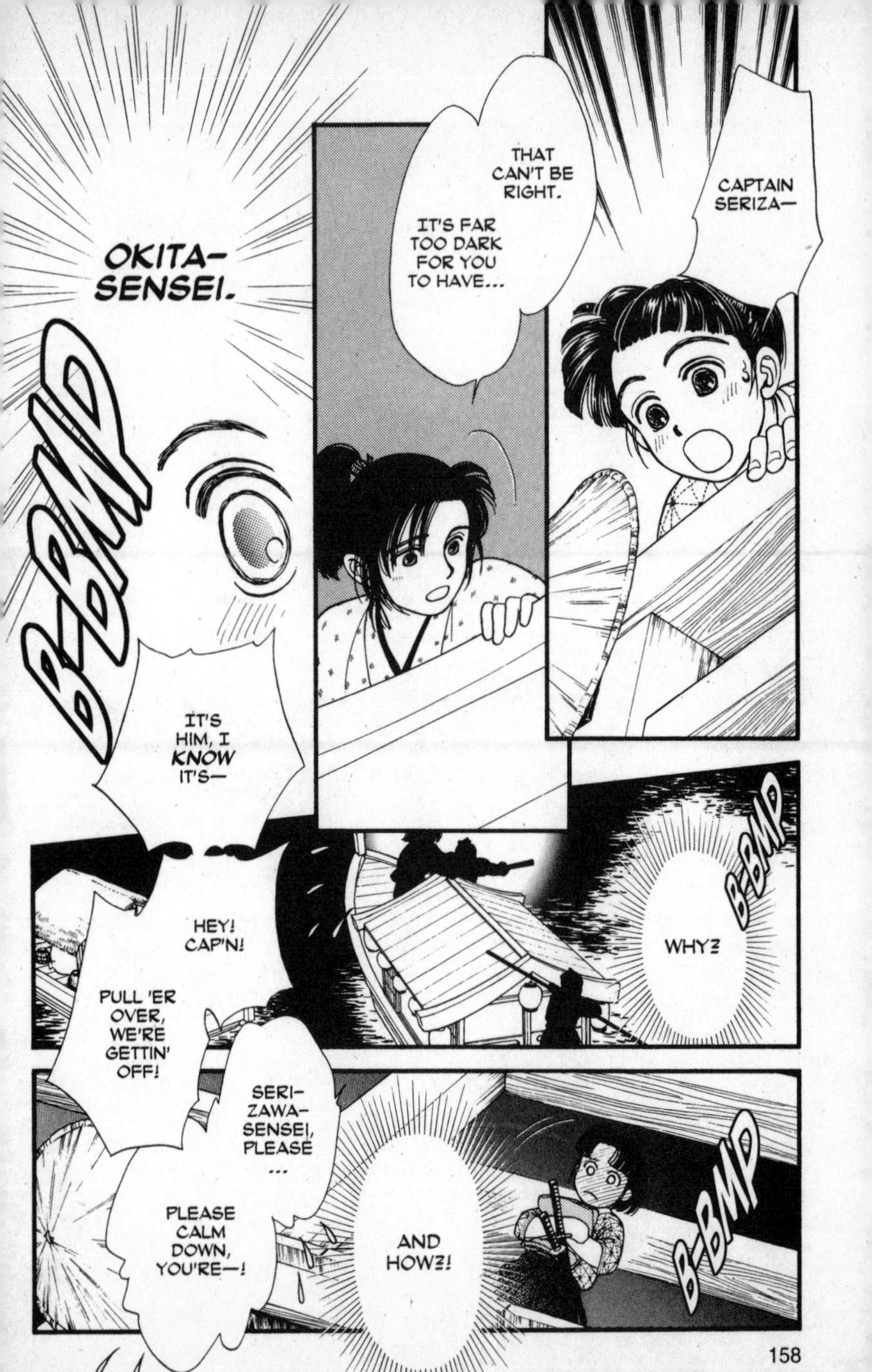
CAPTAIN SERIZA—
THAT CAN'T BE RIGHT.
IT'S FAR TOO DARK FOR YOU TO HAVE...
OKITA-SENSEI.
B-BMP
IT'S HIM, I KNOW IT'S—
B-BMP
WHY?
HEY! CAP'N!
PULL 'ER OVER, WE'RE GETTIN' OFF!
B-BMP
AND HOW?!
SERI-ZAWA-SENSEI, PLEASE...
PLEASE CALM DOWN, YOU'RE—!

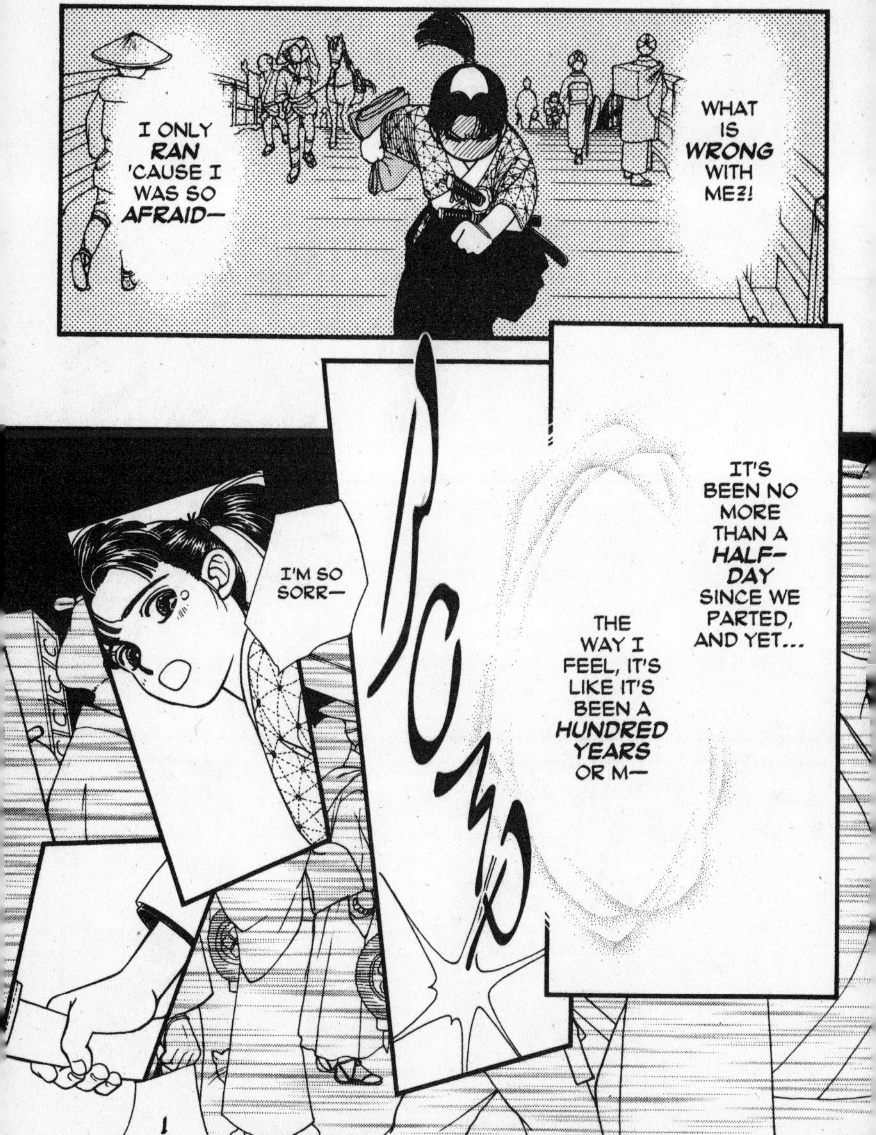
WHAT IS WRONG WITH ME?!
I ONLY RAN 'CAUSE I WAS SO AFRAID—
IT'S BEEN NO MORE THAN A HALF-DAY SINCE WE PARTED, AND YET...
THE WAY I FEEL, IT'S LIKE IT'S BEEN A HUNDRED YEARS OR M—
I'M SO SORR—
!

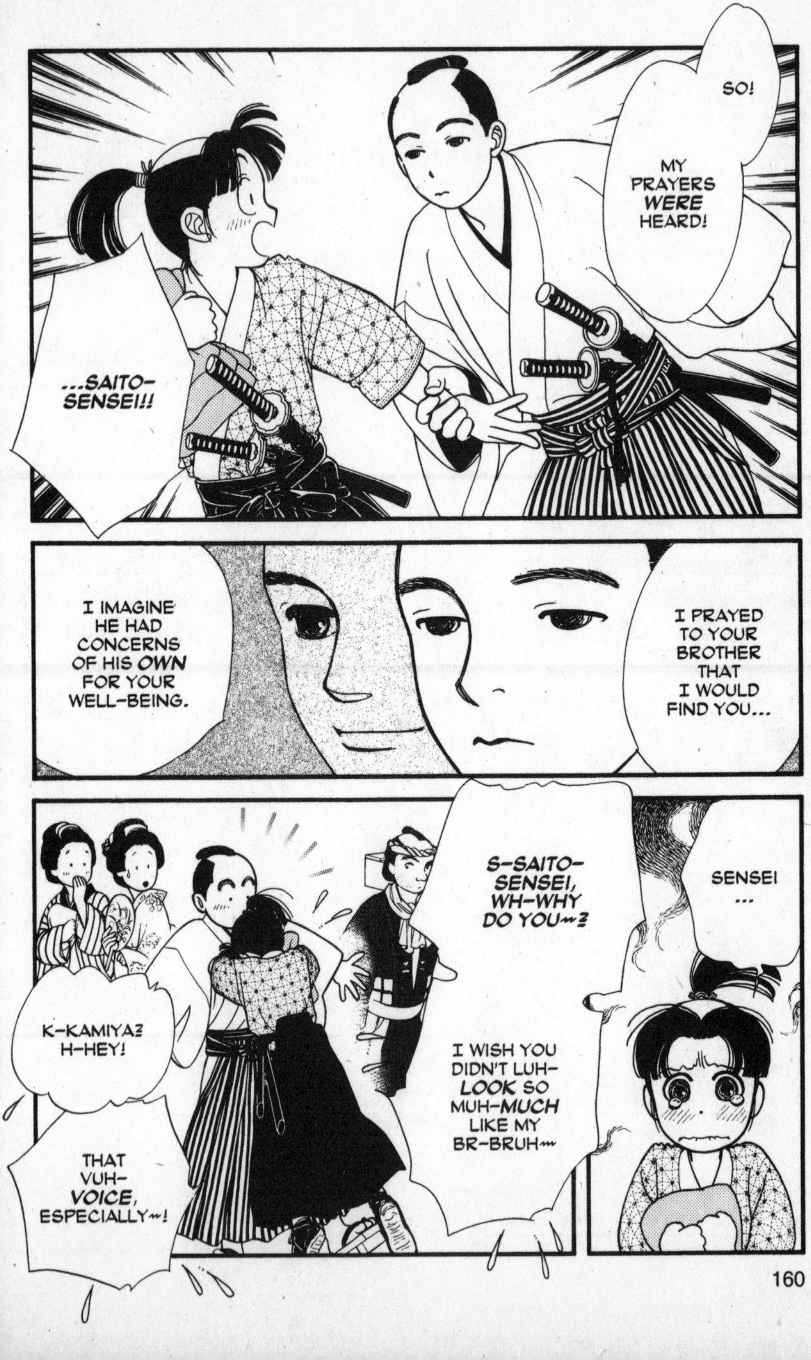
SO!
MY PRAYERS *WERE* HEARD!
...SAITO-SENSEI!!
I PRAYED TO YOUR BROTHER THAT I WOULD FIND YOU...
I IMAGINE HE HAD CONCERNS OF HIS *OWN* FOR YOUR WELL-BEING.
SENSEI ...
S-SAITO-SENSEI, WH-WHY DO YOU~?
I WISH YOU DIDN'T LUH-*LOOK* SO MUH-*MUCH* LIKE MY BR-BRUH~
K-KAMIYA? H-HEY!
THAT VUH-*VOICE*, ESPECIALLY~!

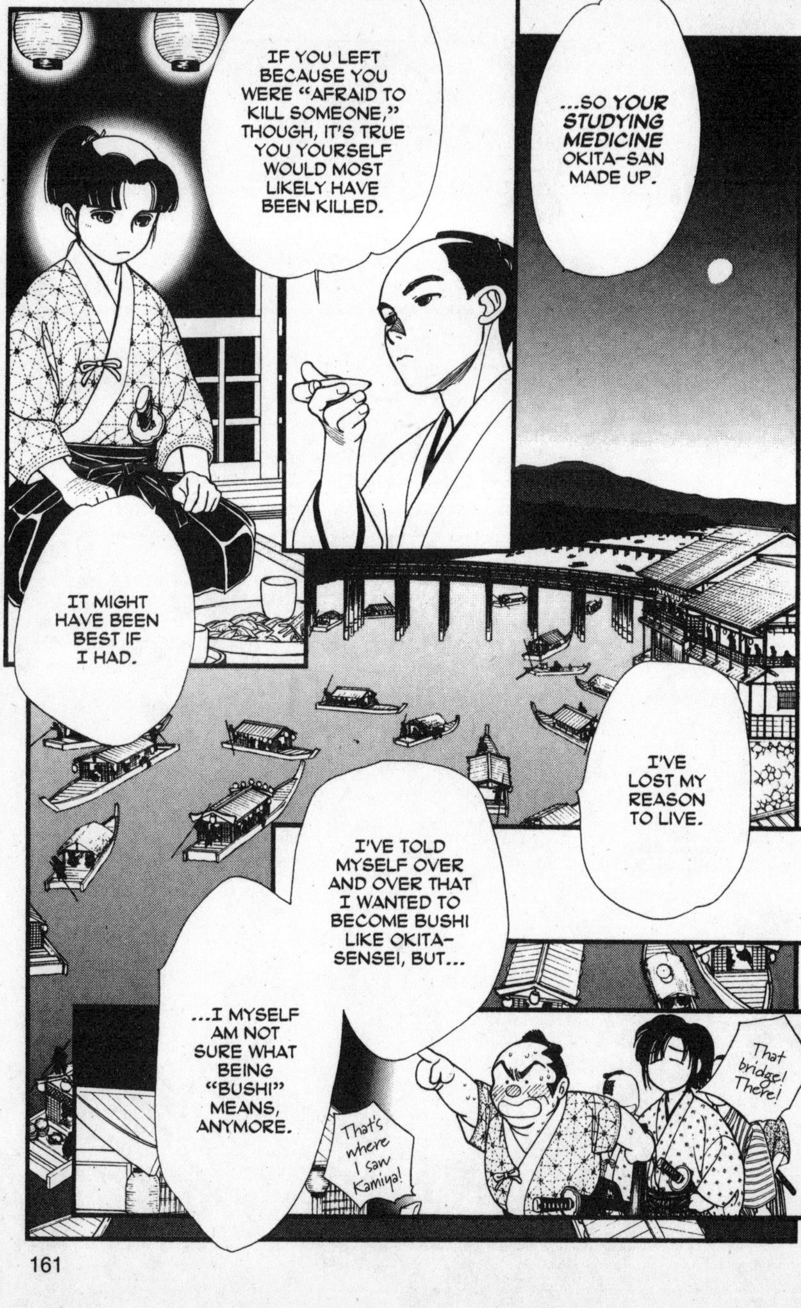
...SO YOUR STUDYING MEDICINE OKITA-SAN MADE UP.
IF YOU LEFT BECAUSE YOU WERE "AFRAID TO KILL SOMEONE," THOUGH, IT'S TRUE YOU YOURSELF WOULD MOST LIKELY HAVE BEEN KILLED.
IT MIGHT HAVE BEEN BEST IF I HAD.
I'VE LOST MY REASON TO LIVE.
I'VE TOLD MYSELF OVER AND OVER THAT I WANTED TO BECOME BUSHI LIKE OKITA-SENSEI, BUT...
...I MYSELF AM NOT SURE WHAT BEING "BUSHI" MEANS, ANYMORE.
That bridge! There!
That's where I saw Kamiya!

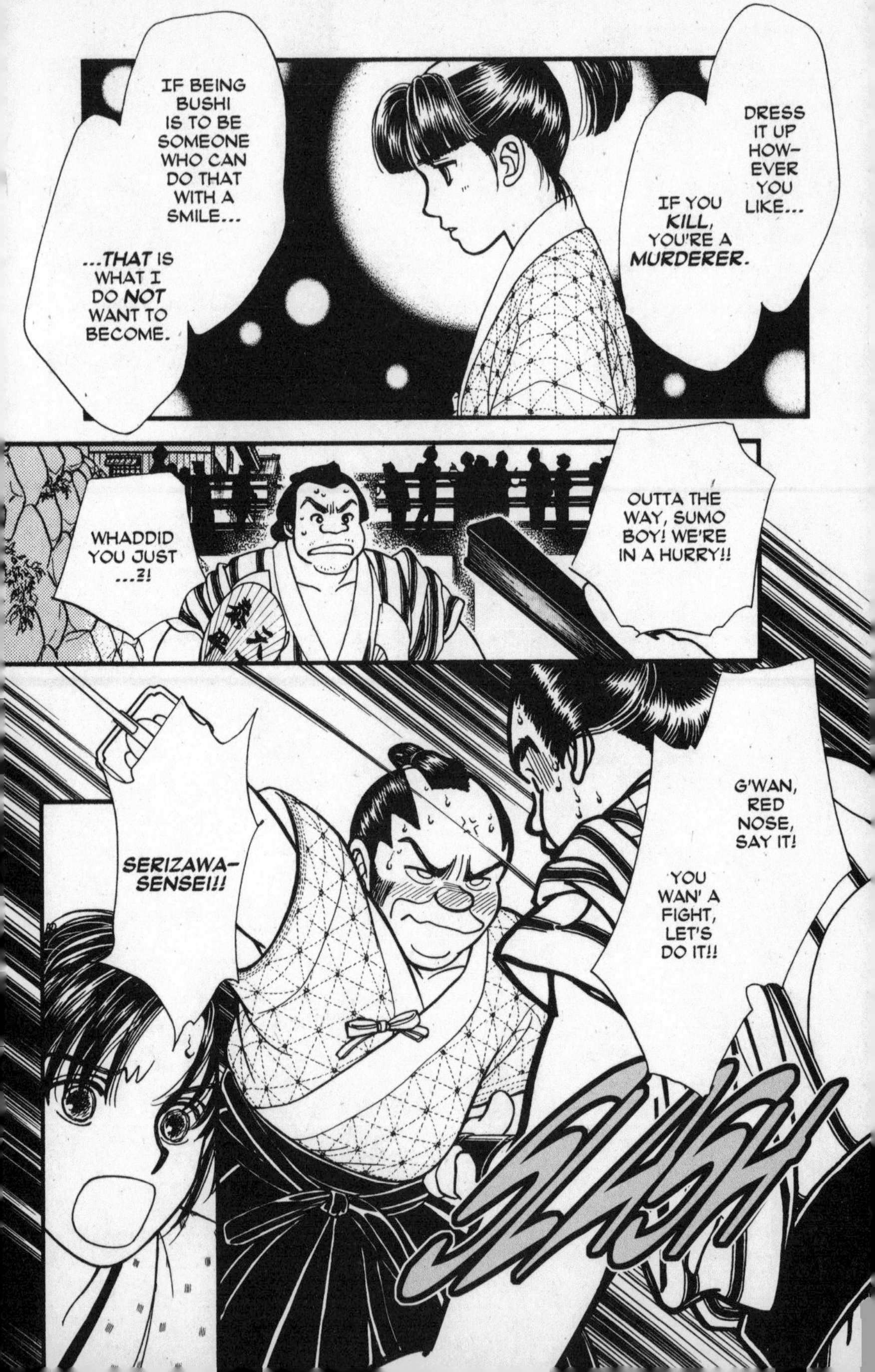
DRESS IT UP HOW-EVER YOU LIKE...
IF YOU KILL, YOU'RE A MURDERER.
IF BEING BUSHI IS TO BE SOMEONE WHO CAN DO THAT WITH A SMILE...
...THAT IS WHAT I DO NOT WANT TO BECOME.
OUTTA THE WAY, SUMO BOY! WE'RE IN A HURRY!!
WHADDID YOU JUST ...?!
G'WAN, RED NOSE, SAY IT!
YOU WAN' A FIGHT, LET'S DO IT!!
SERIZAWA-SENSEI!!

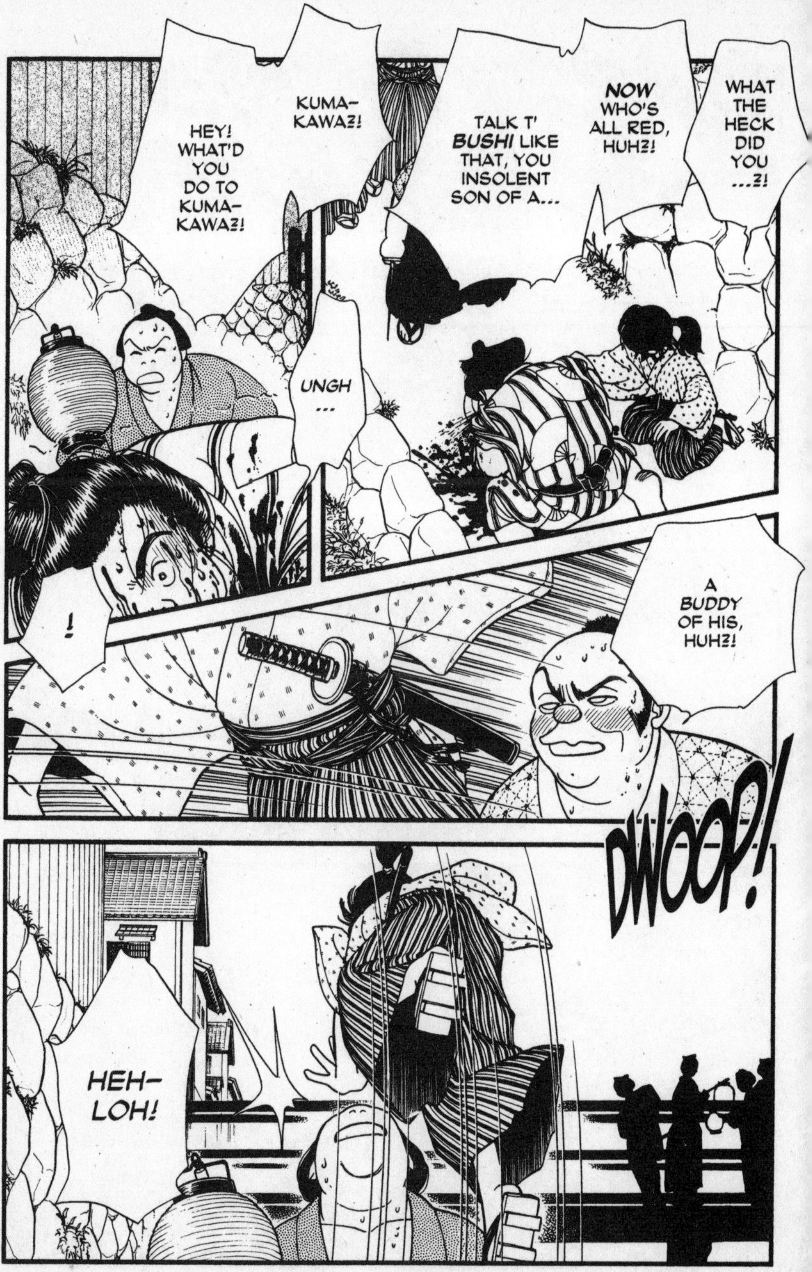
WHAT THE HECK DID YOU ...?!
NOW WHO'S ALL RED, HUH?!
TALK T' BUSHI LIKE THAT, YOU INSOLENT SON OF A...
KUMA-KAWA?!
HEY! WHAT'D YOU DO TO KUMA-KAWA?!
UNGH ...
!
A BUDDY OF HIS, HUH?!
DWOOP!
HEH-LOH!

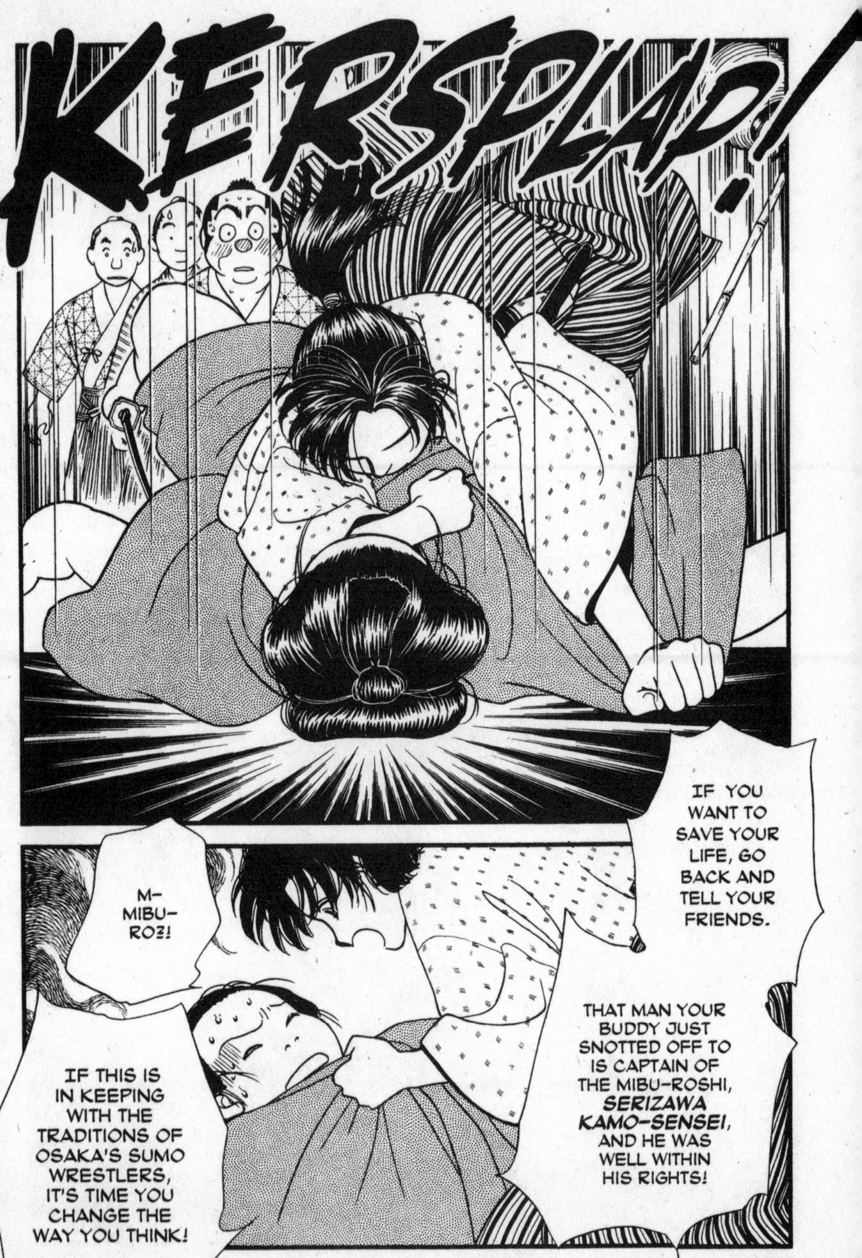
KERSPLAP!
IF YOU WANT TO SAVE YOUR LIFE, GO BACK AND TELL YOUR FRIENDS.
M-MIBU-RO?!
THAT MAN YOUR BUDDY JUST SNOTTED OFF TO IS CAPTAIN OF THE MIBU-ROSHI, SERIZAWA KAMO-SENSEI, AND HE WAS WELL WITHIN HIS RIGHTS!
IF THIS IS IN KEEPING WITH THE TRADITIONS OF OSAKA'S SUMO WRESTLERS, IT'S TIME YOU CHANGE THE WAY YOU THINK!

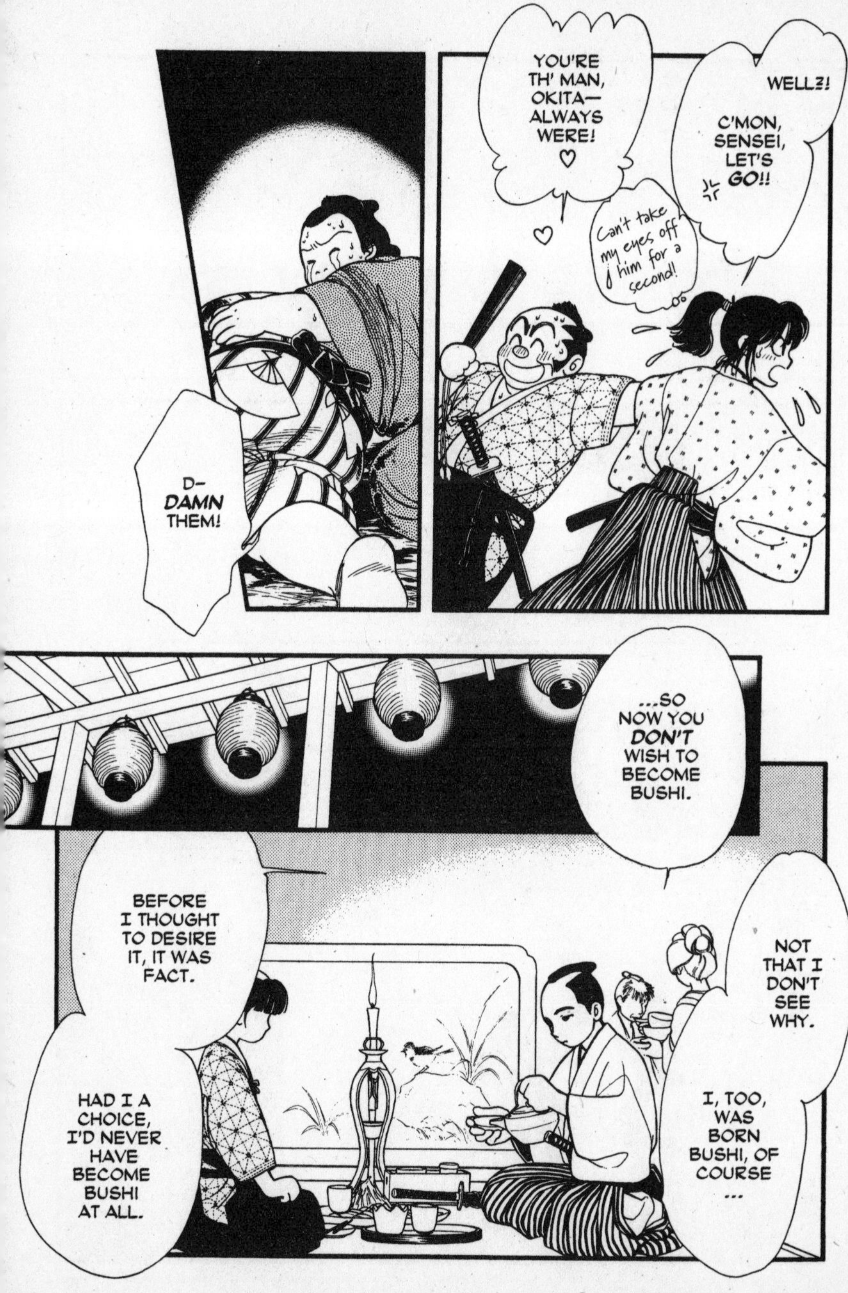
WELL?!
C'MON, SENSEI, LET'S **GO**!!
YOU'RE TH' MAN, OKITA— ALWAYS WERE! ♡
Can't take my eyes off him for a second!
D- **DAMN** THEM!
...SO NOW YOU **DON'T** WISH TO BECOME BUSHI.
NOT THAT I DON'T SEE WHY.
I, TOO, WAS BORN BUSHI, OF COURSE ...
BEFORE I THOUGHT TO DESIRE IT, IT WAS FACT.
HAD I A CHOICE, I'D NEVER HAVE BECOME BUSHI AT ALL.

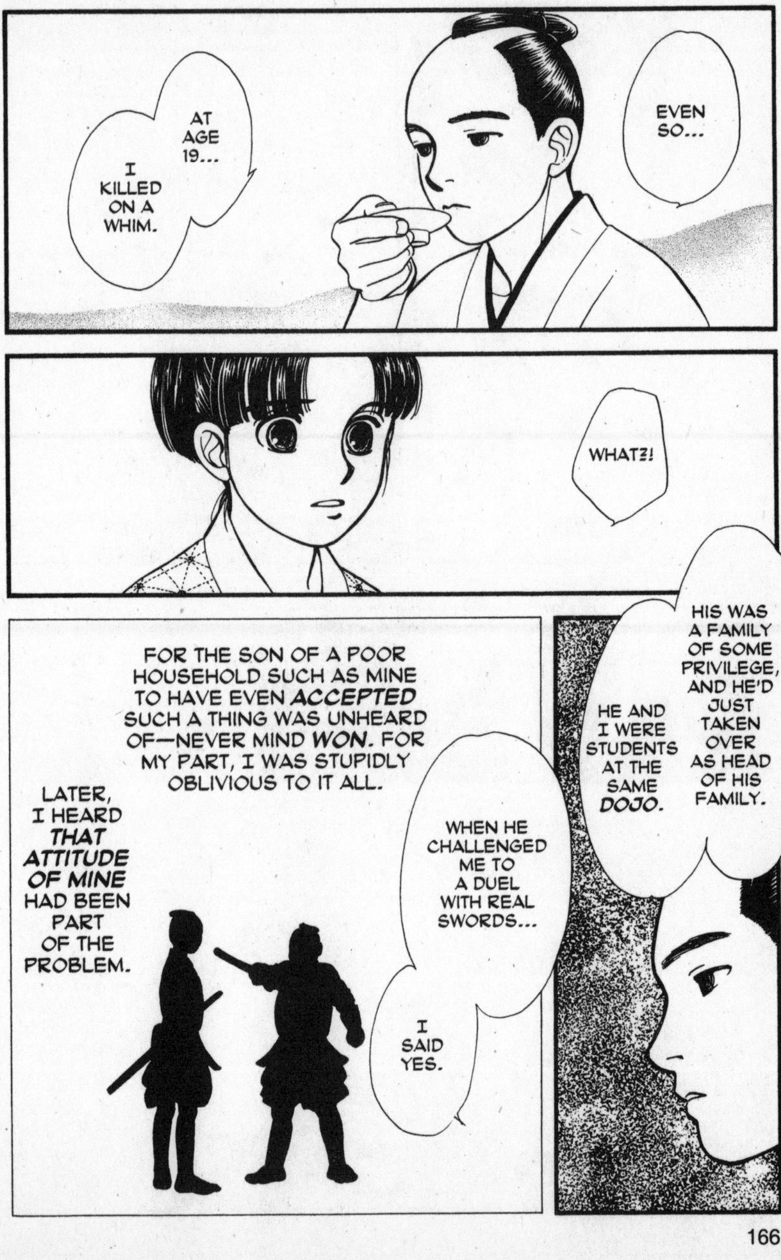
EVEN SO...
AT AGE 19... I KILLED ON A WHIM.
WHAT?!
HIS WAS A FAMILY OF SOME PRIVILEGE, AND HE'D JUST TAKEN OVER AS HEAD OF HIS FAMILY.
HE AND I WERE STUDENTS AT THE SAME *DOJO*.
WHEN HE CHALLENGED ME TO A DUEL WITH REAL SWORDS...
I SAID YES.
FOR THE SON OF A POOR HOUSEHOLD SUCH AS MINE TO HAVE EVEN *ACCEPTED* SUCH A THING WAS UNHEARD OF—NEVER MIND *WON*. FOR MY PART, I WAS STUPIDLY OBLIVIOUS TO IT ALL.
LATER, I HEARD *THAT ATTITUDE OF MINE* HAD BEEN PART OF THE PROBLEM.

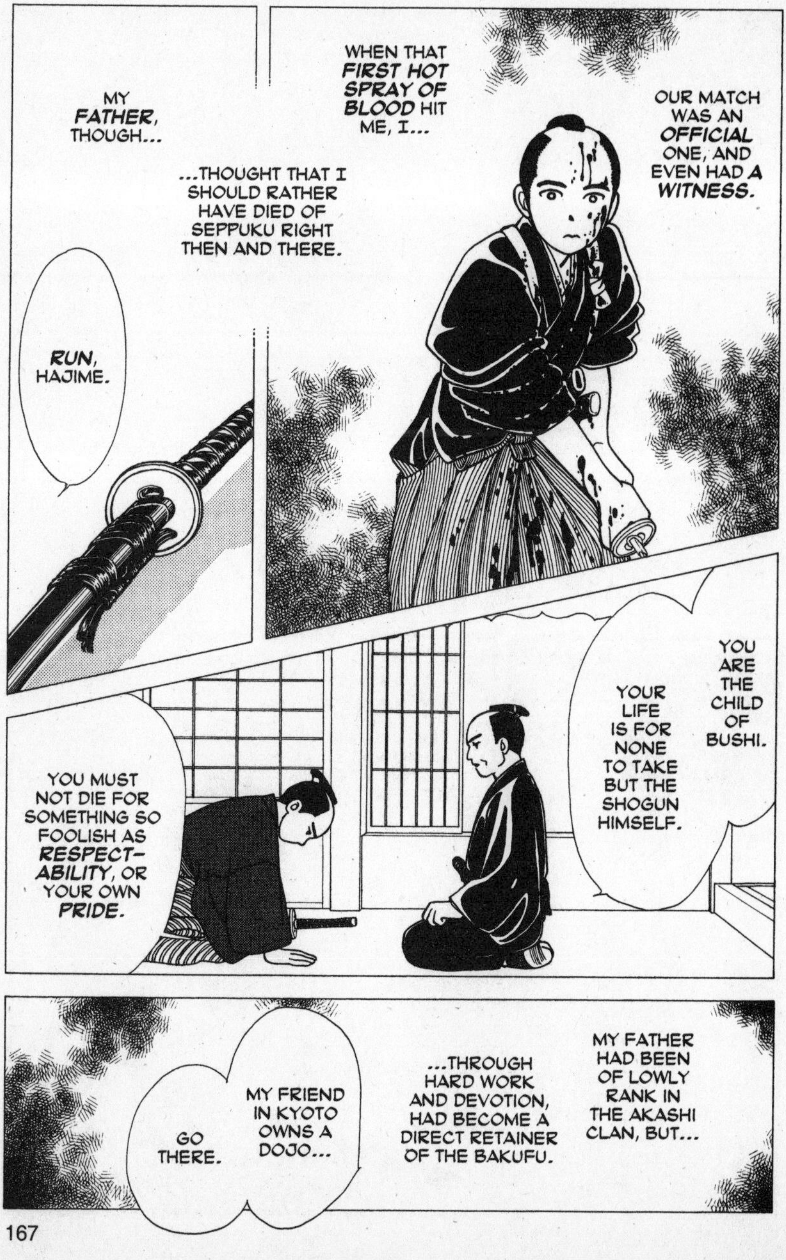
OUR MATCH WAS AN OFFICIAL ONE, AND EVEN HAD A WITNESS.
WHEN THAT FIRST HOT SPRAY OF BLOOD HIT ME, I...
MY FATHER, THOUGH...
...THOUGHT THAT I SHOULD RATHER HAVE DIED OF SEPPUKU RIGHT THEN AND THERE.
RUN, HAJIME.
YOU ARE THE CHILD OF BUSHI.
YOUR LIFE IS FOR NONE TO TAKE BUT THE SHOGUN HIMSELF.
YOU MUST NOT DIE FOR SOMETHING SO FOOLISH AS RESPECTABILITY, OR YOUR OWN PRIDE.
MY FATHER HAD BEEN OF LOWLY RANK IN THE AKASHI CLAN, BUT...
...THROUGH HARD WORK AND DEVOTION, HAD BECOME A DIRECT RETAINER OF THE BAKUFU.
MY FRIEND IN KYOTO OWNS A DOJO...
GO THERE.

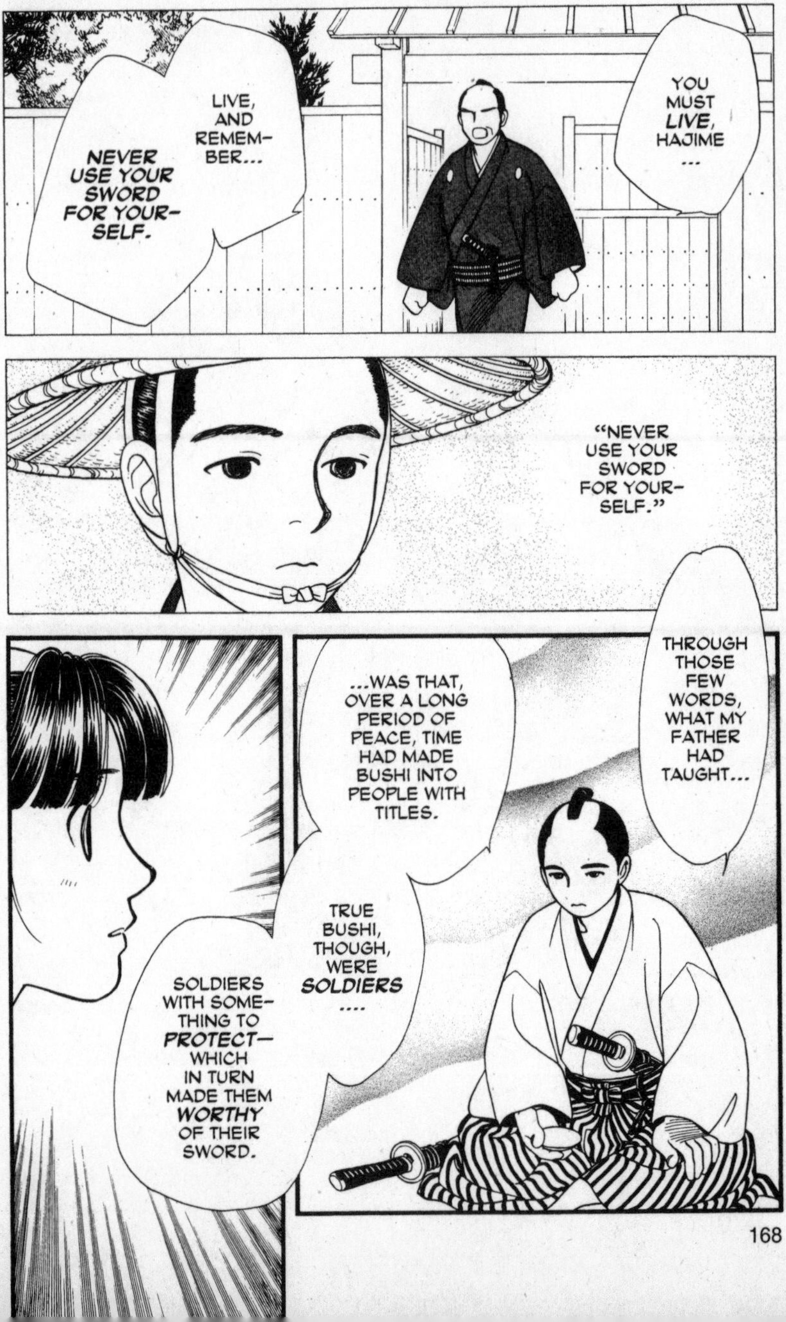

YOU MUST LIVE, HAJIME...
LIVE, AND REMEMBER...
NEVER USE YOUR SWORD FOR YOURSELF.
"NEVER USE YOUR SWORD FOR YOURSELF."
THROUGH THOSE FEW WORDS, WHAT MY FATHER HAD TAUGHT...
...WAS THAT, OVER A LONG PERIOD OF PEACE, TIME HAD MADE BUSHI INTO PEOPLE WITH TITLES.
TRUE BUSHI, THOUGH, WERE SOLDIERS....
SOLDIERS WITH SOMETHING TO PROTECT—WHICH IN TURN MADE THEM WORTHY OF THEIR SWORD.

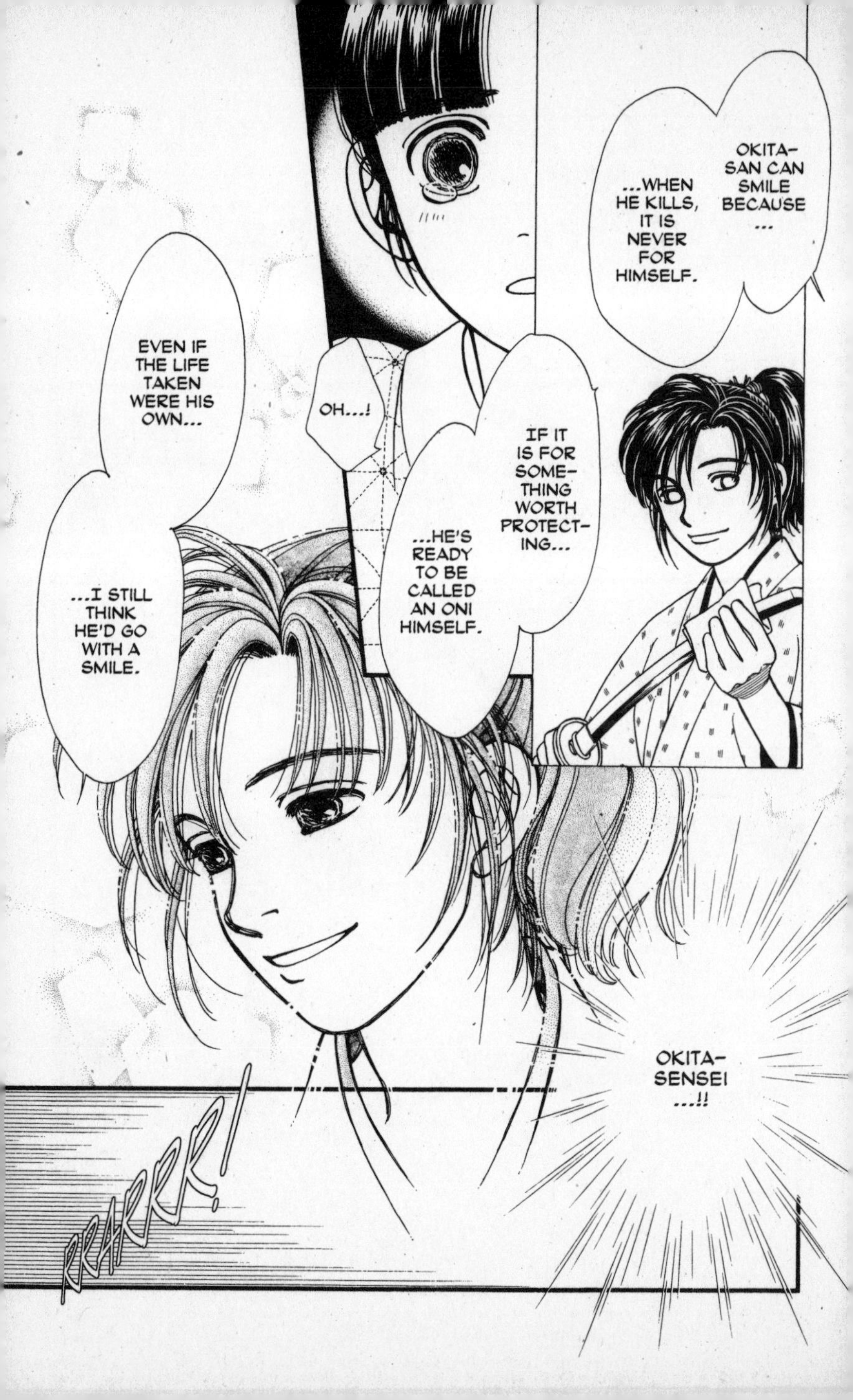
OKITA-SAN CAN SMILE BECAUSE ...
...WHEN HE KILLS, IT IS NEVER FOR HIMSELF.
OH...!
IF IT IS FOR SOME-THING WORTH PROTECT-ING...
...HE'S READY TO BE CALLED AN ONI HIMSELF.
EVEN IF THE LIFE TAKEN WERE HIS OWN...
...I STILL THINK HE'D GO WITH A SMILE.
OKITA-SENSEI ...!!
RRARRR!

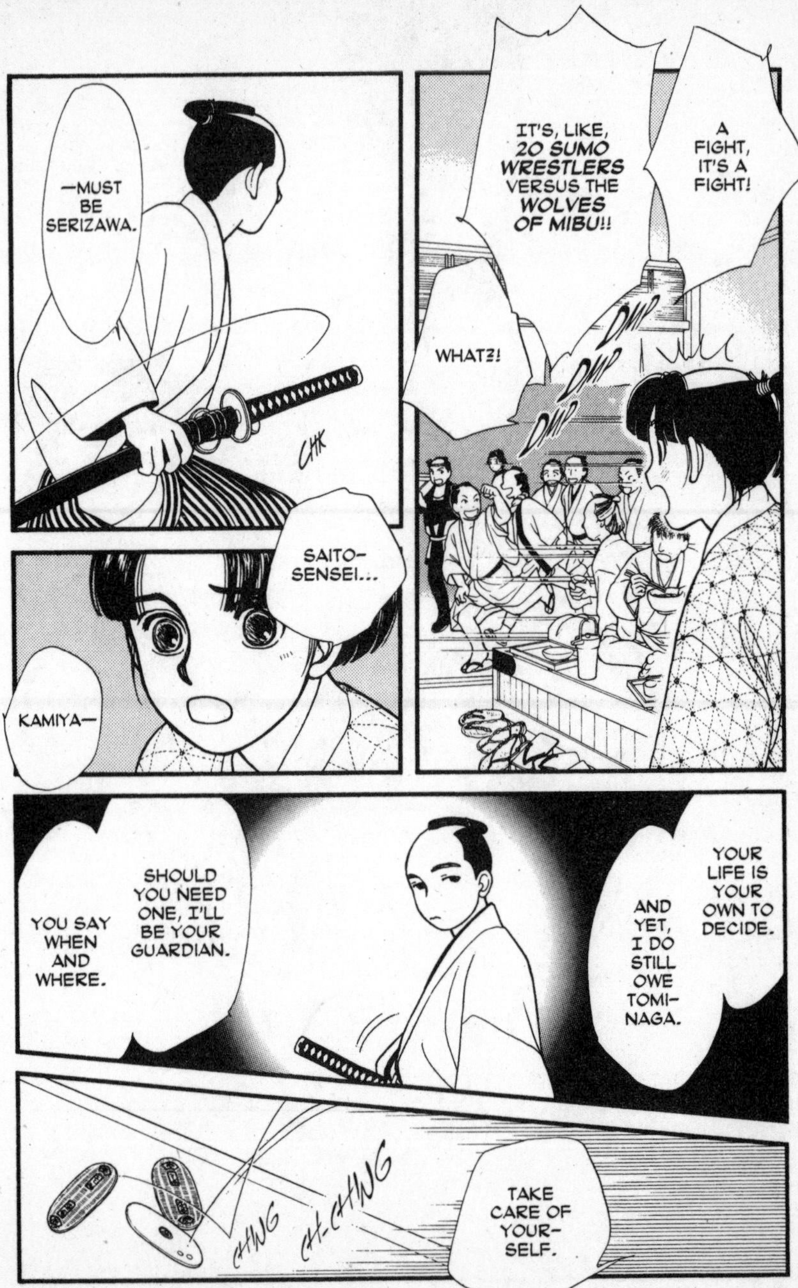
A FIGHT, IT'S A FIGHT!
IT'S, LIKE, 20 SUMO WRESTLERS VERSUS THE WOLVES OF MIBU!!
WHAT?!
DMP DMP DMP DMP
—MUST BE SERIZAWA.
CHK
SAITO-SENSEI...
KAMIYA—
YOUR LIFE IS YOUR OWN TO DECIDE.
AND YET, I DO STILL OWE TOMI-NAGA.
SHOULD YOU NEED ONE, I'LL BE YOUR GUARDIAN.
YOU SAY WHEN AND WHERE.
TAKE CARE OF YOUR-SELF.
CH-CHING
CHING

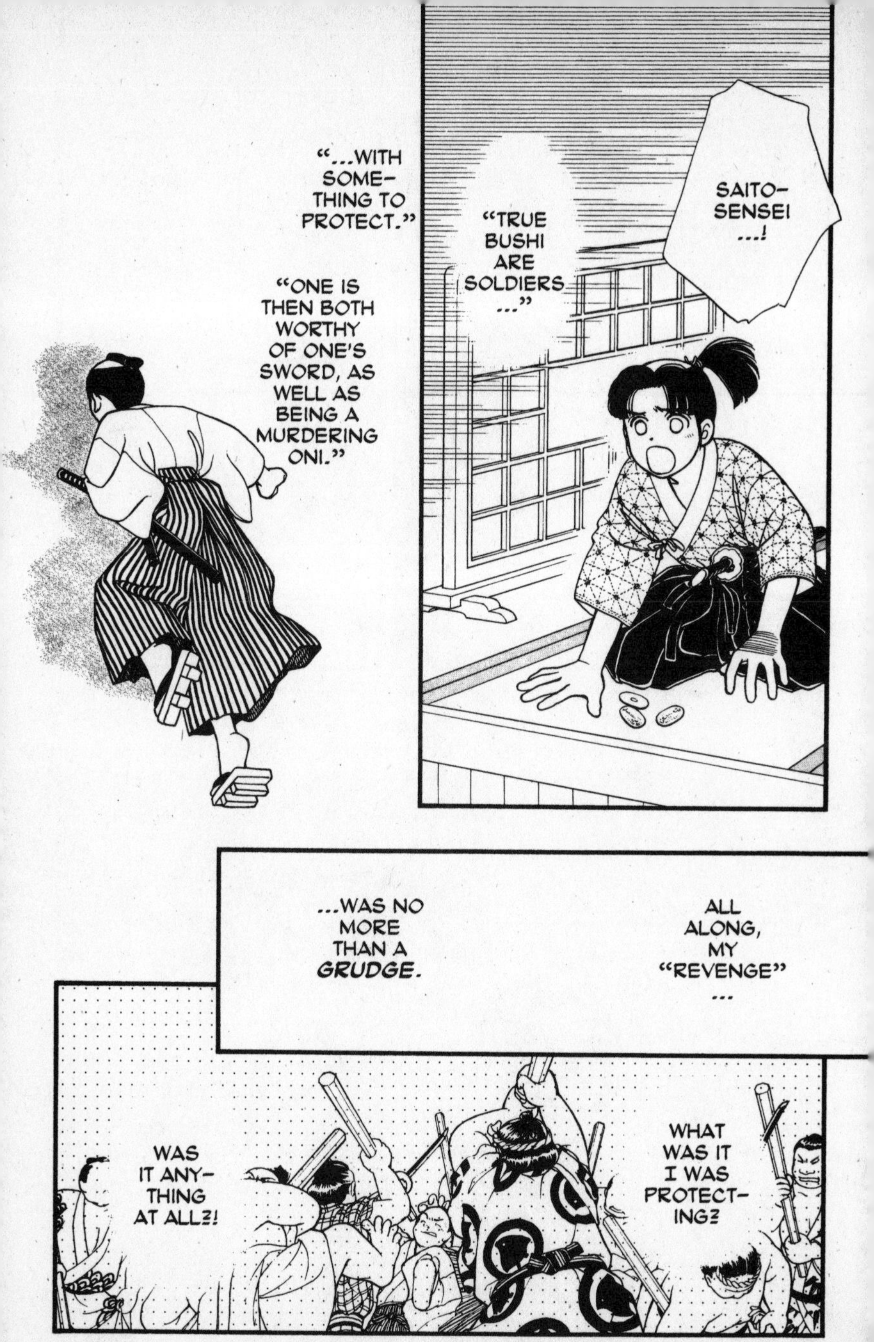
SAITO-SENSEI ...!
"TRUE BUSHI ARE SOLDIERS ..."
"...WITH SOME-THING TO PROTECT."
"ONE IS THEN BOTH WORTHY OF ONE'S SWORD, AS WELL AS BEING A MURDERING ONI."
ALL ALONG, MY "REVENGE" ...
...WAS NO MORE THAN A *GRUDGE*.
WHAT WAS IT I WAS PROTECT-ING?
WAS IT ANY-THING AT ALL?!

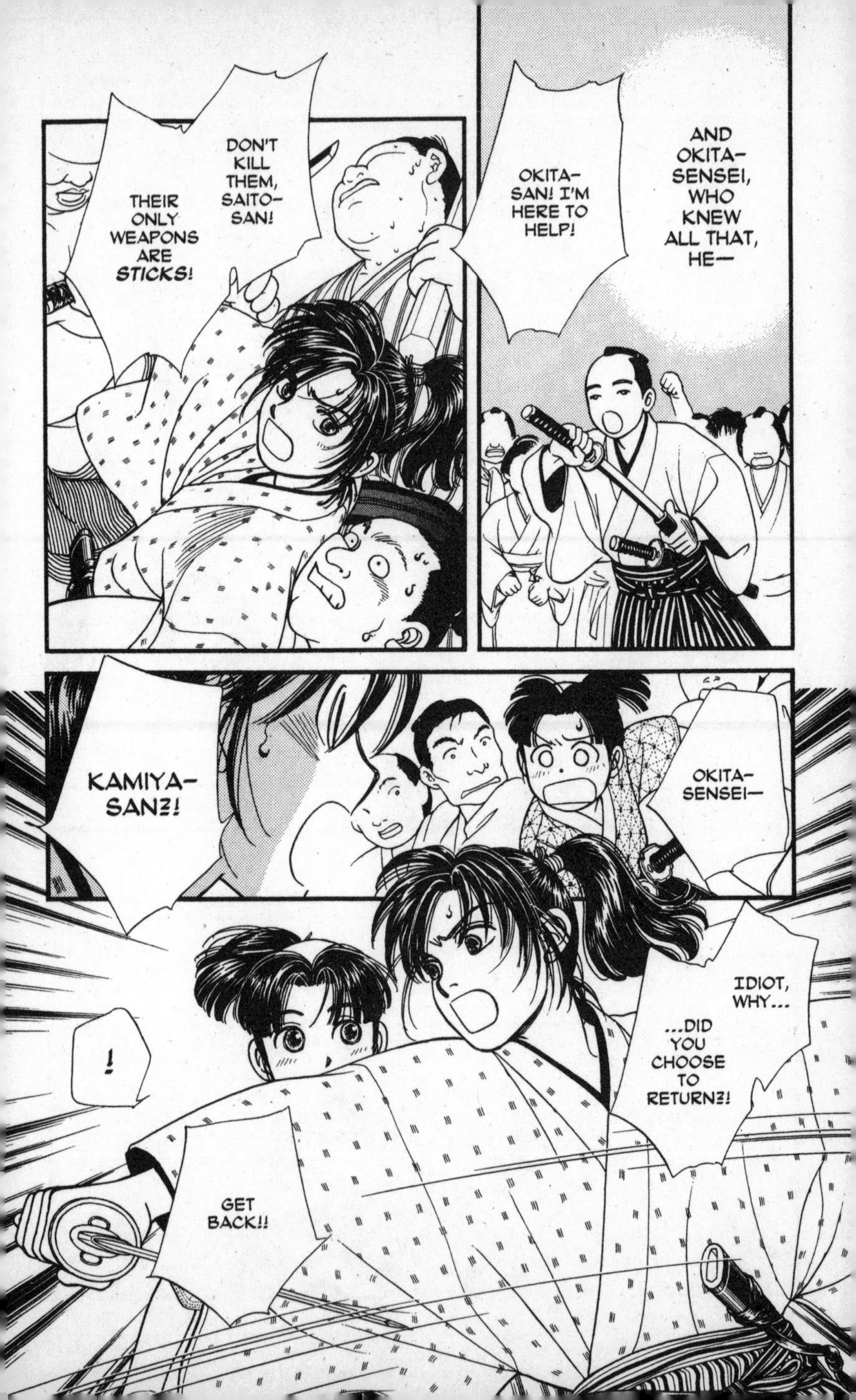
AND OKITA-SENSEI, WHO KNEW ALL THAT, HE—
OKITA-SAN! I'M HERE TO HELP!
DON'T KILL THEM, SAITO-SAN!
THEIR ONLY WEAPONS ARE STICKS!
OKITA-SENSEI—
KAMIYA-SAN?!
IDIOT, WHY...
...DID YOU CHOOSE TO RETURN?!
!
GET BACK!!

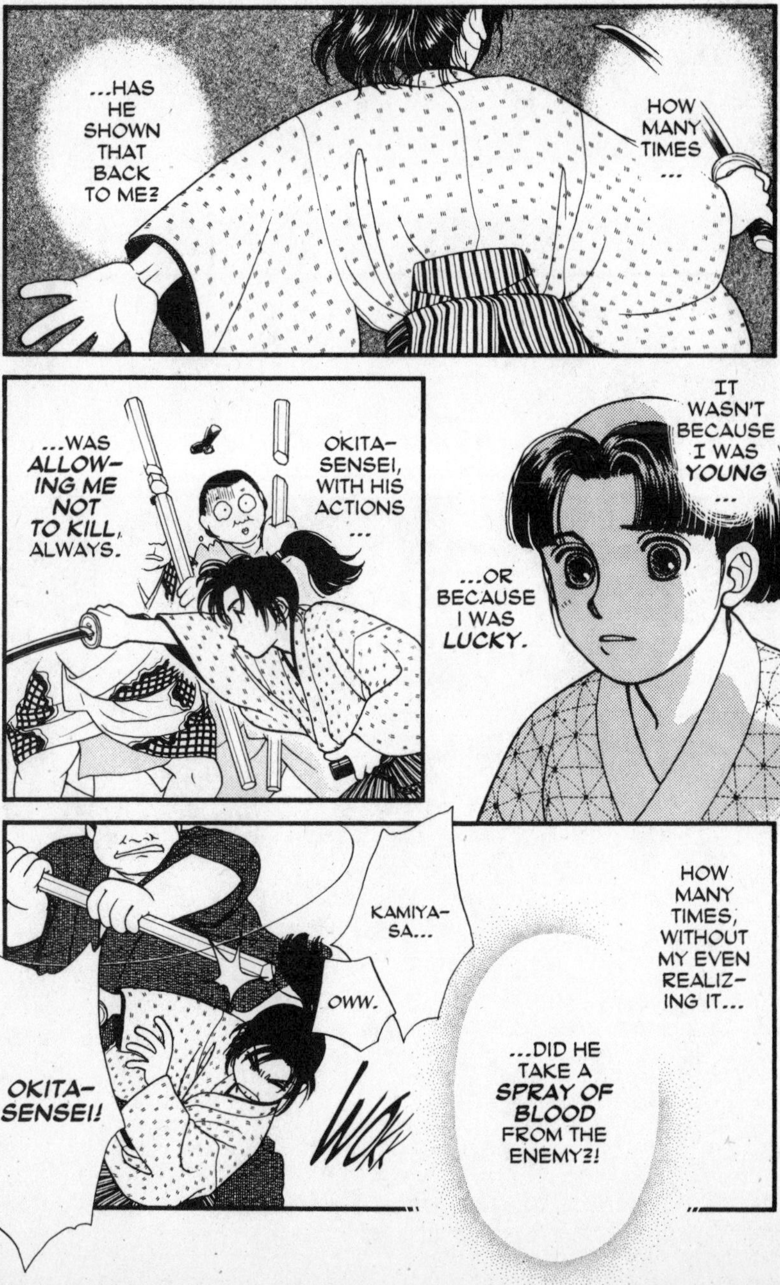

HOW MANY TIMES ...
...HAS HE SHOWN THAT BACK TO ME?
IT WASN'T BECAUSE I WAS **YOUNG** ...
...OR BECAUSE I WAS **LUCKY**.
OKITA-SENSEI, WITH HIS ACTIONS ...
...WAS **ALLOWING ME NOT TO KILL**, ALWAYS.
HOW MANY TIMES, WITHOUT MY EVEN REALIZING IT...
...DID HE TAKE A **SPRAY OF BLOOD** FROM THE ENEMY?!
KAMIYA-SA...
OWW.
WOK
OKITA-SENSEI!

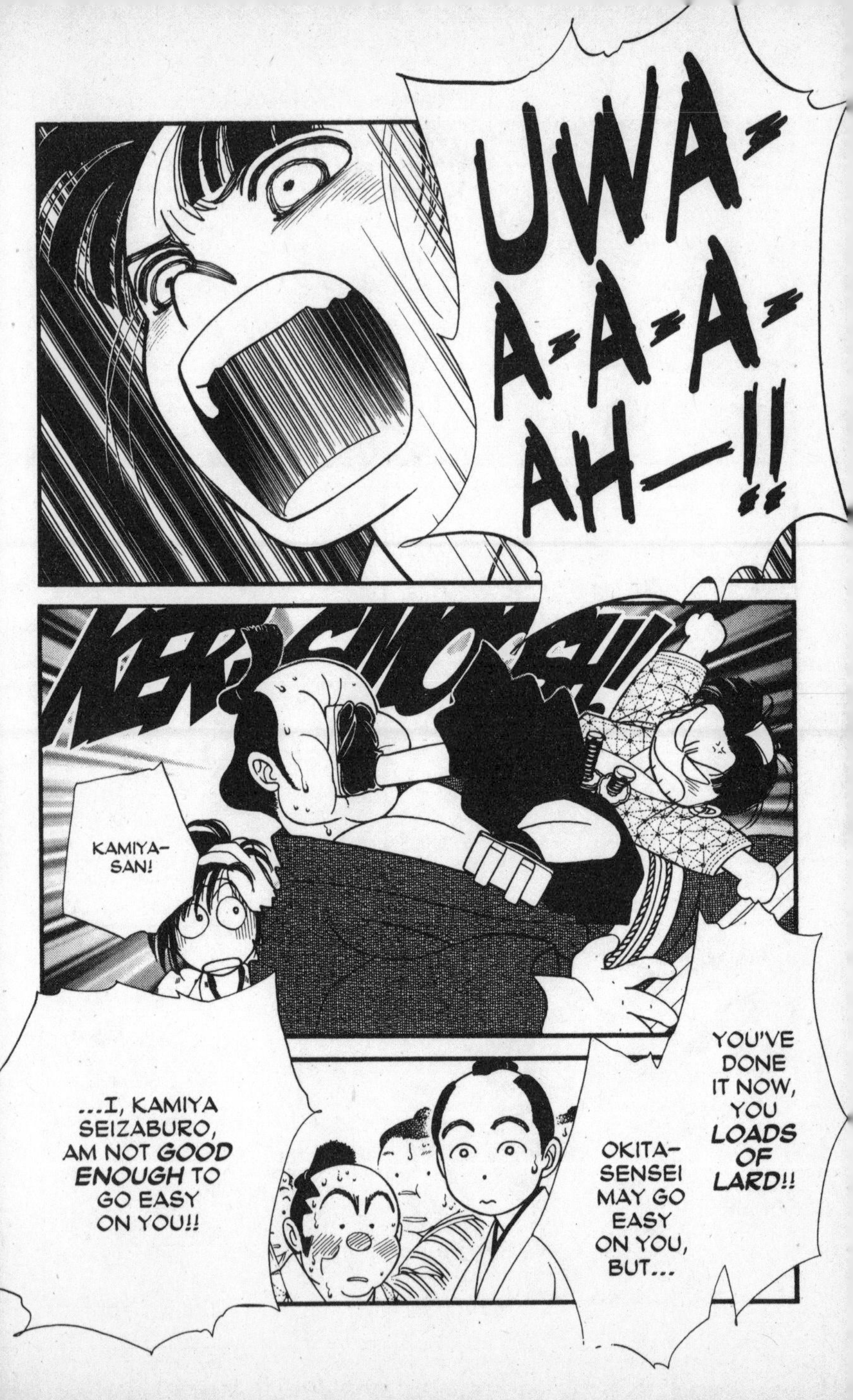
UWA-A-A-AH—!!
KAMIYA-SAN!
YOU'VE DONE IT NOW, YOU **LOADS OF LARD!!**
OKITA-SENSEI MAY GO EASY ON YOU, BUT...
...I, KAMIYA SEIZABURO, AM NOT **GOOD ENOUGH** TO GO EASY ON YOU!!

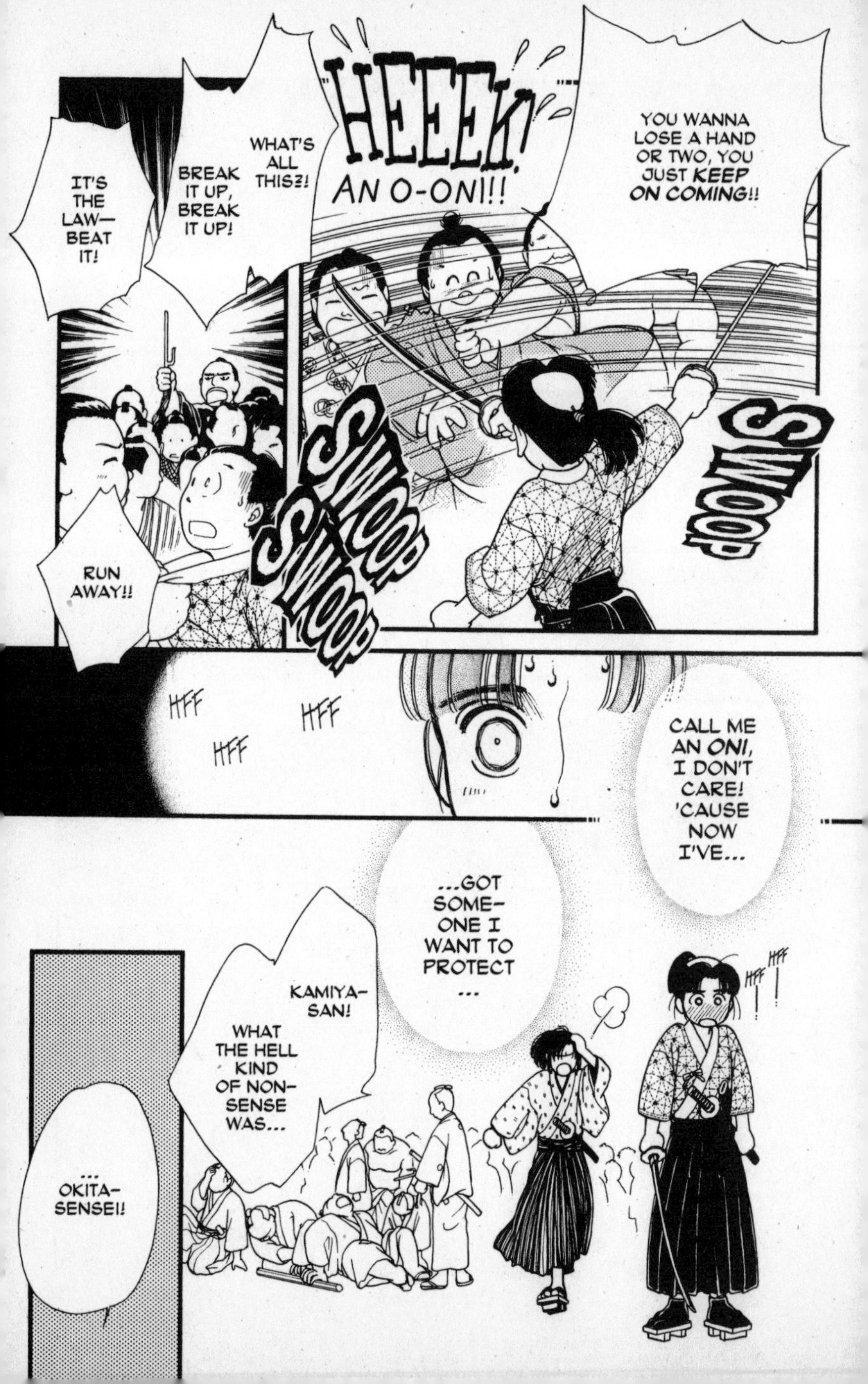
YOU WANNA LOSE A HAND OR TWO, YOU JUST KEEP ON COMING!!
"HEEEK!"
AN O-ONI!!!
WHAT'S ALL THIS?!
BREAK IT UP, BREAK IT UP!
IT'S THE LAW—BEAT IT!
SWOOP
SWOOP SWOOP
RUN AWAY!!
CALL ME AN ONI, I DON'T CARE! 'CAUSE NOW I'VE...
HFF
HFF
HFF
...GOT SOME-ONE I WANT TO PROTECT...
HFF
HFF
KAMIYA-SAN!
WHAT THE HELL KIND OF NON-SENSE WAS...
...OKITA-SENSEI!

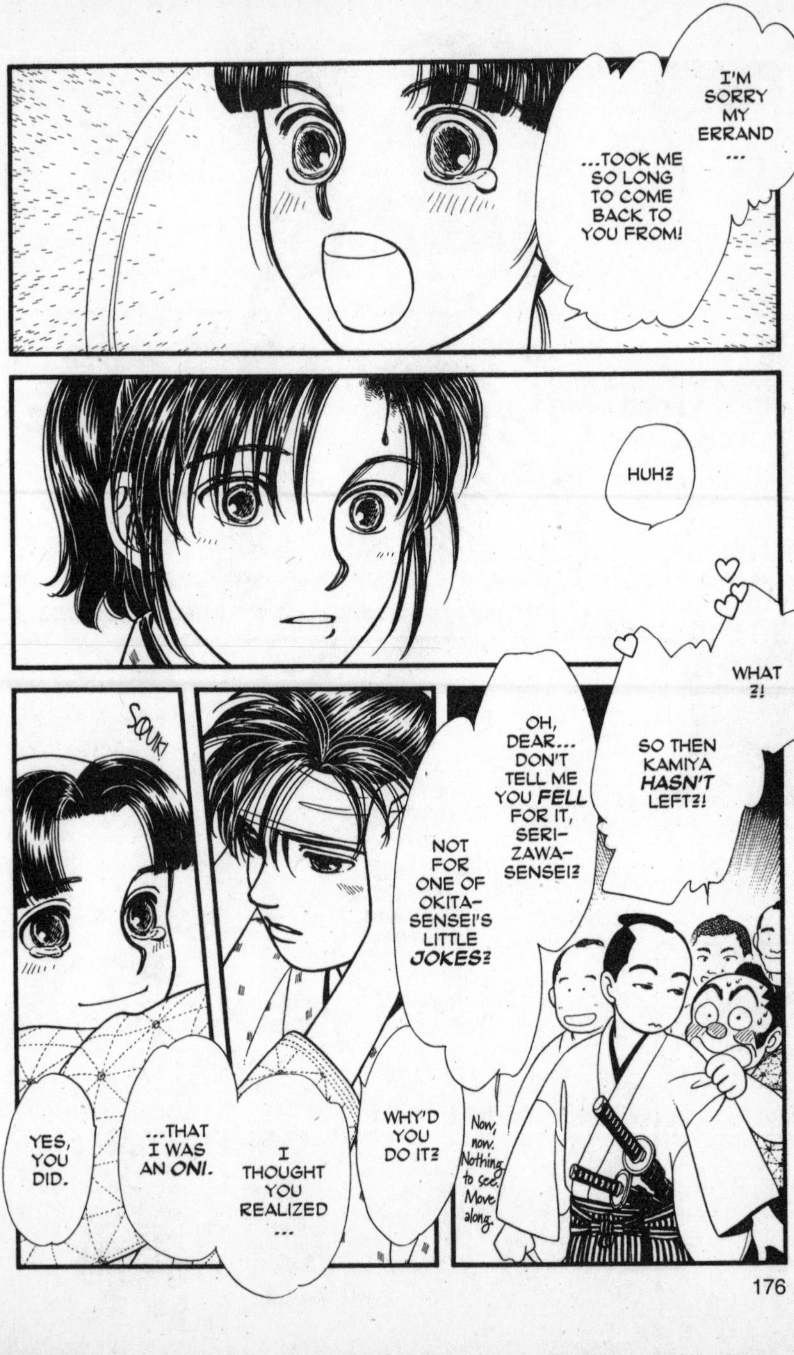
I'M SORRY MY ERRAND ...
...TOOK ME SO LONG TO COME BACK TO YOU FROM!
HUH?
WHAT?!
SO THEN KAMIYA HASN'T LEFT?!
OH, DEAR... DON'T TELL ME YOU FELL FOR IT, SERIZAWA-SENSEI?
NOT FOR ONE OF OKITA-SENSEI'S LITTLE JOKES?
Now, now. Nothing to see. Move along.
WHY'D YOU DO IT?
I THOUGHT YOU REALIZED ...
...THAT I WAS AN ONI.
SQUIK!
YES, YOU DID.

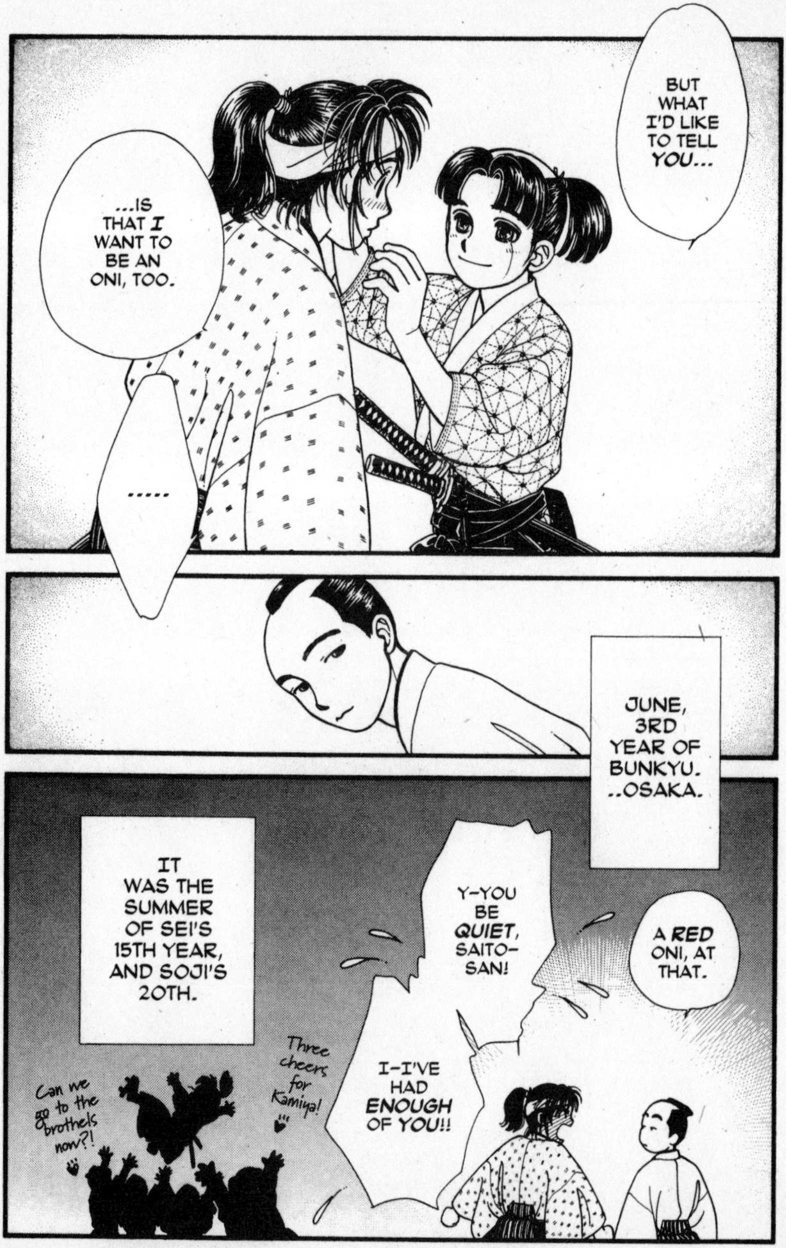
BUT WHAT I'D LIKE TO TELL *YOU*...
...IS THAT *I* WANT TO BE AN ONI, TOO.
.....
JUNE, 3RD YEAR OF BUNKYU. ..OSAKA.
A *RED* ONI, AT THAT.
Y-YOU BE *QUIET*, SAITO-SAN!
I-I'VE HAD *ENOUGH* OF *YOU*!!
IT WAS THE SUMMER OF SEI'S 15TH YEAR, AND SOJI'S 20TH.
Three cheers for Kamiya!
Can we go to the brothels now?!

To Be Continued!

TAEKO WATANABE PRESENTS

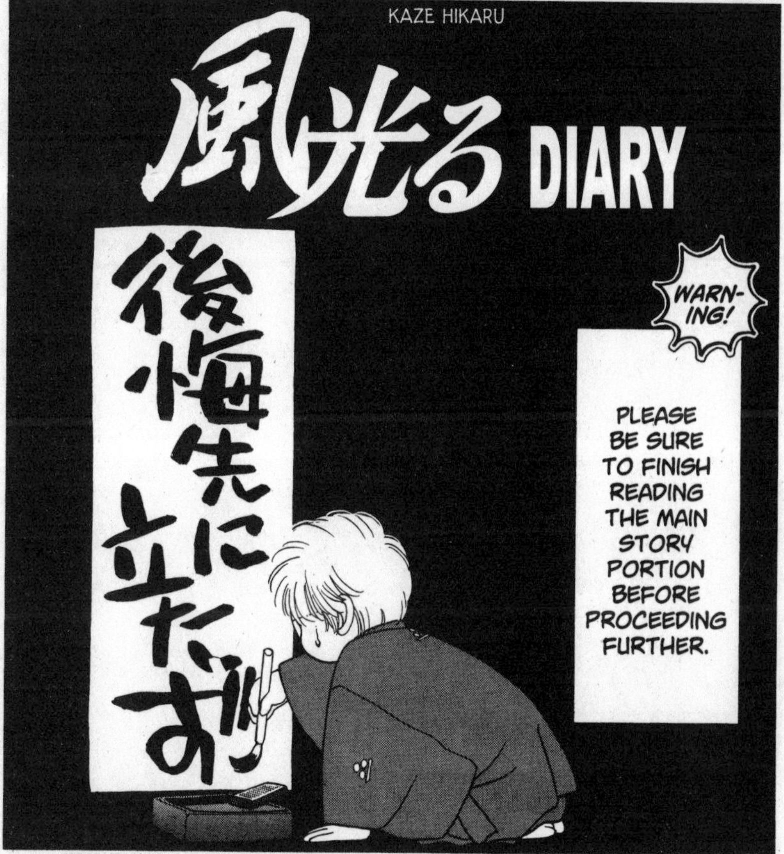
KAZE HIKARU
風光る DIARY
後悔先に立たず
WARN-ING!
PLEASE BE SURE TO FINISH READING THE MAIN STORY PORTION BEFORE PROCEEDING FURTHER.

"REPENTANCE COMES TOO LATE"

THE FOLLOWING IS AN ACCOUNT OF THE ATTEMPT OF A COMPLETELY HISTORY-ILLITERATE MANGA ARTIST TO CREATE A HISTORICAL WORK OF FICTION.

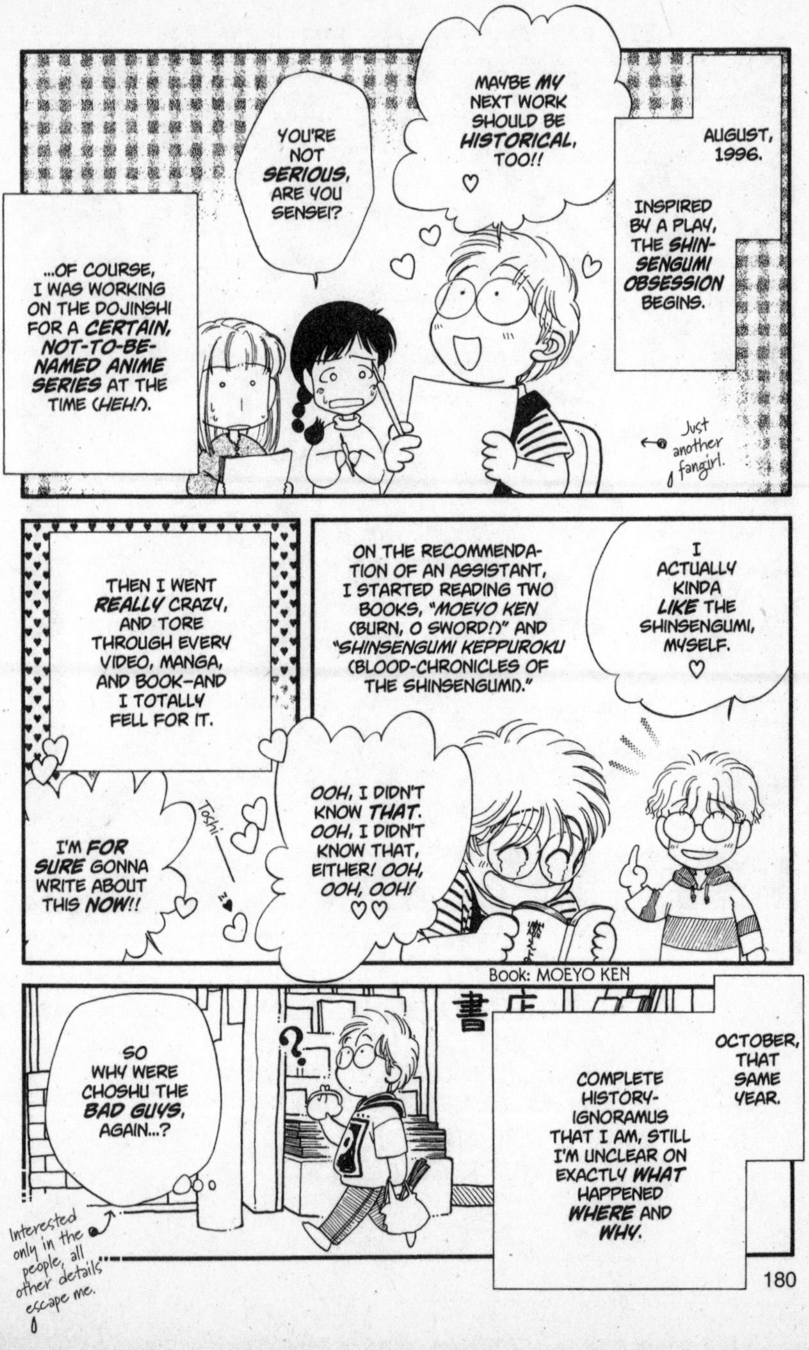

AUGUST, 1996.
INSPIRED BY A PLAY, THE SHINSENGUMI OBSESSION BEGINS.
MAYBE MY NEXT WORK SHOULD BE HISTORICAL, TOO!! ♡
YOU'RE NOT SERIOUS, ARE YOU SENSEI?
...OF COURSE, I WAS WORKING ON THE DOJINSHI FOR A CERTAIN, NOT-TO-BE-NAMED ANIME SERIES AT THE TIME (HEH!).
Just another fangirl.
ON THE RECOMMENDATION OF AN ASSISTANT, I STARTED READING TWO BOOKS, "MOEYO KEN (BURN, O SWORD!)" AND "SHINSENGUMI KEPPUROKU (BLOOD-CHRONICLES OF THE SHINSENGUMI)."
I ACTUALLY KINDA LIKE THE SHINSENGUMI, MYSELF. ♡
OOH, I DIDN'T KNOW THAT. OOH, I DIDN'T KNOW THAT, EITHER! OOH, OOH, OOH! ♡♡
THEN I WENT REALLY CRAZY, AND TORE THROUGH EVERY VIDEO, MANGA, AND BOOK—AND I TOTALLY FELL FOR IT.
I'M FOR SURE GONNA WRITE ABOUT THIS NOW!!
Toshi
Book: MOEYO KEN
OCTOBER, THAT SAME YEAR.
COMPLETE HISTORY-IGNORAMUS THAT I AM, STILL I'M UNCLEAR ON EXACTLY WHAT HAPPENED WHERE AND WHY.
SO WHY WERE CHOSHU THE BAD GUYS, AGAIN...?
Interested only in the people, all other details escape me.

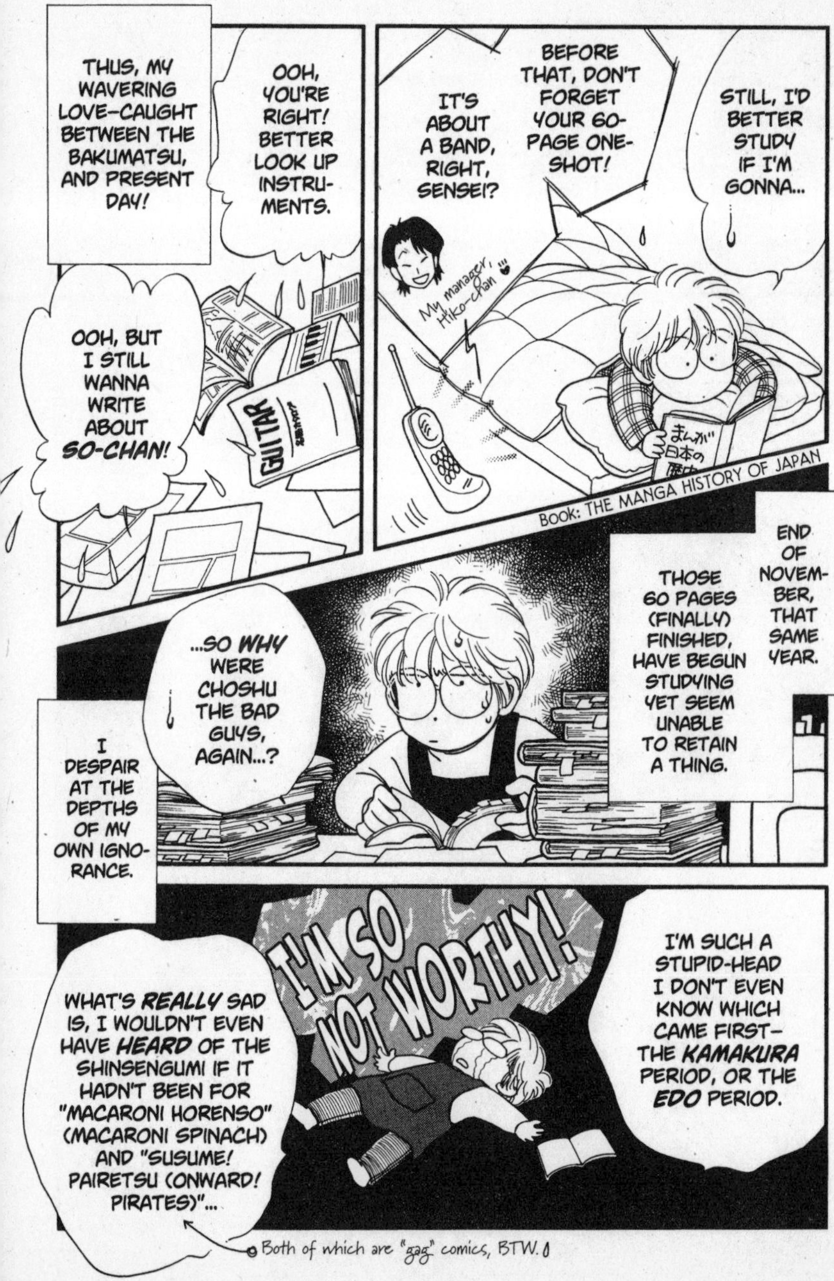
STILL, I'D BETTER STUDY IF I'M GONNA...
BEFORE THAT, DON'T FORGET YOUR 60-PAGE ONE-SHOT!
IT'S ABOUT A BAND, RIGHT, SENSEI?
My manager, Hiko-chan
Book: THE MANGA HISTORY OF JAPAN
OOH, YOU'RE RIGHT! BETTER LOOK UP INSTRUMENTS.
THUS, MY WAVERING LOVE—CAUGHT BETWEEN THE BAKUMATSU, AND PRESENT DAY!
OOH, BUT I STILL WANNA WRITE ABOUT SO-CHAN!
GUITAR
END OF NOVEMBER, THAT SAME YEAR.
THOSE 60 PAGES (FINALLY) FINISHED, HAVE BEGUN STUDYING YET SEEM UNABLE TO RETAIN A THING.
...SO WHY WERE CHOSHU THE BAD GUYS, AGAIN...?
I DESPAIR AT THE DEPTHS OF MY OWN IGNORANCE.
I'M SUCH A STUPID-HEAD I DON'T EVEN KNOW WHICH CAME FIRST—THE KAMAKURA PERIOD, OR THE EDO PERIOD.
I'M SO NOT WORTHY!
WHAT'S REALLY SAD IS, I WOULDN'T EVEN HAVE HEARD OF THE SHINSENGUMI IF IT HADN'T BEEN FOR "MACARONI HORENSO" (MACARONI SPINACH) AND "SUSUME! PAIRETSU (ONWARD! PIRATES)"...
Both of which are "gag" comics, BTW.

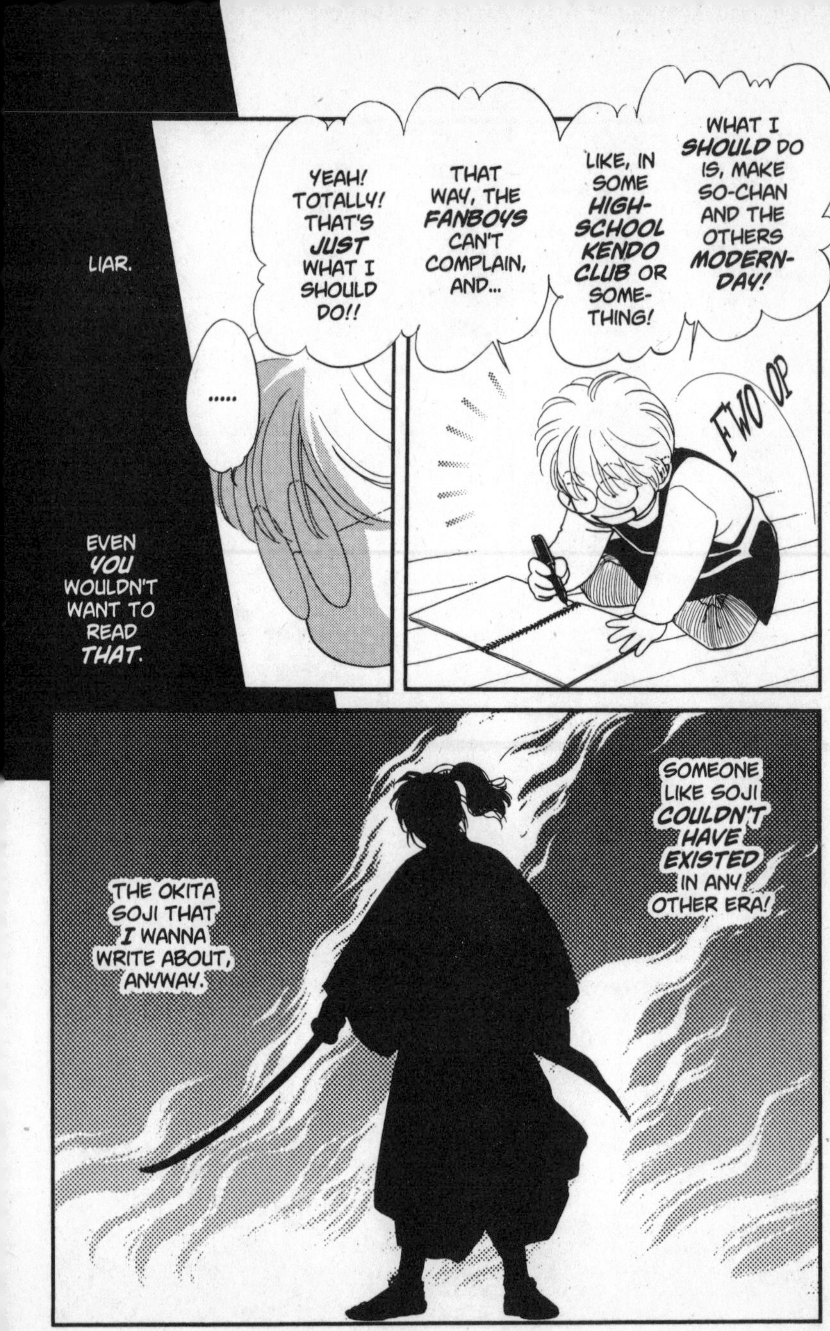
WHAT I SHOULD DO IS, MAKE SO-CHAN AND THE OTHERS MODERN-DAY!
LIKE, IN SOME HIGH-SCHOOL KENDO CLUB OR SOME-THING!
THAT WAY, THE FANBOYS CAN'T COMPLAIN, AND...
YEAH! TOTALLY! THAT'S JUST WHAT I SHOULD DO!!
FWO OP
.....
LIAR.
EVEN YOU WOULDN'T WANT TO READ THAT.
SOMEONE LIKE SOJI COULDN'T HAVE EXISTED IN ANY OTHER ERA!
THE OKITA SOJI THAT I WANNA WRITE ABOUT, ANYWAY.

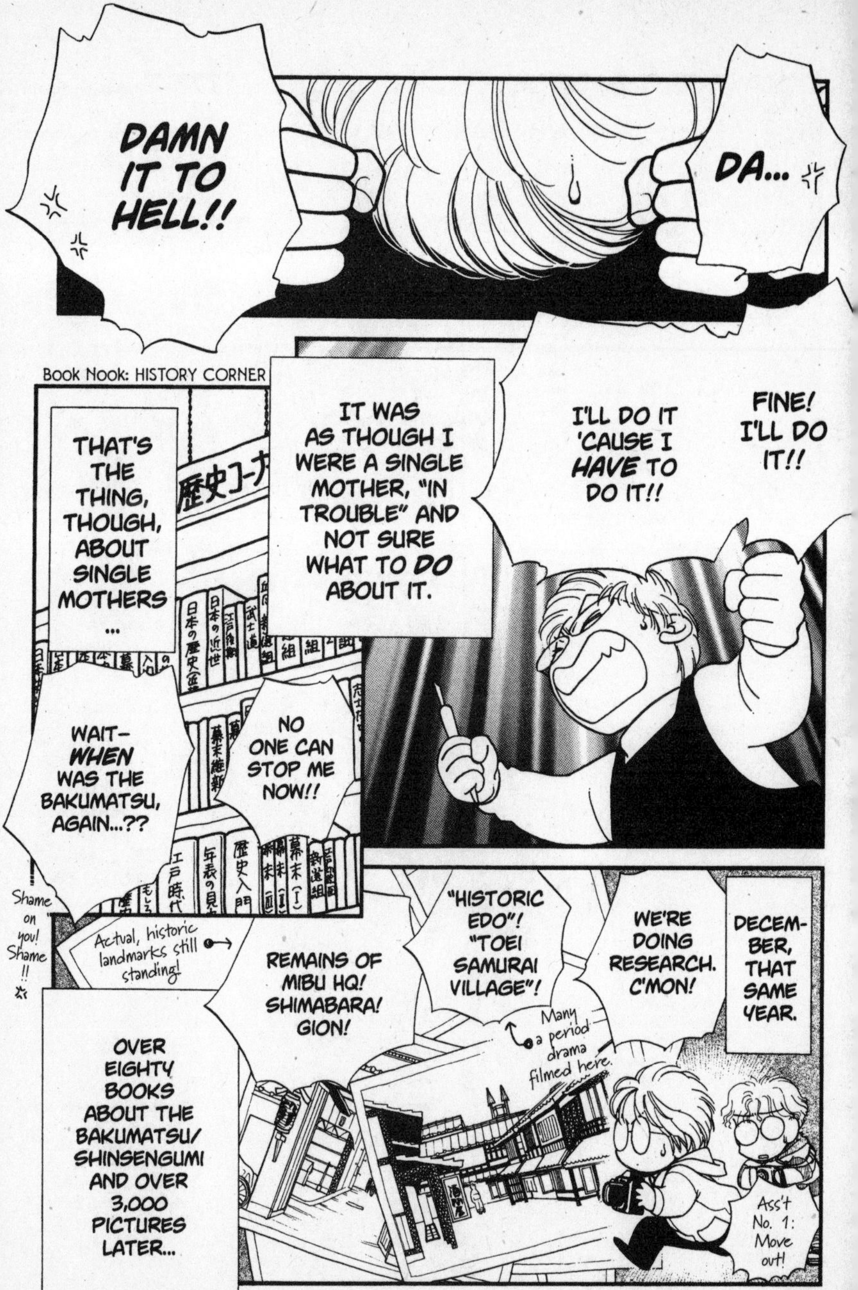
DA...
DAMN IT TO HELL!!
FINE! I'LL DO IT!!
I'LL DO IT 'CAUSE I HAVE TO DO IT!!
IT WAS AS THOUGH I WERE A SINGLE MOTHER, "IN TROUBLE" AND NOT SURE WHAT TO DO ABOUT IT.
Book Nook: HISTORY CORNER
THAT'S THE THING, THOUGH, ABOUT SINGLE MOTHERS ...
NO ONE CAN STOP ME NOW!!
WAIT— WHEN WAS THE BAKUMATSU, AGAIN...??
Shame on you! Shame!!
DECEM-BER, THAT SAME YEAR.
WE'RE DOING RESEARCH. C'MON!
Ass't No. 1: Move out!
"HISTORIC EDO"! "TOEI SAMURAI VILLAGE"!
Many a period drama filmed here.
REMAINS OF MIBU HQ! SHIMABARA! GION!
Actual, historic landmarks still standing!
OVER EIGHTY BOOKS ABOUT THE BAKUMATSU/ SHINSENGUMI AND OVER 3,000 PICTURES LATER...

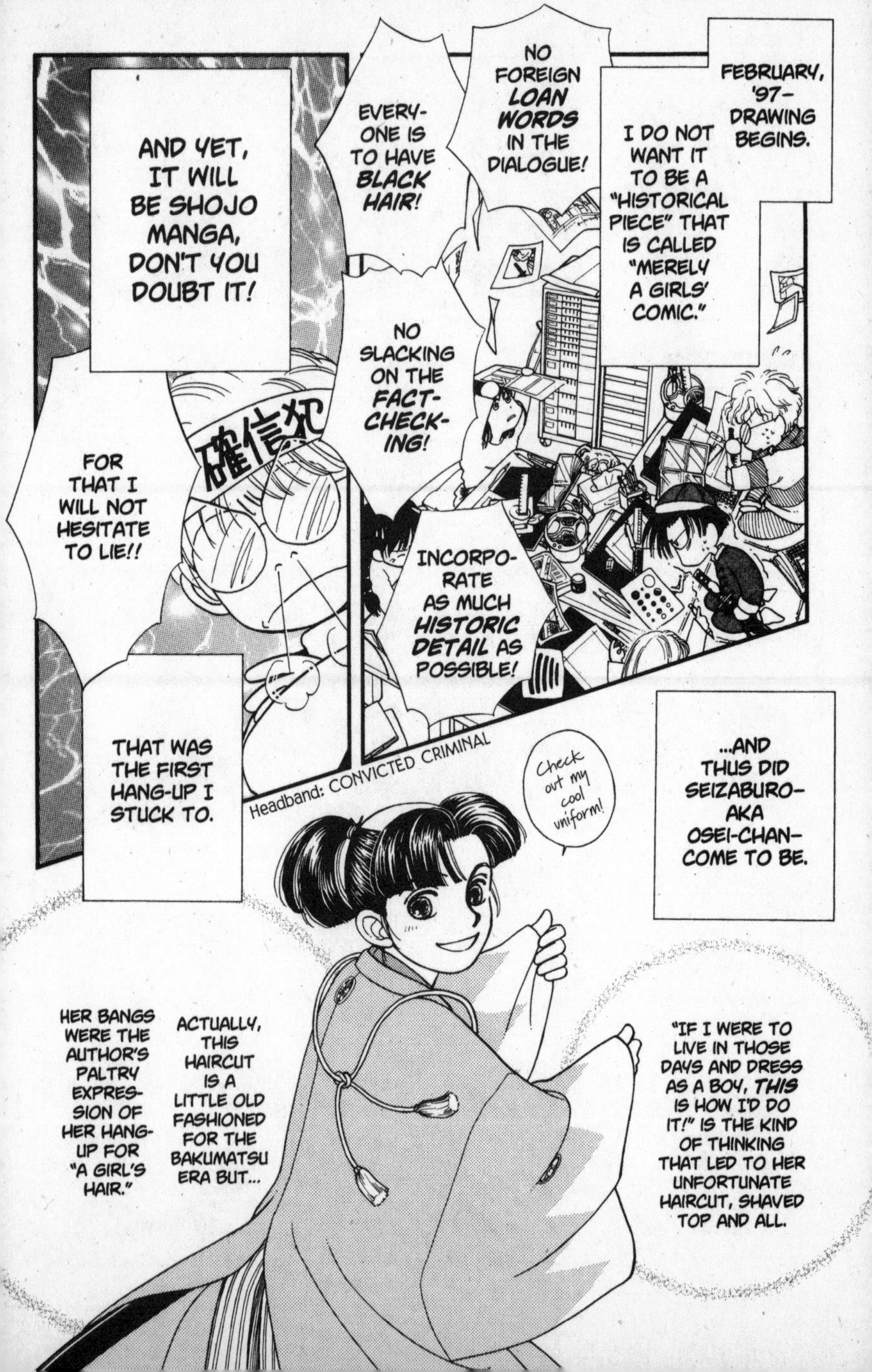
FEBRUARY, '97–DRAWING BEGINS.
I DO NOT WANT IT TO BE A "HISTORICAL PIECE" THAT IS CALLED "MERELY A GIRLS' COMIC."
NO FOREIGN LOAN WORDS IN THE DIALOGUE!
EVERY-ONE IS TO HAVE BLACK HAIR!
NO SLACKING ON THE FACT-CHECKING!
INCORPORATE AS MUCH HISTORIC DETAIL AS POSSIBLE!
AND YET, IT WILL BE SHOJO MANGA, DON'T YOU DOUBT IT!
確信犯
FOR THAT I WILL NOT HESITATE TO LIE!!
THAT WAS THE FIRST HANG-UP I STUCK TO.
Headband: CONVICTED CRIMINAL
...AND THUS DID SEIZABURO–AKA OSEI-CHAN–COME TO BE.
Check out my cool uniform!
"IF I WERE TO LIVE IN THOSE DAYS AND DRESS AS A BOY, THIS IS HOW I'D DO IT!" IS THE KIND OF THINKING THAT LED TO HER UNFORTUNATE HAIRCUT, SHAVED TOP AND ALL.
ACTUALLY, THIS HAIRCUT IS A LITTLE OLD FASHIONED FOR THE BAKUMATSU ERA BUT...
HER BANGS WERE THE AUTHOR'S PALTRY EXPRESSION OF HER HANG-UP FOR "A GIRL'S HAIR."

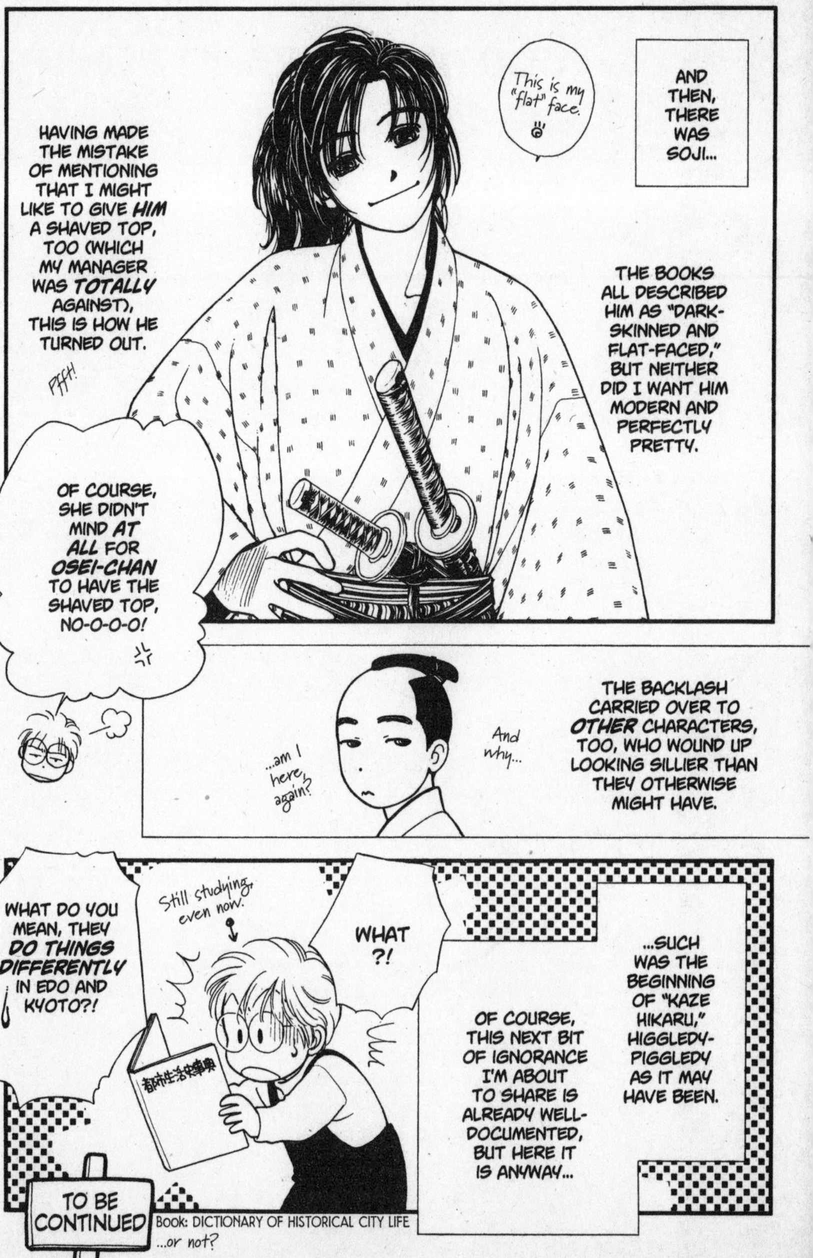

AND THEN, THERE WAS SOJI...
This is my "flat" face.
THE BOOKS ALL DESCRIBED HIM AS "DARK-SKINNED AND FLAT-FACED," BUT NEITHER DID I WANT HIM MODERN AND PERFECTLY PRETTY.
HAVING MADE THE MISTAKE OF MENTIONING THAT I MIGHT LIKE TO GIVE *HIM* A SHAVED TOP, TOO (WHICH MY MANAGER WAS *TOTALLY* AGAINST), THIS IS HOW HE TURNED OUT.
PFFT!
OF COURSE, SHE DIDN'T MIND *AT ALL* FOR *OSEI-CHAN* TO HAVE THE SHAVED TOP, NO-O-O-O!
THE BACKLASH CARRIED OVER TO *OTHER* CHARACTERS, TOO, WHO WOUND UP LOOKING SILLIER THAN THEY OTHERWISE MIGHT HAVE.
And why...
...am I here, again?
...SUCH WAS THE BEGINNING OF "KAZE HIKARU," HIGGLEDY-PIGGLEDY AS IT MAY HAVE BEEN.
OF COURSE, THIS NEXT BIT OF IGNORANCE I'M ABOUT TO SHARE IS ALREADY WELL-DOCUMENTED, BUT HERE IT IS ANYWAY...
WHAT ?!
Still studying even now.
WHAT DO YOU MEAN, THEY *DO THINGS DIFFERENTLY* IN EDO AND KYOTO?!
TO BE CONTINUED
Book: DICTIONARY OF HISTORICAL CITY LIFE
...or not?

Decoding Kaze Hikaru

Kaze Hikaru is a historical drama based in 19th century Japan and thus contains some fairly mystifying terminology. In this glossary we'll break down archaic phrases, terms, and other linguistic curiosities for you so that you can move through life with the smug assurance that you are indeed a know-it-all.

First and foremost, because *Kaze Hikaru* is a period story, we kept all character names in their traditional Japanese form—that is, family name followed by first name. For example, the character Okita Soji's family name is Okita and his personal name is Soji.

AKO-ROSHI:

The ronin (samurai) of Ako; featured in the immortal Kabuki play *Chushingura* (Loyalty), aka *47 Samurai*.

ANI-UE:

Literally, "brother above"; an honorific for an elder male sibling.

BAKUFU:

Literally, "tent government." Shogunate; the feudal, military government that dominated Japan for more than 200 years.

BUSHI:

A samurai or warrior (part of the compound word bushido, which means "way of the samurai").

CHICHI-UE:

An honorific meaning "father above."

DO:

In kendo (a Japanese fencing sport that uses bamboo swords), a short way of describing the offensive single-hit strike to the stomach.

-KUN:

An honorific suffix that indicates a difference in rank and title. The use of *kun* is also a way of indicating familiarity and friendliness between students or compatriots.

MEN:

In the context of *Kaze Hikaru*, *men* refers to one of the "points" in kendo. It is a strike to the forehead and is considered a basic move.

NE'E-SAN:
Can mean "older sister," "ma'am," or "miss."

NI'I-CHAN:
Short for oni'isan or oni'i-chan, meaning older brother.

ONI:
Literally means "ogre." This is Sei's nickname for Vice Captain Hijikata.

RANPO:
Medical science derived from the Dutch.

RONIN:
Masterless samurai.

RYO:
At the time, one *ryo* and two *bu* (four *bu* equaled roughly one *ryo*) were enough currency to support a family of five for an entire month.

-SAN:
An honorific suffix that carries the meaning of "Mr." or "Ms."

SENSEI:
A teacher, master or instructor.

SEPPUKU:
A ritualistic suicide by disembowlment that was considered a privilege of the nobility and samurai elite.

SONJO-HA:
Those loyal to the emperor and dedicated to the expulsion of foreigners from the country.

TAMEBO:
A short version of the name Tamesaburo.

YUBO:
A short version of the name Yunosuke.

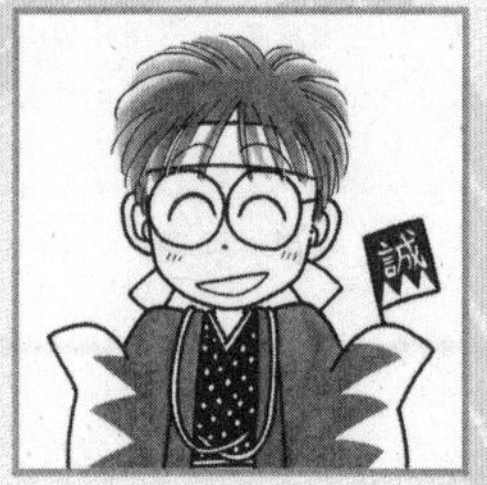
誠

Taeko Watanabe debuted as a manga artist in 1979 with her story *Waka-chan no Netsuai Jidai* (Love Struck Days of Waka). *Kaze Hikaru* is her longest-running series, but she has created a number of other popular series. Watanabe is a two-time winner of the prestigious Shogakukan Manga Award in the girls category—her manga *Hajime-chan ga Ichiban!* (Hajime-chan Is Number One!) claimed the award in 1991 and *Kaze Hikaru* took it in 2003.

Watanabe read hundreds of historical sources to create *Kaze Hikaru.* She is from Tokyo.

KAZE HIKARU VOL. 2
The Shojo Beat Manga Edition

This graphic novel contains material that was originally published in English
in *Shojo Beat* magazine, December 2005–April 2006 issues.

STORY AND ART BY
TAEKO WATANABE

English Adaptation/Annette Garcia
Translation/Mai Ihara
Touch-up Art & Lettering/Gia Cam Luc
Design/Courtney Utt
Editor/Nancy Thistlethwaite

Managing Editor/Megan Bates
Director of Production/Noboru Watanabe
Vice President of Publishing/Alvin Lu
Vice President & Editor in Chief/Yumi Hoashi
Sr. Director of Acquisitions/Rika Inouye
Vice President of Sales & Marketing/Liza Coppola
Publisher/Hyoe Narita

Printed in Canada

Published by VIZ Media, LLC.
P.O. Box 77010
San Francisco, CA 94107

Shojo Beat Manga Edition
10 9 8 7 6 5 4 3 2 1
First printing, June 2006

www.viz.com

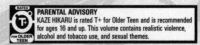

store.viz.com